Key to map pages

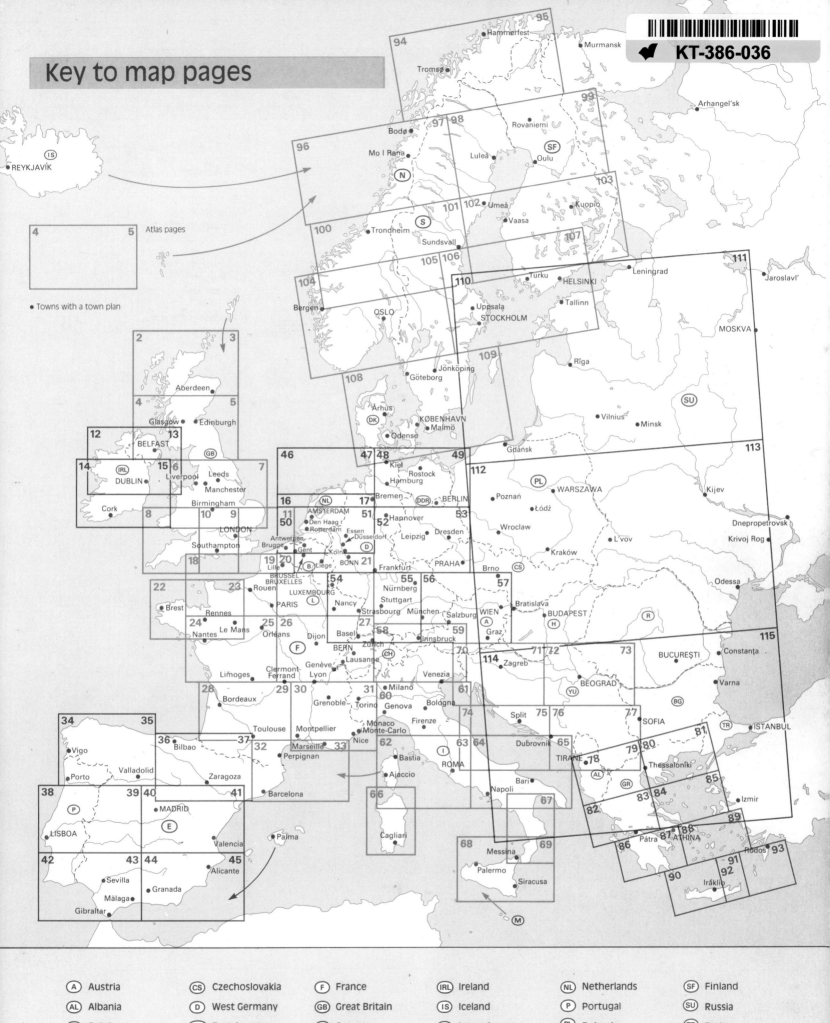

KT-386-036

Atlas pages

• Towns with a town plan

Symbol	Country	Symbol	Country	Symbol	Country	Symbol	Country	Symbol	Country	Symbol	Country
Ⓐ	Austria	ⒸⓈ	Czechoslovakia	Ⓕ	France	ⒾⓇⓁ	Ireland	ⓃⓁ	Netherlands	ⓈⒻ	Finland
ⒶⓁ	Albania	Ⓓ	West Germany	ⒼⒷ	Great Britain	ⒾⓈ	Iceland	Ⓟ	Portugal	ⓈⓊ	Russia
Ⓑ	Belgium	ⒹⒹⓇ	East Germany	ⒼⓇ	Greece	Ⓛ	Luxembourg	ⓅⓁ	Poland	ⓉⓇ	Turkey
ⒷⒼ	Bulgaria	ⒹⓀ	Denmark	Ⓗ	Hungary	Ⓜ	Malta	Ⓡ	Rumania	ⓎⓊ	Yugoslavia
ⒸⒽ	Switzerland	Ⓔ	Spain	Ⓘ	Italy	Ⓝ	Norway	Ⓢ	Sweden		

MICHELIN
Road Atlas of
Europe

First published 1988 by
The Hamlyn Publishing Group Limited
a division of the Octopus Publishing Group
Michelin House, 81 Fulham Road, London SW3 6RB

All maps © Michelin et Cie Propriétaires-Éditeurs 1988

Creation, graphic arrangement, text pages XII-XVI and Index
© The Hamlyn Publishing Group Limited 1988

Mapping of Great Britain on pages 2-11
based upon Ordnance Survey mapping with the permission of
the Controller of Her Majesty's Stationery Office, Crown copyright
reserved.

Mapping of Northern Ireland on pages 12-13
based upon Ordnance Survey mapping with the permission of
the Controller of Her Majesty's Stationery Office, Crown copyright
reserved. Permit No 223.

Mapping of the Republic of Ireland on pages 12-15
based on Ordnance Survey by permission of the Government of
the Republic of Ireland. Permit No 4990.

In spite of the care taken in the production of this
book, it is possible that a defective copy may have
escaped our attention. If this is so, please return it to
your bookseller, who will exchange it for you, or contact
The Hamlyn Publishing Group Limited.

The representation in this atlas of a road is no evidence
of the existence of a right of way.

ISBN   Hardback 0 600 55642 5
ISBN   Softback 0 600 56020 1

Printed and bound in Spain by Cayfosa, Barcelona

MICHELIN
Road Atlas of
Europe

MICHELIN
Touring Services

PAUL HAMLYN

Michelin

MICHELIN tyres and road maps have a reputation unsurpassed throughout Europe for quality and technical excellence in their respective fields.

It is appropriate that, at a time when the twelve member states of the European Economic Community are preparing for a single European market in 1993, Michelin should provide a new Road Atlas of Europe, compiled from their authoritative cartography, designed to meet the needs of the professional driver and holidaymaker alike.

There are over a hundred pages of mapping in this Atlas, showing the road network from North Cape to Gibraltar and from the Atlantic to the Black Sea. A full range of symbols show road categories and widths, towns and cities and places of interest as well as numerous other details, in keeping with Michelin's reputation for accuracy, legibility and up-to-date information.

Seventy town plans are included to help the driver negotiate built-up areas and the 'Driving in Europe' section provides details of national motoring regulations which are useful to know when crossing national frontiers. The comprehensive index locates about 30 000 towns and features.

The map showing 'Climates in Europe' will assist travellers in deciding which is the best season to visit a particular country.

The indispensable road mapping can be used in conjunction with other Michelin publications which provide complementary information on accommodation and sightseeing. The Red Guides, in particular the 'Europe' volume which contains a selection of hotels and restaurants in major European cities, and the Green Guides to the various countries of Europe are ideal companions for this Atlas.

Michelin are always happy to receive suggestions and comments from readers of their publications; taking these into account when preparing new editions can only improve their service to the public.

Thank you in advance and have a good journey!

MICHELIN maps and guides
complement one another:
use them together!

Contents

Plans of cities and principal towns

Route planning

Ísafjörður

Akureyri

REYKJAVÍK (IS)

1 765
△
Vatnajökull

Seyðisfjörður

CERCLE POLAIRE ARCTIQUE

Jan Mayen

SEA

NORVÈGE

DE

MER

NORVEGIAN

Hitra

Kristiansund

Ålesund

2 470
△
Glittertind

Føroyar

OCEAN

ATLANTIQUE

Shetland

Bergen (N)

Stavanger

Skier

Orkney

Kristiansand

ATLANTIC

OCEAN

Hebrides

Skye

Thurso

Inverness
Loch Ness

1 344
△ Ben Nevis

Aberdeen

Dundee

Glasgow

Edinburgh

Skagerrak

NORTH   SEA

DK

Jylland

Londonderry

Belfast

Stanraer

Carlisle

Newcastle

MER   DU   NORD

Esbjerg

Galway

IRL

DUBLIN

Man

IRISH   SEA

Liverpool   Leeds   York

Limerick

Manchester

Sheffield

Cork

St. George's Channel

GB

Nottingham

Birmingham

Coventry

Cardiff

Oxford

Southampton

LONDON

Plymouth

Land's End

Portsmouth

Dover

ENGLISH CHANNEL

LA MANCHE

Norwich

Cambridge

Groningen

Ijsselmeer

NL

AMSTERDAM

Den Haag

Rotterdam

Brugge

Calais

Lille

Gent

Antwerpen

Aachen

Liège

BRUSSEL
BRUXELLES

Bremen

Hannover

Waal

West

Essen   Dortmund

Düsseldorf

Köln

BONN

Kassel

D

Frankfurt a

MER DE BARENTS
BARENTS SEA

Nordkapp

Kanin
Poluostrov

Hammerfest

Kirkenes

Murmansk

Tromsø

LAPLAND

Inarijärvi

Kol'skij
Poluostrov

ARCTIC CIRCLE

MORE

Vesterålen

Ivalo

Lofoten

Narvik

Kiruna

△ 2111
Kebnekaise

Malmberget

Kousomen'

BELOJE

Mezen

Bodø

Rovaniemi

Kuusamo

Kem'

Arhangel'sk

Mo i Rana

Kemi

Dønna

Luleå

Oulu

Oulujärvi

Severnaja Dvina

BOTHNIA
BOTNIE

Pielinen

S

Umeå

SF

Petrozavodsk

Onežkoje Oz.

Vaasa

Kuopio

Joensuu

Trondheim

Östersund

Jyväskylä

GULF

Vologda

Sundsvall

OF

Tampere

Ladozskoje oz.

Čerepovec

GOLFE

Pori

DE

Lahti

Lillehammer

Mora

Turku

Pāijänne

HELSINKI

FINLAND
FINLANDE

Loningrad

Rybinskoje
Vdchr.

Rybinsk

Glomma

Dalälven

Jaroslavl'

OSLO

Uppsala

Åland

GULF OF
GOLFE DE

Tallinn

Novgorod

Moss

Västerås

STOCKHOLM

Saaremaa

Čudskoje Oz.

Kalinin

Örebro

BALTIC

Zagorsk

Norrköping

Vänern

Pskov

MOSKVA

Linköping

SEA

Rižskij
Zaliv

SU

Frederikshavn

Vättern

Jönköping

Gotland

Riga

Tula

Göteborg

Daugava

Ålborg

Öland

Vitebsk

Kattegat

Smolensk

Århus

Karlskrona

Klaipéda

KØBENHAVN

Kaunas

Mogil'ov

Br'ansk

Or'ol

Odense

Malmö

Vilnius

Fyn

Sjælland

Bornholm

Kaliningrad

Minsk

Kursk

Lolland

Rügen

Gdańsk

Nermunas

Gomel'

Kiel

Rostock

Dnepr

Černigov

Lübeck

Szczecin

Toruń

Wisła

Prip'at

Desna

Hamburg

Oder

Poznań

WARSZAWA

Brest

Elbe

BERLIN

Kijev

Magdeburg

Odra

PL

Łódź

Lublin

Žitomir

Poltava

DDR

Dresden

Wrocław

Częstochowa

Kremenčugskoje
Vdchr.

Erfurt

Leipzig

Erzgebirge

Labe

UKRAINA

Vinnica

Dnepropetrovs

L'vov

MER

BALTIQUE

MER BALTIQUE

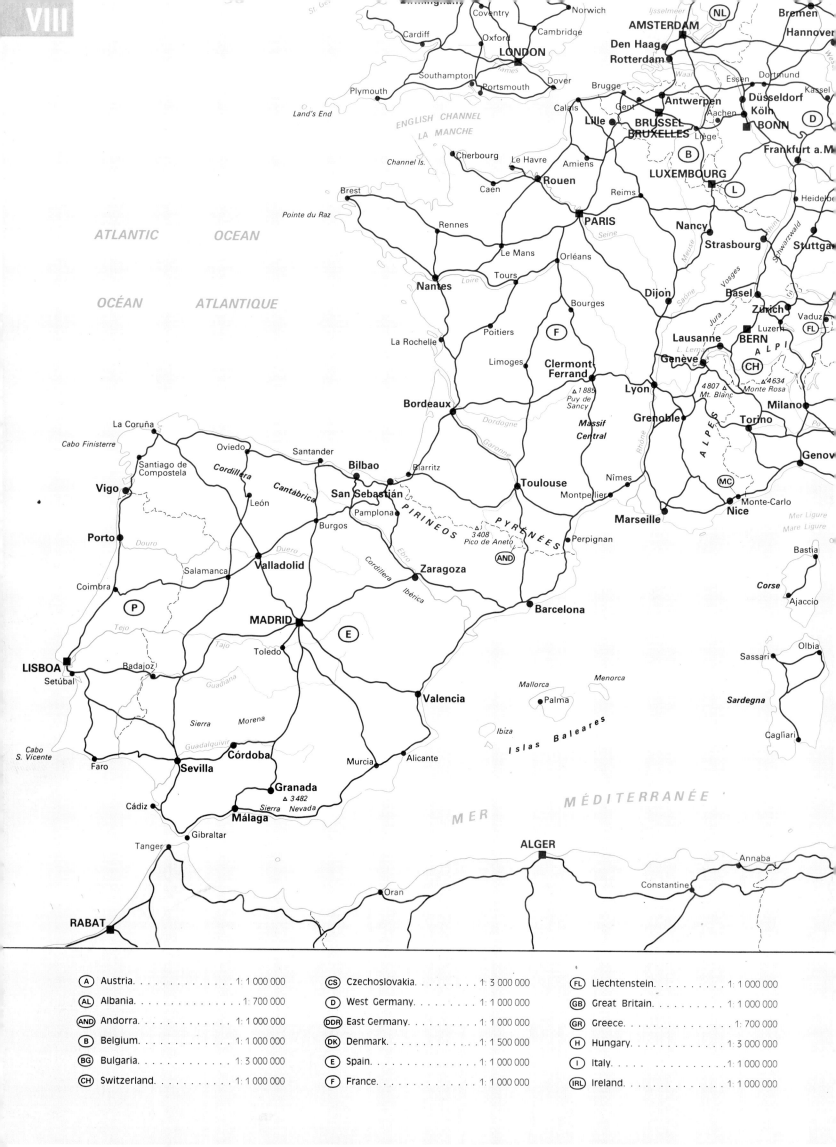

(A)	Austria	1: 1 000 000	(CS)	Czechoslovakia	1: 3 000 000	(FL) Liechtenstein 1: 1 000 000
(AL)	Albania	1: 700 000	(D)	West Germany	1: 1 000 000	(GB) Great Britain 1: 1 000 000
(AND)	Andorra	1: 1 000 000	(DDR)	East Germany	1: 1 000 000	(GR) Greece 1: 700 000
(B)	Belgium	1: 1 000 000	(DK)	Denmark	1: 1 500 000	(H) Hungary 1: 3 000 000
(BG)	Bulgaria	1: 3 000 000	(E)	Spain	1: 1 000 000	(I) Italy 1: 1 000 000
(CH)	Switzerland	1: 1 000 000	(F)	France	1: 1 000 000	(IRL) Ireland 1: 1 000 000

Elbe · Magdeburg · ■ BERLIN · Poznań · Wisła · Prip'at'
DDR · Erfurt · Leipzig · Dresden · Odra · PL · Łódź · Lublin · WARSZAWA · Brest · Kijev · Poltava
Nürnberg · Plzeň · PRAHA · CS · Wrocław · Częstochowa · Żitomir · Kremenčugskoje Vdchr. · UKRAINA
Regensburg · Brno · Kraków · L'vov · Vinnica · Dnepropetrovsk
Augsburg · Linz · Bratislava · KARPATY · Tatry △ 2 655 · Košice · Černovcy · Krivoj Rog
München · Inn · WIEN · Donau · BUDAPEST · Cluj-Napoca · CARPATII · Iaşi · Kišin'ov · Odessa
Salzburg · A · Graz · H · Balaton · Sibiu · Moldoveanu △ 2 543 · Braşov · Cherson
Innsbruck · Großglockner △ 3 797 · ALPEN · Timişoara · R · Carpatii Meridionali
Bolzano · 2 863 △ Triglav · Ljubljana · Duna · Tisza · Novi Sad · Pécs · Dráva · MER NOIRE
Padova · Trieste · Zagreb · Sava · BEOGRAD · BUCURESTI · Constanţa
Verona · Venezia · Rijeka · YU · Drina · Ruse · Varna · BLACK SEA
Parma · Adige · Dunărea · Dunăv · Stara Planina · Veliko Târnovo · Burgas
Bologna · Ravenna · RSM · Sarajevo · 2 376 △ Botev · SOFIA · BG
Pisa · Firenze · Dinara · Split · Titograd · Skopje · Plovdiv · Edirne · Istanbul
Siena · ADRIATIC SEA · Dubrovnik · Drin · 2 764 △ Korab · Rodopi · Évros · TR · Marmara Denizi
Perugia · APPENNINI · MER ADRIATIQUE · Kota · Dalmatska
Gran Sasso 2 914 · Pescara · V · ROMA · I · Bari · Durrës · TIRANË · AL · Thessaloníki · Bursa
Napoli · 1 277 △ Vesuvio · Taranto · Ólimbos △ 917 · Lárissa · AEGEAN SEA · Lésvos · Izmir
MER TYRRHÉNIENNE · TYRRHENIAN SEA · Kérkira · Pindes · Vólos · GR · MER ÉGÉE
Palermo · Messina · Reggio di Calabria · Pátra · ATHÍNA · Kikládes · Dodekánissa
Etna 3 340 △ · Catania · IONIAN SEA · Ionia Nissiá · Kórinthos · Évia · Ródos
Sicilia · MER IONIENNE · Pelopónnissos · Iráklio
TUNIS · Valletta · M · MEDITERRANEAN SEA · Kriti

(IS) Iceland 1: 2 400 000	(P) Portugal 1: 1 000 000	(SU) Russia 1: 3 000 000
(L) Luxembourg 1: 1 000 000	(PL) Poland 1: 3 000 000	(TR) Turkey 1: 3 000 000
(M) Malta 1: 1 000 000	(R) Rumania 1: 3 000 000	(V) Vatican City 1: 140 000
(MC) Monaco 1: 1 000 000	(RSM) San Marino 1: 1 000 000	(YU) Yugoslavia 1: 1 000 000
(N) Norway 1: 1 500 000	(S) Sweden 1: 1 500 000	
(NL) Netherlands 1: 1 000 000	(SF) Finland 1: 1 500 000	

Amsterdam
2836 · Athina
1547 3090 · Barcelona
1971 2621 1792 · Bari
745 2466 1029 1226 · Basel
1341 3874 2046 2690 1508 · Belfast
1718 1118 1972 1503 1348 2756 · Beograd
1817 4017 3178 3244 2187 3112 2899 · Bergen
669 2584 1853 1811 862 1906 1466 1463 · Berlin
1424 3422 607 2124 1174 1755 2304 3196 1990 · Bilbao
782 3316 1487 2131 950 535 2198 2554 1348 1196 · Birmingham
1081 3240 633 1942 831 1412 2122 2853 1647 334 853 · Bordeaux
1098 3501 1242 2278 1096 1244 2383 2870 1664 965 686 622 · Brest
204 2792 1365 1777 551 1150 1674 1969 781 1229 591 886 903 · Brussel/Bruxelles
2221 1238 2611 2142 1987 3259 639 3200 1711 2943 2701 2761 2886 2177 · Bucureşti
1393 1510 1952 1482 1073 2431 392 2372 883 2283 1873 2041 2058 1349 828 · Budapest
902 2752 648 1485 477 1337 1634 2636 1311 706 779 371 752 706 2273 1614 · Clermont-Ferrand
1053 3586 1758 2402 1220 165 2468 2824 1618 1467 247 1124 956 862 2971 2143 1049 · Dublin
2024 1265 2049 1580 1425 2892 525 3204 1771 2381 2333 2199 2480 1970 1164 787 1711 2604 · Dubrovnik
1289 3823 1994 2638 1457 251 2705 3061 1855 1703 484 1360 1193 1098 3208 2380 1286 416 2840 · Edinburgh
1391 2115 1075 720 646 2098 997 2664 1231 1407 1539 1225 1686 1197 1636 976 883 1810 1074 2046 · Firenze
446 2396 1318 1553 327 1549 1278 1864 566 1502 991 1159 1176 402 1781 953 776 1261 1583 1498 973 · Frankfurt A. M.
885 2446 770 1203 259 1492 1328 2446 1121 1102 934 681 1080 703 1967 1307 310 1204 1405 1441 611 586 · Genève
1005 3205 2366 2432 1375 2300 2087 812 651 2384 1742 2041 2058 1157 2388 1560 1824 2012 2392 2249 1852 1052 1634 · Göteborg
441 2780 1802 2007 811 1736 1662 1384 289 1820 1178 1477 1494 593 2026 1198 1260 1448 1967 1685 1427 488 1070 572 · Hamburg
386 2637 1659 1864 668 1623 1519 1527 288 1707 1065 1364 1381 498 2022 1194 1117 1335 1824 1572 1284 345 927 715 151 · Hannover
1204 2540 2388 2346 1397 2441 1422 1186 505 2525 1883 2182 2199 1316 1858 1030 1846 2153 1893 2390 1766 1101 1656 662 776 823 · Helsinki
2665 1171 2919 2450 2295 3703 947 3846 2413 3251 3145 3069 3330 2621 692 1339 2581 3415 1326 3652 1944 2225 2275 3034 2609 2466 2369 · Istambul
2017 2311 3114 2644 2187 3254 1336 2844 1383 3338 2696 2995 3012 2129 1073 1162 2636 2966 1861 3203 2138 1914 2339 2032 1670 1636 1146 489 · Kijev
738 2938 2099 2165 1108 2033 1820 1079 384 2117 1475 1774 1791 890 2121 1293 1557 1745 2125 1982 1585 785 1367 267 305 448 795 2767 1765 · København
264 2579 1342 1714 488 1361 1461 1802 575 1440 803 1097 1114 211 1964 1136 802 1073 1766 1310 1134 189 747 990 426 292 1110 2408 1923 723 · Köln
1637 2973 2821 2779 1830 2874 1855 1619 938 2958 2316 2615 2632 1749 2625 1463 2279 2586 2326 2823 2199 1534 2089 1095 1209 1256 433 2041 1552 1228 1543 · Leningrad
283 2910 1308 1836 610 1046 1792 2055 849 1139 487 796 813 116 2295 1467 617 758 2088 994 1256 520 668 1243 679 566 1384 2739 2197 976 329 1817 · Lille
2322 4320 1285 3022 2072 2653 3202 4094 2888 907 2094 1232 1863 2127 3841 3181 1604 2365 3279 2601 2305 2400 2000 3282 2718 2605 3423 4149 4236 3015 2338 3856 2037 · Lisboa

971 3504 1676 2320 1138 416 2386 2742 1536 1385 165 1042 874 780 2889 2061 967 167 2522 365 1728 1179 1122 1930 1366 1253 2071 3333 2884 1663 991 2504 676 2283 · Liverpool
719 3252 1424 2068 886 722 2134 2490 1284 1133 196 790 622 528 2637 1809 715 434 2270 612 1476 927 870 1678 1114 1001 1819 3081 2632 1411 739 2252 424 2031 · London
391 2637 1148 1560 334 1338 1519 1994 767 1290 779 947 964 218 1993 1165 608 1050 1758 1286 980 248 486 1182 618 484 1302 2466 2115 915 193 1735 334 2188 · Luxembourg
917 2559 630 1292 400 1415 1441 2548 1223 962 857 549 1003 735 2080 1421 178 1127 1518 1364 690 688 141 1736 1172 1029 1758 2388 2548 1469 711 2191 678 1860 · Lyon
1812 3760 686 2462 1562 2143 2642 3584 2378 397 1584 722 1353 1617 3281 2622 1094 1855 2719 2091 1745 1890 1440 2772 2208 2095 2913 3589 3726 2505 1828 3346 1527 658 · Madrid
2360 4086 1012 2788 2025 2691 2968 4132 2849 945 2132 1270 1901 2165 3607 2948 1644 2403 3045 2639 2071 2314 1766 3320 2756 2643 3384 3915 4110 3053 2376 3817 2075 634 · Málaga
1228 2621 493 1323 710 1727 1503 2859 1534 825 1168 643 1315 1046 2142 1483 454 1439 1580 1675 606 999 451 2047 1483 1340 2069 2450 2645 1780 1023 2502 989 1723 · Marseille
1088 2128 973 878 343 1810 1010 2493 1040 1305 1251 1123 1398 894 1649 989 629 1522 1087 1758 298 670 323 1681 1117 974 1575 1957 2151 1414 831 2008 953 2203 · Milano
2463 3169 3630 3306 2639 3700 2194 2313 1829 3784 3142 3441 3458 2575 1931 1918 3088 3412 2705 3649 2800 2360 2898 1789 2116 2082 1127 1347 858 2211 2369 694 2643 4682 · Moskva
837 2063 1370 1224 399 1794 945 2018 585 1615 1236 1272 1421 769 1506 678 918 1506 1184 1743 644 397 599 1206 781 638 1120 1892 1744 939 580 1553 887 2513 · München
887 3290 945 1923 847 1168 2172 2659 1453 669 609 326 296 692 2675 1847 452 802 2125 1116 1331 965 726 1847 1283 1170 1988 3119 2801 1580 903 2421 602 1567 · Nantes
1878 2602 1562 261 1133 2585 1484 3151 1718 1894 2026 1712 2173 1684 2123 1463 1370 2297 1561 2533 490 1460 1098 2339 1914 1771 2253 2431 2625 2072 1621 2686 1743 2792 · Napoli
1387 2434 656 1136 658 1886 1316 2808 1355 988 1327 806 1474 1205 1955 1295 613 1598 1393 1834 419 985 472 1996 1432 1289 1890 2263 2457 1729 1146 2323 1148 1886 · Nice
666 2171 1427 1391 436 1715 1053 1867 434 1668 1157 1325 1342 622 1556 728 885 1427 1351 1664 811 226 695 1055 610 467 969 2000 1759 788 409 1402 740 2566 · Nürnberg
1321 3521 2682 2748 1691 2616 2403 496 967 2700 2058 2357 2374 1473 2704 1876 2140 2328 2708 2565 2168 1368 1950 316 888 1031 690 3350 2348 583 1306 1123 1559 3598 · Oslo
2599 3322 2283 691 1853 3305 2204 3872 2439 2614 2747 2432 2893 2404 2843 2184 2091 3017 2281 3254 1210 2180 1818 3060 2635 2492 2974 3151 3346 2793 2341 3407 2464 3512 · Palermo
504 2912 1091 1735 553 965 1794 2275 1069 922 407 579 596 308 2297 1469 399 677 1937 914 1143 587 537 1463 899 786 1604 2741 2417 1196 520 2037 219 1820 · Paris
2143 4141 1167 2843 1893 2474 3023 3915 2709 728 1915 1053 1684 1948 3662 3002 1425 2186 3100 2422 2126 2221 1821 3103 2539 2426 3244 3970 4057 2836 2159 3677 1858 314 · Porto
950 2154 1711 1596 720 1999 1036 1839 350 1952 1441 1609 1626 906 1361 533 1169 1711 1261 1948 1016 510 979 1027 665 603 859 1983 1389 760 693 1292 1024 2850 · Praha
1665 2389 1349 449 920 2372 1271 2938 1505 1681 1813 1499 1960 1471 1910 1250 1157 2084 1348 2320 277 1247 885 2126 1701 1558 2040 2218 2412 1859 1408 2473 1530 2579 · Roma
2483 4683 3844 3910 2853 3778 3565 2824 2129 3862 3220 3519 3536 2635 3866 3038 3302 3490 3870 3727 3330 2530 3112 1528 2050 2193 837 4512 2557 1745 3288 1005 2721 4760 · Rovaniemi
980 1932 1539 1172 536 1952 814 2161 728 1772 1393 1429 1578 927 1363 535 1076 1664 1052 1900 660 540 736 1349 924 781 1263 1761 1601 1082 723 1696 1045 2670 · Salzburg
2295 4117 1043 2819 2056 2626 2999 4067 2880 880 2067 1205 1836 2100 3638 2979 1577 2338 3076 2574 2102 2345 1797 3255 2691 2578 3415 3946 4141 2988 2311 3848 2010 417 · Sevilla
2104 818 2358 1889 1734 3142 386 3285 1852 2690 2584 2508 2769 2060 420 778 2020 2854 765 3091 1383 1664 1714 2473 2048 1905 1808 561 1493 2206 1847 2241 2178 3588 · Sofia
1368 3568 2729 2795 1738 2663 2450 1021 1014 2747 2105 2404 2421 1520 2751 1923 2187 2375 2755 2612 2215 1415 1997 497 935 1078 165 3397 2395 630 1353 598 1606 3645 · Stockholm
634 2438 1110 1371 145 1450 1320 2076 751 1264 892 921 1077 439 1881 1053 568 1162 1559 1399 791 216 404 1264 700 557 1286 2267 2076 997 377 1719 545 2162 · Strasbourg
622 2302 1258 1404 267 1592 1184 2046 631 1413 1034 1070 1219 558 1745 917 716 1304 1423 1541 824 204 526 1234 670 527 1166 2131 1956 967 365 1599 676 2311 · Stuttgart
2350 511 2604 2135 1980 3388 632 3531 2098 2936 2830 2754 3015 2306 727 1024 2266 3100 779 3337 1629 1910 1960 2719 2294 2151 2054 660 1800 2452 2093 2487 2424 3834 · Thessaloniki
1154 2263 779 997 409 1699 1145 2596 1157 1110 1140 864 1287 905 1784 1124 492 1411 1222 1647 395 736 252 1784 1220 1077 1692 2092 2286 1517 897 2125 961 2008 · Torino
1199 2994 388 1696 933 1611 1876 3082 1757 447 1053 245 853 1003 2515 1856 397 1323 1953 1560 979 1222 674 2270 1706 1563 2292 2823 3018 2003 1246 2725 914 1345 · Toulouse
3041 5241 4402 4468 3411 4336 4123 1893 2687 4420 3778 4077 4094 3193 4424 3596 3860 4048 4428 4285 3888 3088 3670 2570 2608 2751 1367 5070 3087 2303 3026 1535 3279 5318 · Tromsø
1865 4065 3226 3292 2235 3160 2947 717 1511 3244 2602 2901 2918 2017 3248 2420 2684 2872 3252 3109 2712 1912 2494 1394 1432 1575 949 3894 2892 1127 1850 1382 2103 4142 · Trondheim
1892 3435 361 2137 1374 2391 2317 3523 2198 606 1832 771 1402 1710 2956 2297 993 2103 2394 2139 1420 1663 1115 2711 2147 2004 3264 3459 2444 1687 3166 1653 924 · Valencia
1283 1878 1229 760 605 2072 760 2512 1079 1561 1513 1379 1660 1156 1399 739 891 1784 837 2020 254 891 585 1700 1275 1132 1614 1707 1901 1433 1026 2047 1215 2459 · Venezia
1223 2188 2390 2066 1399 2460 1070 2050 589 2544 1902 2201 2218 1335 1506 678 1848 2172 1465 2409 1560 1120 1658 1238 876 842 352 2017 794 971 1129 785 1403 3442 · Warszawa
1150 1862 1833 1341 830 2188 744 2131 642 2141 1630 1798 1815 1106 1071 243 1370 1900 969 2137 835 710 1030 1319 957 951 924 1691 1309 1052 893 1357 1224 3039 · Wien
1337 1499 1591 1122 967 2375 381 2518 1085 1923 1817 1741 2002 1293 1020 350 1253 2087 618 2324 616 897 947 1706 1281 1138 1287 1328 1512 1439 1080 1720 1411 2821 · Zagreb
831 2416 1058 1176 86 1594 1298 2267 852 1260 1036 917 1182 637 1816 988 597 1306 1375 1543 596 412 287 1455 891 748 1387 2245 2054 1188 573 1820 696 2158 · Zürich

Distances in Europe

Distances are calculated from centres and along the best roads from a motoring point of view - not necessarily the shortest

Example: **Luxembourg – Warszawa** 1321 km

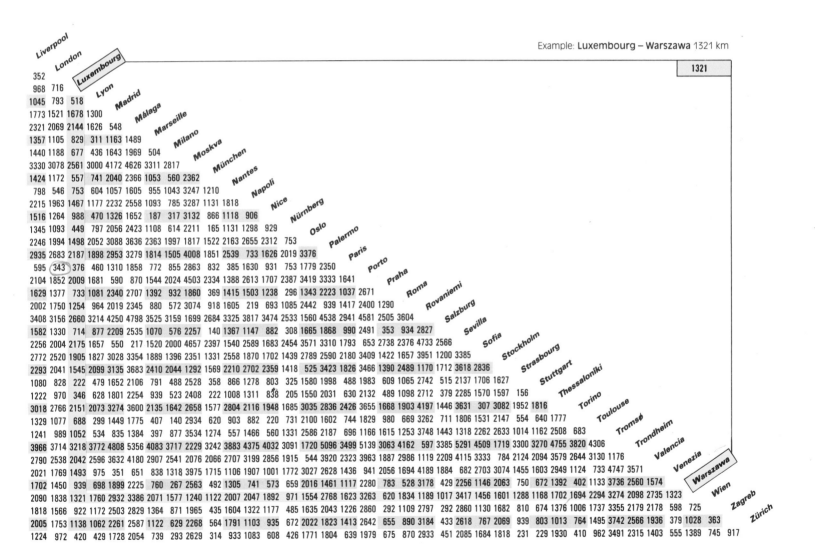

Liverpool |
London | 352 |
Luxembourg | 968 | 716 |
Lyon | 1045 | 793 | 518 |
Madrid | 1773 | 1521 | 1678 | 1300 |
Málaga | 2321 | 2069 | 2144 | 1626 | 548 |
Marseille | 1357 | 1105 | 829 | 311 | 1163 | 1489 |
Milano | 1440 | 1188 | 677 | 436 | 1643 | 1969 | 504 |
Moskva | 3330 | 3078 | 2561 | 3000 | 4172 | 4626 | 3311 | 2817 |
München | 1424 | 1172 | 557 | 741 | 2040 | 2366 | 1053 | 560 | 2362 |
Nantes | 798 | 546 | 753 | 604 | 1057 | 1605 | 955 | 1043 | 3247 | 1210 |
Napoli | 2215 | 1963 | 1467 | 1177 | 2232 | 2558 | 1093 | 785 | 3287 | 1131 | 1818 |
Nice | 1516 | 1264 | 988 | 470 | 1326 | 1652 | 187 | 317 | 3132 | 866 | 1118 | 906 |
Nürnberg | 1345 | 1093 | 449 | 797 | 2056 | 2423 | 1108 | 614 | 2211 | 165 | 1131 | 1298 | 929 |
Oslo | 2246 | 1994 | 1498 | 2052 | 3088 | 3636 | 2363 | 1997 | 1817 | 1522 | 2163 | 2655 | 2312 | 753 |
Palermo | 2935 | 2683 | 2187 | 1898 | 2953 | 3279 | 1814 | 1505 | 4008 | 1851 | 2539 | 733 | 1626 | 2019 | 3376 |
Paris | 595 | 343 | 376 | 460 | 1310 | 1858 | 772 | 855 | 2863 | 832 | 385 | 1630 | 931 | 753 | 1779 | 2350 |
Porto | 2104 | 1852 | 2009 | 1681 | 590 | 870 | 1544 | 2024 | 4503 | 2334 | 1388 | 2613 | 1707 | 2387 | 3419 | 3333 | 1641 |
Praha | 1629 | 1377 | 733 | 1081 | 2340 | 2707 | 1392 | 932 | 1860 | 369 | 1415 | 1503 | 1238 | 296 | 1343 | 2223 | 1037 | 2671 |
Roma | 2002 | 1750 | 1254 | 964 | 2019 | 2345 | 880 | 572 | 3074 | 918 | 1605 | 219 | 693 | 1085 | 2442 | 939 | 1417 | 2400 | 1290 |
Rovaniemi | 3408 | 3156 | 2660 | 3214 | 4250 | 4798 | 3525 | 3159 | 1699 | 2684 | 3325 | 3817 | 3474 | 2533 | 1560 | 4538 | 2941 | 4581 | 2505 | 3604 |
Salzburg | 1582 | 1330 | 714 | 877 | 2209 | 2535 | 1070 | 576 | 2257 | 140 | 1367 | 1147 | 882 | 308 | 1665 | 1868 | 990 | 2491 | 353 | 934 | 2827 |
Sevilla | 2256 | 2004 | 2175 | 1657 | 550 | 217 | 1520 | 2000 | 4657 | 2397 | 1540 | 2589 | 1683 | 2454 | 3571 | 3310 | 1793 | 653 | 2738 | 2376 | 4733 | 2566 |
Sofia | 2772 | 2520 | 1905 | 1827 | 3028 | 3354 | 1889 | 1396 | 2351 | 1331 | 2558 | 1870 | 1702 | 1439 | 2789 | 2590 | 2180 | 3409 | 1422 | 1657 | 3951 | 1200 | 3385 |
Stockholm | 2293 | 2041 | 1545 | 2099 | 3135 | 3683 | 2410 | 2044 | 1292 | 1569 | 2210 | 2702 | 2359 | 1418 | 525 | 3423 | 1826 | 3466 | 1390 | 2489 | 1170 | 1712 | 3618 | 2836 |
Strasbourg | 1080 | 828 | 222 | 479 | 1652 | 2106 | 791 | 488 | 2528 | 358 | 866 | 1278 | 803 | 325 | 1580 | 1998 | 488 | 1983 | 609 | 1065 | 2742 | 515 | 2137 | 1706 | 1627 |
Stuttgart | 1222 | 970 | 346 | 628 | 1801 | 2254 | 939 | 523 | 2408 | 222 | 1008 | 1311 | 838 | 205 | 1550 | 2031 | 630 | 2132 | 489 | 1098 | 2712 | 379 | 2285 | 1570 | 1597 | 156 |
Thessaloniki | 3018 | 2766 | 2151 | 2073 | 3274 | 3600 | 2135 | 1642 | 2658 | 1577 | 2804 | 2116 | 1948 | 1685 | 3035 | 2836 | 2426 | 3655 | 1668 | 1903 | 4197 | 1446 | 3631 | 307 | 3082 | 1952 | 1816 |
Torino | 1329 | 1077 | 688 | 299 | 1449 | 1775 | 407 | 140 | 2934 | 620 | 903 | 882 | 220 | 731 | 2100 | 1602 | 744 | 1829 | 980 | 669 | 3262 | 711 | 1806 | 1531 | 2147 | 554 | 640 | 1777 |
Toulouse | 1241 | 989 | 1052 | 534 | 835 | 1384 | 397 | 877 | 3534 | 1274 | 557 | 1466 | 560 | 1331 | 2586 | 2187 | 696 | 1166 | 1615 | 1253 | 3748 | 1443 | 1318 | 2262 | 2633 | 1014 | 1162 | 2508 | 683 |
Tromsø | 3966 | 3714 | 3218 | 3772 | 4808 | 5356 | 4083 | 3717 | 2229 | 3242 | 3883 | 4375 | 4032 | 3091 | 1720 | 5096 | 3499 | 5139 | 3063 | 4162 | 597 | 3385 | 5291 | 4509 | 1719 | 3300 | 3270 | 4755 | 3820 | 4306 |
Trondheim | 2790 | 2538 | 2042 | 2596 | 3632 | 4180 | 2907 | 2541 | 2076 | 2066 | 2707 | 3199 | 2856 | 1915 | 544 | 3920 | 2323 | 3963 | 1887 | 2986 | 1119 | 2209 | 4115 | 3333 | 784 | 2124 | 2094 | 3579 | 2644 | 3130 | 1176 |
Valencia | 2021 | 1769 | 1493 | 975 | 351 | 651 | 838 | 1318 | 3975 | 1715 | 1106 | 1907 | 1001 | 1772 | 3027 | 2628 | 1436 | 941 | 2056 | 1694 | 4189 | 1884 | 682 | 2703 | 3074 | 1455 | 1603 | 2949 | 1124 | 733 | 4747 | 3571 |
Venezia | 1702 | 1450 | 939 | 698 | 1899 | 2225 | 760 | 267 | 2563 | 492 | 1305 | 741 | 573 | 659 | 2016 | 1461 | 1117 | 2280 | 783 | 528 | 3178 | 429 | 2256 | 1146 | 2063 | 750 | 672 | 1392 | 402 | 1133 | 3736 | 2560 | 1574 |
Warszawa | 2090 | 1838 | 1321 | 1760 | 2932 | 3386 | 2071 | 1577 | 1240 | 1122 | 2007 | 2047 | 1892 | 971 | 1554 | 2768 | 1623 | 3263 | 620 | 1834 | 1189 | 1017 | 3417 | 1456 | 1601 | 1288 | 1168 | 1702 | 1694 | 2294 | 3274 | 2098 | 2735 | 1323 |
Wien | 1818 | 1566 | 922 | 1172 | 2503 | 2829 | 1364 | 871 | 1965 | 435 | 1604 | 1322 | 1177 | 485 | 1635 | 2043 | 1226 | 2860 | 292 | 1109 | 2797 | 292 | 2860 | 1130 | 1682 | 810 | 674 | 1376 | 1006 | 1737 | 3355 | 2179 | 2178 | 598 | 725 |
Zagreb | 2005 | 1753 | 1138 | 1062 | 2261 | 2587 | 1122 | 629 | 2268 | 564 | 1791 | 1103 | 935 | 672 | 2022 | 1823 | 1413 | 2642 | 655 | 890 | 3184 | 433 | 2618 | 767 | 2069 | 939 | 803 | 1013 | 764 | 1495 | 3742 | 2566 | 1936 | 379 | 1028 | 363 |
Zürich | 1224 | 972 | 420 | 429 | 1728 | 2054 | 739 | 293 | 2629 | 314 | 933 | 1083 | 608 | 426 | 1771 | 1804 | 639 | 1979 | 675 | 870 | 2933 | 451 | 2085 | 1684 | 1818 | 231 | 229 | 1930 | 410 | 962 | 3491 | 2315 | 1403 | 555 | 1389 | 745 | 917 |

Driving in Europe

Introduction

The information panels which follow give the principal motoring regulations for all the countries included in this atlas; an explanation of the symbols is given below, together with some additional notes.

🔧 The name, address and telephone number of the national motoring organisation or organisations; the initials FIA and AIT indicate membership of the international touring associations, the Fédération Internationale de l'Automobile and the Alliance Internationale de Tourisme

⊙ Speed restrictions in kilometres per hour applying to:

　🚗 motorways
　🚗 dual carriageways
　🚗 single carriageways
　🏘 urban areas

Where restrictions for 'trailers' or 'towing' are given, it may be assumed that these apply to both trailers and caravans

🍷 The maximum permitted level of alcohol in the bloodstream. This should not be taken as an acceptable level; it is NEVER sensible to drink and drive

🔖 Whether the wearing of seat belts is compulsory

👤 Restrictions applying to children

△ Whether a warning triangle must be carried

✚ Whether a first aid kit must be carried

💡 Whether a spare bulb kit must be carried

🪖 Whether crash helmets are compulsory for motorcyclists

🚗 Whether tolls are payable on motorways and/or other parts of the road network

⛽ Whether petrol concessions or restrictions apply

⊖ The minimum age for drivers

🛂 Documentation required; note that while insurance for driving at home usually provides the legally required minimum third party cover abroad, it will not provide cover against damage, fire, theft or personal accident; for this reason, an International Motoring Certificate (Green Card) is recommended for all countries and essential where 'Green Card required' is given

★ In this section are given any other regulations not falling into the categories above

Andorra

🔧 Automobil Club d'Andorra, FIA,
Babet Camp 4, Andorra-la-Vella   Tel: 20-8-90

🚗	🚗	🚗	🏘
⊙	70	70	40 km/h

🍷 0.08%

🔖 Compulsory if fitted for drivers and front seat passengers

👤 Children under 10 years of age not allowed in front seats

△ Not compulsory unless vehicle exceeds 3000 kg, but advised

✚ Recommended

💡 Compulsory

🪖 Compulsory for motorcyclists and passengers

🚗
⛽ None

⊖ 18

🛂 Valid driving licence; Vehicle registration document or Vehicle on hire certificate; Green Card recommended; National vehicle identification plate

Austria

🔧 Österreicher Automobil-, Motorrad- und Touring Club (ÖAMTC), FIA & AIT, Schubertring 1-3, 1010 Wien 1   Tel: (0222) 72990

🚗	🚗	🚗	🏘
⊙ 130	100	100	50 km/h
70	60	60	50 km/h

if towing trailer over 14.5 cwt

100	100	100	50 km/h

if towing trailer under 14.5 cwt

🍷 0.08%

🔖 Compulsory if fitted for driver and front seat passengers

👤 Children under 12 years of age not allowed in front seats

△ Compulsory

✚ Compulsory

💡

🪖 Compulsory for motorcyclists and passengers

🚗 Tolls payable on most motorways and some roads (especially Austrian trans-Alpine routes)

⛽ None

⊖ 18

🛂 Valid driving licence; Vehicle registration document or Vehicle on hire certificate; Green Card recommended; National vehicle identification plate

Belgium

🔧 Royal Automobile Club de Belgique (RACB),
FIA, 53 rue d' Arlon, 1040 Bruxelles
Tel: (02) 2300810

Touring Club Royal de Belgique (TCB), AIT,
44 rue de la Loi, 1040 Bruxelles
Tel: (02) 2332211

Vlaamse Automobilistenbond,
Sint Jakobs Markt 45, 2000 Antwerpen
Tel: (03) 2003434

🚗	🚗	🚗	🏘
⊙ 120	90	90	60 km/h

🍷 0.08%

🔖 Compulsory if fitted for drivers and front seat passengers

👤 Children under 12 years of age not allowed in front seats

△ Compulsory

✚ Recommended

💡

🪖 Compulsory for motorcyclists

🚗 None at present

⛽ None

⊖ 18

🛂 Valid driving licence; Vehicle registration document or Vehicle on hire certificate; Green Card recommended; National vehicle identification plate

Bulgaria

🔧 Union of Bulgarian Motorists (SBA), FIA & AIT,
6 Sveta Sofia St., Sofia C
Tel: (02) 87 88 01/87 88 02

🚗	🚗	🚗	🏘
⊙ 120	90	90	60 km/h

🍷 0.03%

🔖 Compulsory if fitted for drivers and front seat passengers

👤 Children under 10 years of age not allowed in front seats

△ Compulsory

✚ Compulsory

💡

🪖 Compulsory for motorcyclists

🚗

⛽ Foreign motorists must buy fuel with coupons available in unlimited quantities at border posts and within Bulgaria

⊖ 18

🛂 Valid driving licence plus authorized translation into Bulgarian or International Driving Permit; Vehicle registration document or Vehicle on hire certificate; Green Card required; National vehicle identification plate

Czechoslovakia

🔧 **Ustřední Automotoklub ČSSR**, FIA & AIT,
Na strži 9, 14000 Praha 4   Tel: 432 987

�ūꜛ	🅰ꜛ	🅰	🏭
🅐 110	90	90	60 km/h

🍷 0.0%   any amount of alcohol found in the blood
may result in prosecution

🏷 Compulsory if fitted for drivers and front seat
passengers

🧍 Children under 12 years of age not allowed in
front seats

△ Compulsory

➕ Compulsory

🕯

⬭ Crash helmets and goggles compulsory for
drivers of motorcycles over 50cc; crash helmets
only for passengers

🚏ꜛ

🏮 Tuzex petrol coupons can be purchased with
foreign currency at frontier posts, Tuzex shops
and banks; also from Czech Tourist Bureau Cedok
(London) Ltd

🔄 18

📇 Valid driving licence; Vehicle registration
document or Vehicle on hire certificate; Green
Card recommended; National vehicle
identification plate

Denmark

🔧 **Forenede Danske Motorejere (FDM)**, AIT,
FDM-Huset, Blegdamsvej 124, 2100 København Ø
Tel: (01) 38 21 12

🚏ꜛ	🅰ꜛ	🅰	🏭
🅐 100	80	80	50 km/h
70	70	70	50 km/h if towing

🍷 0.08%

🏷 Compulsory if fitted for drivers and front seat
passengers over 15 years

🧍

△ Compulsory

➕ Recommended

🕯

⬭ Compulsory for motorcyclists and passengers

🚏ꜛ

🏮 None

🔄 17

📇 Valid driving licence; Vehicle registration
document or Vehicle on hire certificate; Green
Card recommended; National vehicle
identification plate

Finland

🔧 **Autoliitto (Automobile and Touring Club of
Finland) (ATCF)**, FIA & AIT, Kansakoulukatu 10,
00101 Helsinki 10   Tel: (90) 6940022

🚏ꜛ	🅰ꜛ	🅰	🏭
🅐 120	60-100	60-100	50 km/h
80	60-80	60-80	50 km/h towing if trailer has brakes
50	50	50	50 km/h towing if trailer unbraked

🍷 0.05%

🏷 Compulsory if fitted for drivers and front and
rear seat passengers

🧍

△ Recommended

➕ Recommended

🕯

⬭ Compulsory for motorcyclists and passengers

🚏ꜛ

🏮 None

🔄 18

📇 Valid driving licence; International Driving Permit
required for car hire or after 3 months; Vehicle
registration document or Vehicle on hire
certificate; Green Card recommended; National
vehicle identification plate

★ Compulsory use of headlights at all times outside
built-up areas

France

🔧 **Automobile Club de France**, FIA, 6-8 Place de
la Concorde, 75008 Paris   Tel: (1) 42 65 08 26
**Association Française des Automobilistes
(AFA)**, FIA & AIT, 9 rue Anatole de la Forge,
75017 Paris   Tel: (1) 42 27 82 00

🚏ꜛ	🅰ꜛ	🅰	🏭
🅐 110-130	110	90	60 km/h
100-110	100	80	60 km/h if wet

🍷 0.08%

🏷 Compulsory if fitted for drivers and front seat
passengers

🧍 Children under 10 years of age not allowed in
front seats

△ Compulsory unless hazard warning lights are
fitted

➕ Recommended

🕯 Compulsory

⬭ Compulsory for motorcyclists and passengers

🚏ꜛ Tolls payable on most motorways although short
urban sections of motorway around Paris and
some other major cities are free; tolls also
payable on some major bridges and in some
tunnels

🏮 None

🔄 18

📇 Valid driving licence; Vehicle registration
document or Vehicle on hire certificate; Green
Card recommended; National vehicle
identification plate

FDR (West Germany)

🔧 **Allgemeiner Deutscher Automobil-Club
(ADAC)**, FIA & AIT, Am Westpark 8,
8000 München 70   Tel: (089) 76760
Automobil-Club von Deutschland (AvD), FIA,
Lyonerstraße 16, 6000 Frankfurt am Main 71
Tel: (069) 66060

🚏ꜛ	🅰ꜛ	🅰	🏭
🅐 130*	100-130	100-130	50 km/h
80	80	80	50 km/h if towing

*recommended

🍷 0.08%

🏷 Compulsory if fitted for drivers and front and
rear seat passengers

🧍 Children under 12 years of age not allowed in
front seats

△ Compulsory

➕ Recommended

🕯

⬭ Compulsory for motorcyclists and passengers

🚏ꜛ None

🏮 None

🔄 17

📇 Valid driving licence; Vehicle registration
document or Vehicle on hire certificate; Green
Card recommended; National vehicle
identification plate

DDR (East Germany)

🔧 **Allgemeiner Deutscher Motorsport Verband
der DDR**, FIA, 60 Charlottenstraße,
108 Berlin (Ost)   Tel: 2071931/2071932

🚏ꜛ	🅰ꜛ	🅰	🏭
🅐 100	80	80	50 km/h
80	80	80	50 km/h if towing

🍷 0.0%   any amount of alcohol found in the blood
may result in prosecution

🏷 Compulsory if fitted for drivers and front seat
passengers

🧍 Children under 7 years of age not allowed in front
seats

△ Compulsory

➕ Compulsory

🕯 Compulsory

⬭ Compulsory for motorcyclists; smoking not
allowed whilst driving

🚏ꜛ Tolls levied on private cars depending on distance
travelled; may be paid in Marks obtained by
currency exchange; information available at
frontier posts

🏮 Reduced price petrol coupons available at main
frontier posts; indefinite validity but cannot be
returned

🔄 17

📇 Valid driving licence; Vehicle registration
document or Vehicle on hire certificate; Green
Card recommended; National vehicle
identification plate

Great Britain

🔧 **Automobile Association (AA)**, FIA & AIT, Fanum House, Basingstoke, Hampshire RG21 2EA
Tel: (0256) 20123
Royal Automobile Club (RAC), FIA & AIT, Lansdowne Road, Croydon CR9 2JA
Tel: (01) 686 2525

🛣	🛤	🅰	🏭
🕐 112	96	96	48 km/h
96	96	80	48 km/h if towing

🍷 0.08%
🪢 Compulsory if fitted for drivers and front seat passengers
👤
△
➕ Recommended
💡
⭕ Compulsory for motorcyclists and passengers
🛣 None
🎫 None
🔄 17
📋 Valid driving licence; Vehicle registration document or Vehicle on hire certificate; Green Card recommended; National vehicle identification plate
★ Drive on the left!

Hungary

🔧 **Magyar Autóklub (MAK)**, FIA & AIT, Rómer Flóris utca 4a, Budapest 11 Tel: (01) 152 040

🛣	🛤	🅰	🏭
🕐 120	80-100	80-100	60 km/h
80	70	70	50 km/h if towing

🍷 0.0% if the alcohol test changes colour, the driver is taken to a hospital for a blood test and his driving licence confiscated
🪢 Compulsory if fitted for drivers and front seat passengers
👤 Children under 6 years of age not allowed in front seats
△ Compulsory
➕ Recommended
💡 Compulsory
⭕ Compulsory for motorcyclists and passengers
🛣
🎫 IBUSZ vouchers available (no price reduction); diesel for foreign vehicles must be bought with coupons paid for in foreign currency from exchange offices and travel agencies; unused coupons not refundable
🔄 18
📋 Valid driving licence; Vehicle registration document; or Vehicle on hire certificate; Green Card strongly recommended; National vehicle identification plate

Ireland

🔧 **Automobile Association (AA)**, FIA & AIT, 23 Suffolk Street, Dublin 2 Tel: (1) 779481
Royal Automobile Club (RAC), FIA & AIT, 34 Dawson Street, Dublin 2 Tel: (1) 775141

🛣	🛤	🅰	🏭
🕐	88	64	48 km/h
	56	56	48 km/h if towing

🍷 0.10%
🪢 Compulsory if fitted for drivers and front seat passengers
👤
△ Recommended
➕ Recommended
💡
⭕ Compulsory for motorcyclists and passengers
🛣 Toll payable on one bridge over River Liffey
🎫 Contact Irish Tourist Board for current information
🔄 17
📋 Valid driving licence; Vehicle registration document or Vehicle on hire certificate; Green Card recommended; National vehicle identification plate
★ Drive on the left!

Greece

🔧 **The Automobile and Touring Club of Greece (ELPA)**, FIA & AIT, 2-4 Messagion, 115 27 Athína Tel: (01) 779 1615
Hellenic Touring Club, AIT, 12 Politechniou, 104 33 Athína Tel: (01) 524 0854

🛣	🛤	🅰	🏭
🕐 100	80	80	50 km/h

🍷 0.05%
🪢 Compulsory if fitted for drivers and front seat passengers
👤 Children under 10 years of age not allowed in front seats
△ Compulsory
➕ Compulsory
💡
⭕ Compulsory for motorcyclists and passengers
🛣 Tolls payable on most 'national' roads
🎫 None
🔄 17
📋 Valid driving licence; Vehicle registration document or Vehicle on hire certificate; Green Card required; National vehicle identification plate
★ Fire extinguisher compulsory

Iceland

🔧 **Felag Islenskra Bifreidaeigenda (FIB)**, FIA & AIT, Borgatun 33, 105 Reykjavik
Tel: (1) 29999

🛣	🛤	🅰	🏭
🕐	70	70	50 km/h

🍷 0.05%
🪢 Compulsory for drivers and front seat passengers; rear seat belts recommended
👤
△ Recommended
➕ Recommended
💡 Recommended
⭕ Compulsory for motorcyclists and passengers
🛣
🎫 None
🔄 17
📋 Driver's passport; Valid driving licence; Vehicle registration document or Vehicle on hire certificate; Green Card required; Temporary importation permit; National vehicle identification plate
★ Vehicle mud flaps are compulsory; headlights must be used at all times

Italy

🔧 **Automobile Club d'Italia (ACI)**, FIA & AIT, Via Marsala 8, 00185 Roma Tel: (06) 49981
Touring Club Italiano (TCI), AIT, Corso Italia 10, 20122 Milano Tel: (02) 85261

🛣	🛤	🅰	🏭
🕐 130-110*	130-110*	90	50 km/h
100	80	80	50 km/h if towing

as at October 1988
* Saturdays, Sundays, public holidays and holiday periods

🍷 Severe penalties for drinking and driving
🪢 Compulsory if fitted
👤
△ Compulsory
➕ Recommended
💡
⭕ Compulsory for motorcyclists
🛣 Tolls payable on most motorways
🎫 Coupons at a discount available at RAC, AA, and Port Offices and frontier Automobile Clubs to personal callers; must be paid for in foreign currency
🔄 18; visitors under 21 years of age may not drive a private car capable of exceeding 180 km/h
📋 Valid driving licence; Vehicle registration document or Vehicle on hire certificate; Green Card recommended; Temporary importation document; National vehicle identification plate

Luxembourg

🔧 Automobile Club du Grand Duché de Luxembourg (ACL), FIA & AIT, 13 rue de Longwy, 8080 Bertrange Tel: 311031

🛣	🛤	🅰	🏙
🚗 120	90	90	60 km/h

🍷 0.08%

🔧 Compulsory if fitted for drivers and front seat passengers

👤 Children under 10 years of age not allowed in front seats

△ Compulsory

➕ Recommended

🔦

🔲 Recommended

🛣 None

⛽ None

⊖ 18

🪪 Valid driving licence; Vehicle registration document or Vehicle on hire certificate; Green Card recommended; National vehicle identification plate

Netherlands

🔧 Koninklijke Nederlandsche Automobiel Club (KNAC), FIA, Westvlietweg 118, Leidschendam   Tel: (070) 99 74 51
Koninklijke Nederlandsche Toeristenbond (ANWB), AIT, Wassenaarseweg 220, Den Haag Tel: (070) 26 44 26

🛣	🛤	🅰	🏙
🚗 100	80	80	50 km/h
80	80	80	50 km/h if towing

🍷 0.05%

🔧 Compulsory if fitted for drivers and front seat passengers

👤 Children under 12 years of age not allowed in front seats unless using child's safety seat and under 4 years of age

△ Compulsory

➕ Recommended

🔦

🔲 Compulsory for motorcyclists and passengers

🛣 Tolls payable on: Zeeland Brug, Kiltunnel (from Dordrecht – Hoekse Waard), Waal Brug, Prins Willem Alexander Brug

⛽ None

⊖ 18

🪪 Valid driving licence; Vehicle registration document or Vehicle on hire certificate; Green Card recommended; National vehicle identification plate

Norway

🔧 Kongelig Norsk Automobilklub (KNA), FIA, Parkveien 68, Oslo 2   Tel: (02) 562690
Norges Automobil-Forbund (NAF), AIT, Storgata 2, Oslo 1   Tel: (02) 429400

🛣	🛤	🅰	🏙
🚗 80-90	80-90	80-90	50 km/h
80	80	80	50 km/h if towing trailer with braking system
60	60	60	50 km/h if towing trailer without braking system

🍷 0.05%

🔧 Compulsory if fitted for drivers and front and rear seat passengers

👤 Children under 12 years of age not allowed in front seats

△ Compulsory

➕ Recommended

🔦

🔲 Compulsory for motorcyclists and passengers

🛣 Tolls payable on most new major roads

⛽ None

⊖ 17 for temporarily imported vehicle; 18 to hire or borrow local vehicle

🪪 Valid driving licence; Vehicle registration document or Vehicle on hire certificate; Green Card recommended; National vehicle identification plate

★ Dipped headlights compulsory at all times

Poland

🔧 Polski Zwiazek Motorowy (PZM), FIA & AIT, Kazimierzowska 66, 02-518 Warszawa Tel: (022) 499361/499212
Auto Assistance, Krucza 6-14, 00-537 Warszawa   Tel: (022) 293541/210467

🛣	🛤	🅰	🏙
🚗 110	90	90	60 km/h
70	70	70	60 km/h if towing

🍷 0.02%

🔧 Compulsory if fitted for drivers and front seat passengers

👤 Children under 10 years of age not allowed in front seats

△ Compulsory

➕ Recommended

🔦

🔲 Compulsory for motorcyclists and passengers

🛣

⛽ Coupons available at frontier offices or branches of Polish Tourist Office (ORBIS) in Poland; also from Fregata Travel Ltd, 100 Dean Street, London; unused coupons refundable

⊖ 18

🪪 Valid driving licence; International Driving Permit after 3 months; Vehicle registration document or Vehicle on hire certificate; Green Card required; National vehicle identification plate

Portugal

🔧 Automóvel Club de Portugal (ACP), FIA & AIT, Rue Rosa Araûje 24-26, 1200 Lisboa   Tel: 563931

🛣	🛤	🅰	🏙
🚗 120	90	90	60 km/h
100	70	70	50 km/h if towing

🍷 0.05%

🔧 Compulsory if fitted for drivers and front seat passengers outside built-up areas

👤

△ Compulsory

➕ Recommended

🔦

🔲 Compulsory for motorcyclists

🛣 Tolls payable in certain directions on some motorways and bridges

⛽ None

⊖ 17

🪪 Valid driving licence; Vehicle registration document or Vehicle on hire certificate; Green Card required; National vehicle identification plate

Romania

🔧 In the event of breakdown or accident contact the National Tourist Office Carpaţi-Bucureşti, Bd Magheru 7, Bucureşti   Tel: 145160

🛣	🛤	🅰	🏙
🚗 70-90*	60-90*	60-90*	60 km/h
*according to cylinder capacity			

🍷 0.0%   any alcohol found in the bloodstream may result in immediate imprisonment

🔧 Recommended if fitted

👤 Children under 12 years of age not allowed in front seats

△ Compulsory

➕ Recommended

🔦

🔲 Compulsory for motorcyclists and passengers

🛣 None

⛽ Coupons compulsory; obtainable with convertible currency only at frontier posts, tourist offices and some hotels; for use at PECO filling stations

⊖ 17

🪪 Valid driving licence; Vehicle registration document or Vehicle on hire certificate; Green Card required; National vehicle identification plate

Spain

🔧 Real Automóvil Club de España (RACE), FIA & AIT, José Abascal 10, Madrid 3
Tel: (01) 447 3200

🚗	🚙	🚗	🏭
⊙ 120	90-100	90-100	60 km/h
80	70	70	70 km/h if towing

these limits are increased by 20 km/h for overtaking

🍷 0.08%

🔧 Compulsory if fitted for drivers and front seat passengers outside built-up areas

👶 Children in front seats not recommended

△ Two are compulsory for vehicles with 9 or more seats; recommended for other vehicles

➕ Recommended

🔦 Compulsory

⭕ Compulsory for motorcycles but not for mopeds

🚗 Tolls payable on most motorways and Cadi tunnel

⛽ None

🔞 18

📋 International Driving Permit required if 'pink' EEC licence not held; Vehicle registration document or Vehicle on hire certificate; Green Card required; Bail Bond strongly recommended; National vehicle identification plate

Switzerland

🔧 Automobile Club de Suisse (ACS), FIA, Wasserwerkgasse 39, 3000 Bern 13
Tel: (031) 22 47 22

Touring Club Suisse (TCS), AIT, 9 rue Pierre-Fatio, 1211 Genève 3   Tel: (022) 37 12 12

🚗	🚙	🚗	🏭
⊙ 120	80	80	50 km/h
80	80	80	50 km/h if towing – up to 20 cwt trailer
60	60	60	50 km/h if towing – over 20 cwt trailer

🍷 0.08%

🔧 Compulsory if fitted for drivers and front seat passengers

👶 Children under 12 years of age not allowed in front seats

△ Compulsory

➕ Compulsory

🔦

⭕ Compulsory for motorcyclists and passengers

🚗 Vignette compulsory: obtainable from frontier posts, post offices, garages, motoring organisations or Swiss National Tourist Office (London); separate vignette required for trailer or caravan

⛽ None

🔞 18

📋 Valid driving licence; Vehicle registration document or Vehicle on hire certificate; Green Card recommended; National vehicle identification plate

USSR

🔧 In the event of breakdown or accident contact officer of State Automobile Inspection (Militia) or nearest office of Intourist (obliged to give tourists assistance)

🚗	🚙	🚗	🏭
⊙	90	90	60 km/h

🍷 0.0%

🔧 Compulsory if fitted for drivers and front seat passengers

👶 Children under 12 years of age not allowed in front seats

△ Compulsory

➕ Compulsory

🔦 Recommended

⭕ Not applicable; motorcycles may not be hired

🚗 Road tax payable on entry to USSR though some foreign cars exempt

⛽ Petrol coupons compulsory; obtainable at border posts

🔞 18

📋 Valid driving licence meeting requirements of International Convention on Road Traffic; Vehicle registration document or Vehicle on hire certificate; Car insurance obtainable on entry to USSR at Ingosstrakh offices; Itinerary card, service coupons and motor routes map issued by Intourist; Customs obligation to take the car out of the country on departure; National vehicle identification plate

★ Fire extinguisher must be carried

Sweden

🔧 Motormännens Riksförbund (M), AIT, Sturegatan 32, Stockholm   Tel: (08) 7 82 38 00

🚗	🚙	🚗	🏭
⊙ 110	70-110	70-110	50 km/h
70	70	70	50 km/h if towing with braking device
40	40	40	40 km/h if towing with no braking device

🍷 0.05%

🔧 Compulsory if fitted for drivers and front and rear seat passengers

👶

△ Recommended

➕ Recommended

🔦

⭕ Compulsory for motorcyclists and passengers

🚗

⛽ None

🔞 18

📋 Valid driving licence; Vehicle registration document or Vehicle on hire certificate; Green Card recommended; National vehicle identification plate

★ Dipped headlights compulsory at all times

Turkey

🔧 Turkiye Turing ve Otomobil Kurumu (TTOK), FIA & AIT, Halaskargazi Cad. 364, 80222 Sisli, Istanbul   Tel: 1314631/6

🚗	🚙	🚗	🏭
⊙	90	90	50 km/h
	70	70	40 km/h if towing

🍷 0.0%

🔧 Compulsory if fitted for drivers and front and rear seat passengers

👶 Children in front seats not recommended

△ Two must be carried – one to place in front of the vehicle, one behind

➕ Recommended

🔦

⭕ Compulsory for motorcyclists

🚗

⛽ None

🔞 Normally 18, but drivers holding a valid foreign driving licence who are not yet 18 are allowed to drive foreign registered vehicles

📋 Valid driving licence; International Driving Permit advised and compulsory if driving Turkish vehicle; Vehicle registration document or Vehicle on hire certificate; Green Card compulsory – must cover European & Asian regions; National vehicle identification plate

Yugoslavia

🔧 Auto-Moto Savez Jugoslavija (AMSJ), FIA & AIT, Ruzveltova 18, 11001 Beograd
Tel: (011) 401699

🚗	🚙	🚗	🏭
⊙ 120	80-100	80-100	60 km/h
80	80	80	60 km/h if towing

🍷 0.05%

🔧 Compulsory if fitted for drivers and front and rear seat passengers

👶 Children under 12 years of age not allowed in front seats

△ Compulsory – two are necessary if towing trailer or caravan

➕ Compulsory

🔦 Compulsory

⭕ Compulsory for motorcyclists and passengers

🚗 Tolls payable on several major roads, Tito Bridge and Ucka tunnel

⛽ Concessionary petrol coupons available at frontier posts for purchase with convertible currency; unused coupons refundable

🔞 18

📋 Valid driving licence; Vehicle registration document or Vehicle on hire certificate; Green Card required; National vehicle identification plate

Signos convencionales

Para más información ver el interior de la cubierta anterior

Importancia de los itinerarios

Autopista con calzadas separadas
con calzada única
Autovía con calzadas separadas
Número de acceso
Accesos: completo – medio acceso
parcial – sin precisión
Carretera de comunicación internacional o nacional asfaltada:
calzadas separadas
4 carriles – 3 carriles
2 carriles anchos – 2 carriles
Carretera de comunicación interregional asfaltada:
calzadas separadas
2 carriles o más – 2 carriles estrechos
Sin asfaltar: transitable, con macadán
Otra carretera asfaltada – sin asfaltar
Pista o camino forestal, sendero
Carretera en construcción
10-1989 Fecha prevista de entrada en servicio

Distancias en kilómetros (totales o parciales)

12 en autopista:
tramo de peaje
12
tramo libre
12 en carretera

Transporte

Línea férrea – Tren-coche
Ⓑ Barcaza – Barcaza (DK, N, S, SF)
Enlace marítimo: permanente – de temporada
✈ Aeropuerto

Segni convenzionali

Vedere la legenda completa all'interno della copertina

Importanza degli itinerari

Autostrada a carreggiate separate
a carreggiata unica
Doppia carreggiata di tipo autostradale
Numero dello svincolo
Svincoli: completo – semi-svincolo
parziale – non precisato
Strada di comunicazione internazionale o nazionale rivestita:
a carreggiate separate
a 4 corsie – a 3 corsie
a 2 corsie larghe – a 2 corsie
Strada di comunicazione interregionale rivestita:
a carreggiate separate
a 2 corsie e più – a 2 corsie strette
Non rivestita: carrozzabile, in macadam
Altre strade con rivestimento – senza rivestimento
Strada per carri, sentiero
Strada in costruzione
10-1989 Apertura prevista

Distanze in chilometri (totali e parziali)

12 su autostrada:
tratto a pedaggio
12
tratto esente da pedaggio
12 su strada

Trasporti

Ferrovia – trasporto automobili per ferrovia
Ⓑ Su chiatta – su chiatta (DK, N, S, SF)
Collegamento via-traghetto: tutto l'anno – stagionale
✈ Aeroporto

Zeichenerklärung

Vollständige Zeichenerklärung siehe Umschlaginnenseite

Verkehrsbedeutung der Straßen

Autobahn mit getrennten Fahrbahnen
mit nur einer Fahrbahn
Schnellstraße mit getrennten Fahrbahnen
Nummer der Anschlußstelle
Anschlußstellen: Autobahnein- und/oder
-ausfahrt – ohne Angabe
Internationale bzw. nationale Hauptverkehrsstraße mit Belag:
getrennte Fahrbahnen
4 Fahrspuren – 3 Fahrspuren
2 breite Fahrspuren – 2 Fahrspuren
Überregionale Verbindungsstraße mit Belag:
getrennte Fahrbahnen
2 u. mehr Fahrspuren – 2 schmale Fahrspuren
Ohne Belag: befahrbar, mit Makadam
Sonstige Straßen: mit Belag, ohne Belag
Wirtschaftsweg – Weg, Pfad
Straße im Bau
10-1989 Voraussichtliches Datum der Verkehrsfreigabe

Entfernungsangaben in Kilometern (Gesamt- und Teilentfernungen)

12 auf der Autobahn:
gebührenpflichtiger Abschnitt
12
gebührenfreier Abschnitt
12 auf anderen Straßen

Transport

Bahnlinie – Autoreisezug
Ⓑ Fähre – Fähre (DK, N, S, SF)
Schiffsverbindung: ganzjährig – während der Saison
✈ Flughafen

Verklaring der tekens

Zie voor de volledige verklaring der tekens de binnenzijde van het omslag

Belang van het wegennet

Autosnelweg met gescheiden rijbanen
met één rijbaan
Dubbele rijbaan van het type autosnelweg
Nummer knooppunt/aansluiting
Knooppunten/aansluitingen : volledig – half
gedeeltelijk – niet nader aangegeven
Internationale of nationale verharde verbindingsweg:
gescheiden rijbanen
4 rijstroken – 3 rijstroken
2 brede rijstroken – 2 rijstroken
Regionale verharde verbindingsweg:
gescheiden rijbanen
2 of meer rijstroken – 2 smalle rijstroken
Onverhard: berijdbaar, macadamweg
Andere weg: verhard – onverhard
Bedrijfsweg, pad
Weg in aanleg
10-1989 Vermoedelijke datum ingebruikneming

Afstanden in kilometers (totaal en gedeeltelijk)

12 op de autosnelweg:
gedeelte met tol
12
tolvrij gedeelte
12 op de weg

Vervoer

Spoorweg – Autotrein
Ⓑ Veerpont – Veerpont (DK, N, S, SF)
Scheepvaartverbinding : permanent – alleen in het seizoen
✈ Luchthaven

Légende

Voir la légende complète à l'intérieure de la couverture

Importance des itinéraires

Autoroute à chaussées séparées
à une seule chaussée
Double chaussée de type autoroutier
Numéro d'échangeur
Échangeurs: complet – demi-échangeur
partiel – sans precision
Route de liaison internationale ou nationale revêtue:
chaussées séparées
4 voies – 3 voies
2 voies larges – 2 voies
Route de liaison interrégionale revêtue:
chaussées séparées
2 voies et plus – 2 voies étroites
Non revêtue: carrossable, en macadam
Autre route revêtue – non revêtue
Chemin d'exploitation, sentier
Route en construction
10-1989 Date de mise en service prévue

Distances en kilomètres (totalisées et partielles)

12 sur autoroute:
section à péage
12
section libre
12 sur route

Transport

Voie ferrée – Train-auto
Ⓑ Bac – Bac (DK, N, S, SF)
Liaison maritime: permanente – saisonnière
✈ Aéroport

Key to symbols

A full key to symbols appears inside the front cover

Road classification

Motorway: dual carriageway
single carriageway
Dual carriageway with motorway characteristics
Interchange number
Interchange: complete – half
limited – unspecified
International and national surfaced road network:
dual carriageway
four lanes – three lanes
two wide lanes – two lanes
Interregional surfaced road network:
dual carriageway
two lanes or more – two narrow lanes
Unsurfaced: suitable for vehicles, macadam
Other surfaced road – unsurfaced
Service road or cart track, footpath
Road under construction
10-1989 Scheduled opening date

Distances in kilometres (total and intermediate)

12 on motorway:
toll section
12
free section
12 on other roads

Transportation

Railway – Motorail
Ⓑ Ferry – Ferry (DK, N, S, SF)
Car ferry: all the year – seasonal
✈ Airport

A   B   C

1

Cape Wrath

Whiten Hea

Durness

Butt of Lewis

Port of Ness

Kinlochbervie

A 838

20

Whiten Hea

A 838

16 A 857

Tongue

908 △ *Foinaven*

31

△ 927

LEWIS

Barvas

A 858

Scourie

A 894

Laxford Bridge

Ben Hope

2

Carloway

A 858

292 △

12

A 857

Eddrachillis Bay

A 838

Kylestrome

Altnaharra

Ben K

34

Garynahine

Stornoway

A 858

Portnaguran

Tiumpan Head

A 837

19

A 894

34

961 △

A 859

A 866

Inchnadamph

40

THE MINCH

12

Eye Peninsula

Lochinver

△ 998

A 838

Ben More Assynt

Flannan I.

△ 574

36

A 859

Kebock Head

Rubha Cóigeach

849 △

Ledmore

A 837

Lai

H E B R I D E S

Hushinish

B 887

Clisham

572 △

W E S T E R N

Coigach

743 △

18

A 835

27 A 839

A 836

799 △

Tarbert

Ullapool

31

A 837

Toe Head

24

Harris

Rubha Réidh

Laide

Gruinard Bay

Bonar Bridge

A 859

Leverburgh

I S L E S

Dundonnell

A 832

12

Rodel

Renish Point

15

△ 1062

1084 △

Beinn Dearg

North Uist

△ 1062

Gairloch

Eastε

Tigharry

A 865

25

Lochmaddy

Loch Maree

Staffin

Sgurr Mór

△ 980

1110

57

19

Ben Wyvis

A 865

9

A 855

20 A 832

92

△ 1046

A 867

13

△ 347

Uig

34

W e s t e r R o s s

15

Garve

Balivanich

A 858

Rona

Torridon

Liathach

Kinlochewe

A 832

Dingwall

Benbecula

The Storr

△ 1054

10 A 896

9

Achnasheen

B

Creagorry

719 △

A 855

Shieldaig

19

Glen Carron

Contin

A 831

A 86

22

16

Sound of Raasay

896 △

A 896

24

1083 △

Dunvegan

A 850

Inner Sound

△ 1058

Lochcarron

Muir of Ord

A 831

A 833

B 862

Idrigill Point

21

Portree

Raasay

15

Stromeferry

Cannich

A 831

Drumnadrochit

South Uist

620 △

SEA OF

Bracadale

9

△ 444

B

Sconser

Kyle of Lochalsh

Stromeferry

29

22

A 865

THE HEBRIDES

Sligachan

Scalpay

A 850

Dornie

△ *Carn Eige*

H I G H L A

Glen More

Daliburgh

Lochboisdale

SKYE

17

A 850

B

5

Eilean Donan Castle

1183

Glen More

Broadford

Kyleakin

A 850

Shiel Bridge

Invermoriston

The Cuillins

14

Kylerhea

B

Glenelg

A' Chràlaig

Foyers

33

△ 993

A 881

Isleornsay

△ 1120

A 897

White Bridge

Barra

A 888

Elgol

17

32

50

16

43

69

Castlebay

383 △

Bayhirivagh

Ardvasar

A 851

80

13

7

Fort Augustus

Canna

Sound of Sleat

Loch Quoich

Monadhliat

△ *Sgurr na Ciche*

Invergarry

Carn Ban

942 △

Mallaig

1040

15

Newtonm

Mingulay

Rhum

812 △

Eigg

19

Arisaig

Loch Morar

76

25

40

Laggan

Barra Head

Muck

46

Glenfinnan

Creag Meagaidh

Dalwhinnie

A 861

882 △

27

A 881

1130 △

30

33

Loch Shiel

10

Spean Bridge

Pas Dru

Kilchoan

528 △

Salen

Strontian

Corran

9

Ben Nevis

△ 1148

Ben Alder

462

B 8007

A 861

13

Inchree

1344 △

S

C

O

M

Coll

Arinagour

Onich

Blackwater Resr

Loch Rannoch

Ballachulish

Tiree

Tobermory

Kentallen

Glen Coe

Kinloch Rannoch

Scarinish

Dervaig

B 8073

A 884

19

Portnacroish

1141 △

33

Bidean nam Bian

Salen

Lochaline

10

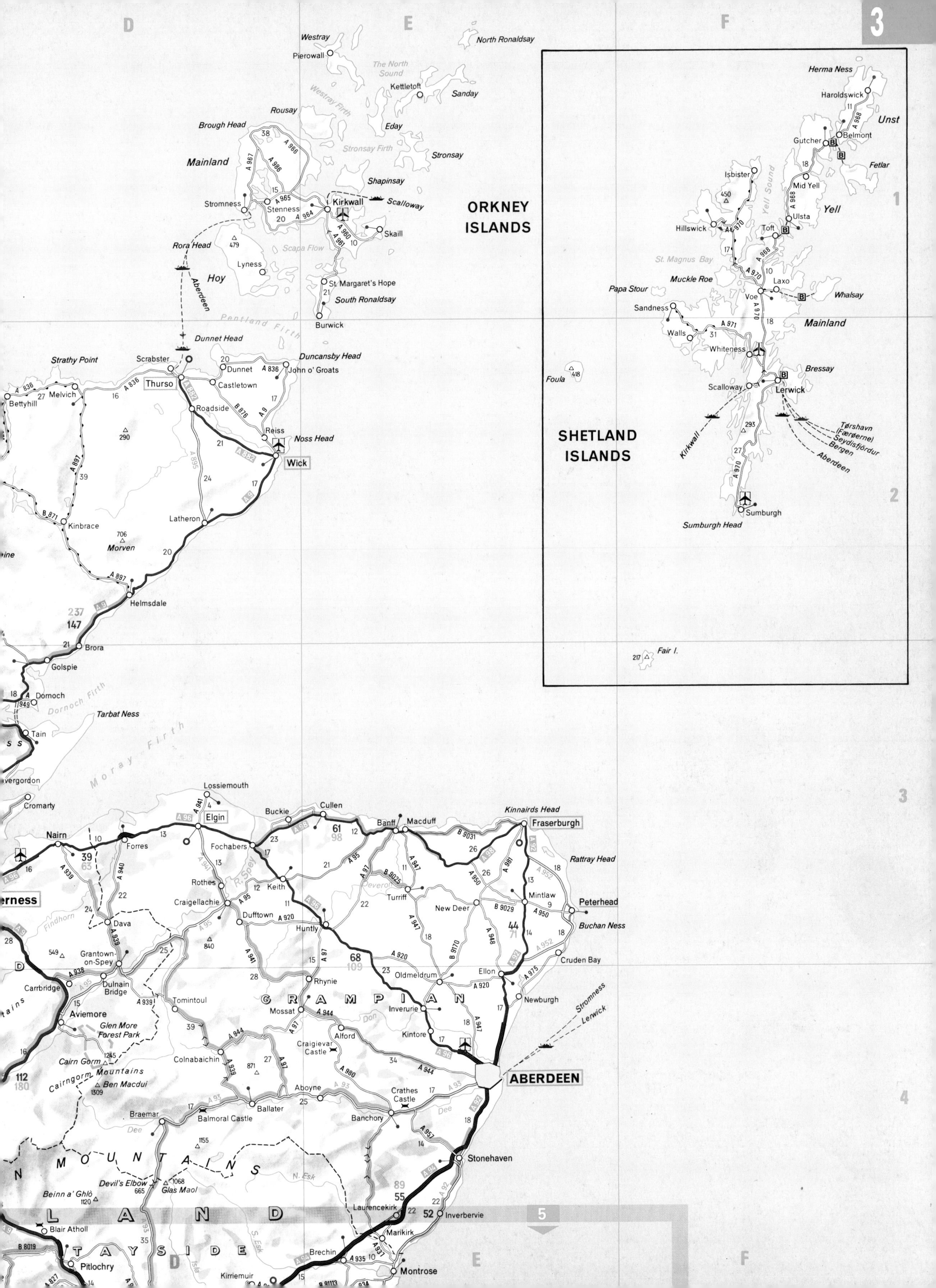

3

ORKNEY ISLANDS

Westray
Pierowall
North Ronaldsay
The North Sound
Kettletoft
Sanday
Rousay
Brough Head
Eday
38 A 966
Mainland
A 967 A 966
Stronsay Firth
Stronsay
Shapinsay
Stromness 15
Stenness A 965
20 A 964 Kirkwall Scalloway
A 960
A 961 10
Skaill
Rora Head
479
Scapa Flow
Hoy
Lyness
St Margaret's Hope
21
South Ronaldsay
Burwick
Aberdeen
Dunnet Head
Pentland Firth

SHETLAND ISLANDS

Herma Ness
Haroldswick
11 A 968 Unst
Gutcher B Belmont
B
Fetlar
Isbister
Mid Yell 18
450
Yell
Hillswick A 970 Toft A 968 B
17 Ulsta
St. Magnus Bay
A 968
Muckle Roe
Papa Stour Laxo
Voe B Whalsay
Sandness A 970
Walls 31 A 971 18 Mainland
Whiteness
Foula 418
Bressay
Scalloway B
Lerwick
293
Kirkwall
Tørshavn (Færøerne)
Seydisfjördur
Bergen
Aberdeen
27
A 970
Sumburgh
Sumburgh Head

217 Fair I.

Strathy Point
Scrabster
Dunnet 20 Duncansby Head
Bettyhill A 836 Melvich 27 16 Thurso A 836 John o' Groats
A 836 A 9 Castletown 17
39 Roadside A 876
290 Reiss Noss Head
21 A 882 Wick
Kinbrace 24 A 9
B 871 706 Latheron 17
Morven 20
A 897
237 Helmsdale
147
21 Brora
Golspie
18 A Dornoch
1949 Dornoch Firth
Tarbat Ness
Tain
Moray Firth

Cromarty
Lossiemouth
A 941 4
vergordon
Nairn A 96 Elgin Buckie Cullen
39 Forres 13 Fochabers 23 A 98 61 Banff Macduff Kinnairds Head
63 A 939 17 A 95 98 12 Fraserburgh
A 940 Rothes 13 A 947 B 9031
Inverness 24 Craigellachie 12 Keith A 96 26 Rattray Head
22 Dava A 95 11 A 95 A 920 Turriff New Deer B 9029 Mintlaw Peterhead
Findhorn A 97 22 A 941 Huntly A 947 18 44 9 Buchan Ness
549 Grantown- 15 A 95 68 A 920 23 Oldmeldrum A 975 Cruden Bay
on-Spey A 939 Dulnain 109 Rhynie Ellon A 920 Newburgh
Carrbridge Bridge 28 GRAMPIAN Stromness
Tomintoul A 939 Mossat A 944 Inverurie 17 Lerwick
Aviemore 840 Alford Kintore 17 A 96
Glen More 39 A 944 34 A 944 ABERDEEN
Forest Park Colnabaichin A 939 871 Craigievar Castle A 980
1245 27 Aboyne Crathes Castle 17 A 93
Cairn Gorm A 93 Castle 25 Banchory Dee 18
112 Cairngorm Mountains Ballater A 957
180 Ben Macdui Braemar 17 Balmoral Castle 14
1309 Dee Stonehaven
MOUNTAINS 1155
Devil's Elbow 1068 N. Esk 89
Beinn a' Ghlò 665 Glas Maol 55
1120 Laurencekirk 22 22 52 Inverbervie
LAND TAYSIDE Marikirk A 937
Blair Atholl 35 Brechin A 935 10 Montrose
B 8019 Kirriemuir
Pitlochry

Stockton-on-Tees

Sedgefield
x9
Billingham
Redcar
Marske-by-the-Sea
Saltburn-by-the-Sea
Brotton
Guisborough
Loftus
Eaglescliffe
A174
Loftus
Middlesbrough
A173
A174
Whitby
A171

Northallerton
Cleveland Hills
454
North York Moors
National Park
A171

A684
A167
A19

Thirsk
Helmsley
Pickering
A170
Scalby
Scarborough

YORKSHIRE
Easingwold
Malton
Norton
Filey

Boroughbridge
B1257
B1363

YORK
Flamborough Head

Wetherby
Tadcaster
Wetwang
Bridlington

H U M B E R S I D E
Gt. Driffield
Beeford

Selby
Barlby
Market Weighton
Leven
B1244
Hornsea

Garforth
Castleford
Howden
M62
Beverley
KINGSTON-UPON-HULL

Pontefract
Snaith
Goole
Barton-upon-Humber
Humber Bridge
Hedon
A1242
Withernsea

wakefield
Thorne
Crowle
A1077
Patrington
Kilnsea

Barnsley
Bentley
Scunthorpe
Immingham Dock
Immingham
Great Grimsby
Spurn Head

Doncaster
Epworth
Brigg
Humberside
Cleethorpes
Rotterdam
Zeebrugge

Rotherham
Bawtry
Caistor
A46

Maltby
Worksop
East Retford
Gainsborough
Market Rasen
Louth
Mablethorpe

Chesterfield
Hardwick Hall
Tuxford
Ollerton
Wragby
Horncastle
Sutton-on-Sea

Mansfield
Newark-on-Trent
Lincoln
Woodhall Spa
Partney
Alford
A52
Skegness

Sutton-in-Ashfield
Southwell
Leadenham
Spilsby
Hucknall

NOTTINGHAM
Bingham
Sleaford
L I N C O L N
Boston

West Bridgford
Grantham
Donington
Sutterton

Long Eaton
Rempstone
Bourne
Holbeach
Long Sutton
Hunstanton
Wells-next-the-Sea
Blakeney
Sheringham
Cromer

Loughborough
Melton Mowbray
Oakham
Spalding
The Wash
Sandringham House
Fakenham
Holt
Mundesley
North Walsham

LEICESTER
Stamford
Crowland
Wisbech
King's Lynn
N O R F O L K
East Dereham
Aylsham
Low Street

Oadby
Uppingham
Eye
Guyhirn
Outwell
Swaffham
Watton
NORWICH
Great Yarmouth

E N G L A N D
Market Harborough
Corby
Weldon
Peterborough
Whittlesey
March
Downham Market
Stradsett
Wymondham
Attleborough
Acle
Gorleston-on-Sea

Lutterworth
Husbands Bosworth
Desborough
Rothwell
Oundle
Chatteris
Littleport
Mundford
Brandon
Thetford
Bungay
Lowestoft
Beccles

Kettering
Thrapston
Ramsey
Ely
Diss
Harleston
Southwold

N O R T H A M P T O N
Higham Ferrers
St. Ives
Soham
C A M B R I D G E
Huntingdon
St. Farith
Ixworth
Scole
Halesworth
Dennington

Wellingborough
Rushden
Godmanchester
St. Neots
Bury St. Edmunds
Yoxford

NORTHAMPTON
B E D F O R D
Bedford
Sandy
Eltisley
Newmarket
Stowmarket
Saxmundham
Leiston

Towcester
Newport Pagnell
Shefford
Biggleswade
Potton
Cambridge
Haverhill
Lavenham
IPSWICH
Aldeburgh

Brackley
Milton Keynes
Buckingham
Bletchley
Woburn
Leighton Buzzard
Letchworth
Hitchin
Baldock
Buntingford
Royston
Saffron Walden
Clare
Sudbury
Finchingfield
Hadleigh
Woodbridge

Zeebrugge

A
B
C
12
1
2
3
4
Achill Island
Keel
Ballycroy
Bangor
Nephin Beg Range
Nephin
Mulrany
Corraun
Newport
Clare Island
Clew Bay
Crossmolina
Ballina / Béal an Átha
Castlebar / Caisleán an Bharraigh
Pontoon
Foxford
Swinford
Charlestown
Tobercurry
Ballymote
Ballysadare
Sligeach
Inishcrone
The Ox Mountains
SLIGO
Dowra
Drumkeeran
Drumshanbo
Keadew
Boyle / Mainistir na Búille
Gorteen
Ballaghaderreen
Frenchpark
Carrick-on-Shannon / Cora Droma Rúisc
Elphin
Strokestown
Tulsk
Castlerea
ROSCOMMON
Ballyhaunis
Kiltamagh
Connaught
Westport / Cathair na Mart
Louisburgh
Croagh Patrick
Inishturk
Inishbofin
Inishshark
Rinvyle Pt.
Mweelrea Mts.
Killary Harbour
Partry Mountains
Ballintober
Claremorris
Letterfrack
Leenane
The Twelve Pins
Clifden / An Clochán
Connemara
Maumturk Mts.
Slyne Head
Roundstone
Maam Cross
Ballinrobe
Lough Mask
Clonbur
Cong
Kilmaing
Lough Corrib
Headford
Tuam / Tuaim
Dunmore
Glennamaddy
Ballymoe
Lanesborough
Roscommon / Ros Comáin
Mount Bellew
Ballyforan
Athlone / Baile Átha Luain
Gortmore
Carna
Oughterard
GALWAY
IRELAND
Kilkieran Bay
Lettermullan
Gorumna Island
Galway / Gaillimh
Spiddle
Barna
Oranmore
Athenry
Ballinasloe / Béal Átha na Sluaighe
Aran Islands
Inishmore
Kilronan
Inishmaan
Inisheer
Galway Bay
Black Head
Craughwell
Loughrea
Clonmacnoise
Ferbane
Clonfert
Ardrahan
Kinvarra
Ballyvaughan
Lisdoonvarna
Kilfenora
Gort
Portumna
Banagher
Cloghan
Kilcormac
Birr
Kinnitty
Slieve Bloom
Cliffs of Moher
Lahinch
Ennistimon
Corrofin
Spanish Point
Milltown Malbay
CLARE
Ennis / Inis
Tulla
Scarriff
Borrisokane
Roscrea
Nenagh / An tAonach
Moneygall
Knappogue Castle
Broadford
Kilmurry
Killaloe
Newmarket on Fergus
Shannon
Bunratty Castle
Creegh
Kilkee
Killadysert
Kilrush
Killimer
Labasheeda
Loop Head
Kilbaha
River Shannon
Mouth of the Shannon
Tarbert
Askeaton
Ballybunnion
Newport
Dolla
Templemore
Thurles / Durlas
TIPPERARY
Milestone
Holycross Abbey
LIMERICK / LUIMNEACH
Adare
Rathkeale
Croom
Kerry Head
Ballyduff
Listowel
Ballyheige
LIMERICK
Newcastle West
Abbeyfeale
Hospital
Tipperary / Tiobraid Árann
Cashel / Caiseal
Killenaule
Fethard
Brandon Head
Brandon Mountain
Sybil Head
Clogher Head
Dingle
Great Blasket I.
Anascaul
Slieve Mish Mts.
Tralee / Trá Lí
Tralee Bay
Slea Head
Castlemaine
Castleisland
Dromcolliher
Kilmallock
Rath Luirc (Charleville)
Galty Mountains
Caher
Slievenamon
Clonmel / Cluain Meala
Dingle Bay
Killorglin
KERRY
Killarney / Cill Airne
Newmarket
Boherboy
Kanturk
Buttevant
Kildorrery
Mitchelstown
Clogheen
Knockmealdown Mts.
Comeragh Mts.
R. Suir
Glenbeigh
Doulus Head
Knight's Town
Valencia Island
Cahersiveen
Ring of Kerry
Iveragh
Carrantuohill
Macgillycuddy's Reeks
Muckross House
Rathmore
Millstreet
Mallow / Mala
Fermoy
Lismore
Cappoquin
CORK
Mangerton Mountain
Derrynasaggart Mts.
Kilgarvan
Waterville
St. Finan's Bay
Bolus Head
Skellig
Sneem
Kenmare
Macroom
Coachford
Blarney
CORK / CORCAIGH
Tallow
Dungarvan / Dún Garbhán
Dungarvan Harbour
Helvick Head
Kenmare River
Lauragh
Beara
Caha Mts.
Glengarriff
Pass of Keimaneigh
Midleton
Youghal / Eochaill
Ardmore
Youghal Bay
Cobh / An Cóbh
Ringaskiddy
Crosshaven
Ballycotton
Castletownbere
Dursey Island
Bere I.
Bantry / Beanntraí
Bantry Bay
Dunmanway
Bandon
Kinsale
Sheep's Head
Dunmanus Bay
Timoleague
Rosscarbery
Clonakilty
Skull
Skibbereen
Roaringwater Bay
Mizen Head
Old Head of Kinsale
Galley Head
Toe Head
Clear Island
Swansea
Roscoff
le Havre

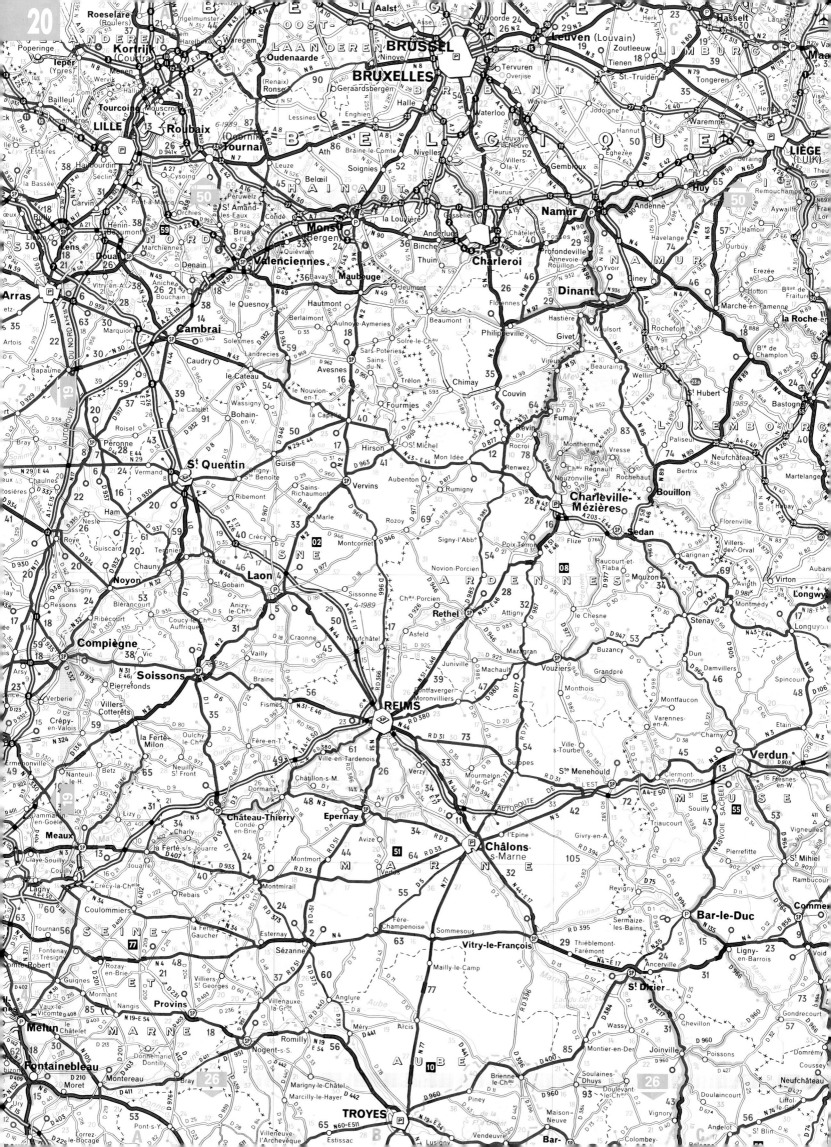

Rosslare   Weymouth   Poole   Portsmouth   St Valery-en-Ca   Veulettes

18   **19**   Fécamp   Cany-Barville

Cap de la Hague   Cap Lévy   St Pierre-Eglise   Pnte de Barfleur   Yport   Valmont   Ourville   Doudevil

Nez de Jobourg   **Cherbourg**   **Etretat**   Cap d'Antifer   Criquetot-l'Esneval   Goderville   Fauville   Yvetot

Beaumont   D901   Barfleur   Montivilliers   St Romain   Bolbec   Caudebec

Quettehou   St Vaast-la-Hougue   Ste Adresse   **LE HAVRE**   Lillebonne   Duclair

Valognes   Montebourg   Villerville   **Honfleur**   Pont-Audemer   Quilleboeuf   Bourgtheroulde

Bricquebec   **Trouville**   **Deauville**   Blonville   **Villers**   Beuzeville

les Pieux   **Houlgate**   **Cabourg**   le Bec-Hellouin

Carteret   Barneville   Ste Mère-Eglise   Grandcamp-Maisy   St Laurent   Port-en-Bessin   St Aubin   Langrune   Luc   Ouistreham   Dives   Cormeille

Portbail   Isigny   Trévières   Arromanches   Courseulles   Lion   Merville   Dozulé   Montfort

la Haye-du-Puits   Carentan   St Jean-de-Daye   **Bayeux**   Creully   Fontaine-Henry   Troarn   Cambremer   Blangy-le-Châu   Lieurey

Lessay   Périers   St Clair-s-l'E.   **CAEN**   Thiberville   le Neubourg

Gorey   St Sauveur-le-V.   Ballroy   **St Lô**   Villers Bocage   Evrecy   Moult   Mézidon   **Lisieux**   la Rivière-Thibouville

St-Hélier   St Malo-de-la-Lande   Marigny   Caumont-l'Eventé   Torigni   Aunay-s-O.   St Pierre-s-D.   Bernay   Beaumont-le-Roger

Coutainville   **Coutances**   Canis   Tessy   Thury-Harcourt   Potigny   Orbec   Broglie   Beaumesnil

Montmartin   Cérisy-la-S.   le Bény-Bocage   Clécy   Livarot   la Neuve-Lyre

I. Chausey   Bréhal   Gavray   Hambye   Percy   Condé-s-Noireau   Vimoutiers   Rugles   Breteuil

Granville   Villedieu-les-Poêles   **Vire**   Vassy   Pont-d'Ouilly   **Falaise**   Trun   la Ferté-Frênel   l'Aigle

St Pair   la Haye Pesnel   St Sever   Exmes   Gacé   Verneuil

St Malo   Paramé   Jullouville   Brécey   St Pois   Tinchebray   **Flers**   Putanges   Ecouché   **Argentan**   Nonant-le-Pin   le Merlerault   Moulins-la-Marche   la Ferté-Vidame

Rothéneuf   Carolles   Sartilly   Sourdeval   Messei   Briouze   Mortrée   Courtomer   Tourouvre

Cancale   **Avranches**   Pontaubault   Juvigny-le-   **Mortain**   **Domfront**   la Ferté-Macé   Sées   la Ferté-Vidame

le Mont-St Michel   le Vivier   Ducey   Barenton   **Bagnoles-de-l'Orne**   Carrouges   Bazoches-s-H.   le Mêle   **Mortagne-au-Perche**

Servon   Dol-de-B.   St Hilaire-du-Harcouet   St James   le Teilleul   Juvigny-s-s-A.   Couptrain   Pré-en-Pail   Mt des Avaloirs   **Alençon**   Pervenchères   Rémalard

Pleine-Fougères   Pontorson   Landivy   Passais   Lassay   Villaines-la-Juhel   **Bellême**

Antrain   Louvigné-du-Désert   Ambrières-les-Vallées   Jarvon   Mamers   **Nogent-le-Rotrou**

Combourg   St Brice-en-Coglès   Gorron   Fresnay-s-S.   Beaumont-s.   Marolles-les-Braults   la Ferté-Bernard

Evran   **Fougères**   Ernée   **Mayenne**   Bais   Sillé-le-Guillaume   Bonnétable   Ballon

Tinténiac   St Aubin-du-Cormier   Chailland   Evron   Conlie   Tuffé   Montmirail

Bécherel   Hédé   St Aubin-d'Aubigné   Champeaux   Montsûrs   Ste Suzanne   **LE MANS**   Boulloire   Mondoubleau

Montauban   Liffré   **Vitré**   Argentré-du-Plessis   **Laval**   Ste Denis-d'Orques   Brûlon   la Suze   Connerré   Vibraye

RENNES   Châteaubourg   Loiron   Vaiges   Loué   St Calais

Mordelles   St Jacques   Châteaugiron   Meslay   Solesmes

Guichen   Janzé   Cossé-le-Vivien   **Sablé**   Malicorne   le Gd Lucé   Savigny-s-B.

Maure   Retiers   la Guerche-de-B.   St Aignan-s-Roë   Craon   Grez-en-Bouère   Pontvallain   Mayet   Château-du-Loir   Château-Renault

Pipriac   Bain-de-Bretagne   Martigné-Ferchaud   Renazé   **Château-Gontier**   Bierné   Châteauneuf-s-S   Ecommoy   la Chartre

la Gacilly   Rougé   Pouancé   Segré   Châteauneuf-s-S.   Baugé   le Lude   Château-Vallière   Neuvy-le-Roi

Redon   Gd Fougeray   **Châteaubriant**   Derval   St Julien-de-Vouvantes   Moisdon   le Lion-d'A   Tiercé   la Flèche   Baugé   Neuillé-Pont-Pierre

Guéméné-Penfao   Nozay   St Mars-la-Jaille   Riaillé   le Louroux   **ANGERS**   Beaufort-en-V.   Vouvray   Montbazon

St Gildas-des-B.   Blain   Ligné   Varades   St Georges   les Ponts-de-Cé   **TOURS**

Pontchâteau   Savenay   **NANTES**   Ancenis   St Florent   Montjean   Chalonnes   Longué   les Rosiers   Langeais   Villandry   Montbazon

Donges   Carquefou   Champtoceaux   Brissac-Quincé   Gennes   **Saumur**   Azay-le-Rideau

Paimboeuf   le Pellerin   Montrevault   Thouarcé   Cunault   Doué   Chinon

St Etienne-de-Montluc   Beaupréau   Chemillé   le Lorgux

MANCHE   **CALVADOS**   **ORNE**   **SARTHE**   **MAYENNE**   **MAINE-ET-LOIRE**   **ILLE-ET-VILAINE**   **LOIRE-ATLANTIQUE**   **INDRE-ET-LOIRE**

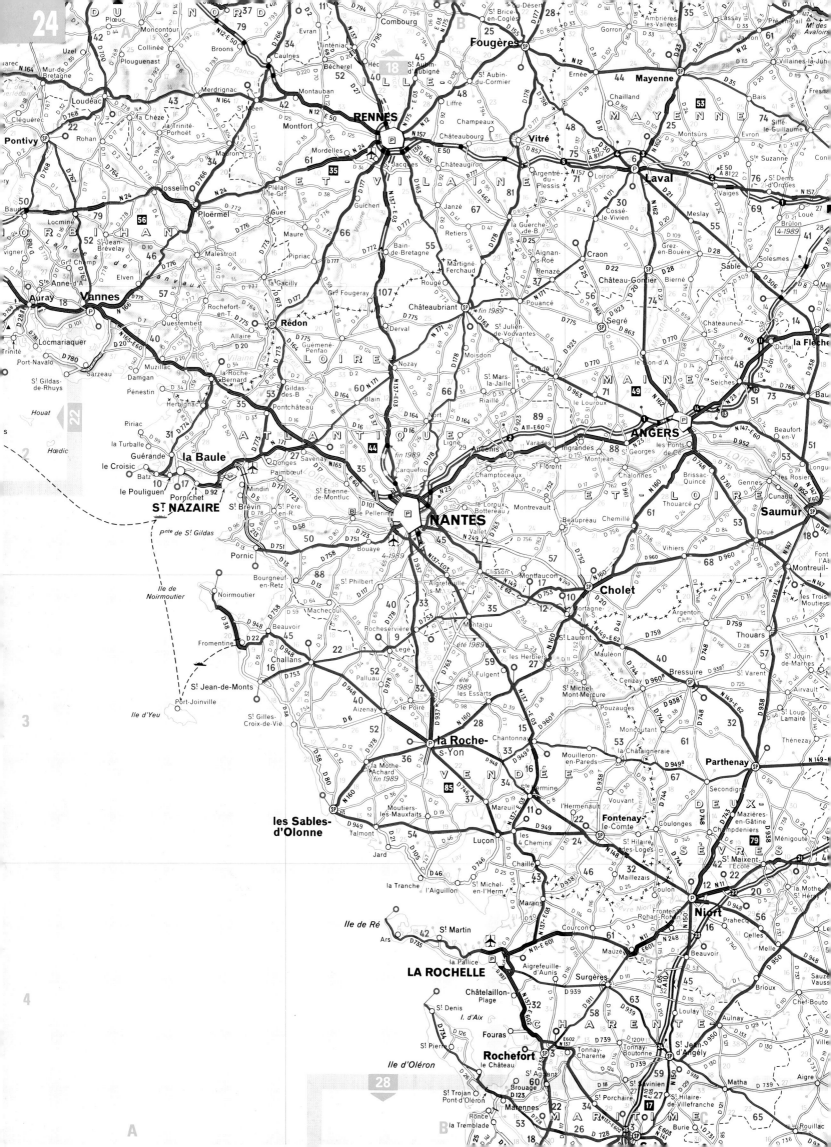

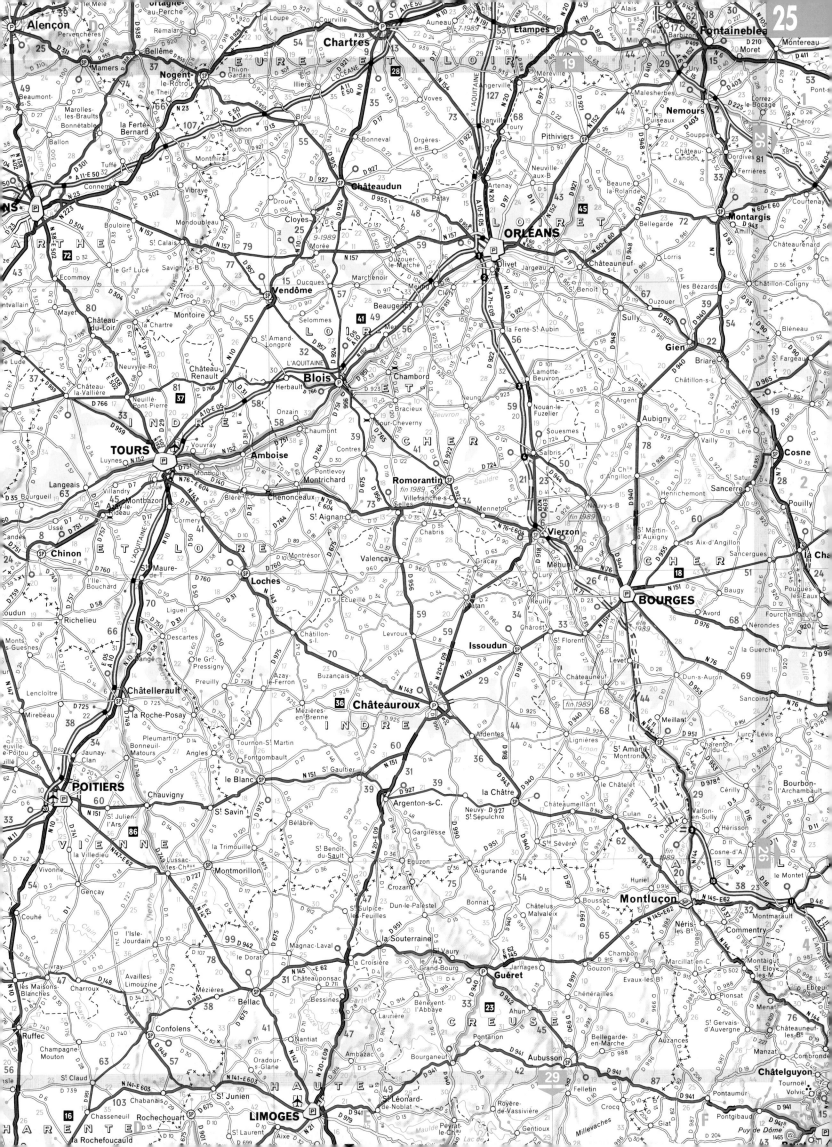

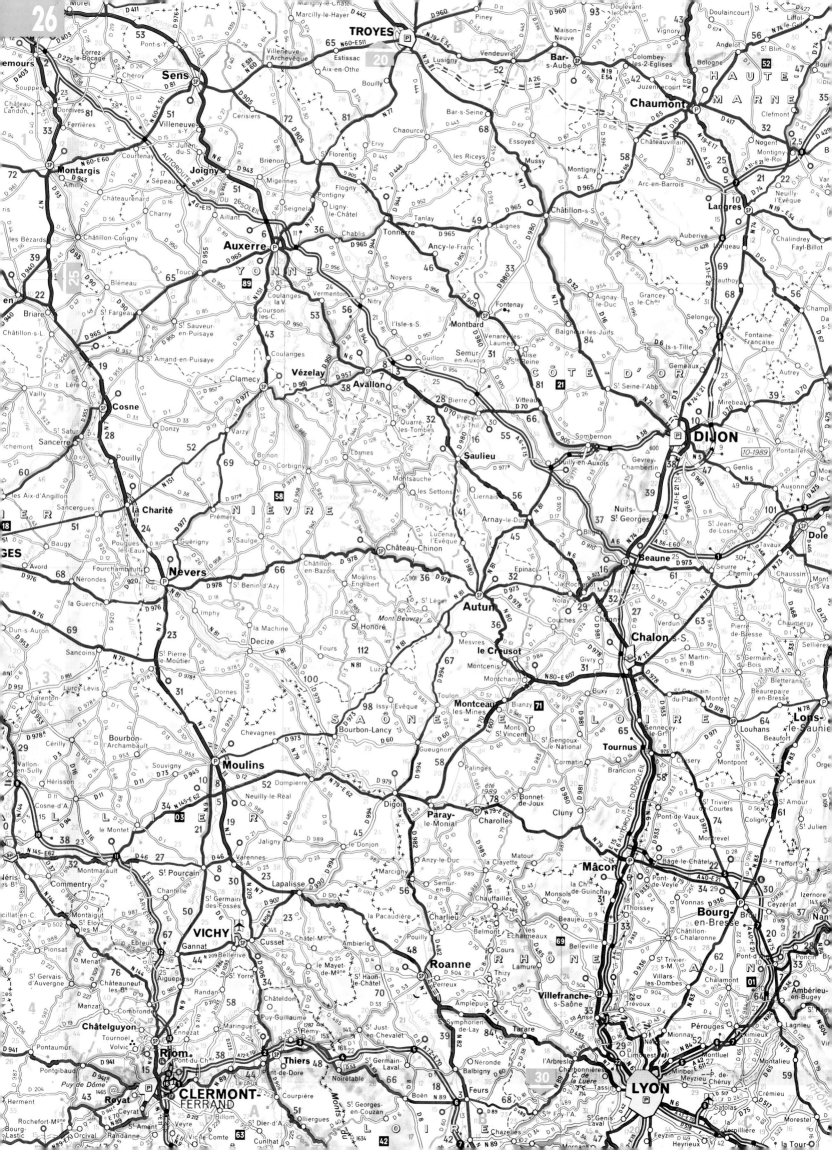

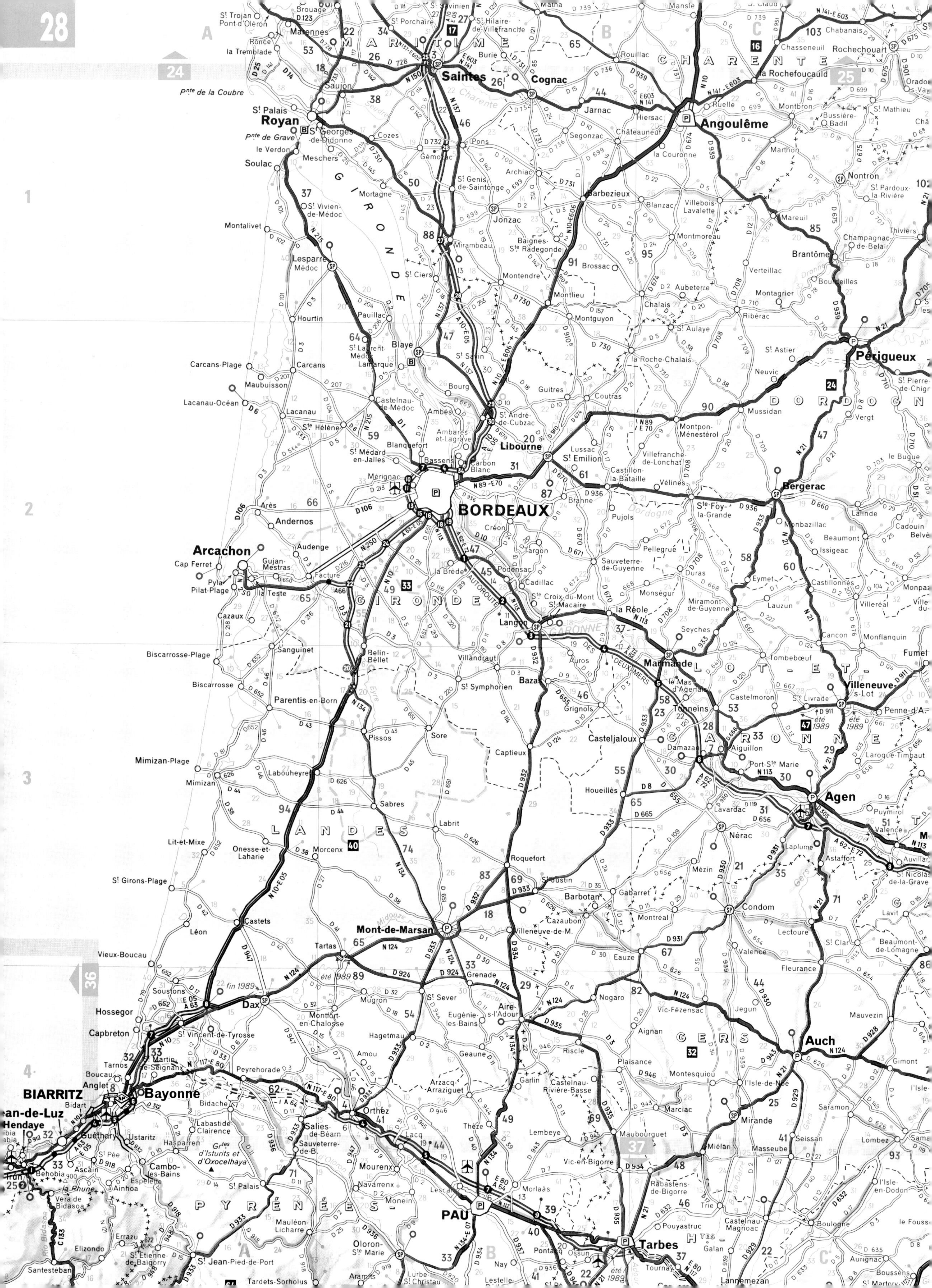

Brouage
St Trojan
Pont-d'Oléron
Marennes
Ronce
la Tremblade
St Porchaire
St Savinien
St Hilaire-de-Villefranche
Matha
Mansle
Chabanais
Chasseneuil
Rochechouart
MARITIME
CHARENTE
Burie
Saintes
Cognac
Rouillac
la Rochefoucauld
Saujon
Pte de la Coubre
St Palais
Royan
St Georges-de-Didonne
Pte de Grave
le Verdon
Soulac
Meschers
Cozes
Pons
Gémozac
Jarnac
Hiersac
Châteauneuf
Segonzac
Angoulême
Ruelle
Montbron
Bussière-Badil
St Mathieu
la Couronne
Marthon
Archiac
St Genis-de-Saintonge
Mortagne
Jonzac
Barbezieux
Blanzac
Villebois-Lavalette
Nontron
St Pardoux-la-Rivière
Mareuil
St Vivien-de-Médoc
Montalivet
Mirambeau
Baignes-Ste Radegonde
Montmoreau
Champagnac-de-Belair
Thiviers
Brantôme
Lesparre-Médoc
St Ciers
Brossac
Montendre
Verteillac
Bourdeilles
Montlieu
Aubeterre
Montagrier
Chalais
Ribérac
Hourtin
Pauillac
Montguyon
St Aulaye
St Laurent-Médoc
Blaye
Lamarque
St Savin
St Astier
Périgueux
Carcans-Plage
Carcans
Maubuisson
Lacanau-Océan
Lacanau
Castelnau-de-Médoc
Bourg
Guitres
Coutras
la Roche-Chalais
Neuvic
St Pierre-de-Chignac
Ste Hélène
St André-de-Cubzac
Ambès
Ambarès-et-Lagrave
Blanquefort
St Médard-en-Jalles
Libourne
Lussac
Montpon-Ménestérol
Mussidan
DORDOGNE
Vergt
St Emilion
Villefranche-de-Lonchat
Bassens
Carbon Blanc
Castillon-la-Bataille
Vélines
Mérignac
Bergerac
le Bugue
BORDEAUX
Branne
Ste Foy-la-Grande
Arès
Andernos
Pujols
Lalinde
Monbazillac
Créon
Beaumont
Cadouin
Arcachon
Cap Ferret
Audenge
Gujan-Mestras
Targon
Sauveterre-de-Guyenne
Pellegrue
Issigeac
Pyla
Pilat-Plage
la Teste
Facture
la Brède
Podensac
Cadillac
Duras
Eymet
Castillonnès
Monpazier
GIRONDE
Ste Croix-du-Mont
St Macaire
Monségur
Miramont-de-Guyenne
Lauzun
Villeréal
Cazaux
Langon
la Réole
Seyches
Cancon
Monflanquin
Biscarrosse-Plage
Sanguinet
Belin-Béliet
Villandraut
Auros
Marmande
Tombebœuf
Fumel
Biscarrosse
St Symphorien
Bazas
le Mas-d'Agenais
LOT-ET-GARONNE
Villeneuve-s-Lot
Parentis-en-Born
Grignols
Tonneins
Castelmoron
Ste Livrade
Penne-d'A.
Sore
Pissos
Casteljaloux
Damazan
Aiguillon
Laroque-Timbaut
Mimizan-Plage
Mimizan
Captieux
Port-Ste Marie
Labouheyre
Houeillès
Agen
Sabres
Lavardac
Puymirol
LANDES
Labrit
Nérac
Valence
Lit-et-Mixe
Onesse-et-Laharie
Morcenx
Roquefort
Laplume
Astaffort
Auvillar
St Nicolas-de-la-Grave
Mézin
St Girons-Plage
St Justin
Barbotan
Gabarret
Condom
Léon
Castets
Cazaubon
Montréal
Lavit
Mont-de-Marsan
Villeneuve-de-M.
Lectoure
Vieux-Boucau
Tartas
Eauze
Valence
St Clar
Beaumont-de-Lomagne
Fleurance
Soustons
Grenade
Hossegor
Dax
St Sever
Aire-s-l'Adour
Nogaro
Vic-Fézensac
Jegun
Mauvezin
Capbreton
St Vincent-de-Tyrosse
Montfort-en-Chalosse
Mugron
Eugénie-les-Bains
Aignan
Hagetmau
Riscle
GERS
Auch
Tarnos
St Martin-de-Seignanx
Peyrehorade
Amou
Geaune
Plaisance
Gimont
Boucau
Anglet
BIARRITZ
Bayonne
Bidart
Bidache
Orthez
Garlin
Castelnau-Rivière-Basse
Montesquiou
l'Isle-de-Noë
Arzacq-Arraziguet
Hendaye
Guéthary
Ustaritz
Labastide-Clairence
Hasparren
Salies-de-Béarn
Sauveterre-de-B.
Lacq
Thèze
Lembeye
Marciac
Mirande
Saramon
St Pée
Ascain
Cambo-les-Bains
Espelette
Grtes d'Isturits et d'Oxocelhaya
Maubourguet
Seissan
Lombez
Behobia
la Rhune
Ainhoa
Vera de Bidasoa
Mourenx
Navarrenx
Monein
Lescar
Vic-en-Bigorre
Miélan
Masseube
PYRÉNÉES
St Palais
Morlaàs
Rabastens-de-Bigorre
Trie
l'Isle-en-Dodon
PAU
Mauléon-Licharre
Pouyastruc
Castelnau-Magnoac
Boulogne
Errazu
St Etienne-de-Baigorry
Elizondo
Oloron-Ste Marie
Pontacq
Ossun
Tarbes
Galan
Santesteban
St Jean-Pied-de-Port
Nay
Tournay
Aurignac
Tardets-Sorholus
Lurbe-St Christau
Aramits
Lestelle
Lannemezan
St Martory
Rio Bidasoa

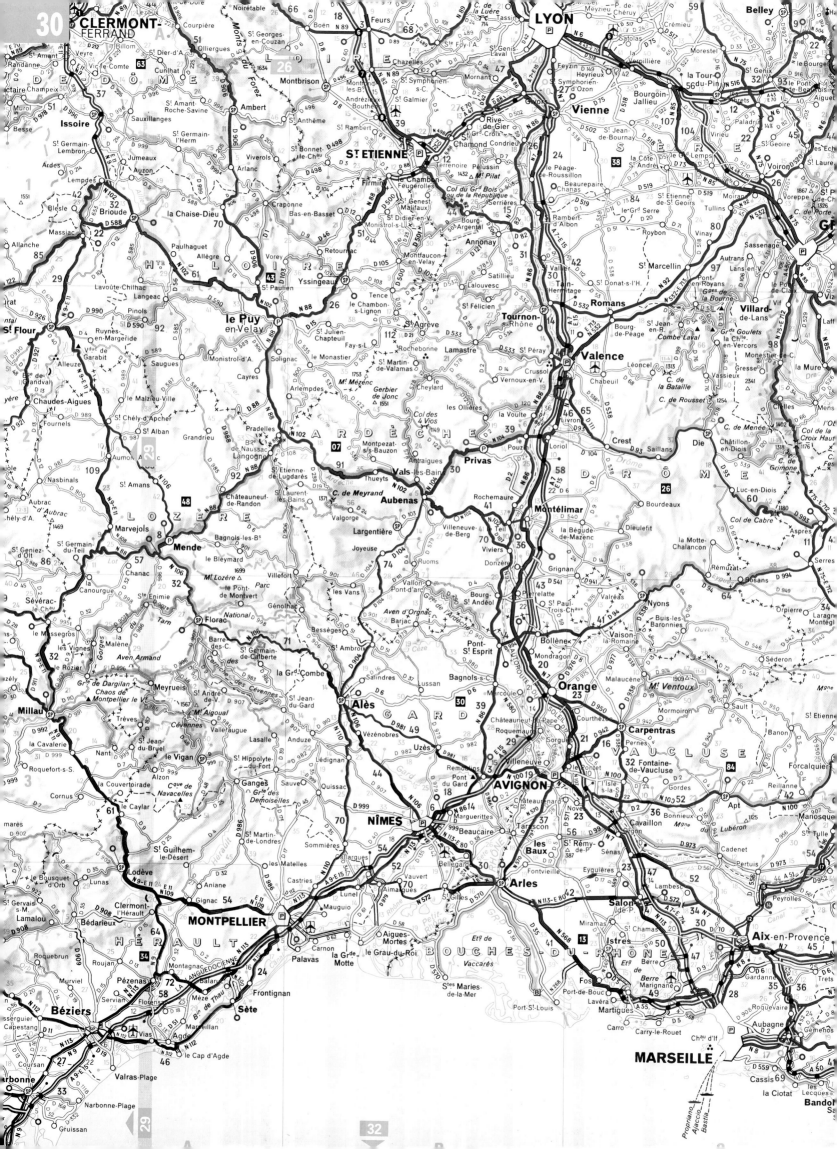

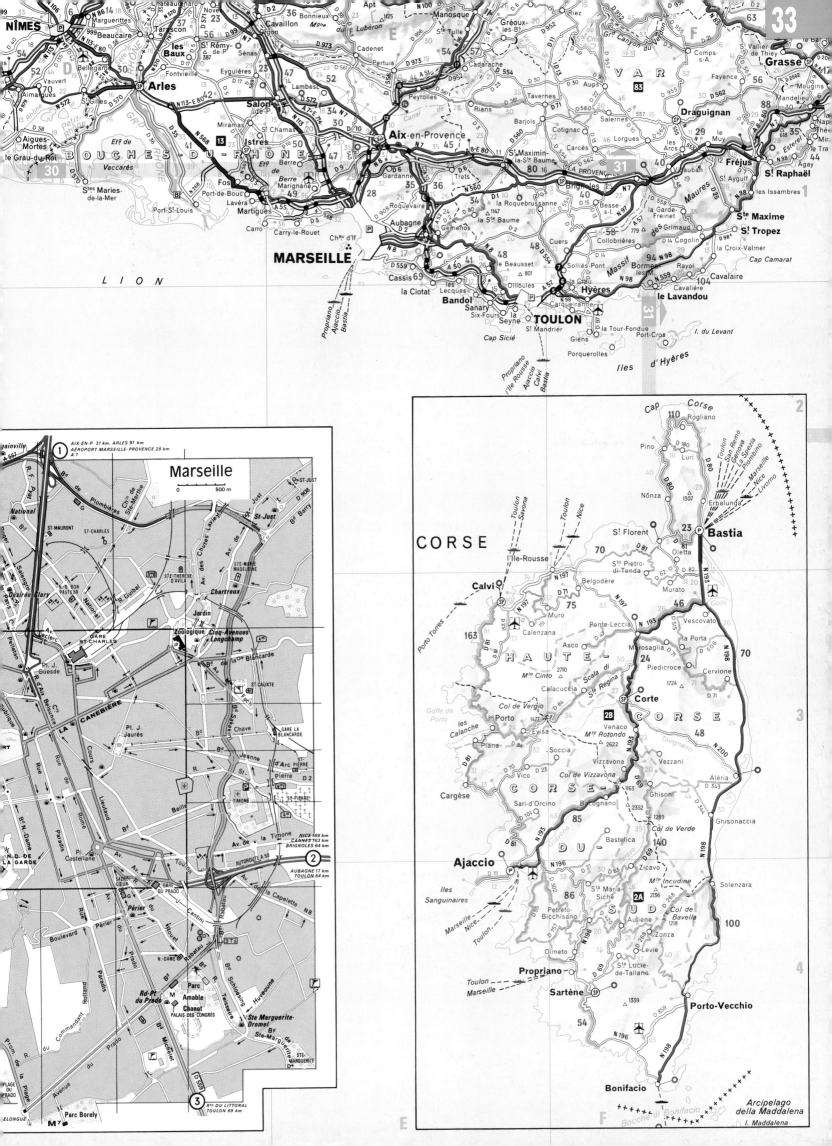

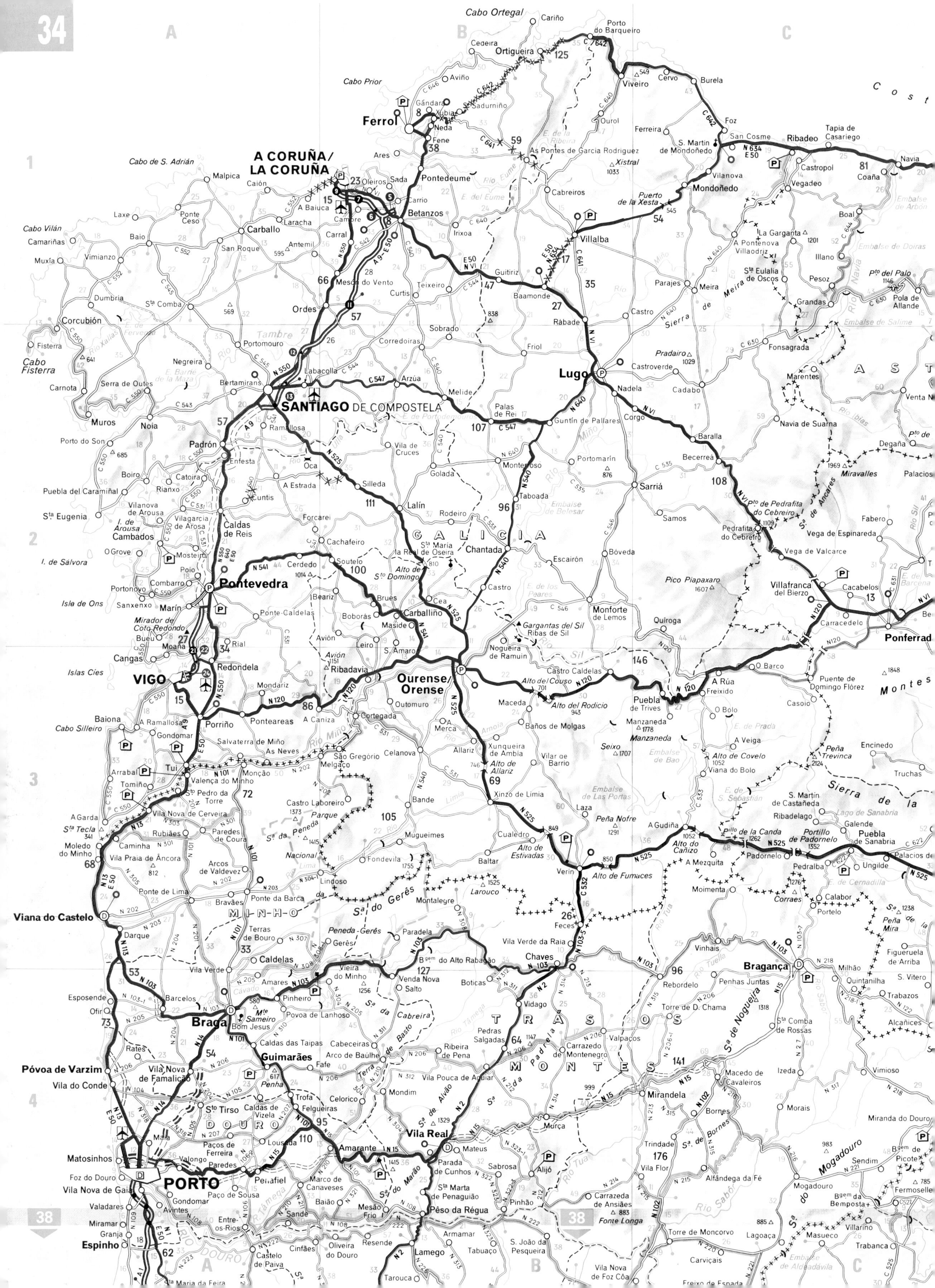
A
B
C
1
2
3
4
Cabo Ortegal
Cariño
Porto do Barqueiro
Cedeira
Ortigueira
Viveiro
Cervo
Burela
Cabo Prior
Aviño
Gándara
Sadurniño
Xubia
Ferrol
Neda
Fene
Ouról
Ferreira
Foz
S. Martin de Mondoñedo
San Cosme
Ribadeo
Tapia de Casariego
Navia
Coaña
Castropol
Vegadeo
A CORUÑA/
LA CORUÑA
Cabo de S. Adrián
Malpica
Caión
Oleiros
Sada
Pontedeume
As Pontes de García Rodriguez
Xistral
Cabreiros
Puerto de la Xesta
Vilanova
Mondoñedo
Ares
A Baiuca
Carrio
Cambre
Betanzos
Laxe
Ponte Ceso
Laracha
Cabo Vilán
Camariñas
Baio
Carballo
Carral
Irixoa
Villalba
Boal
La Garganta
A Pontenova
Villaodriz
Illano
Muxía
Vimianzo
San Roque
Antemil
Sta Eulalia de Oscos
Pesoz
Pto del Palo
Pola de Allande
Dumbria
Sta Comba
Mesón do Vento
Guitiriz
Teixeiro
Curtis
Baamonde
Parajes
Meira
Grandas
Corcubión
Ordes
Rábade
Castro
Sierra de Meira
Fisterra
Cabo Fisterra
Tambre
Portomouro
Sobrado
Corredoiras
Friol
Pradairo
Fonsagrada
Negreira
Castroverde
Lugo
Marentes
Carnota
Serra de Outes
Bertamirans
Labacolla
Arzúa
Melide
Nadela
Cadabo
Venta N
Muros
Noia
SANTIAGO DE COMPOSTELA
Palas de Rei
Guntín de Pallares
Corgo
Navia de Suarna
Porto do Son
Padrón
Ramallosa
Baralla
Degaña
Boiro
Enfesta
Oca
Vila de Cruces
Monterroso
Portomarín
Becerreá
Miravalles
Palacios
Puebla del Caramiñal
Catoira
Rianxo
A Estrada
Silleda
Golada
Sarriá
Pto de Pedrafita do Cebreiro
Sta Eugenia
Vilanova de Arousa
Cuntis
Lalín
Rodeiro
Taboada
Embalse de Belesar
Samos
Fabero
I. de Arousa
Cambados
Vilagarcia de Arosa
Caldas de Reis
Forcarei
Pedrafita do Cebreiro
Vega de Espinareda
O Grove
I. de Sálvora
Mosteiro
Cachafeiro
Sta María la Real de Oseira
GALICIA
Chantada
Bóveda
Vega de Valcarce
Cerdedo
Souteio
Alto de Sto Domingo
Escairón
Portonovo
Combarro
Poio
Pontevedra
Castro
Pico Piapaxaro
Villafranca del Bierzo
Cacabelos
Isla de Ons
Sanxenxo
Marín
Beariz
Brues
Cea
Monforte de Lemos
Quiroga
Carracedelo
Ponferrada
Mirador de Coto Redondo
Ponte-Caldelas
Boborás
Carballiño
Maside
Gargantas del Sil
Ribas de Sil
Bueu
Moaña
Rial
Avión
Leiro
S. Amaro
Nogueira de Ramuín
Cangas
Redondela
Ribadavia
Castro Caldelas
Islas Cíes
VIGO
Mondariz
Ourense/
Orense
Alto del Couso
Alto do Rodicio
Puebla de Trives
A Rúa
Freixido
O Barco
Puente de Domingo Flórez
Montes
Baiona
Cabo Silleiro
A Ramallosa
Gondomar
Porriño
Ponteareas
A Caniza
Cortegada
Outomuro
Maceda
Baños de Molgas
Manzaneda
O Bolo
Casoio
Salvaterra de Miño
As Neves
Merca
Seixo
A Veiga
Encinedo
Arrabal
Tui
Valença do Minho
Monção
São Gregório
Melgaço
Celanova
Allariz
Xunqueira de Ambia
Alto de Allariz
Vilar de Barrio
Embalse de Bao
Alto de Covelo
Viana do Bolo
Peña Trevinca
Truchas
Tominõ
Sto Pedro da Torre
Xinzo de Limia
Sierra de la
S. Martin de Castañeda
A Garda
Vila Nova de Cerveira
Castro Laboreiro
Parque
Bande
Embalse de Las Portas
Laza
E. de S. Sebastián
Ribadelago
Lago de Sanabria
Sta Tecla
Caminha
Rubiães
Paredes de Coura
Sa da Peneda
Mugueimes
Peña Nofre
A Gudiña
Pto de la Canda
Portillo de Padornelo
Galende
Puebla de Sanabria
Moledo do Minho
Vila Praia de Âncora
Arcos de Valdevez
Nacional
Fondevila
Cualedro
Alto de Estivadas
Baltar
Verín
Alto de Fumaces
Alto do Cañizo
Padornelo
Palacios de
Pedralba
Ungilde
A Mezquita
Moimenta
Corraes
E. de Cernadilla
Lindoso
Larouco
Ponte de Lima
Ponte da Barca
Bravães
Montalegre
Calabor
Portelo
Viana do Castelo
Sa do Gerês
MINHO
Peña Mira
Darque
Terras de Bouro
Peneda-Gerês
Paradela
Feces
Vila Verde da Raia
Chaves
Vinhais
Bragança
Figueruela de Arriba
Milhão
Vila Verde
Caldelas
Bgem do Alto Rabagão
S. Vitero
Amares
Vieira do Minho
Venda Nova
Salto
Boticas
Rebordelo
Penhas Juntas
Quintanilha
Esposende
Barcelos
Pinheiro
Vidago
Torre de D. Chama
Trabazos
Ofir
Braga
Mte Sameiro
Bom Jesus
Póvoa de Lanhoso
Sa da Cabreira
TRÁS-OS-MONTES
Sta Comba de Rossas
Alcañices
Rates
Caldas das Taipas
Cabeceiras
Arco de Baulhe
Pedras Salgadas
Valpaços
Carrazedo de Montenegro
Sa da Padrela
Póvoa de Varzim
Vila Nova de Famalicão
Guimarães
Fafe
Ribeira de Pena
Vila Pouca de Aguiar
Macedo de Cavaleiros
Izeda
Vimioso
Vila do Conde
Penha
Celorico
Mondim
Sa de Alvão
Mirandela
Sa de Nogueira
Sto Tirso
Caldas de Vizela
Trofa
Felgueiras
Bornes
Morais
DOURO
Maia
Lousada
Paços de Ferreira
Amarante
Vila Real
Murça
Sa de Bornes
Miranda do Douro
Matosinhos
Valongo
Paredes
Mateus
Sabrosa
Alijó
Trindade
Vila Flor
Sendim
Bgem de Picote
Foz do Douro
Vila Nova de Gaia
PORTO
Penafiel
Marco de Canaveses
Sa do Marão
Sta Marta de Penaguião
Alfândega da Fé
Mogadouro
Sa do Mogadouro
Fermoselle
Valadares
Gondomar
Paço de Sousa
Avintes
Baião
Mesão Frio
Pêso da Régua
Pinhão
Carrazeda de Ansiães
Fonte Longa
Bgem da Bemposta
Miramar
Granja
Espinho
Entre-os-Rios
Sande
Armamar
S. João da Pesqueira
Torre de Moncorvo
Lagoaça
Masueco
Villarino
Trabanca
Castelo de Paiva
Cinfães
Oliveira do Douro
Resende
Lamego
Tabuaço
Carviçais
Sta Maria da Feira
Tarouca
Vila Nova de Foz Côa
Freixo de Espada
Embalse de Aldeadávila
38
38

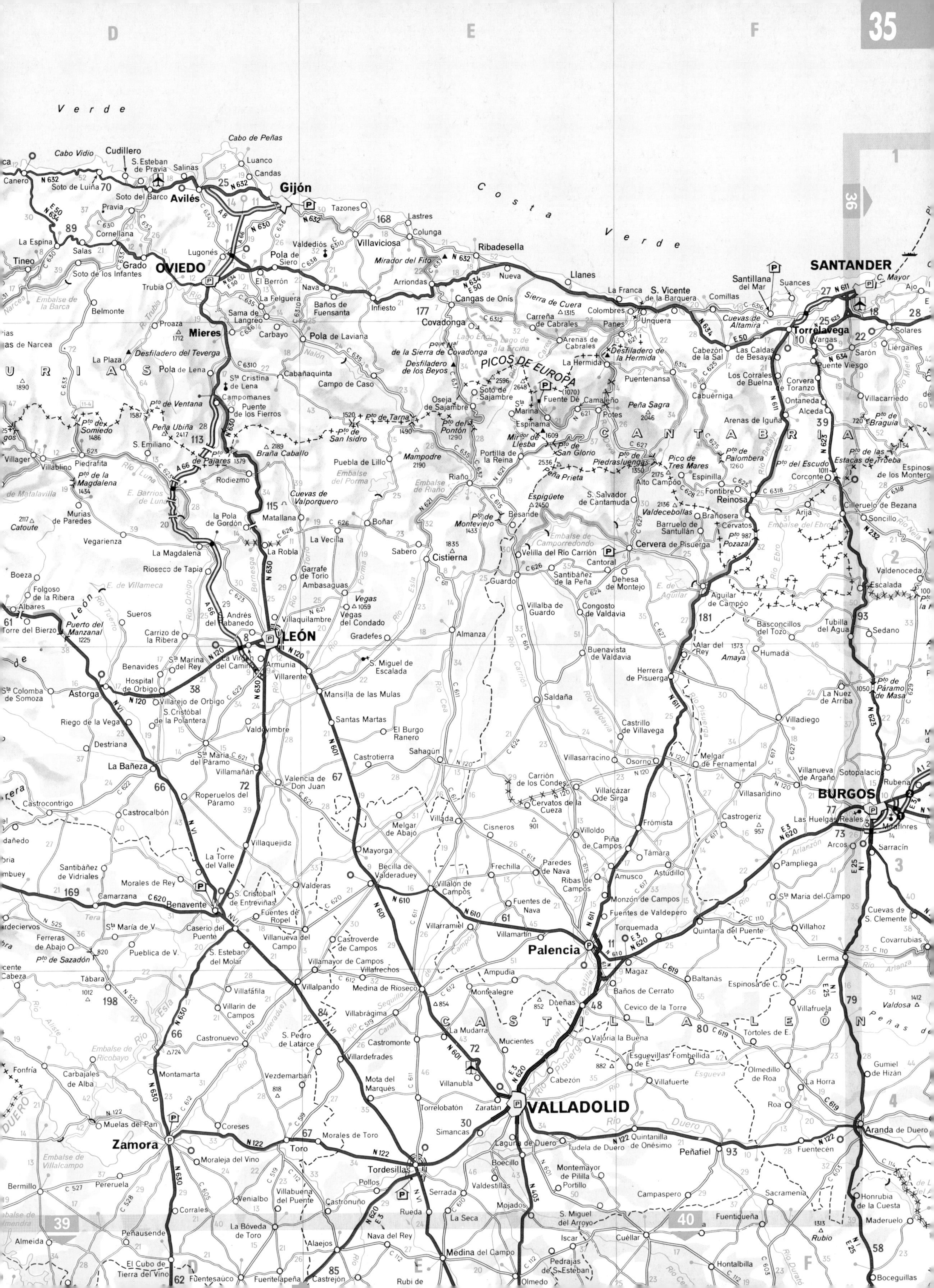

Verde

Costa Verde

Cabo Vidio
Cudillero
Canero
N 632
Soto de Luiña 70
S. Esteban de Pravia
Salinas
Cabo de Peñas
Luanco
Candas
Gijón
N 632
89
E 50 N 634
Soto del Barco
Pravia
Avilés
25 N 632
14 11
Tazones
168
Lastres
Colunga
30
Cornellana
Grado
Lugones
Pola de Siero
Valdediós
Villaviciosa
Ribadesella
52
Tineo
Salas 21
Trubia
OVIEDO
El Berrón
Nava
Mirador del Fito
N 632
La Espina
39
Belmonte
Proaza
Mieres
La Felguera
Sama de Langreo
Baños de Fuensanta
177
Arriondas
N 634
Nueva
Llanes
La Franca
S. Vicente de la Barquera
Santillana del Mar
Comillas
SANTANDER
Embalse de la Barca
Soto de los Infantes
Covadonga
Cangas de Onís
Carreña de Cabrales
Colombres
Unquera
C-6316
27 N 611
C. Mayor
Ajo
La Plaza
Desfiladero del Teverga
Pola de Lena
Sª Cristina de Lena
Cabañaquinta
Campo de Caso
pque N'l de la Sierra de Covadonga
Arenas de Cabrales
Panes
Desfiladero de la Hermida
Cabezón de la Sal
Las Caldas de Besaya
Torrelavega
10 Vargas
Solares
28
Liérganes
Sarón
Puente Viesgo

PICOS DE EUROPA
Desfiladero de los Beyos
La Hermida
Puentenansa
Los Corrales de Buelna
Corvera de Toranzo
Villacarriedo

Peña Ubiña
S. Emiliano
Pto de Pajares 1379
Rodiezmo
Pto de Tarna
Pto del Pontón
Oseja de Sajambre
Soto de Sajambre
Sta Marina
Fuente Dé
Camaleño
Espinama
Peña Sagra
2046
Arenas de Iguña
Ontaneda
Alceda
39
Pto de las Estacas de Trueba
Espinos de los Monteros

CANTABRIA

Puebla de Lillo
Mampodre
Riaño
Portilla de la Reina
Mirador de Llesba
Pto de San Glorio
Peña Prieta
Pto de Piedrasluengas
Pico de Tres Mares
Pto de Palombera
Espinilla
Fontibre
Arija
Soncillo
N 232

la Pola de Gordón
Matallana
Boñar
Embalse del Porma
Riaño
Espigüete
S. Salvador de Cantamuda
Alto Campoo
Reinosa
Valdecebollas
Brañosera
Cervatos
Pto 987 Pozazal
Cillamuelo de Bezana

La Robla
La Vecilla
Sabero
Cistierna
Pto de Monteviejo
Besande
Velilla del Río Carrión
Cervera de Pisuerga
Barruelo de Santullán
Embalse del Ebro
Valdenoceda
Escalada
93

LEÓN
Garrafe de Torio
Ambasaguas
Vegas
Vegas del Condado
Gradefes
Almanza
Guardo
Villalba de Guardo
Congosto de Valdavia
Santibáñez de la Peña
Dehesa de Montejo
E. de Aguilar
Aguilar de Campoo
181
Basconcillos del Tozo
Tubilla del Agua
Sedano

Armunia
Villarente
S. Miguel de Escalada
Saldaña
Buenavista de Valdavia
Villasarracino
Osorno
Melgar de Fernamental
Villadiego
La Nuez de Arriba
Pto de Páramo de Masa
N 623

Mansilla de las Mulas
Santas Martas
El Burgo Ranero
Sahagún
Carrión de los Condes
Frómista
Castrogeriz
E 3 E 620
Las Huelgas Reales
BURGOS
77
Mirafores

Sta Marina del Rey
Astorga
Hospital de Orbigo
Villarejo de Orbigo
S. Cristóbal de la Polantera
Valdevimbre
Valencia de Don Juan
67
Castrotierra
Cervatos de la Cueza
Villalcázar de Sirga
Támara
Támara
Astudillo
Villanueva de Argaño
Sotopalacio
Rubena
73

La Bañeza
Villamañán
Roperuelos del Páramo
72
Villaquejida
Becilla de Valderaduey
Villada
Cisneros
901
Villoldo
Piña de Campos
Frómista
Paredes de Nava
Amusco
Monzón de Campos
Pamplega
Sta Maria del Campo
Cuevas de S. Clemente
Covarrubias

Castrocontrigo
Castrocalbón
La Torre del Valle
Valderas
Mayorga
Frechilla
Ribas de Campos
Fuentes de Nava
61
Fuentes de Valdepero
Torquemada
Quintana del Puente
Villahoz
38

169
Camarzana
Benavente
C 620
S. Cristóbal de Entreviñas
Fuentes de Ropel
Villanueva del Campo
Castroverde de Campos
Villalón de Campos
Villarramiel
Villamartín
PALENCIA
11 E 3 N 620
Magaz
Baltanás
Espinosa de C.
Lerma
79

Sta María de V.
Caserío del Puente
S. Esteban del Molar
Villamayor de Campos
Villafrechos
Medina de Rioseco
Montealegre
852 854
Ampudia
Dueñas
48
Baños de Cerrato
Cevico de la Torre
80
Valoria la Buena
Tórtoles de E.
Villafruela
Valdosa

Tábara
1012
198
Villafáfila
Villarín de Campos
Villalpando
Villabrágima
84
La Mudarra
S. Pedro de Latarce
Castromonte
Mucientes
72
Cabezón
Esguevillas de E.
Fombellida
Olmedillo de Roa
La Horra
La Mudarra

66
Castronuevo
Vezdemarbán
Villardefrades
Mota del Marqués
Villanubla
Simancas
VALLADOLID
30
Zaratán
Laguna de Duero
Tudela de Duero
Peñafiel 93
Roa
Gumiel de Hizán
Aranda de Duero

ZAMORA
Montamarta
Muelas del Pan
Coreses
Torrelobatón
67
Morales de Toro
Toro
Tordesillas
Pollos
Simancas
Boecillo
Montemayor de Pililla
Portillo
Quintanilla de Onésimo
Campaspero
Sacramenia
Honrubia de la Cuesta

Embalse de Ricobayo
Embalse de Villalcampo
Bermillo
Pereruela
Carbajales de Alba
Fonfría
Almeida
El Cubo de Tierra del Vino
62 Fuentesaúco
85
Peñausende
La Bóveda de Toro
Corrales
Venialbo
Villabuena del Puente
Castronuño
Venialbo
Rueda
La Seca
Nava del Rey
Mojados
S. Miguel del Arroyo
Cuéllar
1313
Maderuelo

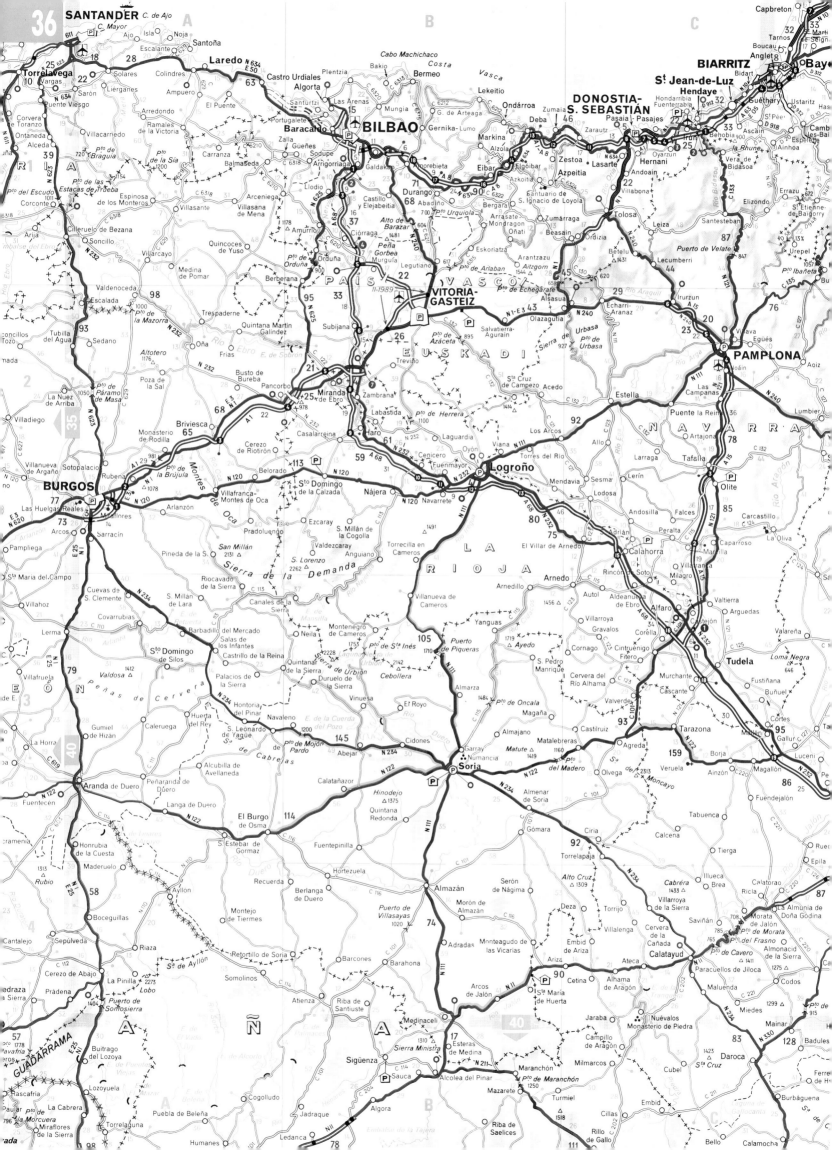

A   B   C

34   34   42

Miramar
Granja
Espinho
Entre-os-Rios
Oliveira do Douro
Resende
Armamar
S. João da Pesqueira
Penedono
Castelo de Paiva
Cinfães
Lamego
Tabuaço

Sta Maria da Feira
Arouca
S. João de Tarouca
Tarouca
Moimenta da Beira
Sernancelhe

S. João da Madeira
Vale de Cambra
Castro Daire
Vila Nova de Paiva
Aguiar da Beira
Vila Nova da Beira

Furadouro
Ovar
Oliveira de Azeméis
Sever do Vouga
S. Pedro do Sul
Penalva do Castelo
Trancoso

Torreira
Estarreja
Angeja
Vouzela
Viseu
Campo de Beisteros
Nelas
Mangualde
Fornos de Algodres
Celorico da Beira

Murtosa
S. Jacinto
Aveiro
Albergaria-a-Velha
Oliveira de Frades
Caramulo
Tôndela
Canas de Senhorim
Carregal do Sal
Gouveia
Vale de Estrela
Guarda

Praia da Barra
Ílhavo
Águeda
Mortágua
Seia
Manteigas
Valhelhas
Pega

Vagos
Anadia
Luso
Buçaco
Pampilhosa
Oliveira do Hospital
S. Romão
Penhas da Saúde
Belmonte

Praia de Mira
Mira
Mealhada
Sta Comba Dão
Tábua
Loriga
Unhais da Serra
Caria
Sto Estêvão

Praia de Tocha
Cantanhede
Penacova
Vila Nova de Poiares
Arganil
S. Pedro de Açor
Covilhã
Tortosendo

Cabo Mondego
Buarcos
Montemor-o-Velho
COIMBRA
Condeixa-a-Nova
Miranda do Corvo
Lousã
Góis
Paúl
Meimoa

Figueira da Foz
Arazede
Soure
Degracias
Penela
Castanheira de Pêra
Pampilhosa da Serra
Orvalho
Silvares
Fundão
Vale de Prazeres

Pedrógão
Louriçal
Penela
Pedrógão Grande
Cambas
S. Vicente da Beira
Alpedrinha
Medelim

Praia da Vieira
Vieira
Monte Redondo
Pombal
Sicó
Pontão
Figueiró dos Vinhos
Bgem do Cabril
Oleiros
Salgueiro do Campo
Alcains
Escalos de Cima
Idanha a Nova

Monte Real
Ansião
Alvaiázere
Barqueiro
Cernache de Bonjardim
Sertã
Sarzedas
Idanha a Nova

S. Pedro de Moel
Marinha Grande
Leiria
Sobreira Formosa
Castelo Branco
Ladoeiro

Martingança
Batalha
Cruz da Légua
Vila Nova de Ourém
Ferreira do Zêzere
Proença-a-Nova
Vila de Rei
Rosmaninhal

Nazaré
Alcobaça
Cova da Iria
Pôrto de Mós
Fátima
Vila Velha de Ródão
Bgem de Cedillo
Malpica

S. Martinho do Porto
Mira de Aire
Tomar
Sardoal
Mação
Fratel
Cedillo
Herrera de Alcántara
Santiago de Alcántara

Alfeizerão
Serra de Aire
Torres Novas
Castelo de Bode
Abrantes
Nisa
Montalvão

Foz do Arelho
Baleal
Caldas da Rainha
Alcanena
Alcanede
Entroncamento
Constância
Almourol
Rossio
Gavião
Arez
Castelo de Vide
Marvão
Valencia de Alcántara

Ilha Berlenga
Cabo Carvoeiro
Peniche
Óbidos
Rio Maior
Golegã
Vila Nova da Barquinha
Tramagal
Tolosa
Alpalhão
Galegos

Atouguia da Baleia
Lourinhã
Bombarral
Cadaval
Chamusca
Bemposta
Flor da Rosa
Portalegre
S. Vicente de Alcántara

Praia de Sta Cruz
Cercal
Santarém
Alpiarça
Almeirim
Ponte de Sor
Crato
La Codosera

Torres Vedras
Atalaia
Cartaxo
Aveiras de Cima
Muge
Galveias
Alter do Chão
Arronches

Ericeira
Alenquer
Sobral de Mte Agraço
Azambuja
São José da Lamarosa
Montargil
Cabeço de Vide
Fronteira
Pto de los Conejeros

Mafra
Sapataria
Arruda dos Vinhos
Carregado
Salvaterra de Magos
Benavente
Bgem de Montargil
Avis
Monforte
Bgem do Caia

Malveira
Lousã
Bucelas
Vila Franca de Xira
Samora Correia
Bgem do Maranhão
Mora
Casa Branca
Campo Maior

Cabo da Roca
Colares
Sintra
Loures
Alverca do Ribatejo
Coruche
Couço
Pavia
Sta Eulália
Bgem do Caia

Amadora
Quéluz
Sacavém
Sto Estêvão
Brotas
Sousel
Veiros

Estoril
Cascais
Oeiras
LISBOA
Alcochete
Tajpadas
Canha
Lavre
Arraiolos
Estremoz
Vila Boim
Elvas

Cabo Raso
Trafaria
Almada
Montijo
Cruzamento de Pegões
Vimieiro
Évoramonte
Borba
Vila Viçosa
Caya

Costa da Caparica
Barreiro
Seixal
Moita
Pinhal Novo
Vendas Novas
Arraiolos
Azaruja
Borba
Juromenha

Santana
Vila Fresca de Azeitão
Palmela
Montemor-o-Novo
Bgem do Divor
Redondo
Alandroal
Olivença

Cabo Espichel
Sesimbra
Portinho
Setúbal
Azeitão
S. Miguel de Machede
Terena
Monsaraz

Península de Tróia
Comporta
Santiago do Escoural
S. Cristóvão
Évora
Alcáçovas
Reguengos

Cabo Espichel
Alcácer do Sal
Alcáçovas
Bgem de Pego do Altar
Montoito
Cheles

PORTUGAL

BEIRA ALTA
BEIRA LITORAL
BEIRA BAIXA
SERRA DA ESTRELA
RIO DOURO
RIO TEJO
RIO GUADIANA

38

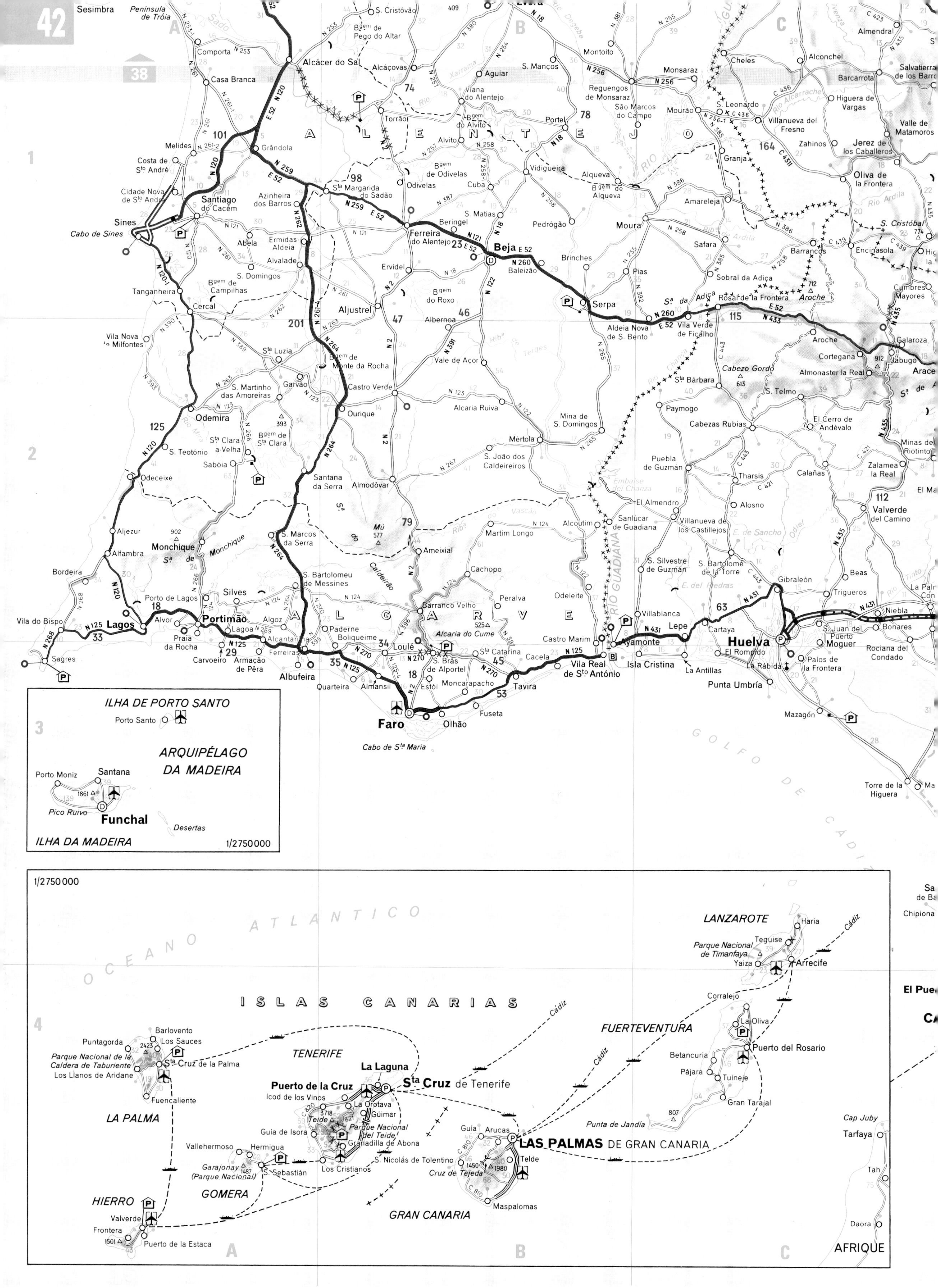

Main map (Southern Portugal / Andalucía region)

Sesimbra
Península de Tróia
A
Comporta N 253
Casa Branca
S. Cristóvão
409
Alcácer do Sal
B gem de Pego do Altar
Alcáçovas
Aguiar
Montoito
Cheles
Alconchel
Almendral
Barcarrota
Higuera de Vargas
Valle de Matamoros
Melides
101
Grândola
A L E N T E J O
74
Viana do Alentejo
S. Manços
Montoito
Reguengos de Monsaraz
S. Leonardo
Mourão
Monsaraz
Villanueva del Fresno
Granja
164
Jerez de los Caballeros
Costa de Sto André
Alvito
Portel
N 18
S. Marcos do Campo
Alqueva
Zahinos
Oliva de la Frontera
Cidade Nova de Sto André
Santiago do Cacém
N 120
E 52
N 259
98
Sta Margarida do Sádão
Odivelas
B gem de Odivelas
Vidigueira
Cuba
B gem de Alqueva
Amareleja
Moura
N 386
S. Cristóbal
Encinasola
Sines
Cabo de Sines
Abela
Ermidas-Aldeia
N 259 E 52
N 262
Ferreira do Alentejo
23 E 52
Beja E 52
Beringel
S. Matias
Pedrógão
Safara
Barrancos
Aroche
Alvalade
N 121
Ervidel
N 260
Brinches
Pias
Sobral da Adiça
Rosa de la Frontera
712
Cumbres Mayores
Aroche
Galaroza
Tanganheira
B gem de Campilhas
Cercal
Aljustrel
201
Albernoa
46
B gem do Roxo
Baleizão
Serpa
N 260
Aldeia Nova de S. Bento
E 52 Vila Verde de Ficalho
115
N 433
Sta Bárbara
Cortegana
912 Jabugo
Vila Nova de Milfontes
N 261
Sta Luzia
47
N 2
Vale de Açor
Castro Verde
N 265
Cabezo Gordo 613
Almonaster la Real
Odemira
125
S. Martinho das Amoreiras
Garvão
393
B gem de Monte da Rocha
N 123
Alcaria Ruiva
Mina de S. Domingos
S. Telmo
Paymogo
Cabezas Rubias
El Cerro de Andévalo
Sta Clara a-Velha
Sabóia
N 266
Ourique
Almodôvar
N 122
Mértola
N 265
Puebla de Guzmán
Tharsis
Calañas
Zalamea la Real
Minas de Riotinto
112
Valverde del Camino
S. Teotónio
Santana da Serra
S. João dos Caldeireiros
C 421
Odeceixe
N 264
Mú 577
79
Vasco
N 124
Martim Longo
Alcoutim
Sanlúcar de Guadiana
El Almendro
Villanueva de los Castillejos
Alosno
Beas
Aljezur
902
Monchique Sa de
S. Marcos da Serra
Cal derão
Ameixial
Cachopo
Peralva
S. Silvestre de Guzmán
Odeleite
Gibraleón
Triguero
La Palm
Niebla
Alfambra
Bordeira
N 120
N 266 Monchique
Silves
A L G A R V E
S. Bartolomeu de Messines
N 124
Barranco Velho
525
Alcaria do Cume
RIO GUADIANA
S. Bartolomé de la Torre
63
N 431
Cartaya
Huelva
El Rompido
Palos de la Frontera
Rociana del Condado
Porto de Lagos
18
Alvor
Portimão
Algoz
Lagoa N 269
Paderne
Boliqueime
34
Loulé
S. Brás de Alportel
Sta Catarina
Cacela
Castro Marim
Villablanca
Lepe
Ayamonte
N 431
Vila do Bispo
N 268
N 125 Lagos
33
Praia da Rocha
29
N 125
Carvoeiro
Armação de Pêra
Ferreiras
Alcantarilha
35 N 125
Albufeira
Quarteira
Almansil
N 2
270
18
Estói
45
Moncarapacho
N 270
Tavira
53
Vila Real de Sto António
Isla Cristina
La Antillas
Puerto Moguer
La Rábida
Sagres
P
Faro
Olhão
Fuseta
Cabo de Sta Maria
Punta Umbría
Mazagón
GOLFO DE CÁDIZ

Inset: Madeira

ILHA DE PORTO SANTO
Porto Santo

ARQUIPÉLAGO DA MADEIRA

Porto Moniz
Santana
1861
Pico Ruivo
Funchal
Desertas
ILHA DA MADEIRA
1/2 750 000

Inset: Canary Islands

1/2 750 000

OCEANO ATLANTICO

ISLAS CANARIAS

LANZAROTE
Haria
Cádiz
Parque Nacional de Timanfaya
Teguise
Yaiza
Arrecife
Corralejo
FUERTEVENTURA
La Oliva
Puerto del Rosario
Betancuria
Pájara
Tuineje
Gran Tarajal
Punta de Jandía
Cap Juby
Tarfaya

Barlovento
Los Sauces
Puntagorda
2423
Parque Nacional de la Caldera de Taburiente
Los Llanos de Aridane
Sta Cruz de la Palma
TENERIFE
La Laguna
Puerto de la Cruz
Icod de los Vinos
La Orotava
Sta Cruz de Tenerife
LA PALMA
3718
Teide
Parque Nacional del Teide
Güimar
Granadilla de Abona
Fuencaliente
Guía de Isora
Guía
Arucas
LAS PALMAS DE GRAN CANARIA
Telde
807
Vallehermoso
Hermigua
Garajonay (Parque Nacional) 1487
S. Sebastián
Los Cristianos
S. Nicolás de Tolentino
1450
Cruz de Tejeda
1980
GOMERA
HIERRO
Valverde
Frontera
1501
Puerto de la Estaca
GRAN CANARIA
Maspalomas
Daora
Tah

AFRIQUE

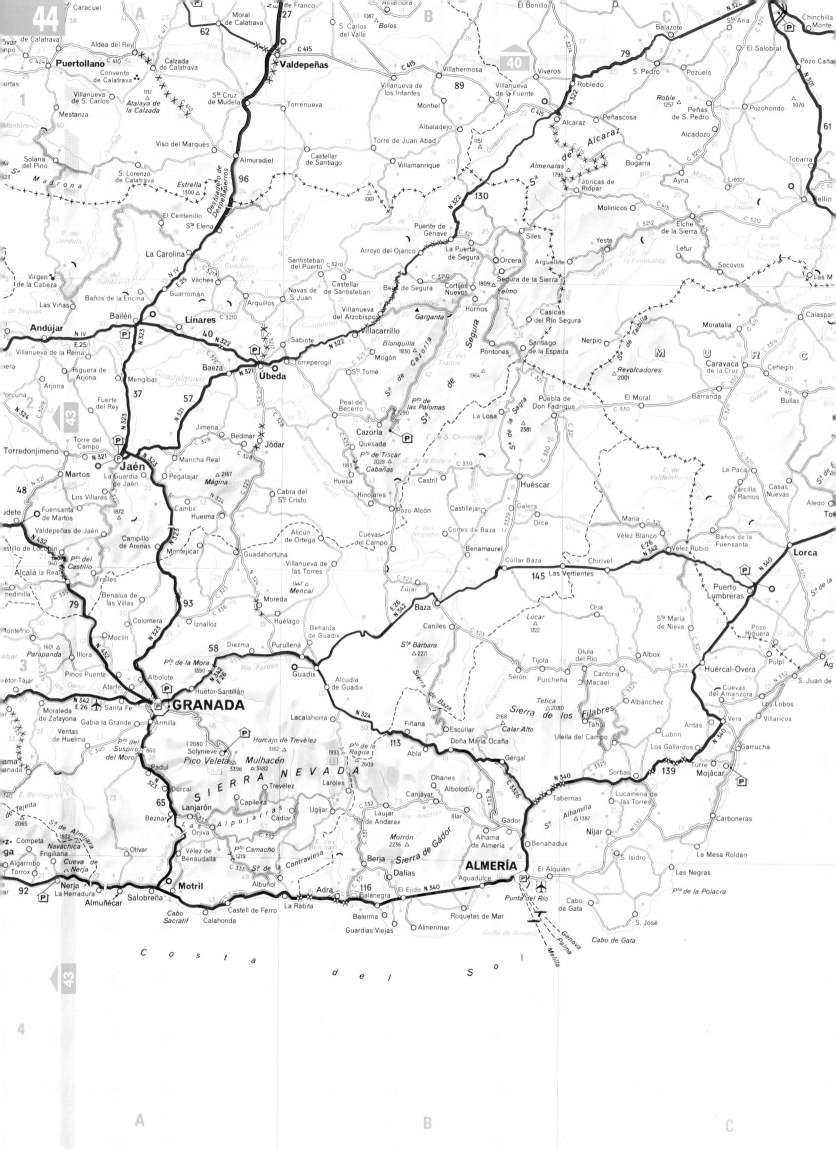

Hamburg

Bremen

0   2 km

0   3 km

46

B

C

Enkhuizen

Urk

HOLLAND

Bergen

Bergen aan Zee

Alkmaar

Hoorn

Egmond aan Zee

Markermeer

Beverwijk

Purmerend

Edam

Volendam

Lelystad-Haven

IJmuiden

Zaandam

Monnickendam

Marken

FLEVOLAND

Zuidelijk-Flevoland

Haarlem

AMSTERDAM

5-1989

Almere-Haven

Harderwijk

Zandvoort

Heemstede

Amstelveen

Bussum

Spakenburg

Nijkerk

Voorthuizen

Noordwijk aan Zee

Hillegom

Keukenhof

Lisse

Sassenheim

Aalsmeer

Uithoorn

Abcoude

HILVERSUM

Baarn

Soest

Soestdijk

Katwijk aan Zee

Great Yarmouth

Leiden

Alphen a/d Rijn

UTRECHT

Zeist

Amersfoort

Wassenaar

Voorschoten

Boskoop

Bodegraven

Woerden

SCHEVENINGEN

DEN HAAG ('S-GRAVENHAGE)

Zoetermeer

Gouda

E 30

Driebergen

Doorn

Amerongen

Veenendaal

Rhenen

Hoek van Holland

Kingston upon Hull Harwich

Delft

Schiedam

Schoonhoven

N 210

Culemborg

Europoort

Maassluis

Krimpen

Vlaardingen

Brielle

ROTTERDAM

Leerdam

Gorinchem

Zaltbommel

Tiel

Oss

Goeree

Spijkenisse

Oud Beijerland

Zwijndrecht

Sliedrecht

's Gravendeel

Ouddorp

Helvoetsluis

HOLLAND

Dordrecht

Biesbosch

Hellevoetsluis

Middelharnis

Geertruidenberg

's-Hertogenbosch

Haamstede

Overflakkee

Willemstad

Waalwijk

Kaatsheuvel

Schouwen Duiveland

Steenbergen

Oosterhout

Dongen

Tilburg

Boxtel

St.-Oedenrode

Zierikzee

Oudenbosch

NOORD BRABANT

Oisterwijk

Oirschot

Nd Beveland

Stavenisse

Tholen

Etten

Breda

A 58

Gilze

Goirle

Domburg

Veere

ZEELAND

Halsteren

Roosendaal

Hilvarenbeek

Veldhoven

Walcheren

Goes

Bergen op Zoom

Zundert

Baarle Nassau

EINDHOVEN

Middelburg

Zd Beveland

Kruiningen

Woensdrecht

Brecht

Reusel

Valkenswaard

Vlissingen

Hoedekenskerke

Wuustwezel

Turnhout

Lommel

Sheerness

Breskens

Terneuzen

Brasschaat

Oostmalle

Kasterlee

Mol

Knokke-Heist

Zeebrugge

Heist

Oostburg

IJzendijke

Hulst

ANTWERPEN (ANVERS)

Herentals

Geel

Blankenberge

De Haan

BRUGGE

Zelzate

Stekene

Beveren

Lier

Heist-o-d.B.

Westerlo

Beringen

Leopoldsburg

Genk

Oostende

Middelkerke-Bad

Jabbeke

Oostkamp

Eeklo

St.-Niklaas

Mechelen (Malines)

Hasselt

Nieuwpoort

Gistel

Evergem

Lokeren

Temse

Aarschot

Diest

Koksijde-Bad

Torhout

Aalter

GENT (GAND)

Zele

Waasmunster

Wetteren

Willebroek

Keerbergen

Herk

De Panne

Veurne

Diksmuide

Tielt

Deinze

Dendermonde

Leuven (Louvain)

Herselt

Dunkerque

Bergues

Roeselare (Roulers)

Ingelmunster

Waregem

Alost Aalst

Asse

BRUSSEL BRUXELLES

Zoutleeuw

Tienen

Tongeren

Poperinge

Harelbeke

Oudenaarde

Ninove

Tervuren

St.-Truiden

Ieper (Ypres)

Kortrijk (Courtrai)

Menen

Wervik

Ronse (Renaix)

Geraardsbergen

Halle

Waterloo

Wavre

Jodoigne

Waremme

Cassel

Bailleul

Comines

Mouscron

Tourcoing

Roubaix

Tournai (Doornik)

Ath

Enghien

Braine-le-Comte

Nivelles

Hannut

Amay

Hazebrouck

Armentières

LILLE

Leuze

Soignies

Villers-la-V.

Gembloux

Eghezée

Béthune

Seclin

Cysoing

Péruwelz

Beloeil

La Louvière

Fleurus

Namur

Andenne

Huy

Carvin

Hénin-Beaumont

Orchies

St-Amand-les-Eaux

Condé

Mons Bergen

Anderlues

Binche

Châtelet

Charleroi

Fosses

Profondeville

Annevoie-Rouillon

Durbuy

Lens

Douai

Marchiennes

Denain

Valenciennes

Quiévrain

Thuin

Beaumont

Dinant

Havelange

Arras

Vitry-en-A.

Aniche

Bouchain

Bavay

Maubeuge

Jeumont

Philippeville

Yvoir

Marche-en-Fam.

Cambrai

Marquion

Le Quesnoy

Hautmont

Aulnoye-Aymeries

Berlaimont

Solre-le-Châ.

Beauraing

Givet

Doullens

Bapaume

Caudry

Le Cateau

Solesmes

Landrecies

Avesnes

Sars-Poteries

Trélon

Chimay

Couvin

St-Hubert

Wassigny

Le Nouvion-en-Th.

Fourmies

MER DU NORD

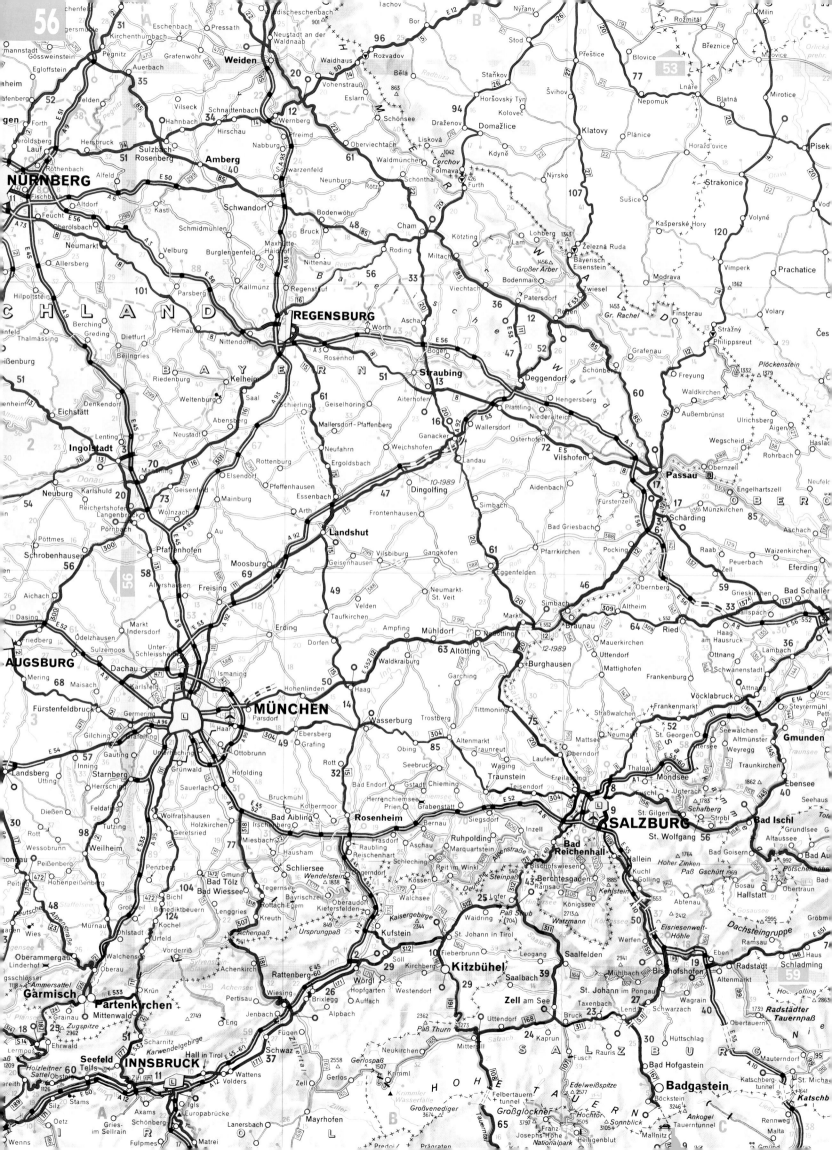

BRNO
WIEN
BRATISLAVA
LINZ
GRAZ
České Budějovice
Jihlava
Pelhřimov
Tábor
Sezimovo-Ústí
Znojmo
Breclav
Krems
St. Pölten
Melk
Baden
Wiener Neustadt
Eisenstadt
Sopron
Szombathely
Leoben
Bruck an der Mur
Kapfenberg
Mariazell
Mürzzuschlag
Semmering-P.
Neunkirchen
Ternitz
Reichenau
Gloggnitz
Knittelfeld
Judenburg
Köflach
Voitsberg
Deutschlandsberg
Wolfsberg
Steyr
Amstetten
Freistadt
Gallneukirchen
Mauthausen
Perg
Gmünd
České Velenice
Třeboň
Trhové Sviny
Dolní Dvořiště
Kaplice
Horn
Zwettl
Eggenburg
Hollabrunn
Stockerau
Korneuburg
Klosterneuburg
Tulln
Mödling
Schwechat
Bruck
Hainburg
Neusiedl
Mattersburg
Mistelbach
Poysdorf
Mikulov
Hodonín
Malacky
Stupava
Körmend
Güssing
Fürstenfeld
Hartberg
Oberwart
Kőszeg
Bük
Szentgotthárd

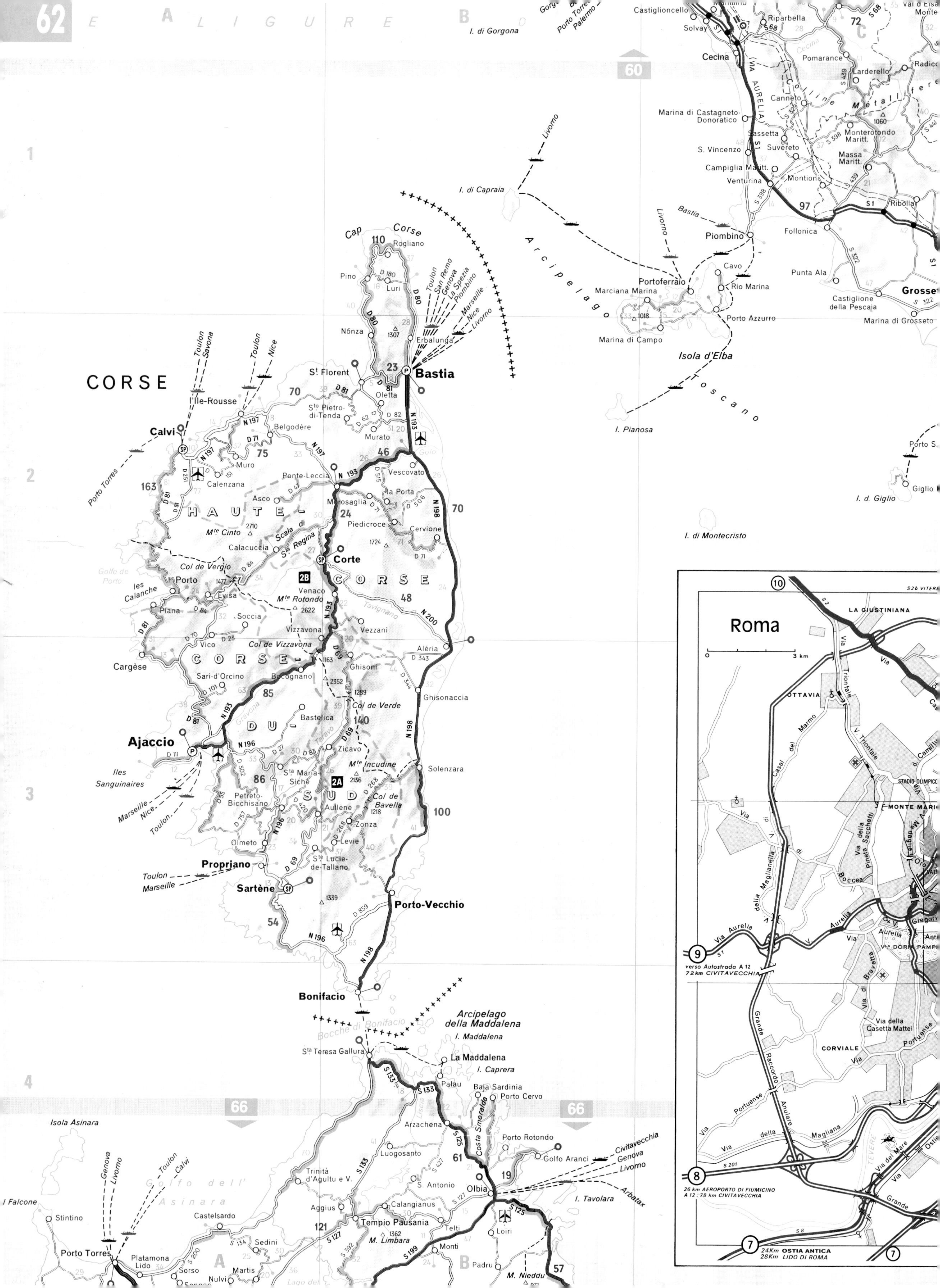

E A L I G U R E B

I. di Gorgona

Gorg...
Porto Torres
Palermo

Castiglioncello
Riparbella
72 S 68
Solvay
S 68 28
Cecina
(VIA AURELIA)
Pomarance
Larderello
Radic...

Marina di Castagneto-
Donoratico
Canneto
Coll...
Metallifere
1060

I. di Capraia
Sassetta
S 1
Monterotondo
Maritt.

Toulon
San Remo
Genova
La Spezia
Piombino
Marseille
Nice
Livorno

S. Vincenzo
Suvereto
Massa
Maritt.

Livorno
Bastia

Arcipelago

Campiglia Maritt.
Montioni
S 439 21

Venturina
97
S 1

Piombino
Follonica
S 322

Portoferràio
Cavo
Rio Marina

Marciana Marina
Punta Ala

Grosse...
S 322

Cap Corse

110 Rogliano

Pino
D 180
Luri

Castiglione
della Pescaia
Marina di Grosseto

Nônza
D 80
1307

Porto Azzurro
Marina di Campo

Erbalunga
Isola d'Elba

CORSE
23
Bastia

I. Pianosa

Toscano

St Florent
81
Oletta

l'Ile-Rousse
70
D 81
Sto Pietro-
di-Tenda
D 82

Calvi
SP
N 197
Belgodère
D 62
Murato
N 193

I. di Giglio

N 197
75
33
N 197
46
Porto S...

D 71
Muro
26
Vescovato
26

163
Calenzana
Ponte-Leccia
N 193
D 515
la Porta

HAUTE-
Asco
Morosaglia
D 71
D 506
N 198

2710
24
Piedicroce
Cervione
70

Mte Cinto
Scala di
Sta Regina
1724
71
D 71
I. d. Giglio

Calacuccia
27
I. di Montecristo

Col de Vergio
D 84
Corte
SP

Porto
1477
Venaco
Mte Rotondo
CORSE
48

les
Calanche
Evisa
D 84
2622
N 193

Plana
D 84
32
Soccia
Vizzavona
Vezzani
N 200

D 81
D 70
Vico
D 23
Col de Vizzavona
Aléria
D 343

Cargèse
CORSE-
1163
D 69
Ghisoni
D 344

Sari-d'Orcino
Bocognano
2352
1289

85
Col de Verde
Ghisonaccia

DU-
Bastelica
140
D 69
N 198

D 81
N 193
Zicavo

Ajaccio
P
N 196
Mte Incudine
Solenzara

86
Sta Maria
Siché
2136

Iles
Sanguinaires
902
2A
Col de
Bavella
1218
100

Petreto-
Bicchisano
Aullène
D 268
Zonza

Marseille
Nice-
Toulon
N 196
Levie
40

Olmeto
Sta Lucie-
de-Tallano

Propriano
D 69

Sartène
SP
1339

54
D 859
Porto-Vecchio

N 196
N 198

Bonifacio

Arcipelago
della Maddalena

Bocche di Bonifacio
I. Maddalena

Sta Teresa Gallura
La Maddalena

I. Caprera

S 133
Palau
Baja Sardinia
Porto Cervo

66
66

Isola Asinara
S 133
Costa Smeralda

Arzachena
S 125
Porto Rotondo

Luogosanto
61
Golfo Aranci
Civitavecchia
Genova
Livorno

Golfo dell'
Asinara
S 133
Trinità
d'Agultu e V.
S 427
19
Olbia
I. Tavolara
Arbatax

Stintino
S. Antonio
S 127

Castelsardo
Aggius
Calangianus
S 125

121
S 134
Sedini
Tempio Pausania
M. Limbara
1362
Telti
Loiri
47

Porto Torres
S 200
Martis
S 127
S 592
Monti
S 199

Platamona
Lido
Sorso
Sennori
Nulvi
Padru
57
M. Nieddu

Roma

10
S 2b VITER...
LA GIUSTINIANA

0
3 km

OTTAVIA
Via
Trionfale

MONTE MARIO

STADIO OLIMPICO

9
S 1
verso Autostrada A 12
72 km CIVITAVECCHIA

Via Aurelia
Aurelia

CORVIALE

Via della
Casetta Mattei
Portuense

8
S 201
26 km AEROPORTO DI FIUMICINO
A 12 : 78 km CIVITAVECCHIA

Grande Raccordo Anulare

7
24 Km OSTIA ANTICA
28 Km LIDO DI ROMA
7

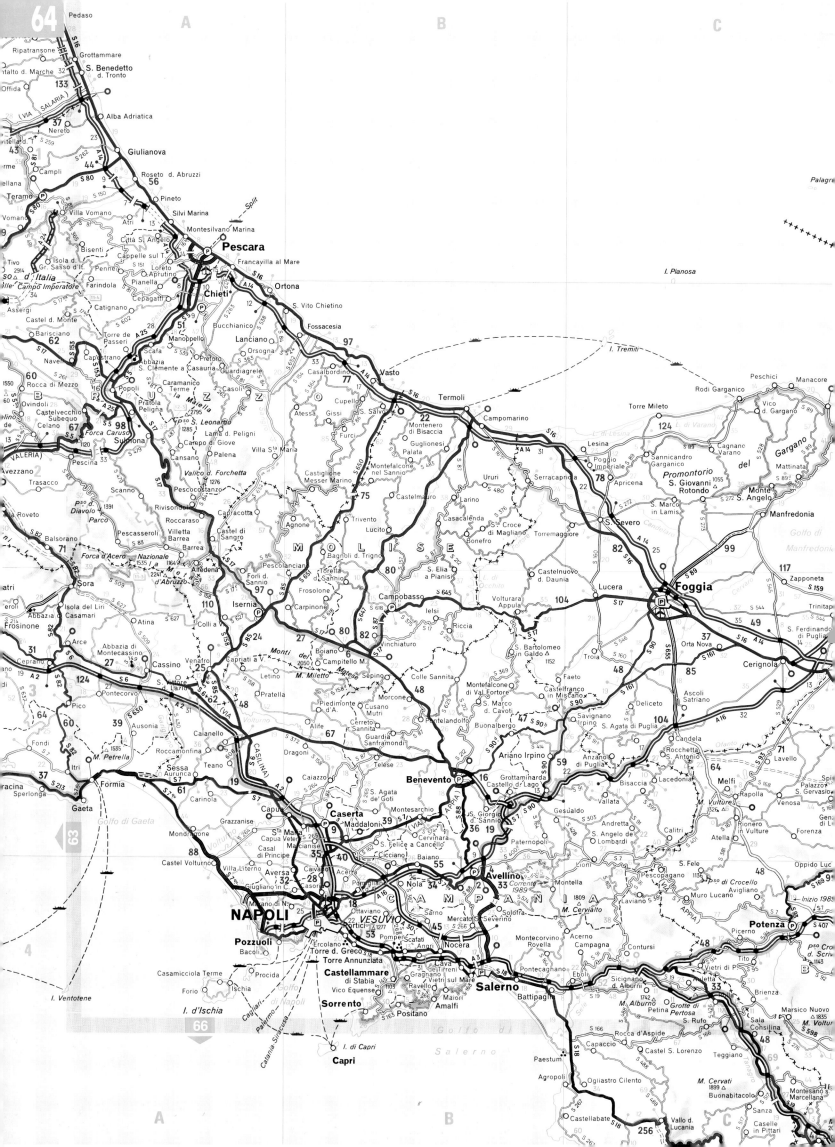

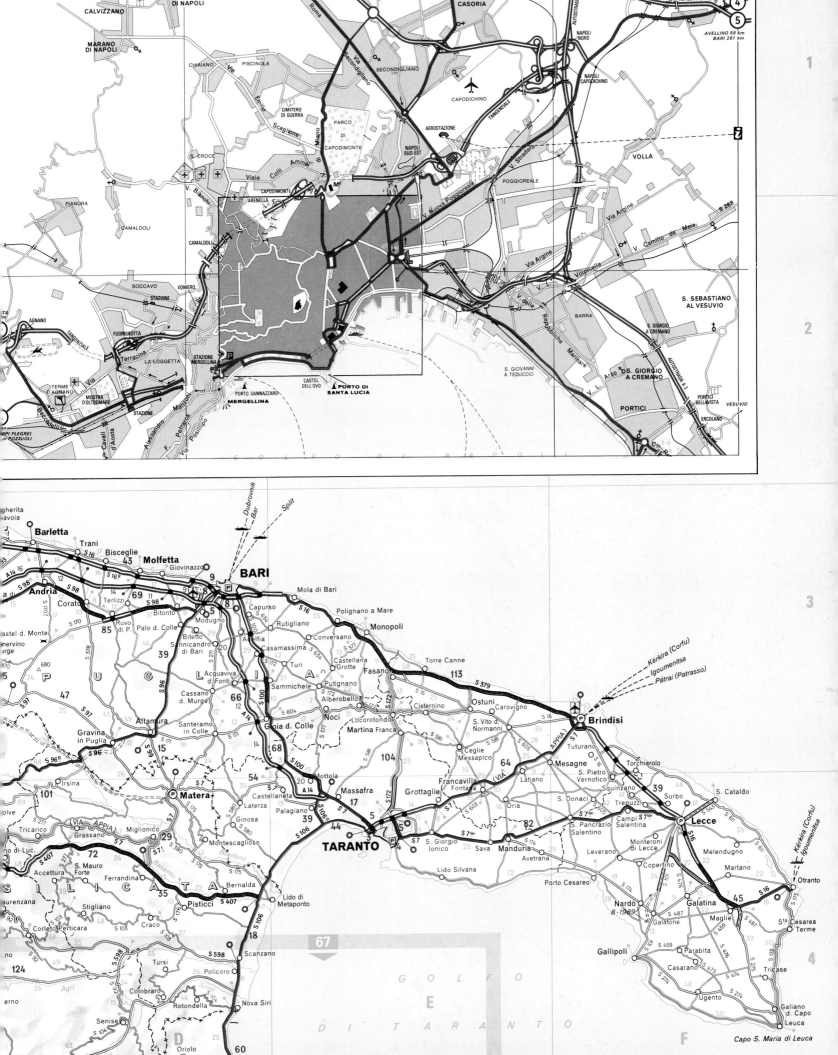

Napoli

2 km

ROMA 239 km S1, verso S7

ROMA 236 km S7BIS

CASERTA 28 km S87

CASERTA 33 km ROMA 219 km

AVELLINO 55 km

AUTOSTRADA A 16

AVELLINO 56 km BARI 261 km

CALVIZZANO

MUGNANO DI NAPOLI

ARZANO

AFRAGOLA

CASALNUOVO DI NAPOLI

MARANO DI NAPOLI

CASORIA

AUTOSTRADA A 2

CHIAIANO

PISCINOLA

SECONDIGLIANO

NAPOLI NORD

NAPOLI CAPODICHINO

CAPODICHINO

VOLLA

CIMITERO DI GUERRA

PARCO DI CAPODIMONTE

AEROSTAZIONE

TANGENZIALE

POGGIOREALE

S. SEBASTIANO AL VESUVIO

S. CROCE

CAMALDOLI

ARENELLA

BARRA

S. GIORGIO A CREMANO

PIANURA

CAMALDOLI

SOCCAVO

VOMERO

STAZIONE

S. GIOVANNI A TEDUCCIO

OS. GIORGIO A CREMANO

PORTICI-BELLAVISTA

AGNANO

FUORIGROTTA

TERRACINA

LA LOGGETTA

STAZIONE MERGELLINA

PORTICI

AUTOSTRADA A 3

VESUVIO

TERME D'AGNANO

MOSTRA D'OLTREMARE

STAZIONE

MERGELLINA

CASTEL DELL'OVO

PORTO DI SANTA LUCIA

ERCOLANO

CAMPI FLEGREI POZZUOLI

PORTO SANNAZZARO

GOLFO DI NAPOLI

Barletta

Trani

Bisceglie

Molfetta

Giovinazzo

BARI

Mola di Bari

Andria

Corato

Terlizzi

Bitonto

Modugno

Capurso

Rutigliano

Polignano a Mere

Monopoli

Ruvo di P.

Palo d. Colle

Bitetto

S. nnicandro di Bari

Adelfia

Turi

Castellana Grotte

Conversano

Fasano

Torre Canne

Kérkira (Corfu)

Igoumenitsa

Pátrai (Patrasso)

Castel d. Monte

Minervino urge

Acquaviva d. Fonti

Sammichele

Putignano

Alberobello

Cisternino

Ostuni

Carovigno

S. Vito d. Normanni

Brindisi

P U G L I A

Cassano d. Murge

Noci

Locorotondo

Martina Franca

Irsina

Altamura

Santeramo in Colle

Gioia d. Colle

Ceglie Messapico

Tuturano

Torchiarolo

Gravina in Puglia

S. Donaci

S. Pietro Vernotico

Squinzano

Mesagne

Surbo

S. Cataldo

Francavilla Fontana

Latiano

Trepuzzi

Lecce

Tricarico

Grassano

Miglionico

Matera

Castellaneta

Laterza

Ginosa

Palagiano

Mottola

Massafra

Grottaglie

Oria

Manduria

S. Pancrazio Salentino

Campi Salentina

Leverano

Monteroni di Lecce

Melendugno

Martano

Accettura

S. Mauro Forte

Ferrandina

Bernalda

Pisticci

Lido di Metaponto

TARANTO

S. Giorgio Ionico

Sava

Avetrana

Copertino

Galatina

Maglie

Sta Cesarea Terme

Otranto

Corleto Perticara

Craco

Scanzano

Lido Silvana

Porto Cesareo

Nardo

Galatone

Parabita

Casarano

Tursi

Policoro

Gallipoli

Ugento

S I L I C A T A

Tricase

Colobraro

Senise

Nova Siri

GOLFO DI TARANTO

Rotondella

Oriolo

Galiano d. Capo Leuca

Capo S. Maria di Leuca

67

60

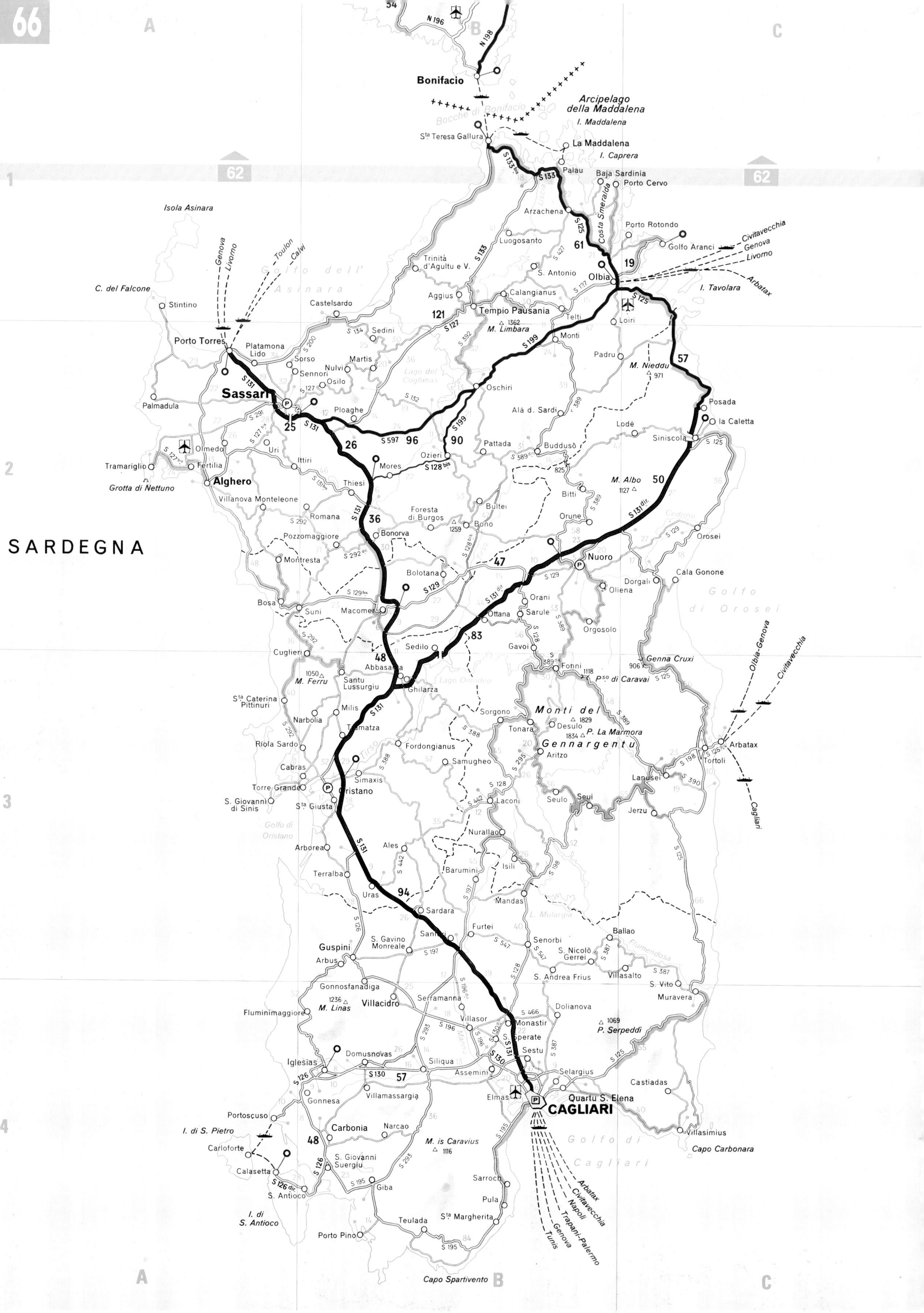

A   B   C

54

N 196   N 198

Bonifacio

Arcipelago
della Maddalena

Bocche di Bonifacio   I. Maddalena

Sta Teresa Gallura   La Maddalena
I. Caprera

S 133 bis   Palau
Baja Sardinia
S 133   Porto Cervo

Isola Asinara   Arzachena
Costa Smeralda   Porto Rotondo
Golfo Aranci   Civitavecchia
Genova
Livorno

Luogosanto   S. Antonio   61   19   Arbatax

C. del Falcone   Trinità
d'Agultu e V.   Olbia   I. Tavolara

Stintino   Castelsardo   Aggius   Calangianus   S 125

Golfo dell'   Tempio Pausania   Telti   Loiri

Asinara   Sedini   121   Monti   Padru   57

Porto Torres   Sorso   Martis   M. Limbara   S 199   M. Nieddu

Platamona   Nulvi   Osilo   Oschiri   Alà d. Sardi   M. Nieddu 971   Posada

Lido   Sennori   Ozieri   Pattada   Buddusò   la Caletta

Palmadula   Sassari   Ploaghe   25   Siniscola   S 125

26   96   90   Lodè   50

Olmedo   Uri   Ittiri   Mores   M. Albo 1127

Tramariglio   Fertilia   S 128 bis   Bitti

SARDEGNA   Alghero   Thiesi   Bultei   Orune   Orosei

Grotta di Nettuno   Villanova Monteleone   Foresta   Bono   Cala Gonone

Romana   di Burgos   47   Nuoro

Pozzomaggiore   36   Bonorva   Golfo

Montresta   Bolotana   Orani   di Orosei

Bosa   Suni   Macomer   Sarule   Dorgali

48   Sedilo   83   Oliena

Cuglieri   M. Ferru   Abbasanta   Gavoi   Orgosolo

Sta Caterina   Santu   Ghilarza   Fonni   Genna Cruxi

Pittinuri   Lussurgiu   Pso di Caravai   Arbatax

Narbolia   Milis   Sorgono   Monti del   Olbia-Genova

Riola Sardo   Tramatza   Fordongianus   Tonara   Desulo   Gennargentu   Civitavecchia

Cabras   Simaxis   Samugheo   P. La Marmora   Tortolì

Torre Grande   Oristano   Aritzo   Arbatax

S. Giovanni   Sta Giusta   Laconi   Lanusei   Cagliari

di Sinis   Golfo di   Nurallao   Seulo   Seui

Oristano   Arborea   Ales   Jerzu

Terralba   Barumini   Isili

Uras   94   Sardara   Mandas   Ballao

Guspini   Sanluri   Furtei   Senorbì   S. Vito

Arbus   S. Gavino   S. Nicolò   Villasalto

Monreale   Gerrei   Muravera

Gonnosfanadiga   Serramanna   S. Andrea Frius   P. Serpeddi

Fluminimaggiore   M. Linas   Villacidro   Villasor   Dolianova

Iglesias   Domusnovas   Siliqua   Monastir   Castiadas

Gonnesa   Villamassargia   57   Assemini   Samassi   Sestu   Selargius

Portoscuso   Carbonia   Narcao   Elmas   CAGLIARI   Quartu S. Elena

I. di S. Pietro   48   Villasimius

Carloforte   S. Giovanni   M. is Caravius   Capo Carbonara

Calasetta   Suergiu   Golfo di

S. Antioco   Giba   Sarroch   Cagliari

I. di   Pula   Arbatax
S. Antioco   Civitavecchia

Porto Pino   Teulada   Sta Margherita   Napoli   Genova

Capo Spartivento   Trapani-Palermo   Tunis

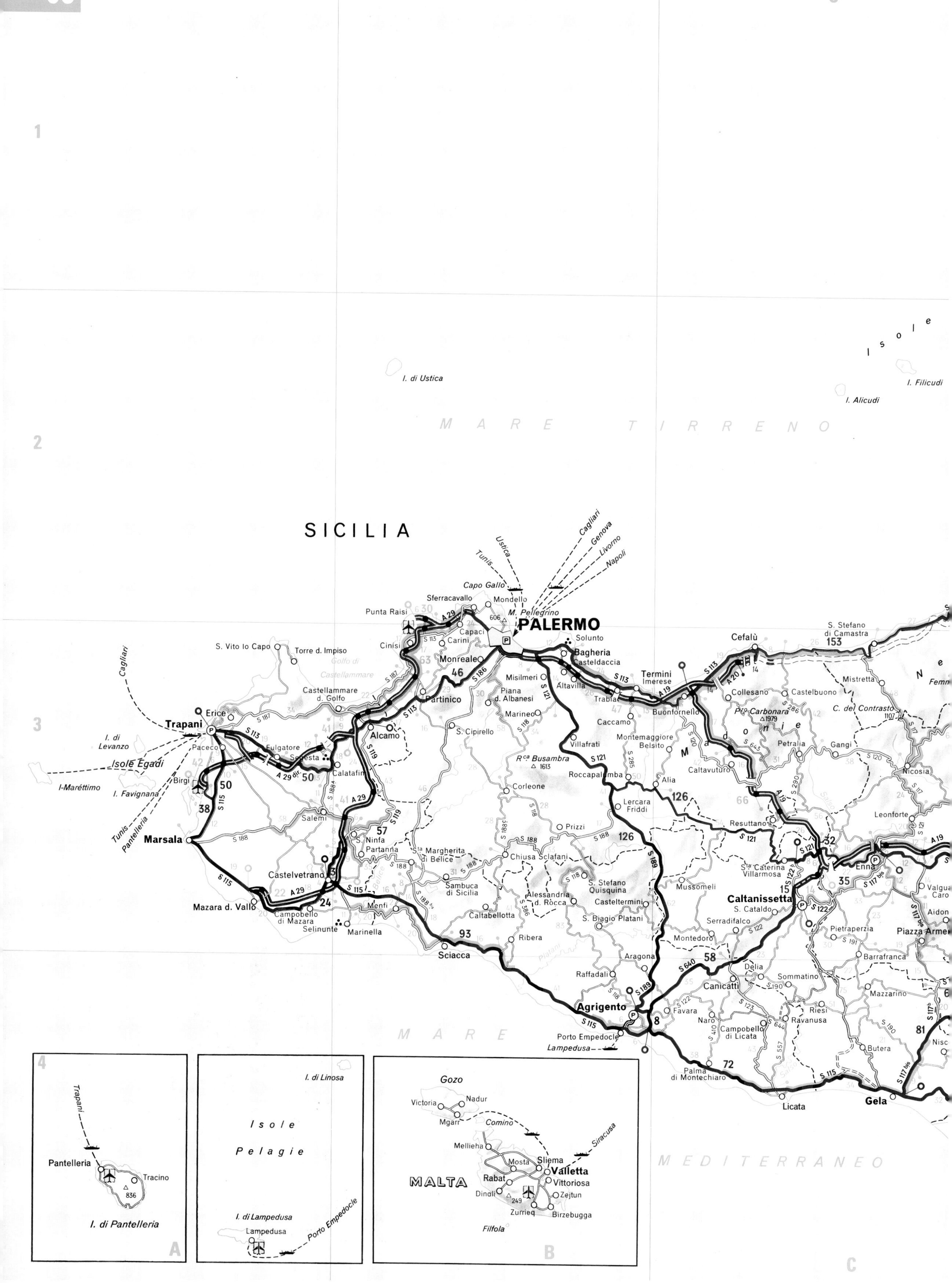

A   B   C

1

2

I s o l e

I. di Ustica

I. Filicudi

I. Alicudi

M A R E   T I R R E N O

S I C I L I A

Cagliari
Genova
Livorno
Napoli
Ustica
Tunis

Capo Gallo

Sferracavallo
Mondello
M. Pellegrino
PALERMO
Solunto
Bagheria
Casteldaccia

Punta Raisi
Capaci
Carini
Termini
Imerese
Cefalù
S. Stefano
di Camastra
153

S. Vito lo Capo
Torre d. Impiso
Cinisi
Monreale
Misilmeri
Altavilla
Trabia
Buonfornello
Collesano
Castelbuono
Mistretta

Golfo di
Castellammare
Castellammare
d. Golfo
Partinico
Piana
d. Albanesi
Marineo
Caccamo
Montemaggiore
Belsito
P.ta Carbonara
C. del Contrasto
Petralia
Gangi

3

Cagliari
Erice
Trapani
Paceco
Fulgatore
Segesta
Alcamo
S. Cipirello
Villafrati
R.ca Busambra
Roccapalumba
Alia
126
Caltavuturo
Resuttano

I. di
Levanzo
Isole Egadi
I-Maréttimo
I. Favignana
Birgi
Calatafimi
Corleone
Lercara
Friddi
66
32
Leonforte
Nicosia

Tunis
Pantelleria
Marsala
Salemi
Prizzi
126
Sta Caterina
Villarmosa
Enna
35
Valgua
Caro

57
S. Ninfa
Partanna
Margherita
di Belice
Chiusa Sclafani
15
Caltanissetta
Aidon
PIAZZA ARME

Castelvetrano
Sambuca
di Sicilia
Alessandria
d. Rocca
S. Stefano
Quisquina
Casteltermini
Mussomeli
S. Cataldo
Serradifalco
Pietraperzia
Barrafranca

Mazara d. Vallo
24
Menfi
Caltabellotta
S. Biagio Platani
Montedoro
Delia
Sommatino
Mazzarino

Campobello
di Mazara
Selinunte
Marinella
93
Ribera
Aragona
58
Canicattì
Riesi
Ravanusa

Sciacca
Raffadali
S 640
Campobello
di Licata
Butera
Nisc

4

I. di Linosa
Gozo
Agrigento
8
Favara
Naro
81

I s o l e
Victoria
Nadur
Mgarr
Comino
Porto Empedocle
Lampedusa
Palma
di Montechiaro
72
Licata
Gela

P e l a g i e
Mellieha
Mosta
Sliema
Siracusa
MALTA
Rabat
Valletta
Vittoriosa
Dingli
Zejtun
M A R E
M E D I T E R R A N E O

M A R E
Pantelleria
Tracino
836
I. di Pantelleria
I. di Lampedusa
Lampedusa
Zurrieq
Birzebugga
Filfola

A   B   C

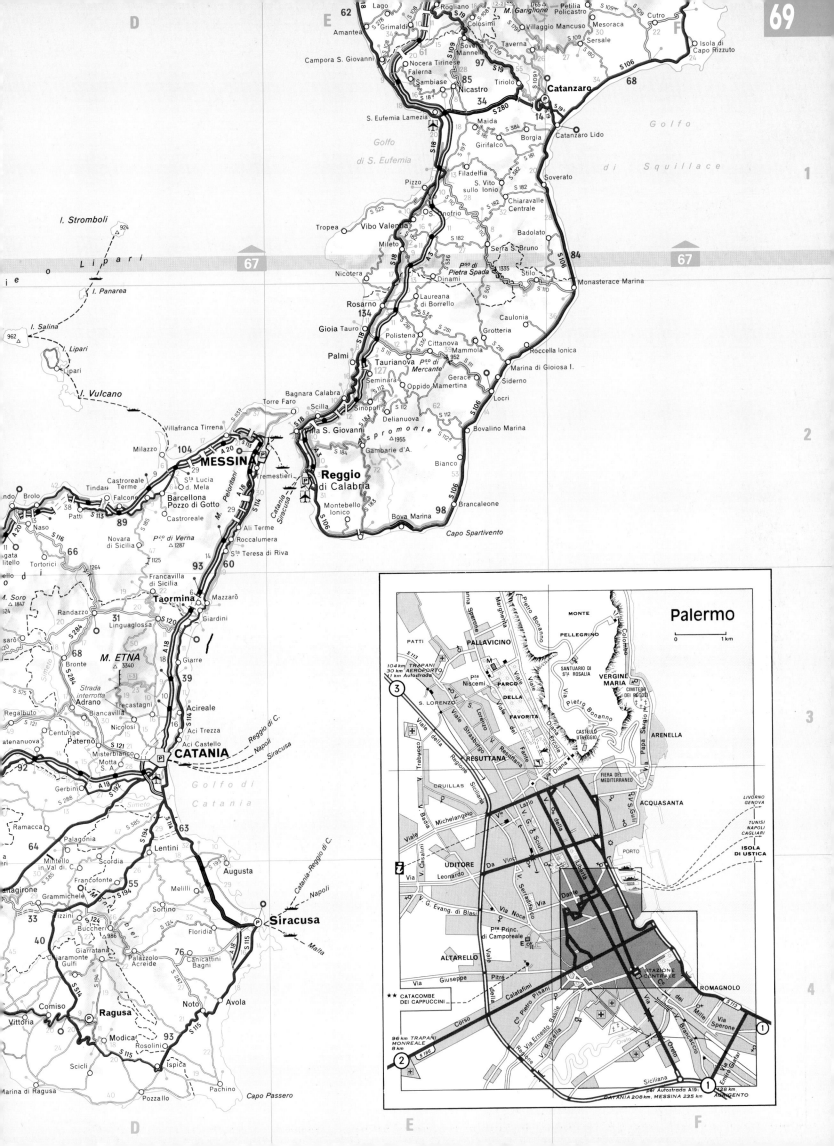

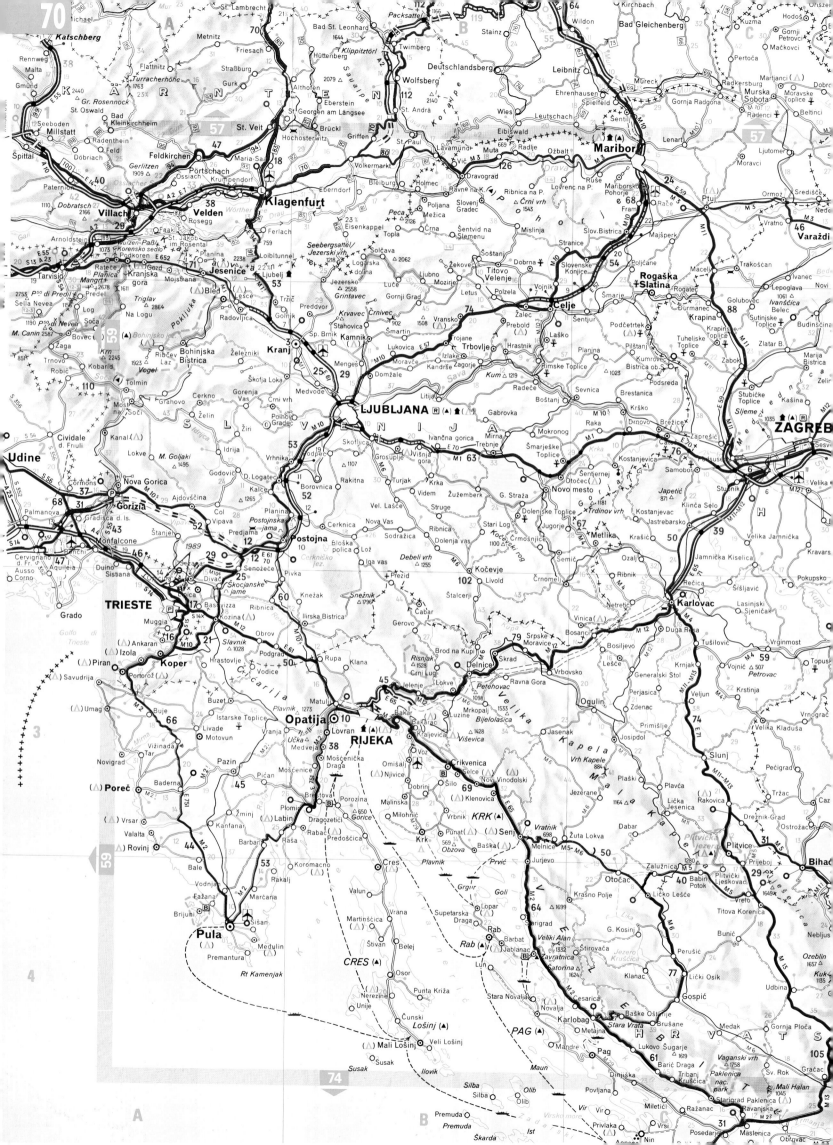

A · B · C

70

1

61

Croatia / Adriatic islands (upper right):
Kruščica nac. park · Mali Halan · Silba · Olib · Povljana · Starigrad Paklenica (Λ) · Miletići · Ražanac · Ravanjska · 31 · Premuda · Škarda · Ist · Vir · Vir · Privlaka · Posedarje · Maslenica · Novigrad · Aenona · Nin · Poličnik · Obrovac · Molat · Molat · Sestrunj · Sestruni · Murvica · Smilčić · Zadar · Ancona · Soline · Ugljan · Preko · Bibinje · Sukošan · Benkovac · Božava · Kali · Kulkjica · Iž · Žderac · Krmčine · Filipjakov · Dugi Otok · Brbinj · Iz Veli · Pašman · Pašman · Biograd · Stank · Luka · Žman · Tkon · Pakošta · Sali · Pirovac · Žut · Murter · Murter · Tijesno · Kornati (Λ) · Kornat · Kaprije · Kakan · Žirje

Italy (Adriatic coast, Marche):
Pesaro · 11 · Fano · VIA FLAMINIA · Marotta · 52 · Mondolfo · Senigallia · Mondavio · Corinaldo · Ostra · Chiaravalle · Falconara Maritt. · 15 · Ancona · 31 · S. Marcello · Jesi · Moie · Osimo · 51 · Numana · Montecarotto · Pergola · Arcevia · Cupramontana · Filottrano · Recanati · Loreto · Porto Recanati · Sassoferrato · Cingoli · Villa Potenza · Potenza Picena · Fabriano · 112 · Borgo Tufico · Treia · Macerata · Civitanova Marche · Porto S. Elpidio · Osteria d. Gatto · S. Severino Marche · Sforzacosta · Corridonia · Montegranaro · S. Elpidio a Mare · Matelica · Tolentino · Porto S. Giorgio · Campodonico · Castelraimondo · Caldarola · Fermo · 67 · Gualdo Tadino · 94 · Camerino · Montegiorgio · S. Ginesio · 84 · Pedaso · Muccia · Fiastra · Sarnano · Monterubbiano · Montefiore d. Aso · Servigliano · Ripatransone · Grottammare · Nocera Umbra · Colfiorito · 136 · Amandola · Montalto d. Marche · 32 · S. Benedetto d. Tronto · Foligno · Visso · Comunanza · Offida · 133 · Trevi · M. Vettore · Montegallo · Ascoli Piceno · Alba Adriatica · Triponzo · Norcia · Arquata d. T. · Civitella d. T. · 37 · Nereto · Spoleto · Castelluccio · Acquasanta Terme · 43 · 23 · Giulianova · Monteluco · Amatrice · Valle Castellana · Campli · 44 · Roseto d. Abruzzi · Cascia · Cittareale · Teramo · 56 · Montorio al Vomano · 69 · Villa Vomano · Pineto · Leonessa · Ceppo · Atri · Silvi Marina · Terni · Posta · Borbona · Montereale · Bisenti · Città S. Angelo · Montesilvano Marina · Piediluco · Prati di Tivo · Gr. Sasso d'If. · Penne · Pescara · Greccio · 37 · Antrodoco · Gran Sasso d'Italia · Campo Imperatore · Farindola · Loreto Aprutino · Francavilla al Mare · Rieti · Cittaducale · 48 · Assergi · Pianella · Ortona · Contigliano · M. Terminillo · Terminillo · Castel d. Monte · Catignano · Chieti · S. Vito Chietino · L'Aquila · 62 · Navelli · Torre de Passeri · Bucchianico · Fossacesia · Rocca Sinibalda · Fiamignano · 116 · 60 · Capestrano · Scafa · Manoppello · Lanciano · 97 · Montenero S. · Pescorocchiano · Rocca di Mezzo · Ovindoli · Castelvecchio Subequo · Popoli · Pratola Peligna · Pretoro · Orsogna · Guardiagrele · Vasto · Poggio Mirteto · 77 · Borgorose · Magliano de Marsi · Celano · 67 · Sulmona · 98 · Caramanico Terme · Casoli · Casalbordino · 77 · Termoli · Orvinio · 112 · Tagliacozzo · 100 · Avezzano · Pescina · Cansano · Lama d. Peligni · Atessa · Gissi · Campomarino · Roma · 82 · TIBURTINA · Carsoli · Trasacco · Scanno · Pescocostanzo · Palena · Villa Sta Maria · Furci · Guglionesi · Tivoli · Mandela · VALERIA · Capistrello · Roccaraso · Rivisondoli · Castiglione Messer Marino · Palata · Larino · Mentana · Guidonia · Subiaco · Civitella Roveto · Balsorano · Pescasseroli · Villetta Barrea · Castel di Sangro · Agnone · Trivento · Casacalenda · Palestrina · Villa Adriana · Castel Madama · Forca d'Acero · Barrea · Bonefro · Lucito · Santa Croce di Magliano · Fiuggi · Nazionale · Bagnoli d. Trigno

Ferry destinations: Zadar · Split · Dubrovnik · Kérkira (Corfou) · Igoumenitsa · Pátrai (Patras)

M A R C H E · A B R U Z Z I · M O L I S E · I T A L I A · A D R I A · Mare

63 · 64 · 73 · 75

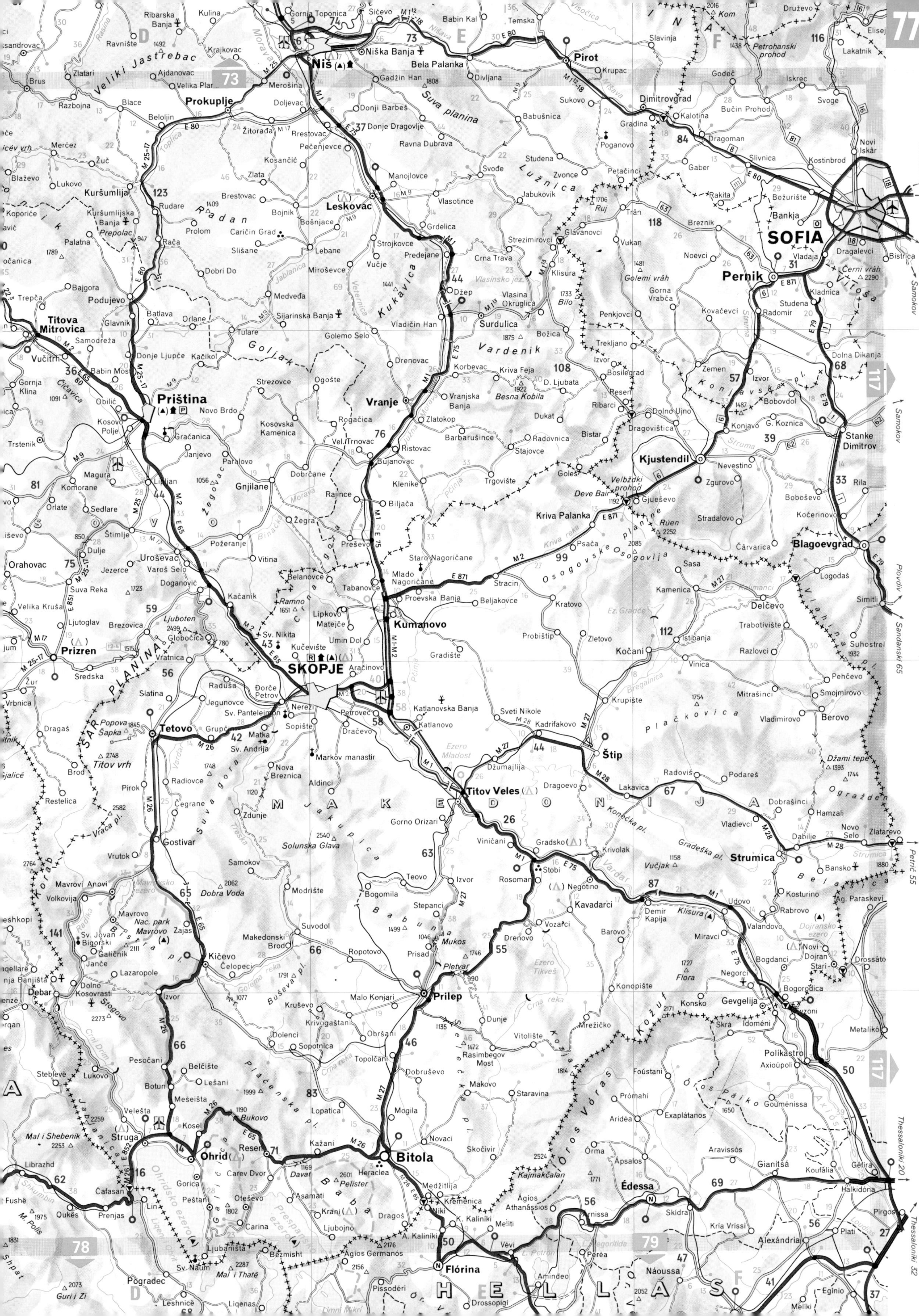

Niš
Niška Banja
Bela Palanka
Pirot
Dimitrovgrad
Prokuplje
Kuršumlija
Leskovac
Vlasotince
Surdulica
Vladičin Han
Vranje
Bujanovac
Preševo
Priština
Titova Mitrovica
Vučitrn
Podujevo
Kosovo Polje
Gnjilane
Uroševac
Kačanik
Prizren
Tetovo
Gostivar
Kičevo
Debar
Struga
Ohrid
Resen
Bitola
Prilep
Kumanovo
SKOPJE
Titov Veles
Štip
Kočani
Kriva Palanka
Kjustendil
Pernik
SOFIA
Dragoman
Slivnica
Kostinbrod
Bankja
Blagoevgrad
Stanke Dimitrov
Dupnica
Delčevo
Berovo
Strumica
Kavadarci
Negotino
Gevgelija
Dojran
Polikastro
Édessa
Flórina
Niki
Pogradec
Librazhd
Kukavica
Radan
Goljak
Vardenik
Osogovske planine
Šar Planina
Jakupica
Babuna
Kožuf
Belasica
Ogražden
Plačkovica
Vitoša
Konjavska pl.
M A K E D O N I J A
H E L L Á S
Veliki Jastrebac
Suva planina
Lužnica
Titov vrh
Pelister
Kajmakčalan
Samokov
Plovdiv
Sandanski
Thessaloniki
Varna
Vraca
Burgas
Petrič

TIRANË - DURRËS

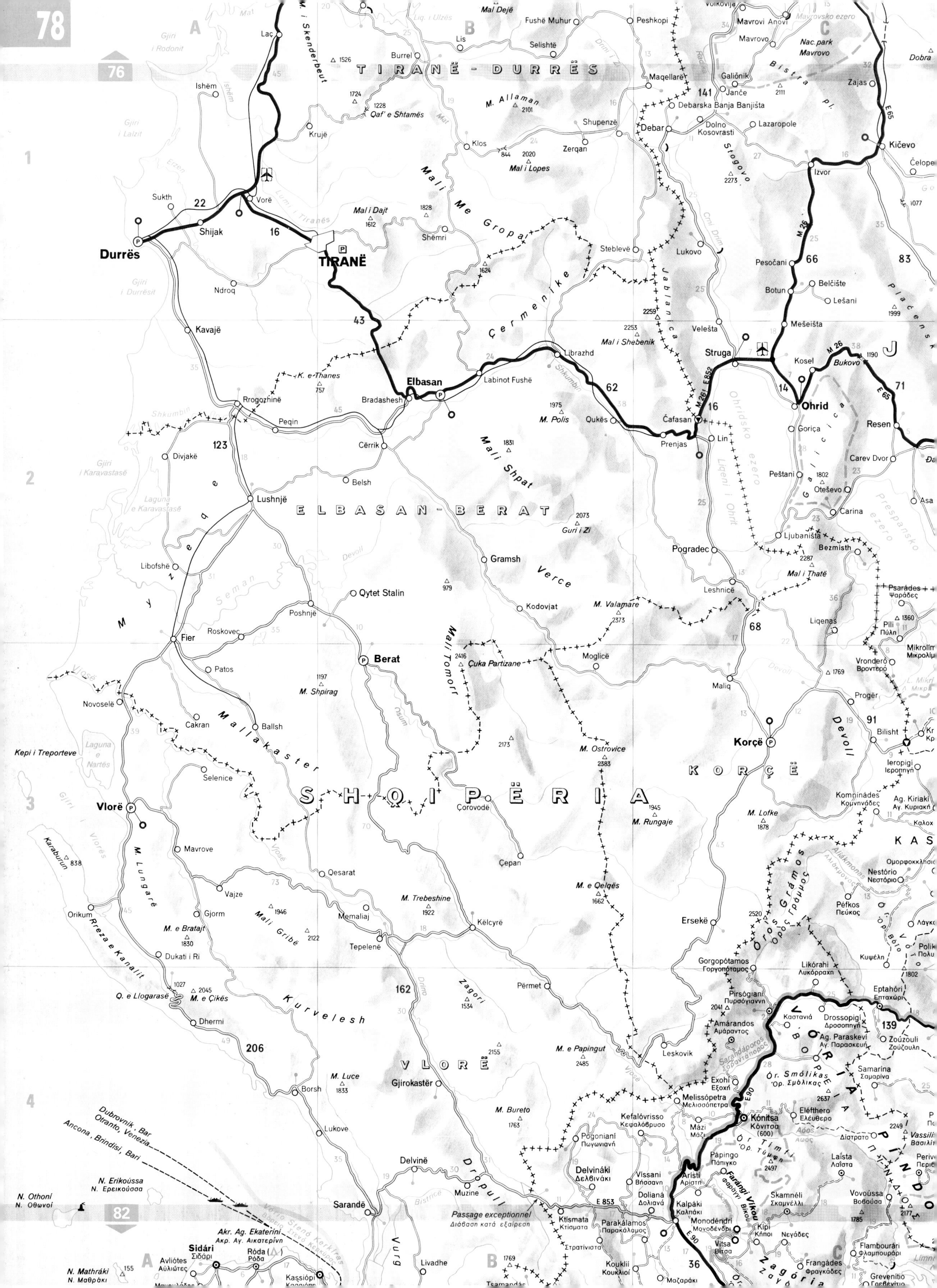

Mal Dejé
Fushé Muhur
Peshkopi
Mavrovi Anovi
Mavrovo
Nac. park Mavrovo
Dobra

Liq. i Ulzës
Lis
Selishtë
Maqellarë
Galiônik
Zajas
Kičevo
Čelopek

Laç
Mal i Skenderbeut
Burrel
1526
M. Allaman
2101
Shupenzë
Debar
Dolno Kosovrasti
Lazaropole
Izvor

Ishëm
1724
1228
Qaf' e Shtamës
Klos
Zerqan
844 2020
Mal i Lopes
Debarska Banja Banjišta
141 Janče
2111
Stogovo
2273

Gjiri i Lalzit
Krujë
Mal i Dajt
1828
Shëmri
Steblevë
Lukovo
Pesočani 66 83
Botun
Belčište
Lešani
1999

Sukth 22
Vorë
1612
Mali Me Gropa
Čermenike
2259
Velešta
Mešeišta
M 26

Durrës
Shijak 16
TIRANË
Jablanica
Mal i Shebenik
2253
Struga
Kosel Bukovo M 26 J
1190

Ndroq
43
Librazhd
Labinot Fushë
Steblevë
1975
62
Čafasan 16
Ohrid 71
E 65

Kavajë
K. e Thanes
757
Elbasan
Bradashesh
24
M. Polis
Qukës
Prenjas
Lin
Goriça
Resen

Rrogozhinë
Peqin
45
Cërrik
1831
Ohridsko ezero
Peštani 1802
Carev Dvor

123
Belsh
Mali Shpat
Otešovo
Carina
Prespansko ezero

Divjakë
Lushnjë
ELBASAN - BERAT
2073
Guri i Zi
Pogradec
Ljubaništa
Bezmisth 2287
Psarádes

Libofshë
Gramsh
979
Verce
2416
Leshnicë
68
Mal i Thatë
Liqenas
Mikrolim

Fier
Roskovec
Qytet Stalin
Poshnjë
Kodoviat
M. Valamare 2373
Moglicë
Maliq
Vronderó 1769
Progër

Novoselë
Patos
Berat
1197
M. Shpirag
Mallakaster
Çuka Partizane
2173
SHQIPËRIA
Korçë 91 Bilisht
Ieropigi

Vlorë
Cakran
Ballsh
M. Ostrovice 2383
KORÇË
M. Lofke 1878
Komninádes

Selenice
Çorovodë
1945
M. Rungaje
Kastaniá
Nestório

Mavrove
Qesarat
Çepan
M. e Oelqës 1662
Ersekë 2520
KAS

Orikum
Vajze
73
Memaliaj
Kurvelesh
Gorgopótamos
Likórahi
Eptahóri 1802

Gjorm
Mali Gribë
1946 2122
Tepelenë
Kelcyrë
18
Pirsógiani 2041
Drossopigi
139

Dukati i Ri
1027 2045
M. e Çikës
162
M. Trebeshine 1922
Përmet
M. e Papingut 2485 2155
Leskovik
Kónitsa
Samarina

Q. e Llogarasë
206
Zagori 1534
Ór. Smólikas 2637
Konitsa (600)
Vassili 2249

Dhermi
M. Luce 1833
Gjirokastër
M. Bureto 1763
Melissópetra
Áristi 2497
Skamnéli

Borsh
V L O R Ë
Kefalóvrisso
Exohi
Mázi
Páпingo

Dubrovnik - Bar, Otranto, Venezia
Ancona, Brindisi, Bari
Lukove
Delvinë
Drópull
Pogoniani
Vissani Delvináki Doliana Kalpáki Monodéndri E 90

N. Othoni
N. Erikoússa
Sidári
Muzine
Sarandë
Passage exceptionnel
Diádosi katá exaíresi
Ktismata Parakálamos
36
Vitsa Zagoria

82

N. Mathráki
155
Avliótes
Róda
Kassiópi
Livadhe
1769
Koukli
Mazaraki
Frángades

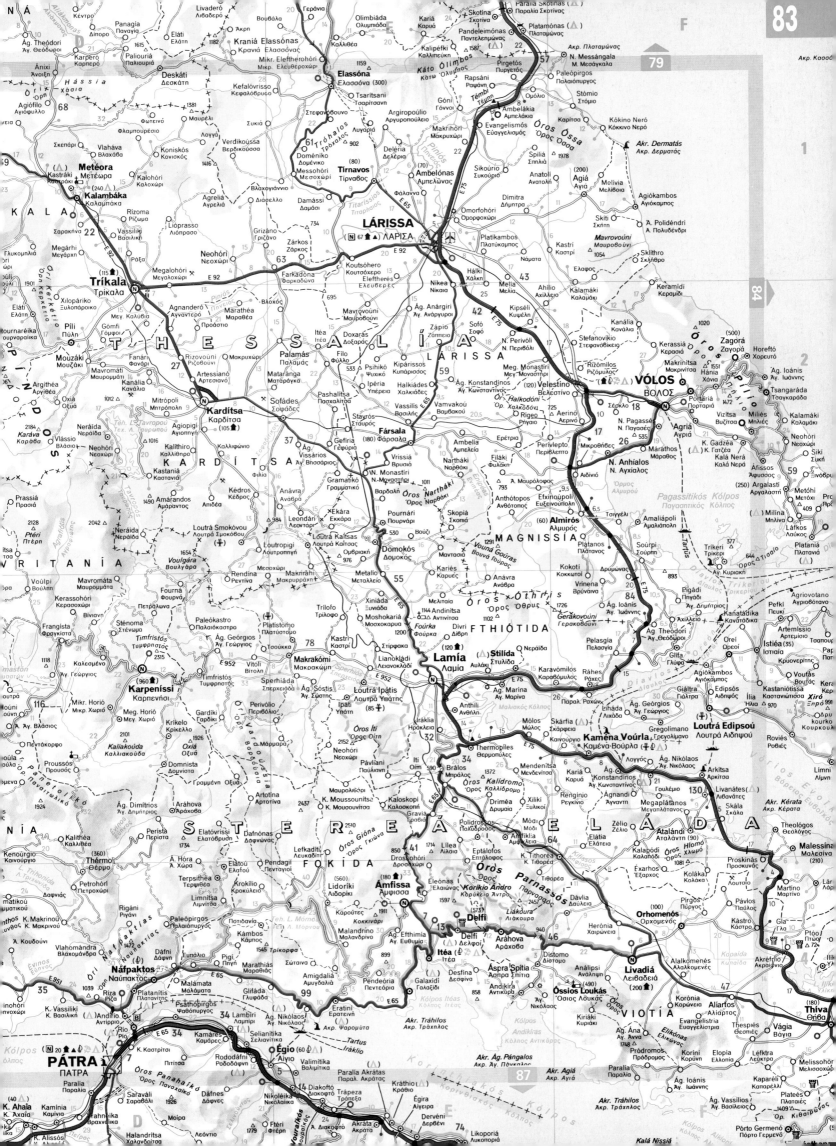

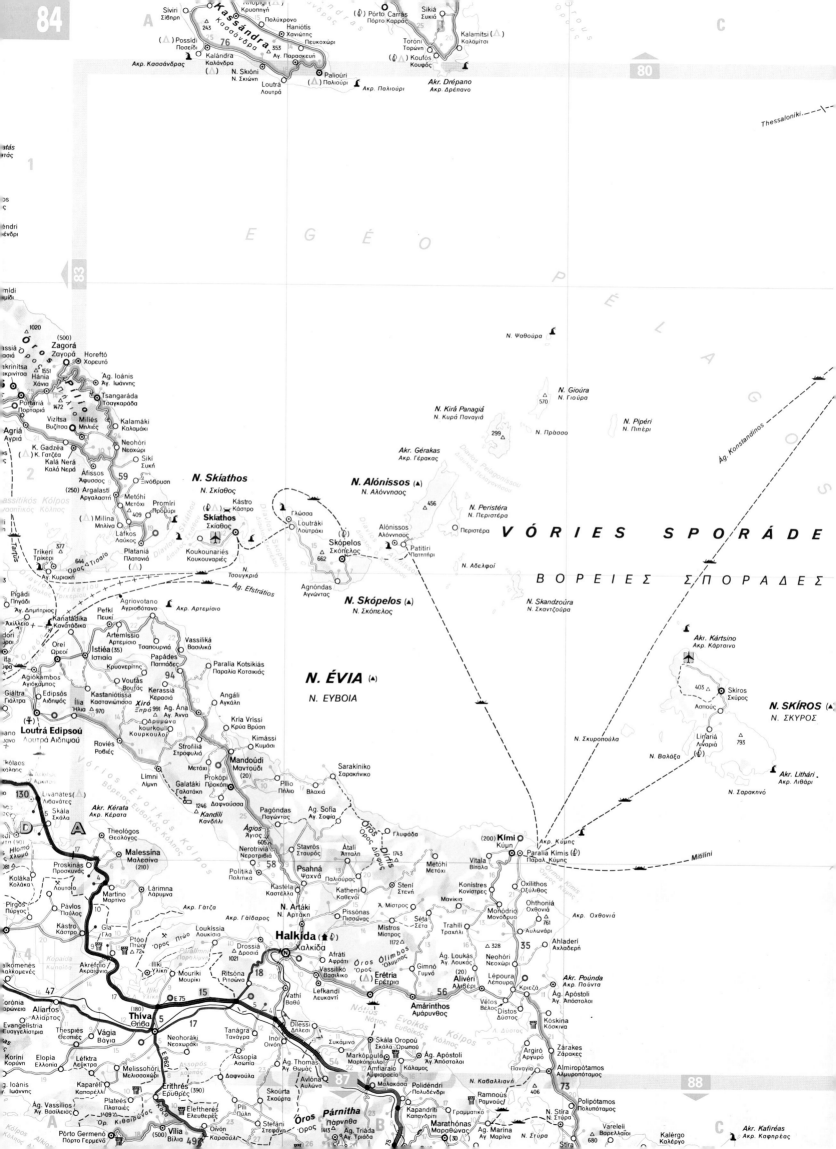

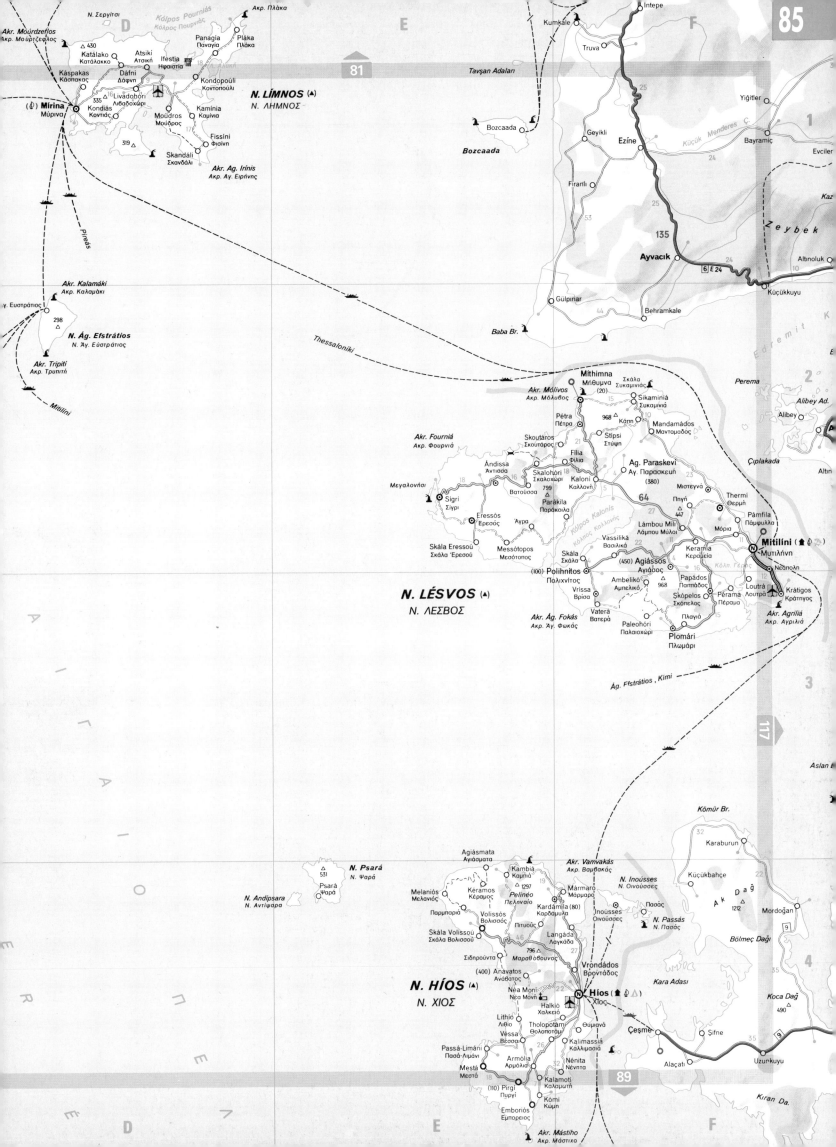

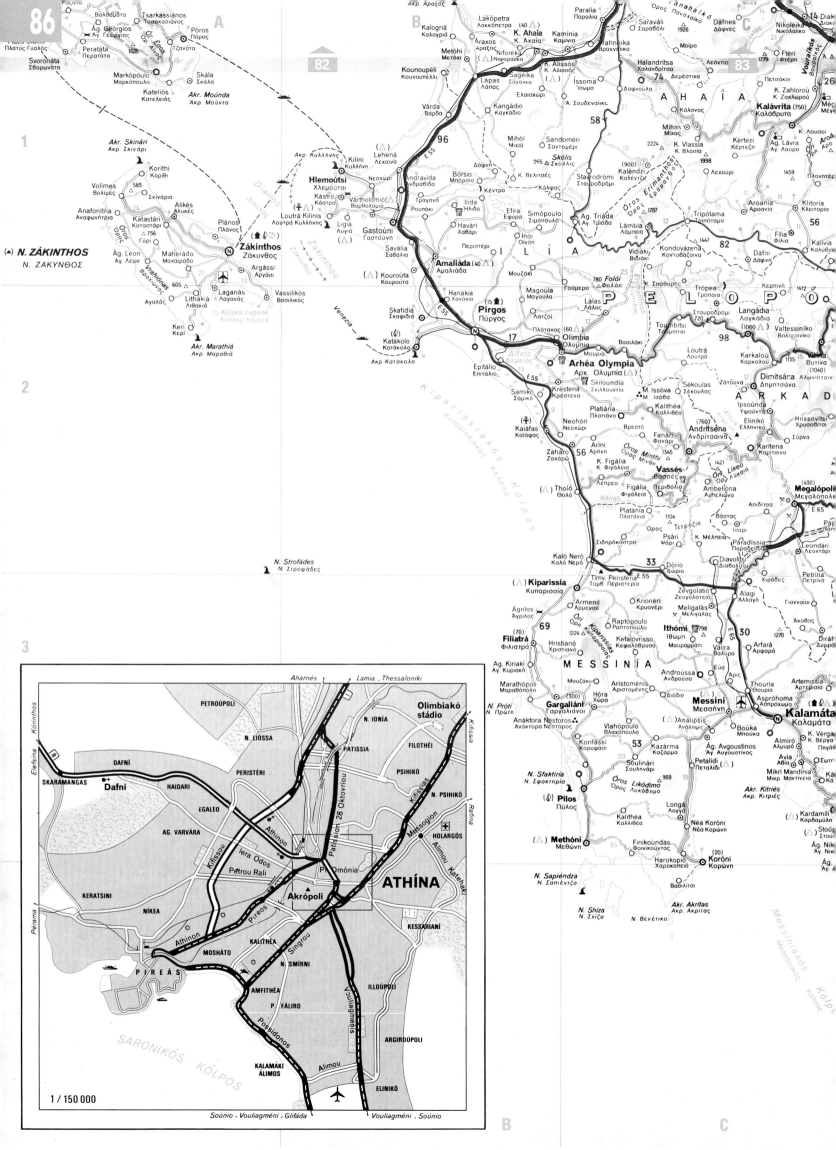

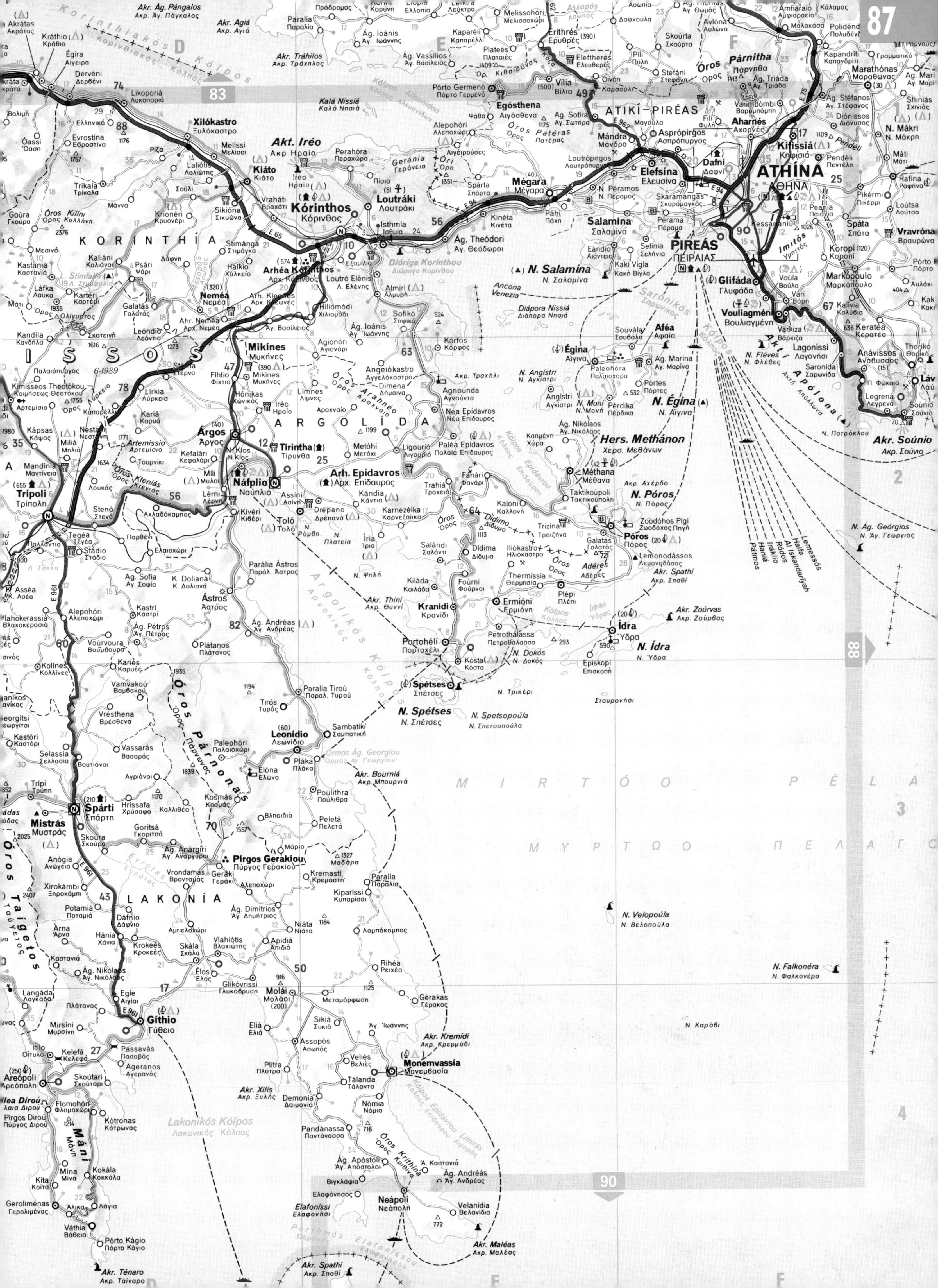

Korinthiakós Kólpos
Κορινθιακός Κόλπος
83
Xilókastro
Ξυλόκαστρο
Kiáto
Κιάτο
Akt. Iréo
Ακρ Ηραίο
Kórinthos
Κόρινθος
Loutráki
Λουτράκι
Dióriga Korínthou
Διώρυγα Κορίνθου
Egósthena
Αιγόσθενα
Mégara
Μέγαρα
Elefsína
Ελευσίνα
ATIKÍ-PIRÉAS
Aspróprirgos
Ασπρόπυργος
Óros Párnitha
Kifissiá
Κηφισιά
ATHÍNA
ΑΘΗΝΑ
Marathónas
Μαραθώνας
Rafína
Ραφήνα
Salamína
Σαλαμίνα
PIREÁS
ΠΕΙΡΑΙΑΣ
Glifáda
Γλυφάδα
Vouliagméni
Βουλιαγμένη
N. Salamína
N. Σαλαμίνα
Saronikós Kólpos
Σαρωνικός Κόλπος
Égina
Αίγινα
N. Égina
N. Αίγινα
Akt. Apólona
Akr. Soúnio
Ακρ. Σούνιο
Lávrio
K O R I N T H Í A
Nemea
Νεμέα
Arhéa Kórinthos
Αρχ. Κόρινθος
P E L O P Ó N I S S O S
Mikínes
Μυκήνες
A R G O L Í D A
Árgos
Άργος
Tírintha
Τίρυνθα
Náfplio
Ναύπλιο
Arh. Epídavros
Αρχ. Επίδαυρος
Paléa Epídavros
Παλαιά Επίδαυρος
Hers. Methánon
Χερσ. Μεθάνων
Méthana
Μέθανα
N. Póros
N. Πόρος
Póros
Πόρος
Trípoli
Τρίπολη
Tolό
Τολό
Ástros
Άστρος
Argolikós Kólpos
Αργολικός Κόλπος
Kranídi
Κρανίδι
Ermióni
Ερμιόνη
Portohéli
Πορτοχέλι
Ídra
Ύδρα
N. Ídra
N. Ύδρα
Spétses
Σπέτσες
N. Spétses
N. Σπέτσες
N. Spetsopoúla
N. Σπετσοπούλα
Óros Párnonas
Όρος Πάρνωνας
Leonídio
Λεωνίδιο
M I R T Ó O   P É L A
M Y P T Ω O   Π E Λ A Γ
Spárti
Σπάρτη
Mistrás
Μυστράς
Pírgos Gerakíou
Πύργος Γερακίου
L A K O N Í A
Óros Taígetos
Ταΰγετος
Gíthio
Γύθειο
Monemvassía
Μονεμβασία
N. Velopoúla
N. Βελοπούλα
N. Falkonéra
N. Φαλκονέρα
Areópoli
Αρεόπολη
Máni
Μάνη
Lakonikós Kólpos
Λακωνικός Κόλπος
Geroliménas
Γερολιμένας
Akr. Ténaro
Ακρ. Ταίναρο
Neápoli
Νεάπολη
Elafoníssi
Ελαφονήσι
Akr. Maléas
Ακρ. Μαλέας
Porthmós Elafoníssou
88
90
2
3
4

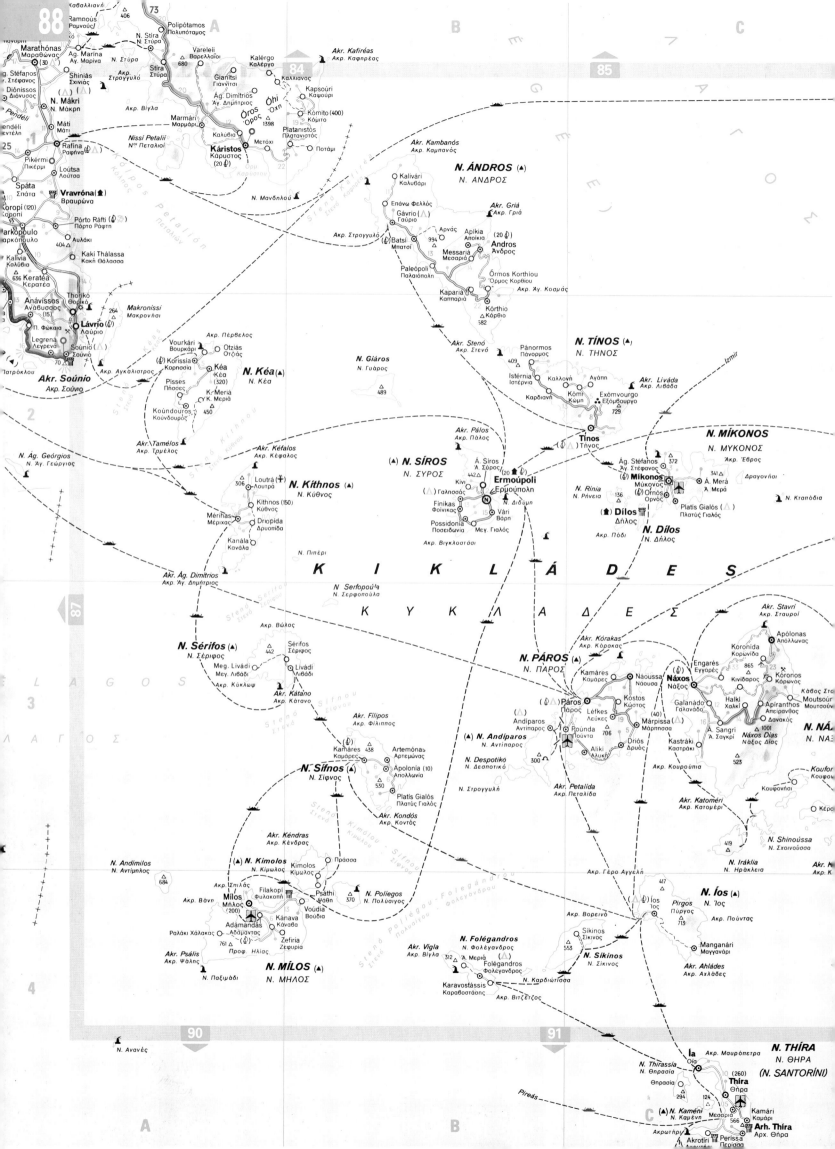

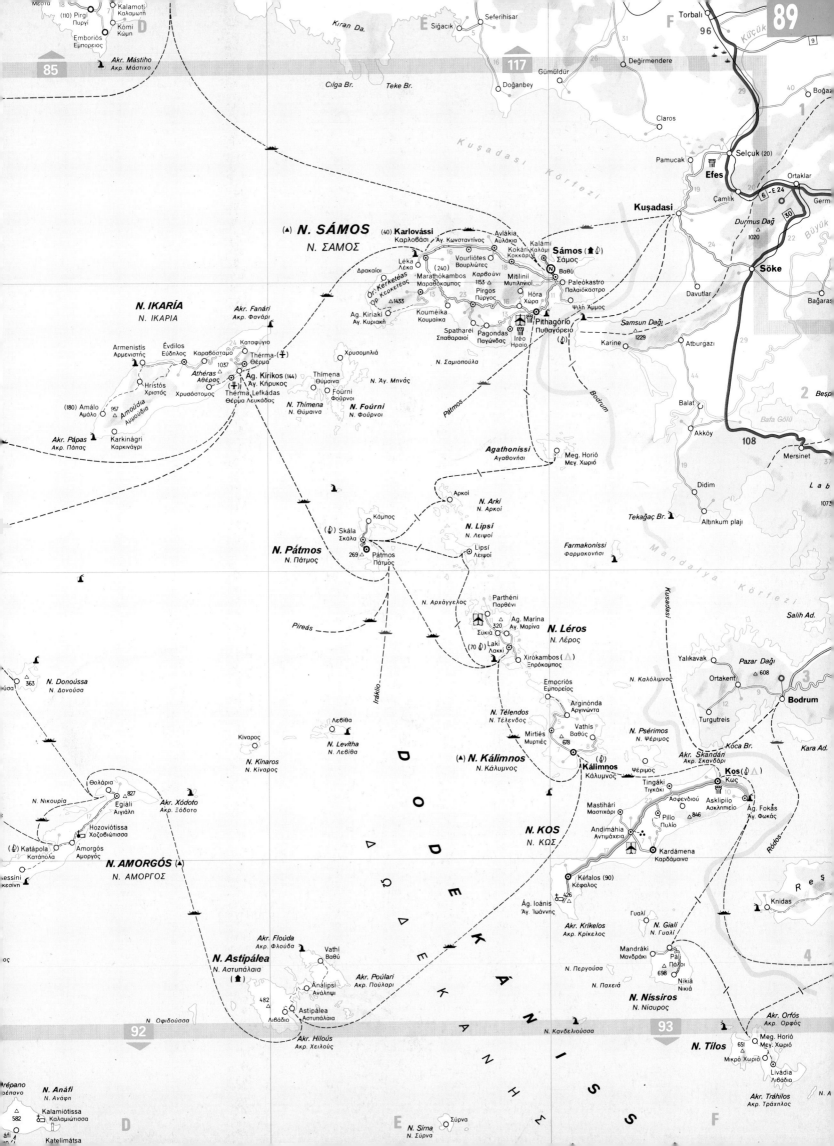

D

E

F

1

Kiran Da.

Seferihisar

Sığacık

5

Torbalı

96

Küçük

9

Çılga Br.

Teke Br.

Değirmendere

31

Claros

Doğanbey

Gümüldür

16

Pamucak

26

Selçuk (20)

19

Efes

6 -E 24

Çamlık

Ortaklar

Germ

30

Kuşadası Körfezi

Kuşadası

Durmuş Dağ
△ 1020

Büyük

Söke

(▲) **N. SÁMOS**
N. ΣΑΜΟΣ

(40) **Karlovássi**
Καρλοβάσι

Avlákia
Αυλάκια

Kalámi
Καλάμι

Sámos (⚓)
Σάμος

74

Davutlar

Bağaras

Áy. Konstantínos
Áγ. Κωνσταντίνος

Kókári Kalámi
Κοκκάρι

Kókkari
Κοκκάρι

N

Vathí
Βαθύ

Léka
Λέκα

Vourliótes
Βουρλιώτες

16

Mitilinií
Μυτιληνιοί

Paleókastro
Παλαιόκαστρο

2

Drakaíoi
Δρακαίοι

(240)

Marathókambos
Μαραθόκαμπος

1153
△

Pírgos
Πύργος

Hóra
Χώρα

11

Psilí Ámmos
Ψιλή Άμμος

Karine

Atburgazı

29

Óri. Kerketéas
Όρ. Κερκετέας
△1433

23

16

13

Samsun Dağı
△ 1229

N. IKARÍA
N. IKAPIA

Akr. Fanári
Aκρ. Φανάρι

24

Katafýgio
Καταφύγιο

Ag. Kiriakí
Áγ. Κυριακή

Koumeíka
Κουμαίικα

Spatharei
Σπαθαραίοι

Pagóndas
Παγώνδας

Iréo
Ιρέο
Ηραίο

Pithagório
Πυθαγόρειο
(⚓)

Armenistís
Αρμενιστής

Évdilos
Εύδηλος

Karavóstamo
Καραβόσταμο

1037

Thérma (✈)
Θέρμα

Hristós
Χριστός

Athéras
Aθέρας △

Ág. Kirikos (144)
Áγ. Κήρυκος

Thérma Lefkádas
Θέρμα Λευκάδας

Chrysómlia
Χρυσομηλιά

N. Samiopoúla
N. Σαμιοπούλα

(180) Amálo
Αμάλο

957
△

Amoúdia
Αμμούδια

Chrysóstomos
Χρυσόστομος

Thimena
Θύμενα
Θύμαινα

Foúrni
Φούρνοι

N. Áy. Mínás
N. Άγ. Μηνάς

Pátmos

Bodrum

44

Akr. Pápas
Aκρ. Πάπας

Karkinágri
Καρκινάγρι

N. Thímena
N. Θύμαινα

N. Foúrni
N. Φούρνοι

Mersinet

Agathoníssi
Αγαθονήσι

Meg. Horió
Μεγ. Χωριό

19

37

Didim

Bafa Gölü

Akköy

108

Balat

3

Lab

1073

Arkoí
Αρκοί

N. Arkí
N. Αρκοί

Tekağaç Br.

Altınkum plajı

Kámpos
Κάμπος

N. Lipsí
N. Λειψοί

Farmakoníssi
Φαρμακονήσι

Mandalya

Körfezi

(⚓) Skála
Σκάλα

Lipsí
Λειψοί

269

Pátmos
Πάτμος

N. Pátmos
N. Πάτμος

Parthéni
Παρθένι

N. Arhángelos
N. Αρχάγγελος

Salih Ad.

N. Donoússa
N. Δονούσσα
△ 363

Pireás

Ag. Marína
Áγ. Μαρίνα

Sikiá
Συκιά

320
△

N. Léros
N. ΛΕΡΟΣ

Kuşadası

Yalıkavak

Pazar Dağı
△ 608

Ortakent

9

3

Bodrum

N. Kalólimnos
N. Καλόλιμνος

12

N. Levítha
N. Λεβίθα

Λεβίθα

Irakhio
Ιράκλιο

(70) (⚓) Laki
Λακκί

Xirókambos (△)
Ξηρόκαμπος

Emporiós
Εμπορειός

Turgutreis

Kínaros
Κίναρος

N. Kínaros
N. Κίναρος

N. Télendos
N. Τέλενδος

Arginónda
Αργινώντα

Vathís
Βαθύς

678
△

N. Psérimos
N. Ψέριμος

Mirtiés
Μυρτιές

Akr. Skándári
Aκρ. Σκανδάρι

Kóca Br.

Kara Br.

Tholária
Θολάρια

827
△

(▲) **N. Kálimnos**
N. Κάλυμνος

Kálimnos
(⚓)
Κάλυμνος

Ψέριμος

Kos (⚓ △)
Κως

N. Nikouría
N. Νικουριά

17

Egiáli
Αιγιάλη

Akr. Xódoto
Aκρ. Ξόδοτο

Tingáki
Τιγκάκι

Asklipiío
Ασκληπιείο

Ág. Fokás
Áγ. Φωκάς

10

(⚓) Katápola
Κατάπολα

Hozoviótissa
Χοζοβιώτισσα

Amorgós
Αμοργός

Mastihári
Μαστιχάρι

Asfendioú
Ασφενδιού

846
△

Andimáhia
Αντιμάχεια

Pilío
Πυλίο

N. AMORGÓS (▲)
N. ΑΜΟΡΓΟΣ

N. KOS
N. ΚΩΣ

Kardámena
Καρδάμαινα

Rádos

Res

Kéfalos (90)
Κέφαλος

426
△

Knidas

Ág. Ioánis
Áγ. Ιωάννης

Gyalí
Γυαλί

N. Giali
N. Γυαλί

Akr. Floúda
Aκρ. Φλούδα

Vathí
Βαθύ

Akr. Krikelos
Aκρ. Κρίκελος

Mandráki
Μανδράκι

Páli
Πάλοι

N. Astipálea
N. Αστυπάλαια
(▲)

Análipsi
Ανάληψη

Akr. Poúlari
Aκρ. Πούλαρι

N. Pergoússa
N. Περγούσα

Nikiá
Νικιά

698
△

4

482

Astipálea
Αστυπάλαια

Livádio
Λιβάδιο

N. Ofidoússa
N. Οφιδούσσα

N. Pahiá
N. Παχειά

N. Níssiros
N. Νίσυρος

Akr. Orfós
Aκρ. Ορφός

Akr. Hiloús
Aκρ. Χειλούς

N. Kandelioússa
N. Κανδελιούσσα

Meg. Horió
Μεγ. Χωριό
651

N. Tílos
N. Τίλος

D

O

D

E

K

A

N

I

S

S

Mikró Horió
Μικρό Χωριό

répano
σέπανο

N. Anáfi
N. Ανάφη

Livádia
Λιβάδια

Akr. Tráhilos
Aκρ. Τράχηλος

582

Kalamiótissa
Καλαμιώτισσα

N. A

Katelimátsa

D

N. Sírna
N. Σίρνα

Sýrna
Σύρνα

E

N. A

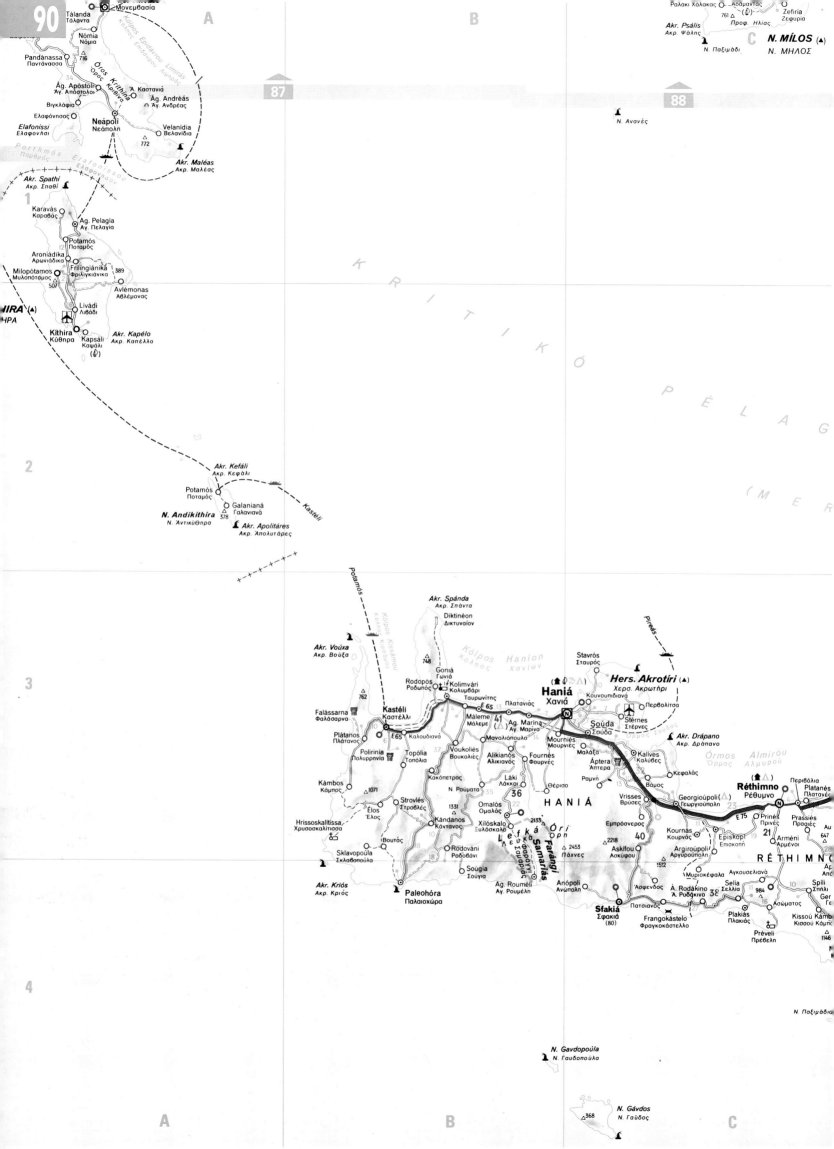

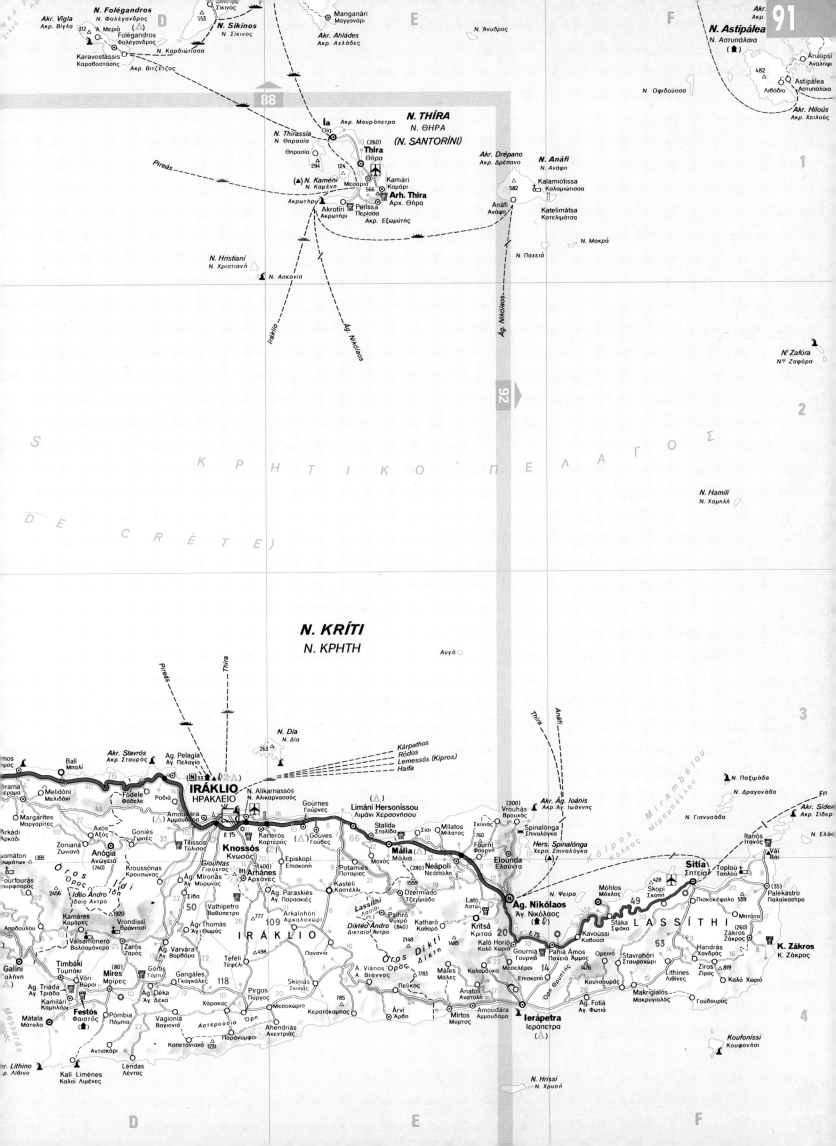

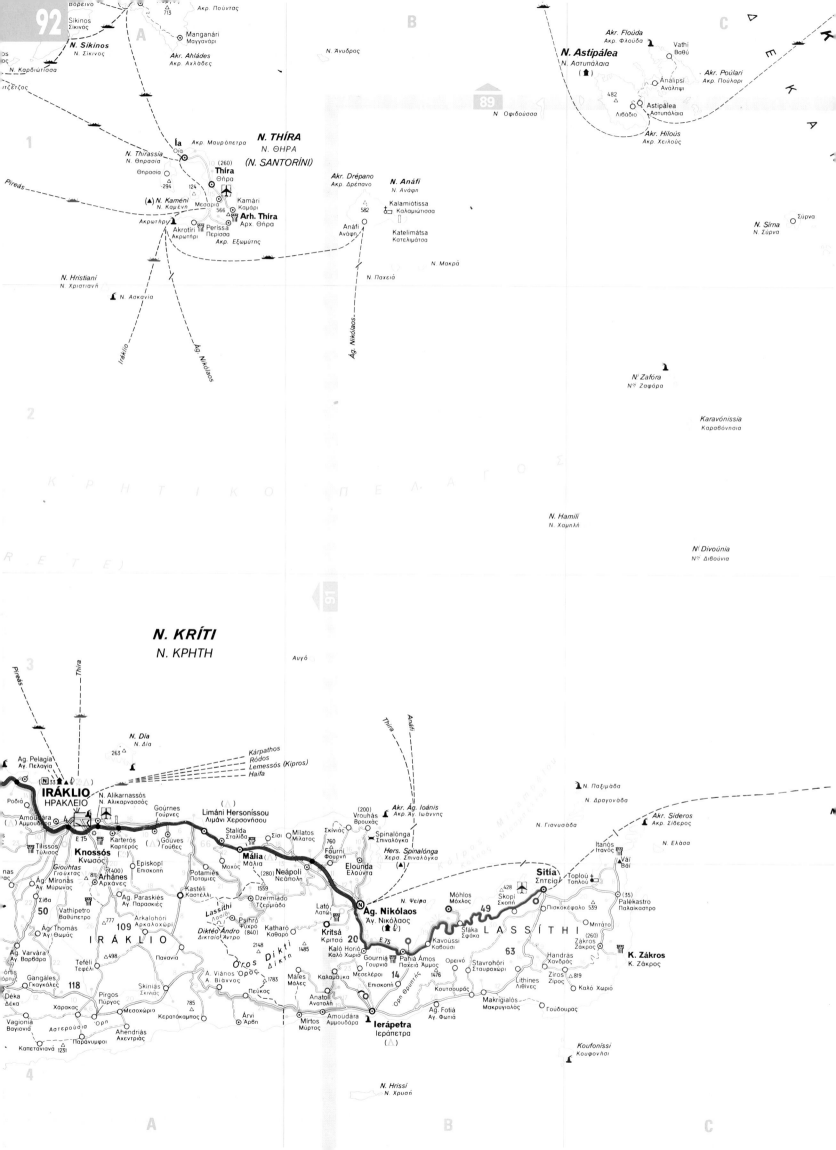

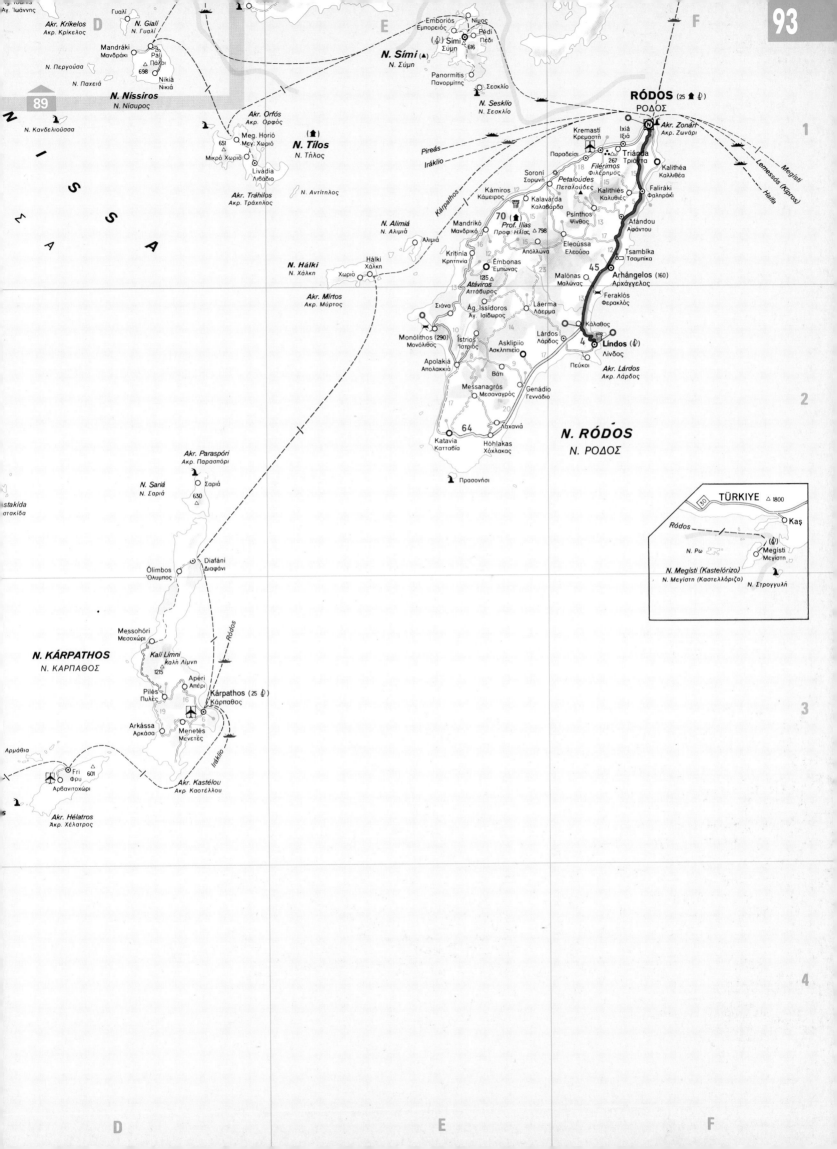

89

D

Akr. Krikelos
Ακρ. Κρίκελος

N. Giali
Ν. Γυαλί

Αγ. Ιωάννης

Mandráki
Μανδράκι

Pali
Πάλοι

698

Nikiá
Νικιά

N. Pergoúsa
Ν. Περγούσα

N. Pahiá
Ν. Παχειά

N. Níssiros
Ν. Νίσυρος

N. Kandelioússa
Ν. Κανδελιούσσα

N I S S A
Σ

E

Emboriós
Εμπορειός

Nímos
Νίμος

Sími
Σύμη

Pédi
Πέδι

616

N. Sími
Ν. Σύμη

Panormitis
Πανορμίτης

Seskliό
Σεσκλιό

N. Sesklío
Ν. Σεσκλιό

Akr. Orfós
Ακρ. Ορφός

651

Meg. Horió
Μεγ. Χωριό

N. Tílos
Ν. Τήλος

Mikró Horió
Μικρό Χωριό

Livádia
Λιβάδια

Akr. Tráhilos
Ακρ. Τράχηλος

N. Antítplos
Ν. Αντίτηλος

N. Alimiá
Ν. Αλιμιά

Alimiá
Αλιμιά

N. Hálki
Ν. Χάλκη

Hálki
Χάλκη

Horió
Χωριό

Akr. Mírtos
Ακρ. Μύρτος

F

RÓDOS (25)
ΡΟΔΟΣ

Akr. Zonári
Ακρ. Ζωνάρι

Lemessós (Kípros)

Megísti

Kremastí
Κρεμαστή

Ixiá
Ιξιά

Paradísi
Παραδείσι

Triánda
Τριάντα

Filérimos
Φιλέρημος

267

Kalithéa
Καλλιθέα

Soroní
Σορωνή

Petaloúdes
Πεταλούδες

18

Kalithiés
Καλυθιές

Faliráki
Φαλιράκι

Kámiros
Κάμειρος

15

Kalavárda
Καλαβάρδα

12

Psinthos
Ψίνθος

13

Afándou
Αφάντου

Mandrikó
Μανδρικό

Prof. Ilias
Προφ: Ηλίας △ 798

15

Eleoússa
Ελεούσα

12

Tsambíka
Τσαμπίκα

70

Kritinía
Κριτηνία

16

12

Apóllona
Απόλλωνα

45

Arhángelos (160)
Αρχάγγελος

Émbonas
Έμπωνας

23

MaloΝas
Μαλώνας

Atáviros
Αττάβυρος

125 △

Láerma
Λάερμα

Feraklós
Φερακλός

Siána
Σιάνα

Ág. Issídoros
Αγ. Ισίδωρος

14

Kálathos
Κάλαθος

Monólithos (290)
Μονόλιθος

10

Ístrios
Ιστριός

Lárdos
Λάρδος

4

Líndos
Λίνδος

Apolakiá
Απολακκιά

8

Asklipiío
Ασκληπιείο

9

Váti
Βάτι

Peúki
Πεύκοι

Akr. Lárdos
Ακρ. Λάρδος

Messanagrós
Μεσαναγρός

17

Genádio
Γεννάδιο

N. RÓDOS
Ν. ΡΟΔΟΣ

20

64

Láhania
Λάχανιά

Katavía
Κατταβία

Hóhlakas
Χόχλακας

Prasonísi
Πρασονήσι

Pireás

Iráklio

Kárpathos

D

Akr. Paraspóri
Ακρ. Παρασπόρι

N. Sariá
Ν. Σαριά

Sariá
Σαριά

630 △

stakída
στακίδα

Ólimbos
Όλυμπος

Diafáni
Διαφάνι

N. KÁRPATHOS
Ν. ΚΑΡΠΑΘΟΣ

Messohóri
Μεσοχώρι

Kalí Limni
Καλή Λίμνη
1215 △

Apéri
Απέρι

Piles
Πυλές

Kárpathos (25)
Κάρπαθος

Arkássa
Αρκάσα

19

6

Menetés
Μενετές

16

Rόdos

Armáthia
Αρμάθια

Fri
Φρύ

601 △

Arvanitohóri
Αρβανιτοχώρι

Akr. Kastélou
Ακρ. Καστέλλου

Iráklio

Akr. Hélatros
Ακρ. Χέλατρος

TÜRKIYE △ 1800

Kaş

Rόdos

N. Ro
Ν. Ρω

Megísti
Μεγίστη

N. Megísti (Kastelórizo)
Ν. Μεγίστη (Καστελλόριζο)

N. Stroungíli
Ν. Στρογγύλη

E

F

1

2

3

4

A   B   C

1

2

3

4

Sørvær

Hasw

Loppa

Øksfjord
120

Nordkvaløy   Vanna   Årviksand   Slettfjellet
△ 1168   Langfjordjøkelen
1064 △

Rebbenesøy   Mikkelvik   Skåningsbukt   Arnøy   Lauksundskaret

Hansnes   Karlsøy   Hurtigrute   Flåten   Skjervøy
Skåningsbukt   Hamneidet

Ringvassøy   Reinøy   Nord Lenangen   292

Futrikelv   Oldervik   Lyngen   Djupvik   Storslett (Nordreisa)

(F ♦ △) TROMSØ   Eidkjosen   Breivikeidet   Svensby   Olderdalen (△)

Sommarøy   (♦)   Tromsdalen   Fagernes   Lyngseidet   E 6   Bæcce

Hillesøy   Kvaløy   Larseng   91   Bilto
Mefjordvær   862   Vikran   E 78   Jiekkevarre
△ 1833   1375 △   865

Skaland (Berg)   Mefjordbotn   861   Gibostad   856   Furuflaten   73   Isfjellet   Skibotn (△)   Raisduoddarhal'di
△ 1365

Gryllefjord (Torsken)   86   858   Målsnes   868   43   Halti-Haldi
(△)   Straumsnes   Tennes   Oteren   45

Senja   (Lenvik)   Storsteinnes   Nordkjosbotn (△)   Mallax
Ånderdalen   Finnsnes   Moen (Målselv)   Kilpisjärvi △ 1024   Raittijärvi
Tranøy   Vangsvik   Heia   Tierbmesvarri

Andenes (△)   Skrolsvik   Stonglandet   Sørreisa   Øverbygd (△)   Kummavuopio
Bleik   Bardufoss   Andselv   857   Saarikoski   E 28 21   Ro

Andøya   Brøstadbotn   854   TROMS   Frihetsli
82   Dverberg   Dyrøya   148   △ 1487   87   Njunis
104   Åse   Bjarkøy   Istindan   1681 △   △ 1713   Øvre Dividalen
Risøyhamn   Grytøya   Sjøvegan (Salangen)   Setermoen (Bardu)   Kirkestinden

Myre (Øksnes)   Vågsfjorden   Andørja   851   E 6   Innset

VESTERÅLEN   867   Harstad   Rolla   Ibestad   848   Fossbakken
Langøya   Borkenes   Sørrollnes   Myrlandshaugen   Lavangen
Straumsjøen   820   (Kvæfjord)   825   848   Gratangen
821   25   Kilbotn   829

Sortland   Flesnes   Refsnes   Grovfjord   Bjerkvik   Vadvetjåkka
Bø   Sigerfjord   19   825   Evenskjær (Skånland)   Bogen   70   Björkliden

Stokmarknes (△)   19   Hinnøya   66   32   98   Vuoskojaure
(▲) Melbu   Kaljord   19   Ramsund   19   Narvik   Abisko
Fiskebøl   99   Tjeldøya   Evenes   Liland   ▲   Riksgränsen   Abisko   176   Laimoluokta

Eggum   77   Kongselva   Lødingen   Beisfjord   Abisko   713 △   Kuortovare
Austvågøy   Digermulen   Ballangen   E 6   Kungsleden
Vestvågøy   815   Svolvær   Leiknes   Skarberget   △ 1901   Rensjön

knes   19   Stamsund   Bognes   Kjøpsvik   Rautas
Gravdal   Hurtigrute   Skutvik   Vuistasvággi
Ballstad   97   81   Hamarøy   Drag   Kebnekaise   98

Engeløya   Bjørntoppen   1520   Nikkaluokta   Jukkasjärvi
(△) Steigen   248   Innhavet   Kebnekaise   Kiruna   (▲)
Bogøy   △ 2111   98

Nordfold   E 6   Kebnekaise   98   48
△ 1361   △ 1810   Kårsatjåkka   Svappavaara

Kjerringøy △ 854   Vaisaluokta   Kallaktjåkká   Stora   △ 1491   Nieras
Bonnåsjøen   Padjelanta   Araslukta   Sjøfallet   2089 △   Vietas   Fjällåsen

Festvåg   Rago   Saltoluokta
Røsvik   Vastenjaure   Skaulo

(F ♦ △) BODØ   63 (△)   Lødina   80   Straumen (△)   N O R R B O T T E N S   66

VESTFJORDEN   Folda

97

98

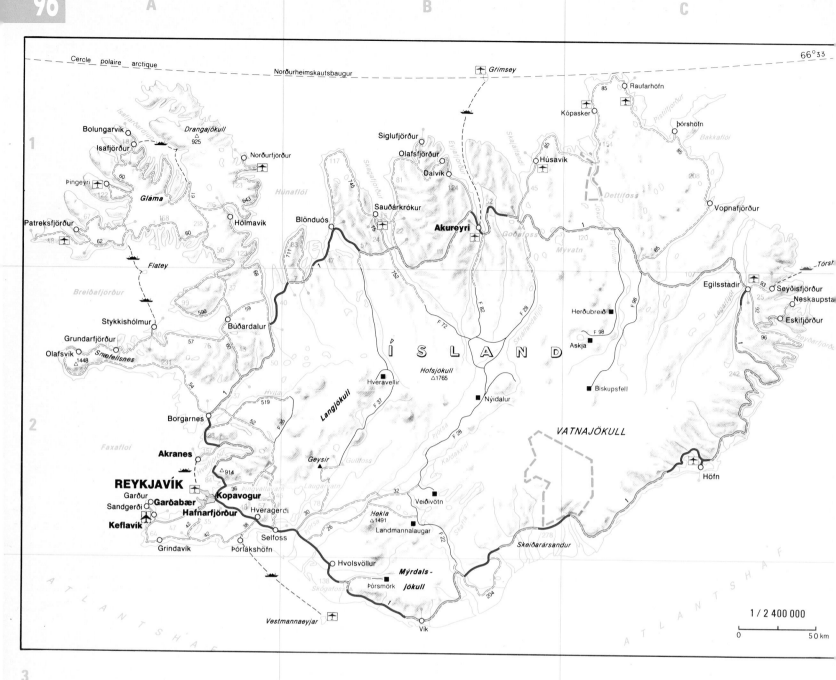

Cercle polaire arctique
Norðurheimskautsbaugur
66°33

Grímsey

Bolungarvík
Ísafjörður
Drangajökull
△ 925
Norðurfjörður

Raufarhöfn
85
Kópasker
Þórshöfn
Bakkaflói

Siglufjörður
Ólafsfjörður
Húsavík
Dalvík

Þingeyri
Gláma
Hólmavík
Blönduós
Sauðárkrókur
Akureyri
Vopnafjörður

Patreksfjörður
ÍSLAND

Flatey
Breiðafjörður
Herðubreið ■
Egilsstaðir
Seyðisfjörður
Neskaupsta
Eskifjörður

Stykkishólmur
Búðardalur
Askja
F 98

Grundarfjörður
Hofsjökull
△ 1765
Biskupsfell ■

Ólafsvík
Snæfellsnes
△ 1448
Hveravellir ■

Langjökull
Nýidalur ■

Borgarnes
VATNAJÖKULL

Faxaflói
Akranes
△ 914
Geysir ▲
Höfn

REYKJAVÍK
Garður
Kópavogur
Veiðivötn ■

Sandgerði
Garðabær
Hafnarfjörður
Hveragerði
Hekla
△ 1491

Keflavík
Landmannalaugar

Grindavík
Þorlákshöfn
Selfoss
Skeiðarársandur

Hvolsvöllur
Mýrdals-
jökull
Þórsmörk ■

Vestmannaeyjar
1 / 2 400 000

Vík
0   50 km

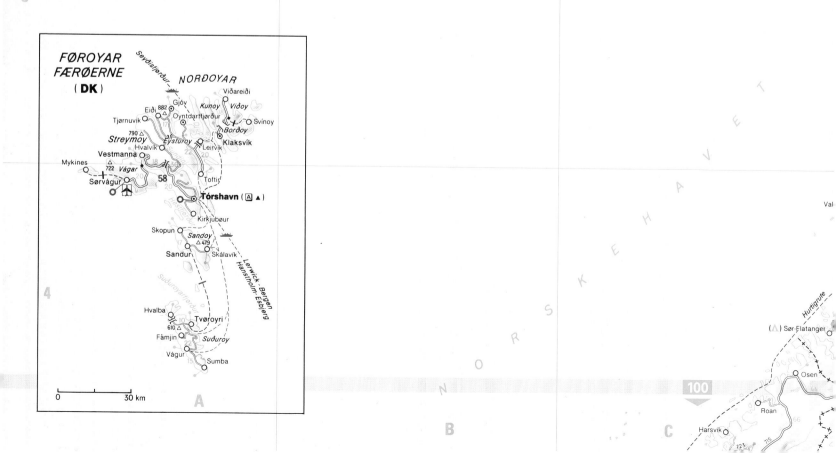

FØROYAR
FÆRØERNE
(DK)
Seyðisfjørður
NORÐOYAR

Viðareiði
Eiði
882 △
Gjógv
Kunoy
Viðoy
Tjørnuvík
Oyndarfjørður
Svínoy

790 △
Borðoy
Streymoy
Hvalvík
Eysturoy
Klaksvík
Leirvík

Vestmanna
Mykines
722 △
Vágar
Toftir

Sørvágur
58

Tórshavn (Ⓐ ▲)

Kirkjubøur

Skopun
Sandoy
△ 479

Sandur
Skálavík

Hvalba
Tvøroyri

610 △
Fámjin
Suðuroy

Vágur
Sumba

Leirvík - Bergen
Hanstholm - Esbjerg

NORSKEHAVET
Hurtigrute

(△) Sør-Flatanger

100

Osen

Roan

Harsvík

Kajaani
Paltaniemi
Oulujärvi
Vuolijoki
Otanmäki
Kestilä
Pulkkila
Piippola
Pyhäntä
Haapavesi
Kärsämäki
Sotkamo
Vuokatti
Kuhmo
Tipasoja
Hiidenportti
Maanselkä
Sukeva
Nissilä
Valtimo
Nurmes
Vieremä
Sonkajärvi
Iisalmi
Kiuruvesi
Pyhäsalmi
Pyhäjärvi
Haapamäki
Rautavaara
Lieksa
Pankakoski
Hattuvaara
Reboly
Tulivaara
Lendery
Pielinen
Juuka
Varpaisjärvi
Lapinlahti
Nilsiä
Pielavesi
Maaninka
Pihtipudas
Kärväskylä
Kinnula
Viitasaari
Keitele
Siilinjärvi
Juankoski
Kaavi
POHJOIS-KARJALAN
LÄÄNI
KUOPION
Koli
Ukkola
Uimaharju
Eno
Kontiolahti
Joensuu
Ilomantsi
Mökö
Kuopio
Outokumpu
Tuusniemi
Riistavesi
Vehmersalmi
Karttula
Tervo
Vesanto
Kannonkoski
Kerkonkoski
Konginkangas
Saarijärvi
Äänekoski
Suolahti
Sumiainen
Konnevesi
Rautalampi
Suonenjoki
Heinävesi
Valamen
Liperi
Pyhäselkä
Ylämylly
Kovero
Tuupovaara
Kiihtelysvaara
Tohmajärvi
Vartsila
Onkamo
Rääkkylä
Kitee
Puhos
Keski-Suomen
Jyväskylä
Laukaa
Hankasalmi
Varkaus
Pieksämäki
Joroinen
Kangaslampi
Savonranta
Enonkoski
Muurame
Säynätsalo
Toivakka
MIKKELIN
LÄÄNI
Kangasniemi
Haukivuori
Juva
Rantasalmi
Savonlinna
Kerimäki
Punkaharju
Kesälahti
Uukuniemi
Sortavala
Mänttä
Jämsä
Korpilahti
Leivonmäki
Joutsa
Mikkeli
Anttola
Puumala
Sulkava
Särkisalmi
Parikkala
Lahdenpoh
Hartola
Sysmä
Kuhmoinen
Pertunmaa
Ristiina
Mäntyharju
Ruokolahti
Imatra
Rautjärvi
Kurkijoki
Ladožskoe
Heinola
Padasjoki
Savitaipale
Taipalsaari
Lappeenranta
Joutseno
Svetogorsk
Priozërsk
Kamennogorsk
Lahti
Hollola
Nastola
Kuusankoski
Kouvola
Valkeala
Luumäki
Ylämaa
Nuijamaa
Vainikkala
Vyborg
RSFSR
KYMEN
LÄÄNI
Anjalankoski
Elimäki
Orimattila
Hamina
Virolahti
Vaalimaa
Kotka
Karhula
Pyhtää
Loviisa
Lapinjärvi
Myrskylä
Mäntsälä
Riihimäki
Hyvinkää
Järvenpää
Sibbo
Pernå
Porvoo
Primorsk
Zelenogorsk
Sestroreck
Sovetskij
Kamenka
Pervomajskoe
Krasnosel'skoe
Sosnovo
Kondrat'evo
Kirkonmaanselkä

A   B   C

Kalvåg   Smørhamn   Lote   Stryn   Nyseter   31
Svelgen   Hyen   Innvik   Loen   Pollfoss   *Tverrfjellet*   Dombås   Fokstuho   1716
(F) **Florø**   Sandane   92   122   55   100   Bismo   15   (*) **Vågåmo**   47   Høvringen   Dovre
Naustdal   Byrkjelo   Sotaseter   Lom (*)   38   Otta
69   Skei   Fonn   Briksdal   Elvekrok   Bøverdal   Lalm   15   Kvam
Askvoll   Ringstad   609   14   **Førde**   Lunde   165   2470   *Glittertind*   Vinstra
Dale   Viksdalen   Fjærland   2469   *Galdhøpiggen*   255
SOGN OG FJORDANE   Høgbru   *Jotunheimen*   Gjendesheim   Skåbu
39   95   Luster   125   Espedal   *Peer Gynt*
Krakhella   Vadheim   Høyanger   Solvorn   Eidsbugarden   *Valdres Flya*   *veien*
48   Nordeide   88   Drågsvik   Leikanger   Urnes (*)   Øvre Årdal   Bygdin   *Ormtjernkampen*
Rysjedalsvika   Lavik   Balestrand   Hella   Sogndal   Kaupanger   125   Beitostølen   **OPPLAND**
Rutledal   Leirvåg   Ortnevik   Vangsnes   Hermansverk   Årdalstangen   Hurum   Hegge
Brekke   Hopperstad   Vik   Revsnes   Naddvik   *Fille-*   Øye   Lomen   179
Steine   6-1989   1660   Lærdalsøyri   E68   Borgund   *fjell*   Grindaheim   153
Duesund   *Fresvikbreen*   80   Tyin   100   Fagernes   Leira   Aurdal
Lindås   Gudvangen   Undredal   Hemsedal   Hovet   Hol   Gol   53   Reinli
Radøy   Sævråsvåg   *Stølsheimen*   Aurland   Flåm   *Hallingskarvet*   288   Torpo   7   Hedal   122
91   Vikanes   Stamnes   *Hardanger-*   Hovet   Ål   Nesbyen   Nes
Tjeldstø   Manger   Dale   **Voss**   Ulvik   *jøkulen*   1862   Ustaoset   Geilo   53
Knarvik   Tysseboth   26   Granvin   Bruravik   Dagali   **BUSKERUD**
Steinestø   *Osterøya*   **HORDALAND**   11   Kvanndal   Eidfjord   101   Fossli   Uvdal   Rødberg   *Norefjell*
Askøy   Vaksdal   138   Åivik   Utne   Brimnes   Nore   Noresund   138
Kleppestø   Samnanger   Øystese   Kinsarvik   *Hardangervidda*   163
BERGEN   Tysse   E68   Norheimsund   Lofthus   *Hårteigen*   1691   Rødberg   Rollag   Flesberg   78
Hjelstad   Strandebarm   Tørvikbygd   77   Jondal   *Haukelifjell*   Tinn   Austbygd   Prestfoss   Tyristrand
Klokkarvik   Eikelandsosen   552   Tyssedal   Rjukan   287   Sokna
Steinsland   Vengjaneset   Halhjem   **Odda**   Skinnarbu   Bønsnes
Krokeide   Søyri   Rosendal   *Folgefonna*   E76   Rauland   Flesberg   Vikersund
Storebø   Husavik   Gjermundshavn   Røldal   80   Edland   Hjartdal   Sauland   Åmot   Sylling
Huftarøy   Sandvikvåg   99   *Tysnesøy*   Løfallstrand   72   Vinje   Hovden   Åmot   Heddal   Hokksund   **Drammen**
Flatråker   Jektevik   Husnes   Skånevik   46   Haukeligrend   76   Seljord   **Kongsberg**   40   Mjøndalen
Rubbestadneset   Sagvåg   Leirvik   Utåker   Etne   **Sauda**   Brunkeberg   **TELEMARK**   106   **Notodden**   108   Eidsfoss
Bømlo   Skjersholmane   Valevåg   Ølen   49   Sandeid   Vikedal   Kviteseid   Eidsborg   Dalen   96   Bø   Garvik   Hvittingfoss   Horten
Siggjarvåg   *Stord*   Sunde   Førde   Etne   Sand   *Setesdalsheiene*   Bykle   Vrådal   Gvarv   Akkerhaugen   Svarstad   97
Mosterhamn   Utbjoa   Buavåg   14   184   Vindsvik   *Bykleheiene*   Valle   Lunde   Ulefoss   **SKIEN**   **VESTFOLD**
Langevåg   *Tysvær*   Nedstrand   Jelsa   Nesvik   Tøtlandsvik   181   Fyresdal   117   **Porsgrunn**   Siljan   Andebu
Haugesund   Avaldsnes   *Ryfylke*   Hjelmeland   Drangedal   Herre   **Sandefjord**
Åkrehamn   Kopervik   52   Føresvik   *Setesdalen*   8-1989   Fyresdal   Treungen   Brevik   20   Langangen
Karmøy   Bokn   Finnøy   Judaberg   Valle   **ROGALAND**   **AUST-AGDER**   Åmli   Langesund   **Larvik**   Stavern
Skudeneshavn   *Rennesøy*   Vikevåg   *Lyseheiene*   Bygland   105   Nevlunghavn
Kvitsøy   Randaberg   Tau   Jørpeland   *Prekestolen*   Dølemo   Søndeled   Kragerø   *Frederikshavn*
STAVANGER   Hommersåk   597   Oanes   Lauvvik   Svartevatn   **VEST-AGDER**   Åseral   Evje   Vegårshei   415   Risør
Sola   Sandnes   Oltedal   6-89   Byglandsfjord   45   Tvedestrand
Kleppe   Ålgård   53   Vikeså   Tonstad   Eiken   Iveland   30   Eydehavn
Bryne   *Jæren*   68   Varhaug   Risnes   150   Konsmo   **Arendal**   (F)
Nærbø   Vigrestad   *Dalane*   Sira   Hægebostad   62   Rykene   70   **Grimstad**
Brusand   Bjerkreim   10   61   Kvinesdal   Vennesla   Vik   68   Lillesand
Sirevåg   Hellvik   44   69   Hauge   Feda   Birkeland
Egersund   Åna Sira   **Flekkefjord**   Lyngdal   Mosby   Hamre
Vestbygda   125   Nodeland   Søgne   Vigeland   Høllen
Farsund   Lindesnes   **Mandal**   Skålevik   **Kristiansand**   108

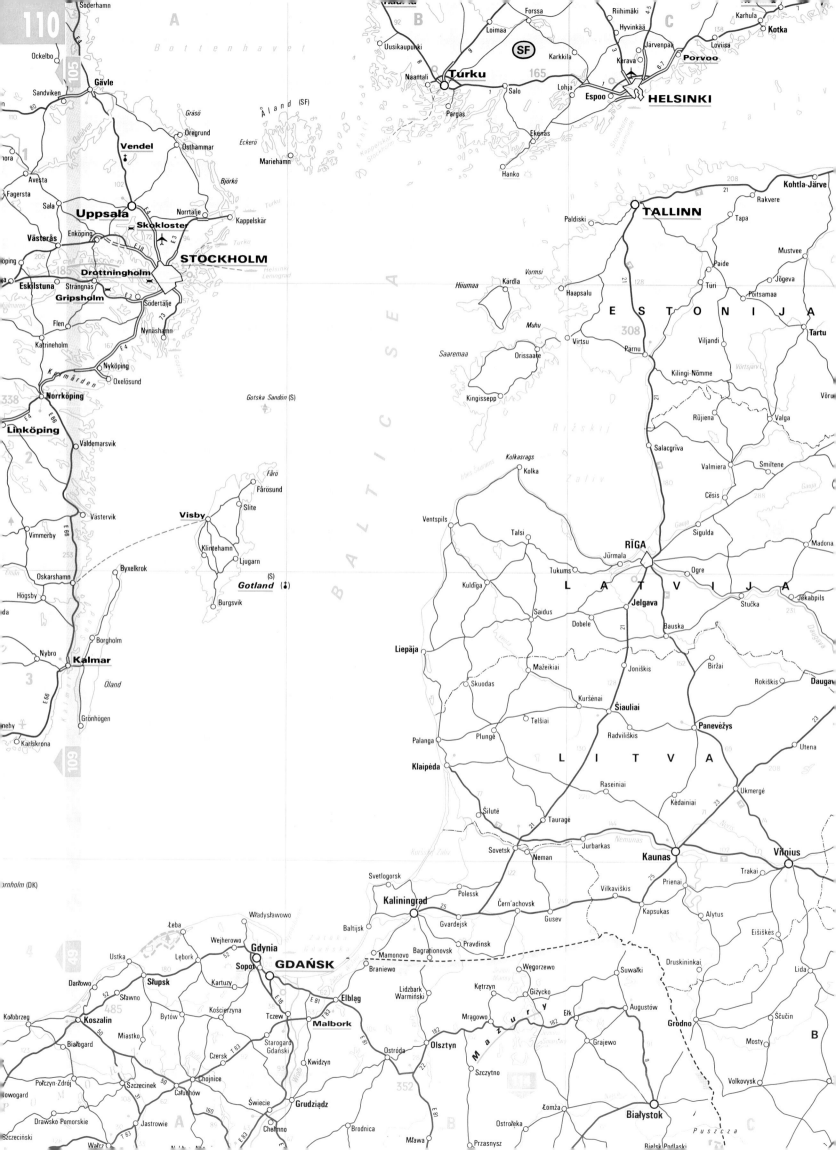

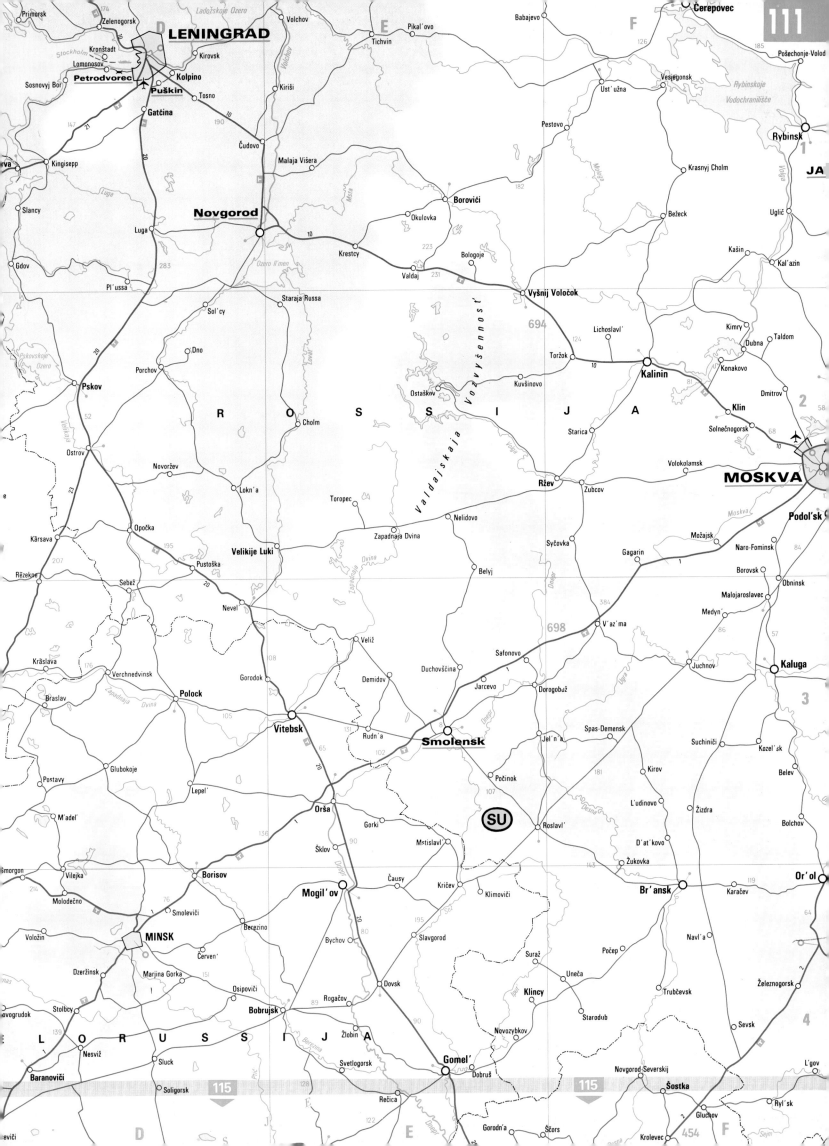

Index Register Índice Indice

(F) Lorsqu'un nom figure plusieurs fois dans l'index, une précision est ajoutée entre parenthèses pour permettre de l'identifier plus facilement: pays, région ou ville la plus proche, élément géographique d'après les abréviations ci-dessous.

(GB) Where there are two or more identical place names, the name of the distinguishing country or region or nearest large town is given in brackets; geographical features are indicated by the abbreviations below.

(D) Tritt ein Name mehrfach im Register auf, wird er durch eine in Klammern gesetzte nähere Bestimmung genauer definiert. Sie finden folgende Zusätze: Land, Region oder nächstgelegene Stadt, geographische Gegebenheiten, ggf. abgekürzt

(NL) Bij namen die meermalen in het register voorkomen, staat tussen haakjes een aanduiding ter verklaring: het land, de streek, de dichtstbijgelegen stad of een geografisch gegeven (zie de afkortingen hieronder).

(E) Para poder localizar más fácilmente un nombre que figura varias veces en el índice, se añade entre paréntesis el país, la región o ciudad más cercana, o un elemento geográfico, con las abreviaturas siguientes.

(I) Quando un nome figura più volte nell'indice, una precisazione viene aggiunta tra parentesi per permettere d'identificarlo più facilmente: nazione, regione o città la più vicina, elemento geografico come da abbreviazioni qui di seguito.

Ákr	Ákra, Akrotírion	Liq	Liquen	Pk	Park		
B	Bay, Baie, Bucht, Bahia, Baia, Bukt(en), Bugt, Bukhta	Meg	Méga, Megál, -a, -i, -o	Pl	Planina		
		Mikr.	Mikr-í, -ón	Pque	Parque		
Bgem	Barragem	Mgne(s)	Montagne(s)	Prov	Province		
C	Cape, Cap, Cabo, Capo	M, Mte(s)	Maj, Maj'e, Monte(s)	Pso	Passo		
Co	County	Mt(s), *Mt(s)*	Mount(s), Mountain(s), Mont(s)	Pt(e)	Point(e)		
Ch	Chaîne			Rib	Ribeirão		
Chan	Channel	Mti	Monti, Muntii	R, *R*	River, Rivière, Rio, Ria, Rijeka		
Dépt	Département	Nac	Nacional(e)	Reg	Region, Région		
Emb	Embalse	Nat	National	Res	Reservoir, Reservoire		
Ez	Ezero	Naz	Nazionale	Sa	Sierra, Serra		
G	Gulf, Golfe, Golfo	N	Nissi, Nissos	Sd	Sound, Sund		
Gges	Gorges	Ni	Nissiá, Nissi	St	Saint, Sankt, Sint		
I(s), *I(s)*	Isles(s), Island(s), Ile(s), Ilha(s), Isla(s), Isola(e)	Os	Ostrov(a)	Ste(s)	Sainte(s)		
		Ot	Otok(i), Otoci	Teh L	Tehniti Limni		
Jez	Jezoro, Jezioro	Oz	Ozero(a)	V	Valley, Vale, Vallée, Val, Valle, Vall		
K	Kanal, Kanaal	P	Pass				
L, *L*	Lake, Loch, Lough, Llyn, Lac, Laguna, Lago, Limni	Pal	Paleós, á, ó				
		Pen	Peninsula, Penisola				

A

Aachen	51 D3	Abanilla	45 D2	Abcoude	16 C2	Aberhonddu	8 C1	Aboyne	3 E4
Aalen	55 E2	Abano Terme	61 D1	Abejar	36 B3	Aberlady	5 D2	Abrantes	38 B3
Aalsmeer	16 C2	Abbadia		Abejuela	41 E3	Aberpennar	8 C2	Abreschviller	21 E4
Aalst	50 B3	San Salvatore	63 D1	Abela	42 A1	Aberporth	8 B1	Abrets, les	30 C1
Aalten	17 D3	Abbasanta	66 B3	Abelvær	97 D4	Abersoch	6 A3	Abriès	31 E2
Aalter	50 B3	Abbazia di		Abenberg	55 E2	Abertawe	8 C2	Abruzzo	63 F2
Äänekoski	103 D2	Casamari	63 F3	Abenójar	39 F4	Aberteifi	8 B1	Abruzzo, Parco	
Aapajärvi	95 F4	Abbazia di		Åbenrå	108 A4	Abertillery	9 D2	Nazionale d'	64 A2
Aarau	27 F2	Fossanova	63 F3	Abensberg	55 F2	Aber-Wrac'h, I'	22 A2	Abstadt-	
Aarberg	27 F2	Abbazia di		Aberaeron	8 C1	Aberystwyth	8 C1	Tailfingen	55 D3
Aarburg	27 F2	Montecassino	64 A3	Aberdâr	8 C2	Abetone	60 C3	Abtenau	59 E1
Aare	58 A3	Abbazia San Clemente		Aberdare	8 C2	Abiego	37 E3	Åby	105 F4
Aargau	27 F2	a Casauria	64 A2	Aberdaron	6 A3	Abingdon	9 E2	Åbybro	108 B2
Aarlen	21 D2	Abbeville	19 E2	Aberdaugleddau	8 B2	Abington	5 D3	A Caniza	34 A3
Aarschot	50 C3	Abbeyfeale	14 B3	Aberdeen	3 E4	Abisko	94 B3	Acceglio	31 E2
Aavasaksa	98 C2	Abbeyleix	12 C4	Aberdeen	3 E4	Abisko (Nat park)	94 B4	Accettura	65 D4
Abades	40 A1	Abbey Town	5 D4	Aberdovey	4 C1	Abla	44 B3	Acciaroli	67 D1
Abadiño	36 B1	Abbiategrasso	60 A1	Aberfeldy	4 C1	Ablis	19 E4	Accous	37 D1
A Baiuca	34 A1	Abborrträsk	98 B3	Aberfoyle	4 C2	Åbo	107 D2	Accrington	6 C2
		Abbots Bromley	6 C3	Abergavenny	9 D2	Abondance	27 E3	Acebo	39 D2
		Abbotsbury	9 D3	Abergele	6 B2	Abony	112 B4	Acedo	36 B2
				Abergwaun	8 B1				

Acehuche	39 D3	Afjord	100 C1
Acerno	64 B4	Åfjorden	104 A1
Acerra	64 B4	Aflenzer	
Aceuchal	39 D4	Seeberg	57 E3
Ache	59 E1	Aflenz Kurort	57 E3
Achenkirch	59 D1	Afráti	84 B4
Achenpaß	56 A4	Afsluitdijk	16 C1
Achensee	59 D1	A Garda	34 A3
Achern	54 C3	Agathonissi	89 E2
Acheux	19 F2	Agay	31 E4
Achill I	12 A2	Agazzano	60 B2
Achim	17 F1	Agde	30 A4
Achnacroish	4 B1	Agdenes	100 C1
Achnasheen	2 C3	Agen	28 C3
A'Chràlaig	2 C4	Åger	37 F3
Aci Castello	69 D3	Ager	56 C3
Acıpayam	115 F4	Ageranós	87 D4
Acireale	69 D3	Agerbæk	108 A3
Aci Trezza	69 D3	Agger	17 E4
Acle	7 F3	Aggius	66 B1
A Coruña	34 B1	Aggsbach-Dorf	57 E2
Acqualagna	61 E4	Aggsbach-Markt	57 E2
Acquapendente	63 D1	Agiá	83 F1
Acquasanta		Agiá, Akr	83 F4
Terme	63 F1	Agia Ána (Évia)	84 A3
Acquasparta	63 E1	Agia Ána	
Acquaviva dei		(Viotia)	83 F4
Fonti	65 D3	Agía Efimía	82 B4
Acqui-Terme	60 A2	Agia Efthimía	83 E4
Acri	67 E2	Agia Ekaterini, Akr	82 A1
Ada	72 C1	Agia Fotiá	91 F4
Adaja, R	39 F2	Agia Galini	91 D4
Adak	98 A3	Agia Kiriaki	
Ådalsel	104 C2	(Makedonia)	78 C3
Adamandás	88 A4	Agia Kiriaki	
Adamclisi	115 E1	(Pelopónissos)	86 B3
Adamello	58 C3	Agia Kiriaki	
Adamello Brenta,		(Sámos)	89 E2
Parco Naturale	58 C3	Agia Lávra	86 C1
Adamello, Mont'	58 C3	Agia Marina	
Adamuz	43 F2	(Égina)	87 F2
Adanero	39 F1	Agia Marina (Kríti)	90 B3
Adapazarı	115 F3	Agia Marina (Léros)	89 E3
Adare	14 B3	Agia Marina	
Adaševci	72 B3	(Stereá Eláda)	83 E3
Adda	60 B2	Agia Marina	
Adelboden	27 E3	(Stereá Eláda)	88 A1
Adelfia	65 D3	Agia Paraskevi	
Adelsheim	55 D1	(Lésvos)	85 F2
Ademuz	41 D3	Agia Paraskevi	
Adenau	51 E4	(Makedonia)	80 C2
Ádendro	79 F3	Agia Paraskiés	91 E4
Adéres, Óros	87 E2	Agia Pelagía	
Adiça, Sa da	42 C1	(Kithira)	90 A1
Adige	61 D1	Agia Pelagía (Kríti)	91 D3
Adjud	113 E4	Agia Rouméli	90 B4
Admont	57 D3	Agiasma	80 C2
Adolfström	97 F3	Agiásmata	85 E4
Adorf	53 D3	Agia Sofia (Évia)	84 B3
Adour	28 B4	Agia Sofía	
Adra	44 B4	(Pelopónissos)	87 D2
Adradas	36 B4	Agia Sotíra	87 E1
Adrall	32 A3	Agiássos	85 F2
Adrano	69 D3	Agía Triáda (Kríti)	91 D4
Adria	61 D2	Agía Triáda	
Adriatic Sea	114 A3	(Makedonía)	79 F3
Adzaneta	41 E3	Agía Triáda	
Aegean Sea	115 E4	(Pelopónissos)	86 C1
Aenona	74 C1	Agía Triáda	
Aerinó	83 F2	(Stereá Eláda)	87 F1
Ærø	108 B4	Agia Varvára	91 D4
Ærøskøbing	108 B4	Agiófilo	83 D1
A Estrada	34 A2	Agiókambos	
Aetópetra	82 B1	(Évia)	83 F3
Aetós (Kefaloniá)	82 B4	Agiókambos	
Aetós		(Thessalía)	83 F1
(Makedonía)	79 D3	Agionóri	87 E2
Aetós		Ágio Óros	80 C4
(Stereá Eláda)	82 C3	Agiopigi	83 D2
Aetsä	107 D2	Ágios	84 A3
Afándou	93 F1	Ágios Anárgiri	
Åfarnes	100 B2	(Pelopónissos)	87 D3
Aféa	87 F2	Ágios Anárgiri	
Affi	60 C1	(Thessalía)	83 E2
Afiónas	82 A1	Ágios Andónios	80 A3
Áfissos	83 F2	Ágios Andréas	
Áfitos	80 B4	(Arkadía)	87 D2

Ágios Andréas (Lakonía) 87 E4
Ágios Apóstoli (Évia) 84 B4
Ágios Apóstoli (Pelopónissos) 87 E4
Ágios Apóstoli (Stereá Eláda) 84 B4
Ágios Athanássios (Dráma) 80 C2
Ágios Athanássios (Péla) 79 D2
Ágios Avgoustínos 86 C3
Ágios Déka 91 D4
Ágios Dimítrios, Akr 88 A3
Ágios Dimítrios (Évia) 88 A1
Ágios Dimítrios (Lakonía) 87 D3
Ágios Dimítrios (Makedonía) 79 E4
Ágios Dimítrios (Messinía) 87 D4
Ágios Dimítrios (Stereá Eláda) 83 D3
Ágios Dionissíos 79 E4
Ágios Efstrátios, N 85 D2
Ágios Fokás 89 F3
Ágios Fokás, Akr 85 F3
Ágios Geórgios (Évia) 83 F3
Ágios Geórgios, N 87 F2
Ágios Geórgios (Stereá Eláda) 83 D3
Ágios Geórgios (Zákinthos) 86 A1
Ágios Georgíou, Órmos 87 E3
Ágios Germanós 79 D2
Ágios Górdis 82 A1
Ágios Harálambos 81 E2
Ágios Ioánis, Akr 91 F3
Ágios Ioánis (Dodekánissa) 89 F4
Ágios Ioánis (Pelopónissos) 87 E2
Ágios Ioánis (Stereá Eláda) 83 F4
Ágios Ioánis (Thessalía) 83 F3
Ágios Ioánis (Thessalía) 83 F2
Ágios Irínis, Akr 85 D1
Ágios Issídoros 93 E2
Ágios Kírikos 89 D2
Ágios Konstandínos (Stereá Eláda) 83 F3
Ágios Konstandínos (Thessalía) 83 E2
Ágios Kosmás (Grevená) 79 D4
Ágios Kosmás (Kavála) 80 C2
Ágios Léon 86 A1
Ágios Loukás 84 B4
Ágios Mámas 80 A4
Ágios Márkos 80 A2
Ágios Mathéos 82 A2
Ágios Míronas 91 D4
Ágios Nikítas 82 B3
Ágios Nikólaos (Etolía-Akarnanía) 82 B3
Ágios Nikólaos (Fokída) 83 E4
Ágios Nikólaos (Fthiótida) 83 F3
Ágios Nikólaos (Hers.Methánon) 87 E2
Ágios Nikólaos (Ípiros) 82 B1
Ágios Nikólaos (Kríti) 91 E4
Ágios Nikólaos (Lakonía) 87 D3
Ágios Nikólaos (Makedonía) 80 B4
Ágios Nikólaos (Messinía) 86 C3
Ágios Pandeleímonos 79 D3
Ágios Pángalos, Akr 83 E4
Ágios Paraskeví (Ípiros) 78 C4
Ágios Paraskeví (Makedonía) 79 F2
Ágios Pávlos 80 A3
Ágios Pétros 87 D2
Ágios Pnévma 80 B2
Ágios Pródromos 80 A3
Ágios Sóstis 83 E3
Ágios Stéfanos (Kikládes) 88 C2
Ágios Stéfanos (Stereá Eláda) 87 F1
Ágios Theódori (Makedonía) 79 D4
Ágios Theódori (Pelopónissos) 87 E1
Ágios Theódori (Thessalía) 83 F3
Ágios Thomás (Kríti) 91 D4
Ágios Thomás (Stereá Eláda) 84 B4
Ágios Vassílios (Makedonía) 80 A3
Ágios Vassílios (Stereá Eláda) 84 A4
Ágios Vissários 83 E2
Agíou Órous, Kólpos 80 C4
Agira 68 C3
Agly 32 B2
Ágnanda 82 C2
Agnanderó 83 D2
Ágnandi 83 F3
Agnóndas 84 B3
Agnone 64 B2
Agnoúnda 87 E2
Agorá 80 C2
Agordo 59 D3
Agost 45 E1
Agout 29 D4
Agrafiótis 83 D2
Agramunt 37 F3
Agrate Br. 60 A1
Agreda 36 C3
Agreliá 83 D1
Agri 65 D4
Agriá 83 F2
Agrigento 68 B4
Agriliá 82 C4
Agriliá, Akr 85 F3
Ágrilos 86 B3
Agrinio 82 C3
Agriovótano 83 F3
Agropoli 64 B4
Agskaret 97 E2
Aguadulce (Almeria) 44 B4
Aguadulce (Sevilla) 43 E3
Aguas Vivas, R 37 D4
Aguaviva 41 E2
A Gudiña 34 C3
Agudo 39 F4
Agueda 38 B1
Agueda, R 39 D2
Aguiar 42 B1
Aguiar da Beira 38 C1
Aguilafuente 40 A1
Aguilar 43 F2
Aguilar de Campóo 35 F2
Aguilar del Alfambra 41 E2
Aguilar, Emb de 35 F2
Águilas 44 C3
Ahaïa 86 C1
Aharnés 87 F1
Ahaus 17 E3
Åheim 100 A3
Ahelóos 82 C4
Ahendriás 91 E4
Ahérondas 82 B2
Ahigal 39 D2
Ahílio (Kérkira) 82 A1
Ahílio (Thessalía) 83 E2
Ahinós 80 B2
Ahjärvi 103 F3
Ahladeri 84 B4
Ahládes, Akr 88 C4
Ahladohóri 80 B1
Ahlainen 102 B3
Ahlbeck 49 E2
Ahlen 17 E3
Ahlhorn 17 F1
Ahrensbök 48 B2
Ahrensburg 48 B2
Ahrweiler 51 E4
Ähtäri 102 C2
Ähtärinjärvi 102 C2
Ahtävänjoki 102 C2
Ahtopol 115 E2
Ahun 25 E4
Åhus 109 D3
Ahvenanmaa 106 C3
Ahvenselkä 99 E1
Aichach 55 F3
Aidenbach 56 B2
Aidone 68 C3
Aigen 56 C2
Aigle 27 E3
Aigle, Bge de l' 29 E1
Aigle, l' 19 D4
Aignan 28 C4
Aignay-le-Duc 26 C2
Aigoual, Mt 29 F3
Aigre 24 C4
Aigrefeuille-d'Aunis 24 B4
Aigrefeuille-sur-Maine 24 B3
Aiguablava 32 C3
Aiguebelette 30 C1
Aiguebelle 31 D1
Aigueperse 26 A4
Aigues 30 C3
Aigues-Mortes 30 B4
Aigües Tortes, Parque Nac de 37 F2
Aiguilles 31 E2
Aiguillon 28 C3
Aiguillon, l' 24 B4
Aigurande 25 E4
Ailefroide 31 D2
Aillant 26 A1
Ailly-le-Haut-locher 19 E2
Ailly-sur-Noye 19 F2
Ailsa Craig 4 B3
Aimargues 30 B4
Aime 31 D1
Ain 27 D3
Ain (Dépt) 26 C4
Ainhoa 28 A4
Ainsa 37 E2
Ainsdale 6 B2
Ainzón 36 C3
Airaines 19 E2
Airasca 31 E2
Airdrie 4 C2
Aire *R* 7 D2
Aire 19 F1
Aire, I del 45 F2
Aire, Sa de 38 B3
Aire-sur-l'Adour 28 B4
Airisto 107 D3
Airolo 58 A3
Airvault 24 C3
Aisne 20 A3
Aisne (Dépt) 20 A2
Aitana 45 E1
Aiterhofen 56 B2
Aitrach 55 E3
Aitzgorri 36 B1
Aiud 112 C4
Aix-d'Angillon, les 26 A2
Aixe 29 D1
Aix-en-Othe 26 B1
Aix-en-Provence 30 C4
Aix, I d' 24 B4
Aix-les-Bains 27 D4
Aizenay 24 B3
Ajaccio 33 E4
Ajaureforsen 97 F3
Ajdanovac 77 D1
Ajdovščina 70 A2
Ajka 112 A4
Ajo 35 F1
Ajo, C de 36 A1
Ajos 99 D3
Ajtos 115 E2
Akarnaniká, Óri 82 C3
Äkäsjokisuu 95 D4
Äkäskero 95 D4
Äkäslompolo 95 D4
Akçakoca 115 F3
Aken 53 D1
Åkersberga 106 B3
Akershus 105 D3
Åkers styckebruk 106 B4
Akhisar 115 F4
Åkirkeby 109 D4
Akkajaure 94 B4
Akkerhaugen 104 C3
Akku 95 E3
Akranes 96 A2
Akráta 87 D1
Ákrathos, Akr 80 C4
Akréfnio 83 F4
Åkrehamn 104 A3
Akrestrømmen 100 C3
Akritas 79 D2
Akritas, Akr 86 C4
Akrogiáli 80 B3
Akropótamos 80 B3
Akrotíri 91 E1
Akrovoúni 80 C2
Aktí Apólona 87 F2
Akujärvi 95 F3
Akureyri 96 B1
Ål 104 C2
Ala 60 C1
Ala di Stura 31 E1
Alà d. Sardi 66 B2
Alaejos 35 E4
Alagí 86 C3
Alagna Valsesia 27 F4
Alagnon 29 F2
Alagón 37 D3
Alagón, R 39 D2
Alagonia 86 C3
Alahärmä 102 C2
Ala-Honkajoki 102 B3
Alaior 45 F2
Alajärvi 102 C2
Alakylä 99 D1
Alalkomenés 83 F4
Alameda 43 F3
Alamillo 43 F1
Alanäs 101 F1
Aland 48 C3
Åland 106 C3
Alandroal 38 C4
Alange 39 D4
Alange, Emb de 39 D4
Alanís 43 E2
Alapitkä 103 E2
Alaraz 39 E1
Alarcón 40 C3
Alarcón, Emb de 40 C3
Alar del Rey 35 F3
Alaşehir 115 F4
Alassio 31 F3
Alastaro 107 D2
Alatoz 41 D4
Alatri 63 F3
Alavieska 102 C1
Ala-Vuokki 99 F4
Alavus 102 C2
Alba 31 F2
Alba Adriatica 64 A1
Albacete 40 C4
Albacken 101 F2
Alba de Tormes 39 E1
Albæk 108 B1
Albaida 45 E1
Albaida, Pto de 45 E1
Alba Iulia 114 C1
Albaladejo 44 B1
Albalate de Cinca 37 E3
Albalate del Arzobispo 37 D4
Albalate de las Nogueras 40 C2
Alban 29 E3
Albánchez 44 C3
Albano di Lucania 65 D4
Albano Laziale 63 E3
Albarca 37 F4
Albarella, I 61 D1
Albares 35 D2
Albarracín 41 D2
Albarracín, Sa de 41 D2
Albatana 45 D1
Albatera 45 D2
Albena 115 E2
Albenga 31 F3
Albens 27 D4
Alberche, R 39 F2
Alberga 105 F4
Albergaria-a-Velha 38 B1
Alberique 41 E4
Albernoa 42 B1
Alberobello 65 E3
Albersdorf 48 A2
Albert 19 F2
Albert Kanaal 50 C3
Albertville 27 D4
Albestroff 21 E3
Albi 29 E3
Albiano 31 F1
Albinia 63 D2
Albino 58 B4
Albisola Marina 60 A3
Albocácer 41 F2
Albolodúy 44 B3
Albolote 44 A3
Albo, M 66 C2
Alborea 41 D4
Ålborg 108 B2
Ålborg Bugt 108 B2
Albox 44 C3
Albstadt-Ebingen 55 D3
Albufeira 42 A3
Albujón 45 D2
Albulapass 58 B3
Albuñol 44 A4
Alburno, Mte 64 C4
Alburquerque 38 C3
Alby (F) 27 D4
Alby (S) 101 E3
Alcácer do Sál 42 A1
Alcáçovas 42 B1
Alcadozo 44 C1
Alcafozes 38 C2
Alcains 38 C2
Alcalá de Chivert 41 F2
Alcalá de Guadaira 43 D3
Alcalá de Henares 40 B2
Alcalá de la Selva 41 E2
Alcalá del Júcar 41 D4
Alcalá de los Gazules 43 D4
Alcalá del Río 43 D2
Alcalá la Real 44 A3
Alcamo 68 B3
Alcampel 37 E3
Alcanadre, R 37 E3
Alcanar 41 F2
Alcanede 38 A3
Alcanena 38 B3
Alcanhões 38 B3
Alcañices 34 C4
Alcañiz 37 E4
Alcántara 39 D3
Alcántara, Emb de 39 D3
Alcantarilha 42 A2
Alcantarilla 45 D2
Alcaracejos 43 E1
Alcaraz 44 B1
Alcaraz, Sa de 44 C1
Alcaria do Cume 42 B2
Alcaria Ruiva 42 B2
Alcarrache, R 42 C1
Alcarràs 37 E4
Alcaudete 43 F3
Alcaudete de la Jara 39 F3
Alcázar de San Juan 40 B4
Alceda 35 F2
Alcester 9 E1
Alcoba 39 F4
Alcobaça 38 A3
Alcoba de los Montes 39 F4
Alcobendas 40 B2
Alcoceber 41 F3
Alcochete 38 A4
Alcolea 43 F2
Alcolea de Cinca 37 E3
Alcolea del Pinar 36 B4
Alcolea del Río 43 E2
Alconchel 42 C1
Alcora 41 E3
Alcorisa 41 E2
Alcorlo, Emb de 40 B1
Alcoutim 42 B2
Alcover 37 F4
Alcoy 45 E1
Alcubierre 37 D3
Alcubierre, Sa de 37 D3
Alcubilla de Avellaneda 36 A3
Alcublas 41 E3
Alcudia 45 F2
Alcudia de Crespins 41 E4
Alcudia de Guadix 44 B3
Alcuéscar 39 D4
Aldeacentenera 39 E3
Aldeadávila, Emb de 34 C4
Aldea del Cano 39 D3
Aldea del Fresno 40 A2
Aldea del Rey 44 A1
Aldeanueva de Ebro 36 C3
Aldeanueva de la Vera 39 E2
Aldeanueva del Camino 39 E2
Aldeburgh 11 E1
Aldeia da Ponte 39 D2
Aldeia Nova de São Bento 42 C1
Alderney 18 A2
Aldershot 9 F3
Aldinci 77 E3
Aldocer 40 C2
Aledo 44 C2
Aleksandrija 113 F2
Aleksandrovac (Srbija) 73 D3
Aleksandrovac (Srbija) 77 D1
Aleksa Šantić 72 B1
Aleksinac 73 E4
Alençon 23 F3
Alenquer 38 A3
Alentejo 42 B1
Alepohóri (Pelopónissos) 87 D2
Alepohóri (Stereá Eláda) 87 E1
Aléria 33 F3
Alès 30 B3
Ales 66 B3
Aleşd 112 C4
Alessandria 60 A2
Alessandria d. Rocca 68 B3
Ålestrup 108 A2
Ålesund 100 A2
Aletschhorn 27 F3
Alexandria (GB) 4 C2
Alexándria (GR) 79 F3
Alexandria (RO) 115 D2
Alexandroúpoli 81 E2
Alf 51 E4
Alfajarín 37 D3
Alfambra (E) 41 D2
Alfambra (P) 42 A2
Alfambra, R 41 E2
Alfândega da Fé 34 C4
Alfaro 36 C3
Alfarrás 37 E3
Alfaz del Pi 45 E1
Alfedena 64 A2
Alfeizerão 38 A3
Alfeld (Bayern) 55 F1
Alfeld (Niedersachsen) 52 B1
Alfiós 86 B2
Alfonsine 61 D2
Alfonso XIII, Emb de 44 C2
Alford (Grampian) 3 E4
Alford (Lincs) 7 E3
Alfreton 7 D3
Alfta 101 F4
Algaida 45 F3
Algar 43 D4
Älgård 104 A4
Algar de Palancia 41 E3
Algarinejo 43 F3
Algarrobo 43 F4
Algarve 42 B2
Algatocín 43 E4
Algeciras 43 D4
Algemesí 41 E4
Alghero 66 A2
Alginet 41 E4
Algodonales 43 E3
Algodor, R 40 A3
Algora 40 C1
Algorta 36 B1
Algoz 42 A2
Alhama de Almería 44 B3
Alhama de Aragón 36 C4
Alhama de Granada 43 F3
Alhama de Murcia 45 D2
Alhambra 40 B4
Alhamilla, Sa 44 B3
Alhaurín el Grande 43 E4
Alhóndiga 40 B2
Alia (E) 39 E3
Alia (I) 68 C3
Aliaga 41 E2
Aliaguilla 41 D3
Aliákmona, L 79 E4
Aliákmonas 79 D4
Aliartos 83 F4
Alibunar 73 D2
Alicante 45 E2
Alicudi, I 68 C2
Alicún de Ortega 44 B2
Alife 64 B3
Alijó 34 B4
Alikés 86 A1
Alikianós 90 B3
Alikí (Kiklády) 88 C3
Alikí (Thássos) 81 D3
Alimiá, N 93 E1
Alingsås 108 C1
Alinyà 32 A3
Aliseda 39 D3
Alise-Ste-Reine 26 B2
Aliste, R 35 D4
Alistráti 80 B2
Ali Terme 69 D2
Alivéri 84 B4
Aljezur 42 A2
Aljibe 43 D4
Aljucén 39 D4
Aljustrel 42 B1
Alkionídon, Kólpos 87 E1
Alkmaar 16 C2
Allaire 22 C4
Allaman, M 76 C4
Allanche 29 E2
Alland 57 E3
Allariz 34 B3
Alleen 104 B4
Alleghe 59 D3
Allègre 29 F2
Allen, L 12 C2
Allensbach 55 D4
Allentsteig 57 E2
Allepuz 41 E2
Aller 48 A4
Allersberg 55 F1
Allershausen 55 F3
Alleuze 29 F2
Allevard 31 D1
Allier (Dépt) 26 A3
Allier *R* 26 A3
Allinge-Sandvig 109 D4
Allo 36 C2
Alloa 5 D2
Allonnes 23 F4
Allos 31 D3
Allos, Col d' 31 D3
Alloza 41 E1
Allstedt 52 C2
Almacelles 37 E3
Almáchar 43 F3
Almada 38 A4
Almadén 39 F4
Almadén de la Plata 43 D2
Almadenejos 43 F1
Almagro 40 A4
Almajano 36 B3
Almansa 45 D1
Almansil 42 B3
Almanza 35 E2
Almanzora, R 44 B3
Almanzor, Pico 39 E2
Almaraz 39 E3
Almargen 43 E3
Almarza 36 B3
Almazán 36 B4
Almazora 41 E3
Almedinilla 43 F3
Almeida (E) 35 D4
Almeida (P) 39 D1
Almeirim 38 B3

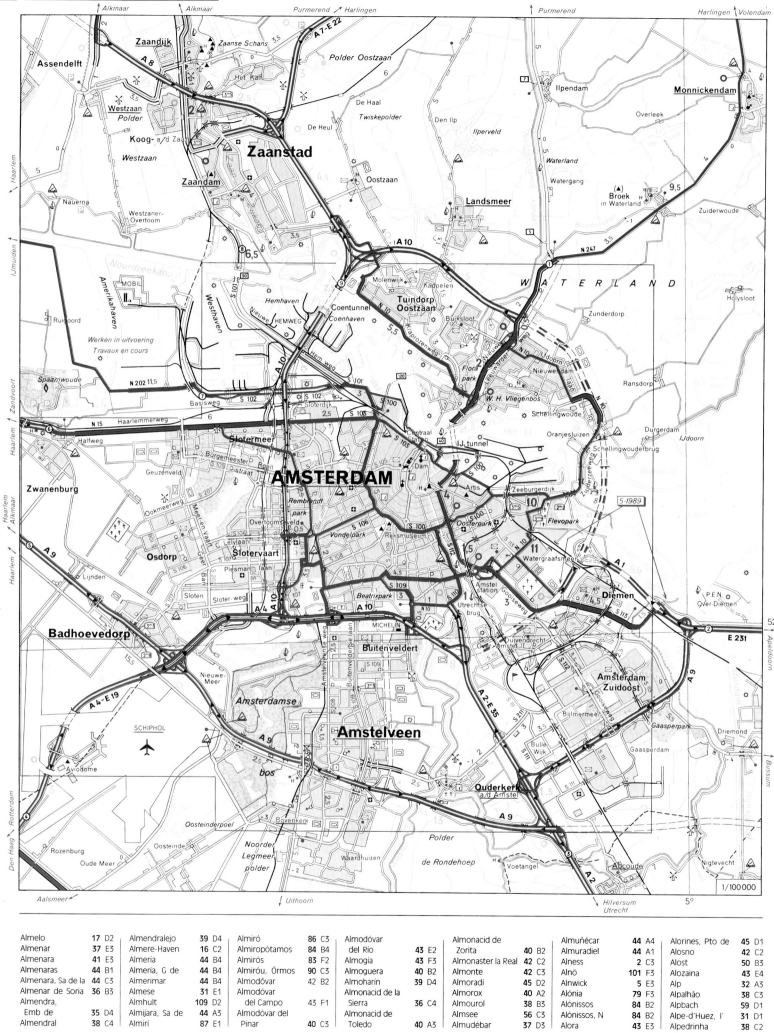

Alpera 41 D4
Alpes-de-Haute-Provence 31 D3
Alpes-Maritimes 31 E3
Alpe Veglia 58 A3
Alphen aan den Rijn 16 C3
Alpi Apuane 60 B3
Alpiarça 38 B3
Alpignano 31 E1
Alpi Orobie 58 B3
Alpirsbach 54 C3
Alpua 99 D4
Alqueva 42 B1
Alqueva, Bgem de 42 B1
Alquézar 37 E3
Als 108 B2
Als (Reg) 108 B4
Alsasua 36 B2
Alsdorf 17 D4
Alsen 101 E2
Alsfeld 52 A3
Alstahaug 97 D3
Alston 5 E4
Alta 95 D2
Altaelva 95 D2
Altafjorden 95 D2
Altamura 65 D3
Alta, Sa 41 D2
Altastenberg 17 F4
Altaussee 56 C3
Altavilla 68 B3
Altdöbern 53 E1
Altdorf (CH) 58 A2
Altdorf (D) 55 F1
Altea 45 E1
Altedo 61 D2
Altena 17 E4
Altenahr 51 E4
Altenau 52 B2
Altenberg 53 E3
Altenberge 17 E3
Altenburg 53 D3
Altenholz 48 A1
Altenhundem 17 F4
Altenkirchen (D) 51 E3
Altenkirchen (DDR) 49 D1
Altenmarkt (D) 56 B3
Altenmarkt (Salzburg) 59 F1
Altenmarkt (Steiermark) 57 D3
Altenstadt 55 E3
Altensteig 54 C3
Altentreptow 49 D2
Altenwalde 47 F2
Alte Oder 49 E3
Alter do Chão 38 C3
Altglashütten 54 C4
Altheim 56 C3
Althofen 70 B1
Altkirch 27 E1
Altlandsberg 49 E4
Altlengbach 57 E2
Altmühl 55 F2
Altmühlsee 55 E2
Altmünster 56 C3
Altnaharra 2 C2
Alto Campó 35 F2
Alto Cruz 36 C4
Alto de Allariz 34 B3
Alto de Barazar 36 B1
Alto de Covelo 34 C3
Alto de Estividas 34 B3
Alto de Fumaces 34 B3
Alto del Couso 34 B3
Alto del Portalé 37 E4
Alto del Rodicio 34 B3
Alto de Santo Domingo 34 B2
Alto do Cañizo 34 C3
Alto Laza 37 D2
Altomira 40 B2
Alton 9 F3
Altopascio 60 C3
Alto Rabagão, Bgem do 34 B3
Altorricon 37 E3
Altotero 36 A2
Altötting 56 B3
Altrincham 6 C2
Alt Ruppin 49 D3
Altshausen 55 D4
Altstätten 58 B2
Altura 41 E3
Altweilnau 51 F4
Alustante 41 D2
Alva 4 C2
Alvaiázere 38 B2
Alvalade 42 A1
Alvão, Sa de 34 B4
Alva, R 38 B2
Alvdal 100 C3
Älvdalen 101 E4
Alvelos, Sa de 38 B2
Alverca do Ribatejo 38 A4
Alvesta 109 D2
Alvignac 29 D2
Ålvik 104 B2
Alvito 42 B1
Alvito, Bgem do 42 B1
Älvkarleby 106 B2
Alvor 42 A2
Älvros 101 E3
Älvsborgs Län 108 C1
Älvsbyn 98 B3
Alyth 5 D1
Alytus 110 C4
Alz 56 B3
Alzenau 52 A4
Alzey 54 C1
Alzira 41 E4
Alzola 36 B1
Alzon 29 F3
Alzonne 32 B1
Amadora 38 A4
Åmål 105 E4
Amalfi 64 B4
Amaliáda 86 B1
Amaliápoli 83 F2
Amálo 89 D2
Amance 27 D1
Amancey 27 D2
Amandola 61 F4
Amantea 67 E3
Amárandos (Ípiros) 78 C4
Amárandos (Thessalía) 83 D2
Amarante 34 B4
Amareleja 42 C1
Amares 34 A4
Amárinthos 84 B4
Amatrice 63 F1
Amay 50 C4
Amaya 35 F3
Ambarès-et-Lagrave 28 B2
Ambasaguas 35 E2
Ambazac 25 E4
Ambelákia (Thessalía) 83 E1
Ambelákia (Thráki) 81 F1
Ambelia 83 E2
Ambelikó 85 F3
Ambelióna 86 C2
Ambelónas 83 E1
Amberg 55 F1
Ambérieu-en-Bugey 26 C4
Ambert 29 F1
Ambès 28 B2
Ambierle 26 B4
Amble 5 E3
Ambleside 5 D4
Amblève 51 D4
Amboise 25 D2
Ambra 61 D4
Ambrières-les-Vallées 18 C4
Ameixial 42 B2
Ameland 16 C1
Amelia 63 E2
Amélie-les-Bains-Palalda 32 B3
Amelinghausen 48 B3
Amer 32 B3
A Merca 34 B3
Amerongen 16 C3
Amersfoort 16 C3
Amersham 9 F2
Amesbury 9 E3
A Mezquita 34 C3
Amfiaraio 84 B4
Amfiklia 83 E3
Amfilohia 82 C3
Amfipoli 80 B2
Ámfissa 83 E4
Amiata, Mont' 63 D1
Amiens 19 F2
Amigdaleónas 80 C2
Amigdaliá 83 E4
Amindeo 79 D3
Åmli 104 B4
Amlwch 6 A2
Ammanford 8 C2
Ämmänsaari 99 E3
Ammarfjället 97 F3
Ammarnäs 97 F3
Ammel 56 A4
Ammersattel 55 F4
Ammersee 56 A3
Amohóri 79 D3
Amolianí 80 B4
Amorbach 55 D1
Amorebieta 36 B1
Amorgós 89 D3
Amorgós, N 89 D3
Amório 81 F1
Åmot (Buskerud) 104 C3
Åmot (S) 105 F2
Åmot (Telemark) 104 B3
Åmotfors 105 D3
Amótopos 82 C2
Amou 28 B4
Amoudára 91 D3
Amoudára 91 E4
Amoúdia 89 D2
Ampezzo 59 E3
Ampfing 56 B3
Amphion 27 D3
Amplepuis 26 B4
Amposta 41 F2
Ampthill 9 F2
Ampudia 35 E4
Ampuero 36 A1
Amriswil 58 B1
Amrum 47 F1
Amsele 98 B4
Amstelveen 16 C2
Amsterdam 16 C2
Amstetten 57 D3
Amungen 101 E4
Amurrio 36 B1
Amusco 35 F3
Amvrakia, L 82 C3
Amvrakikós Kólpos 82 C3
Anadia 38 B1
Anáfi 91 E1
Anafi, N 91 F1
Anafonitria 86 A1
Anagni 63 F3
Anáktora Néstoros 86 B3
Análipsi 83 F4
Análipsi 92 C1
Análipsis 86 C3
Ananjev 113 E3
Anaráhi 79 D3
Anárgiri 79 D3
Änarjohka 95 E2
Anascaul 14 A3
Ånaset 102 B1
Åna Sira 104 A4
Anatolí (Ípiros) 82 C1
Anatolí (Kríti) 91 E4
Anatolí (Thessalía) 83 F1
Anatolikí Rodópi 81 D2
Anatolikó 79 D3
Änättijärvi 99 F4
Anávatos 85 E4
Anávissos 87 F2
Anávra (Karditsa) 83 E2
Anávra (Magnissía) 83 E3
An Cabhán 13 D3
Ancares, Sa de 34 C2
Ancenis 23 D4
Ancerville 20 C4
Anchuras 39 F3
An Clochán 12 A3
An Cóbh 14 C4
Ancona 61 F3
Ancy-le-Franc 26 B1
Anda 100 A3
Andalo 58 C3
Åndalsnes 100 B2
Andalucía 43 E2
Andarax, R 44 B3
Andartikó 79 D2
Andebu 104 C3
Andelot 26 C1
Andelys, les 19 E3
Andenes 94 A3
Andenne 50 C4
Anderlues 50 B4
Andermatt 58 A3
Andernach 51 E4
Andernos 28 A2
Anderstorp 109 D2
Andfjorden 94 B3
Andigonos 79 D3
Andikira 83 E4
Andikiras, Kólpos 83 E4
Andikíthira, N 90 A2
Andimáhia 89 F3
Andimilos, N 88 A4
Andinitsa 83 E3
Andiparos 88 B3
Andiparos, N 88 B3
Andipaxi, N 82 B2
Andipsara, N 85 E4
Andirio 83 D4
Ándissa 85 E2
Andoain 36 C1
Andorno Micca 31 F1
Andorra 41 E1
Andorra la Vella 32 A2
Andosilla 36 C2
Andover 9 E3
Andøya 94 A3
Andratx 45 E3
Andravida 86 B1
Andretta 64 C3
Andrézieux-Bouthéon 30 B1
Andria 65 D3
Andrijevica 76 C2
Andritsena 86 C2
Andros 88 B1
Ándros, N 88 B1
Androússa 86 C3
Andselv 94 B3
Andújar 43 F2
Anduze 30 B3
Aneby 109 D1
Ånes 100 B2
Anet 19 E4
Aneto, Pico de 37 E2
Angáli 84 A3
Ånge (Jämtlands Län) 101 E2
Ånge (Västernorrlands Län) 101 E3
Angeja 38 B1
Ängelholm 108 C3
Angeli 95 E3
Angelohóri 79 E3
Angelókastro (Pelopónissos) 87 E2
Angelókastro (Stereá Eláda) 82 C4
Anger 57 E4
Angera 58 A4
Ångermanälven 101 F2
Angermünde 49 E3
Angern 57 F2
Angers 23 E4
Angerville 25 E1
Ängesån 98 C2
Anghiari 61 D4
Angistis, Stathmós 80 B2
Angistri 87 E2
Angistri, N 87 E2
Ángistro 80 B1
Angitis 80 B2
Angles 25 D3
Anglès (E) 32 B3
Anglès (F) 32 B1
Anglesey, I of 6 A2
Anglesola 37 F3
Anglet 28 A4
Anglure 20 B4
Angoulême 28 C1
Angri 64 B4
Ängsö 106 C3
Angüés 37 E3
Anguiano 36 B2
Anguillara Veneta 61 D1
Angvik 100 B2
Anholt 108 C2
Aniane 30 A4
Aniche 20 A1
Aniene 63 F2
Ánixi 79 D4
Anizy-le-Château 20 A3
Anjalankoski 107 F2
Anjum 47 D3
Ankaran 70 A3
Ankarsrum 109 E1
Anklam 49 E2
Ankogel 59 E2
An Longfort 12 C3
An Muileann gCearr 13 D3
Ånn 101 D2
Ånn *L* 101 D2
Annaberg 57 E3
Annaberg-Buchholz 53 E3
Annaburg 53 E1
Annan 5 D3
Annan *R* 5 D3
Anndalsvågen 97 D3
Annecy 27 D4
Annemasse 27 D4
Annevoie-Rouillon 50 C4
Annonay 30 B1
Annone Veneto 59 E4
Annot 31 D3
Annweiler 54 C2
Áno Drossiní 81 E2
Anógia 87 D3
Anógia 91 D3
Áno Hóra 83 D4
Anoia, R 32 A4
Áno Kalendíni 82 C2
Áno Kaliníki 79 D2
Áno Kómi 79 E4
Áno Lefkími 82 A2
Áno Melás 79 D3
Áno Merá 88 C2
Anópoli 90 C4
Áno Polidéndri 83 F1
Áno Poróïa 80 A2
Áno Rodákino 90 C4
Áno Sangrí 88 C3
Áno Siros 88 B2
Añover de Tajo 40 A3
Áno Viános 91 E4
Áno Vrondoú 80 B2
Áno Zervohóri 79 E3
Ansbach 55 E1
Anse 26 C4
Ansedonia 63 D2
Ansião 38 B2
Ansnes 100 C1
Ansó 37 D2
Anstruther 5 D2
An tAonach 12 C4
Antas 44 C3
Antegnate 60 B1
Antemil 34 A1
Antequera 43 F3
Anterselva 59 D2
Anthia 81 E2
Anthili 83 E3
Anthis 80 B2
Antholz 59 D2
Anthótopos 83 E2
Antibes 31 E4
Antifer, Cap d' 19 D3
An tInbhear Mór 15 E3
Antnäs 98 C3
Antraigues 30 B2
Antrain 18 B4
Antrim 13 E2
Antrim (Co) 13 E2
Antrim Coast 13 E1
Antrim Mts 13 E1
Antrodoco 63 F2
Anttola 103 E3
Antwerpen 50 B3
Antwerpen (Prov) 50 C3
An Uaimh 13 D3
Anvers 50 B3
Anzano di Puglia 64 C3
Anzio 63 E3
Anzola d'Ossola 58 A4
Anzy-le-Duc 26 B4
Aoiz 36 C2
Aóos 78 C4
Aosta 27 E4
Aoste 27 E4
Apatin 72 B2
Apatovac 71 D2
Apecchio 61 E4
Apeldoorn 17 D2
Apen 47 E3
Apéri 93 D3
Aphrodisias 115 F4
Apidiá 87 D3
Apíkia 88 B1
Apiranthos 88 C3
Apolakiá 93 E2
Apolda 52 C3
Apolitáres, Akr 90 A2
Apólonas 88 C3
Apolonia (Kiklådes) 88 B3
Apolonia (Makedonia) 80 B3
A Pontenova Villaodriz 34 C1
Apóstoli 90 C4
Äppelbo 105 E2
Appenweier 54 C3
Appenzell 58 B2
Appiano 59 D3
Appingedam 47 D3
Appleby 5 D4
Aprica 58 C3
Apricena 64 C2
Aprilia 63 E3
Ápsalos 79 E2
Apt 30 C3
Áptera 90 C3
Aquileia 59 F3
Aquitaine, L' 25 E2
Arabba 59 D3
Aracena 42 C2
Aracena, Emb de 43 D2
Aracena, Sa de 42 C2
Aračinovo 77 E3
Arad 112 C4
Årådalsfjorden 104 B1
Arada, Sa de 38 B1
Aragón 37 D3
Aragona 68 B4
Aragón, R 36 C2
Arahnéo, Óros 87 E2
Aráhova (Etolía-Akarnanía) 83 D3
Aráhova (Viotía) 83 E4
Arákinthos, Óros 83 D4
A Ramallosa 34 A3
Aramits 37 D1
Aranda de Duero 36 A3
Aranđelovac 73 D3
Aran I 12 C1
Aran Is 12 A4
Aranjuez 40 B3
Arantzazu 36 B1
Aran, Vall d' 37 F2
Araquil, R 36 C2
Ara, R 37 E2
Aras de Alpuente 41 D3
Arasluokta 97 F1
Árahthos 82 C2
Áratos 81 E2
Aravaca 40 A2
Aravis, Col des 27 D4
Aravissós 79 E2
Áraxos 86 B1
Áraxos, Akr 86 B1
Arazede 38 B2
Arba, R 36 C3
Arbatax 66 C3
Arbeca 37 F4
Arbesbach 57 D2
Arboga 105 F3
Arbois 27 D3
Arbon 58 B1
Arbón, Emb de 34 C1
Arborea 66 B3
Arborio 31 F1
Arbrå 101 F4
Arbroath 5 E1
Arbresle, l' 26 B4
Arbúcies 32 B4
Arbus 66 B3
Arc 31 D1
Arcachon 28 A2
Arce 64 A3
Arcen 17 D3
Arc-en-Barrois 26 C1
Arceniega 36 A1
Arcevia 61 E4
Archena 45 D2
Arches 27 D1
Archiac 28 B1
Archidona 43 F3
Arcidosso 63 D1
Arcipelago Toscano 62 B1
Arcis 20 B4
Arciz 113 E4
Arco 58 C4
Arco de Baúlhe 34 B4
Arcos 35 F3
Arcos de Jalón 36 B4
Arcos de la Frontera 43 D3
Arcos de Valdevez 34 A3
Arcouest, Pte de l' 22 C2
Arcs, les (Savoie) 31 D1
Arcs, les (Var) 31 D4
Arcusa 37 E2
Arda 115 E3
Ardales 43 E3
Årdalstangen 104 B1
Ardánio 81 F2
Ardara 12 C1
Árdas 81 F1
Ardbeg 4 B2
Ardèche (Dépt) 30 B2
Ardèche *R* 30 B2
Ardèche, Gges de l' 30 B3
Ardee 13 D3
Ardennes (Dépt) 20 B3
Ardennes, Canal des 20 C3
Ardentes 25 E3
Ardentinny 4 C2
Ardes 29 F1
Ardez 58 B2
Ardglass 13 E2
Ardila, R 42 C1
Ardila, Rib de 42 C1
Ardisa 37 D3
Ardlussa 4 B2
Ardmore 14 C4
Ardrahan 12 B4
Ardres 19 E1
Ardrishaig 4 B2
Ardrossan 4 C2
Ards Pen 13 E2
Arduaine 4 B1
Ardvasar 2 B4
Åre 101 D2
Arenas de Cabrales 35 E2
Arenas de Iguña 35 F2
Arenas de San Juan 40 B4
Arenas de San Pedro 39 F2
Arendal 104 C4
Arendonk 50 C3
Arendsee 48 C3
Arenos, Emb de 41 E3
Arenys de Mar 32 B4
Arenzano 60 A3
Areópoli 87 D4
Arès 28 A2
Ares (Galicia) 34 B1
Ares (Valencia) 41 E2
Ares, Col des 37 F2
Ares, Pto de 32 B3
Åreskutan 101 D2
Aréthoussa 80 B3
Aretí 80 A3
Arévalo 39 F1
Arez 38 C3
Arezzo 61 D4
Arfará 86 C3
Argalastí 83 F2
Argamasilla de Alba 40 B4
Argamasilla de Calatrava 44 A1
Arganda 40 B2
Arganil 38 B2
Arga, R 36 C2
Argássi 86 A2
Argelès 32 B2
Argelès-Gazost 37 E1
Argens 31 D4
Argent 25 F2
Argenta 61 D2
Argentan 19 D4
Argentario, Mte 63 D2

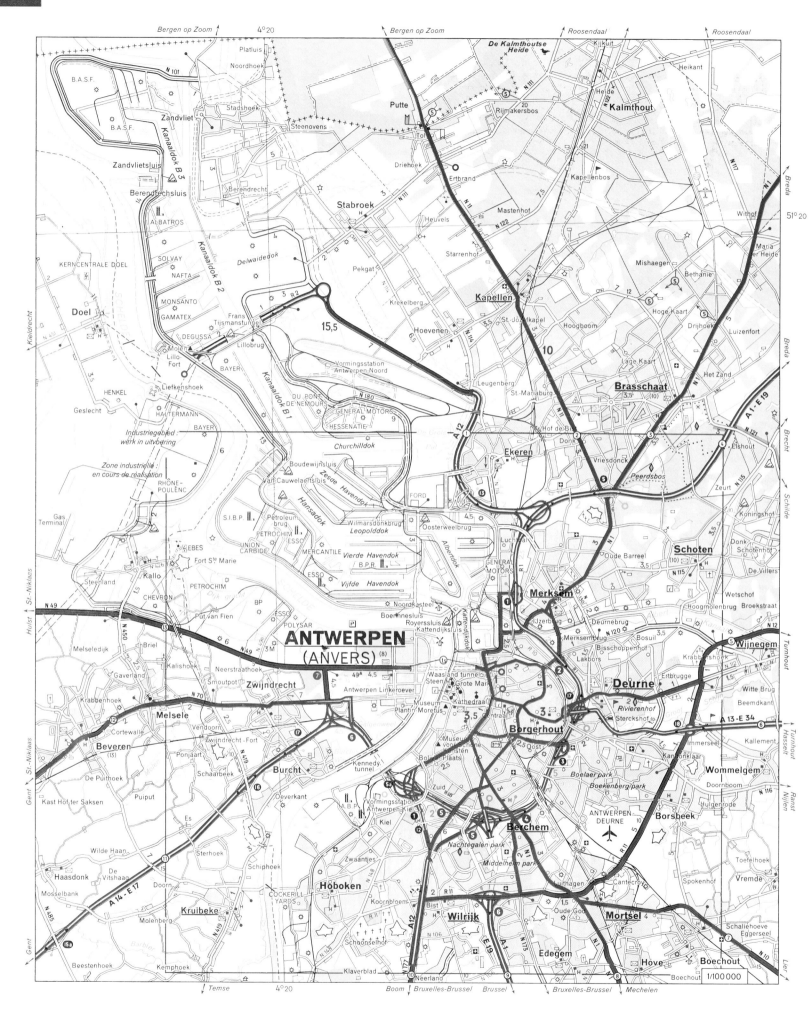

ANTWERPEN
(ANVERS) (8)

1/100 000

Argentat 29 D2
Argente 41 D2
Argentera 31 E3
Argentière 27 E4
Argentière-la-Bessée, l' 31 D2
Argentona 32 B4
Argenton-Château 24 C3
Argenton-sur-Creuse 25 E3
Argentré-du-Plessis 23 E3
Arginónda 89 F3
Argirádes 82 A2
Argiró 84 B4
Argiropoúlio 83 E1
Argiroúpoli 90 C3
Argithéa 83 D2
Argolida 87 E2
Argolikós Kólpos 87 E2
Árgos 87 D2
Árgos Orestikó 79 D3
Argos, R 44 C2
Argostóli 82 B4
Arguedas 36 C3
Argueil 19 E3
Arguellite 44 B1
Arguis 37 D2
Argyll 4 B1
Argyll Forest Park 4 C2
Arhánes 91 D4
Arhángelos (Makedonía) 79 E2
Arhángelos (Ródos) 93 F1
Arhéa Epídavros 87 E2
Arhéa Kleonés 87 D1
Arhéa Kórinthos 87 E1
Arhéa Neméa 87 D1
Arhéa Olympía 86 C2
Arhéa Thíra 91 E1
Århus 108 B3
Arianá 81 E2
Ariano Irpino 64 B3
Ariano nel Polesine 61 D2
Aridéa 79 E2
Ariège (Dépt) 32 A2
Ariège *R* 32 A2
Arija 35 F2
Arild 108 C3
Arilje 72 C4
Arinagour 2 B4
Aríni 86 C2
Ariño 37 D4
Arinthod 27 D3
Arisaig 2 B4
Arisaig, Sd of 2 B4
Arísti 78 C4
Aristoménis 86 C3
Arísvi 81 E2
Aritzo 66 B3
Arive 36 C2
Ariza 36 B4
Årjäng 105 D3
Arjeplog 98 A3
Arjona 44 A2
Arkádi 91 D3
Arkadía 86 C2
Arkaig, L 2 C4
Arkalohóri 91 E4
Arkássa 93 D3
Arkessíni 89 D3
Arki, N 89 E2
Arkitsa 83 F3
Arklow 15 E3
Arkona, Kap 49 D1
Arkoúdi, N 82 B4
Arlaban, Pto de 36 B1
Arlanc 29 F1
Arlanda 106 B3
Arlanza, R 36 A3
Arlanzón 36 A2
Arlanzón, R 35 F3
Arlbergpaß 58 B2
Arlberg-Straßentunnel 58 B2
Arlempdes 30 A2
Arles (Bouches-du-Rhône) 30 B4
Arles (Pyrénées-Orientales) 32 B3
Arlesheim 27 E2
Arlon 21 D2
Arlsleben 52 C2
Armacão de Pêra 42 A3
Armadale 5 D2
Arma di Taggia 31 F3
Armagh 13 D2
Armagh (Co) 13 D2
Armamar 34 B4
Arméni 90 C3
Armenií 86 C3
Armenistís 89 D2
Armentières 19 F1
Armilla 44 A3
Armólia 85 E4
Armunia 35 D3
Árna 87 D3
Arnac-Pompadour 29 D1
Arnay-le-Duc 26 B2
Arnéa 80 B3
Arneburg 48 C4
Arnedillo 36 B3
Arnedo 36 C3
Arnes 41 F2
Årnes 105 D3
Arnhem 17 D3
Arni 60 B3
Árnissa 79 E2
Arno 60 C4
Arnoldstein 59 F2
Arnon 25 F3
Arnøy 94 C2
Arnsberg 17 F3
Arnstadt 52 C3
Arnstein 52 B4
Aroania, Óri 86 C1
Aroche 42 C2
Aroche *Mt* 42 C1
Arogí 81 D2
Arolsen 52 A2
Arona 58 A4
Aroniádika 90 A1
Aronkylä 102 B3
Åros 104 C3
Arosa 58 B2
Arouca 38 B1
Arousa, I de 34 A2
Årøysund 104 C3
Arpajon 19 F4
Arpela 99 D3
Arquata del Tronto 63 F1
Arques (Pas-de-Calais) 19 F1
Arques (Seine-Maritime) 19 E2
Arquillos 44 A2
Arrabal 34 A3
Arrábida, Sa da 38 A4
Arracourt 21 D4
Arraiolos 38 B4
Arran 4 B2
Arras 19 F2
Arrasate-Mondragon 36 B1
Arreau 37 E2
Arrecife 42 C4
Arredondo 36 A1
Arrée, Mts d' 22 B2
Arrens 37 E2
Arrifana 38 C1
Arrigorriaga 36 B1
Arriondas 35 E1
Arrochar 4 C2
Arromanches 18 C3
Arronches 38 C4
Arroux 26 B3
Arrow, L 12 C2
Arroyo de la Luz 39 D3
Arroyo del Ojanco 44 B1
Arroyo de San Serván 39 D4
Arroyomolinos de León 43 D1
Arroyomolinos de Montánchez 39 D4
Arruda dos Vinhos 38 A3
Års 108 A2
Ars (Charente-Maritime) 24 B4
Ars (Moselle) 21 D3
Arsiè 59 D3
Arsiero 59 D4
Arsunda 106 B2
Arsy 19 F3
Artà 45 F2
Árta 82 C2
Artajona 36 C2
Árta (Nomos) 82 C2
Arta Terme 59 E3
Arteaga, G de 36 B1
Artemissía 86 C3
Artemíssio (Évia) 83 F3
Artemíssio (Pelopónissos) 87 D2
Artemónas 88 B3
Artena 63 F3
Artenay 25 E1
Artern 52 C2
Artesa de Segre 37 F3
Artessianó 83 D2
Artfjället 97 E3
Arth (CH) 58 A2
Arth (D) 56 B2
Arthurstown 15 D4
Arties 37 F2
Artjärvi 107 F2
Artotína 83 D3
Artruix, C de 45 F2
A Rúa 34 C3
Arucas 42 B4
Arudy 37 D1
Arundel 9 F3
Arve 27 E4
Árvi 91 E4
Arvidsjaur 98 A3
Årvik 100 A2
Arvika 105 E3
Årviksand 94 C2
Arzachena 66 B1
Arzacq-Arraziguet 28 B4
Arzano 22 B3
Aržano 75 E1
Arzberg 53 D4
Arzignano 60 C1
Árzos 81 F1
Arzúa 34 B2
As 50 C3
Aš 53 D4
Åsa 108 C2
Asamati 77 D4
Åsarna 101 E2
Åsarp 109 D1
Ascain 28 A4
Ascha 56 B2
Aschach 56 C2
Aschaffenburg 52 A4
Aschau 56 B3
Aschbach Markt 57 D3
Ascheberg (Nordrhein-Westfalen) 17 E3
Ascheberg (Schleswig-Holstein) 48 B2
Aschendorf 17 E1
Aschersleben 52 C2
Asciano 61 D4
Ascione, Colle d' 67 F3
Asco 33 F3
Ascó 37 E4
Ascoli Piceno 63 F1
Ascoli Satriano 64 C3
Ascona 58 A3
Ascot 9 F2
Åse 94 A3
Åseda 109 E2
Åsele 101 F1
Åsen 101 D1
Asenovgrad 115 D3
Åseral 104 B4
Asfáka 82 B1
Asfeld 20 B3
Åsgårdstrand 104 C3
Ashbourne (GB) 6 C3
Ashbourne (IRL) 13 D3
Ashburton 8 C4
Ashby de la Zouch 6 C3
Ashford 11 D3
Ashington 5 E3
Ashton-under-Lyne 6 C2
Asiago 59 D4
Asikkala 107 F2
Asin 37 D3
Asinara, G dell' 66 B1
Asinara, I 66 A1
Ask 105 D3
Askainen 107 D2
Askeaton 14 B3
Askersund 105 F4
Askifou 90 C3
Askim 105 D3
Áskio, Óros 79 D3
Askja 96 C2
Asklipiío (Dodekánissa) 89 F3
Asklipiío (Ródos) 93 E2
Askola 107 F2
Askós 80 A3
Askøy 104 A2
Askvoll 104 A1
Asmunti 99 D3
Asnæs 108 B3
Åsnen 109 D2
As Neves 34 A3
Asola 60 B1
Asolo 59 D4
Aspang 57 F3
Aspatria 5 D4
Aspe 45 D2
Aspe, Gave d' 37 D1
Asperg 55 D2
Aspet 37 F2
Aspin, Col d' 37 E2
As Ponte de Garcia Rodriguez 34 B1
Áspra Spítia 83 E4
Aspres 30 C2
Áspro 79 E3
Aspróhoma 86 C3
Asprókavos, Akr 82 A2
Aspromonte 67 E4
Asprópirgos 87 F1
Asprovália 80 B3
Asse 50 B3
Assemini 66 B4
Assen 17 D1
Assens 108 B3
Assergi 63 F2
Assini 87 E2
Assisi 63 E1
Aßmannshausen 51 F4
Assomáton 91 D3
Assopia 84 A4
Assopós (Korinthía) 87 D1
Assopós (Lakonía) 87 E4
Assopós *R* 87 E1
Ássos (Ípiros) 82 B2
Ássos (Kefaloniá) 82 B4
Astaffort 28 C3
Astafjorden 94 B3
Astakída, N 93 D2
Astakós 82 C4
Asten 57 D3
Asti 31 F2
Astipálea 92 C1
Astipálea, N 92 C1
Astorga 35 D3
Åstorp 108 C3
Ástros 87 D2
Astudillo 35 F3
Asturias 34 C2
Asvestádes 81 F1
Asvestohóri 82 B1
Asvestópetra 79 D3
Atalaia 38 A3
Atalándi 83 F3
Atalaya de la Calzada 44 A1
Atalayassa 45 D4
Atáli 84 B3
Ataquines 39 F1
Atarfe 44 A3
Atáviros 93 E2
Ateca 36 C4
Atella 64 C3
Atessa 64 B2
Ath 50 B4
Athamánon, Óri 82 C2
Athánio 82 B3
Athboy 13 D3
Athenry 12 B3
Athéras 89 D2
Athéras, Akr 82 B4
Atherstone 9 E1
Athína 87 F1
Áthira 79 F2
Athlone 12 C3
Áthos 80 C4
Athy 13 D4
Atienza 36 B4
Atikí-Piréas 87 F1
Atina 64 A3
Átokos, N 82 C4
Atouguia da Baleia 38 A3
Ätran 108 C2
Ätran *R* 108 C2
Atri 64 A1
Atsikí 85 D1
Attendorn 17 F4
Attersee 56 C3
Attersee *L* 56 C3
Attigliano 63 E2
Attigny 20 B3
Attleborough 11 D1
Attnang 56 C3
Åtvidaberg 109 E1
Au 55 F2
Aub 55 E1
Aubagne 30 C4
Aubange 21 D2
Aube 20 B4
Aube (Dépt) 20 B4
Aubenas 30 B2
Aubenton 20 B2
Auberive 26 C1
Aubeterre 28 C1
Aubigny (Cher) 25 F2
Aubigny (Pas-de-Calais) 19 F2
Aubin 29 E3
Aubisque, Col d' 37 E1
Aubonne 27 D3
Aubrac 29 F2
Aubrac, Mts d' 29 F2
Aubusson 25 F4
Auch 28 C4
Auchencairn 4 C3
Auchterarder 5 D1
Auchtermuchty 5 D1
Aude (Dépt) 32 B2
Aude *R* 32 B1
Audenge 28 A2
Audeux 27 D2
Audierne 22 A3
Audincourt 27 E2
Audlem 6 C3
Audruicq 19 F1
Audun-le-Roman 21 D3
Audun-le-Tiche 21 D3
Aue *R* 48 A4
Aue 53 D3
Auer 59 D3
Auerbach (D) 55 F1
Auerbach (DDR) 53 D3
Auffach 59 D1
Aughnacloy 13 D2
Aughrim 13 D4
Augsburg 55 F3
Augusta 69 D4
Augustenborg 108 B4
Augustów 110 C4
Augustusburg 53 E3
Aukan 100 B2
Aukra 100 B2
Aulanko 107 E2
Auletta 64 C4
Aulla 60 B3
Aullène 33 F4
Aulnay 24 C4
Aulne 22 B3
Aulnoye-Aymeries 20 B2
Ault 19 E2
Aulus-les-Bains 37 F2
Auma 53 D3
Aumale 19 E2
Aumetz 21 D3
Aumont-Aubrac 29 F2
Aunay-sur-Odon 18 C3
Auneau 19 E4
Auneuil 19 E3
Auning 108 B2
Aups 31 D4
Aura 107 D2
Aurajoki 107 D2
Auray 22 C4
Aurdal 104 C2
Aure 100 B2
Aurich 47 E3
Aurignac 37 F1
Aurillac 29 E2
Aurland 104 B2
Auron 31 E3
Auron *R* 25 F3
Auronzo di Cadore 59 E2
Auros 28 B3
Aursjøen 100 B3
Aursunden 101 D2
Ausonia 64 A3
Außernbrünst 56 C2
Ausso Corno 59 F3
Aust-Agder 104 B4
Austbygd 104 C3
Austvågøy 94 A3
Auterive 37 F1
Authie 19 F2
Autol 36 C3
Autrans 30 C1
Autrey 26 C2
Auttoinen 107 E1
Autun 26 B3
Auvézère 28 C2
Auvillar 28 C3
Auxerre 26 A1
Auxi-le-Château 19 E2
Auxonne 26 C2
Auzances 25 F4
Auzon 29 F1
Availles-Limouzine 25 D4
Avaía 73 D3
Avaldsnes 104 A3
Avallon 26 B2
Avaloirs, Mt des 23 E3
Ávas 81 E2
Avaviken 98 A3
Ávdira 81 D2
Avebury 9 E2
A Veiga 34 C3
Aveiras de Cima 38 A3
Aveiro 38 B1
Aveiro, R de 38 B1
Avellino 64 B4
Aven Armand 29 F3
Aven d'Orgnac 30 B3
Averøya 100 B2
Aversa 64 B4
Avesnes 20 B2
Avesnes-le-Comte 19 F2
Avesta 105 F3
Avetrana 65 E4
Aveyron 29 D3
Aveyron (Dépt) 29 E3
Avezzano 63 F2
Avgerinós 79 D4
Avgó 82 C2
Avía 86 C3
Aviano 59 E3
Aviémonas 90 A2
Aviemore 3 D4
Aviés 79 E4
Avigliana 31 E1
Avigliano 64 C4
Avignon 30 B3
Ávila 39 F2
Ávila, Sa de 39 F2
Avilés 35 D1
Aviño 34 B1
Avintes 34 A4
Avión 34 B2
Avioth 20 C3
Avis 38 B4
Avisio 59 D3
Avize 20 B3
Avlákia 89 E1
Avlí 80 C2
Avliótes 82 A1
Avlóna 84 B4
Avlum 108 A2
Avola 69 D4
Avon (Co) 9 D2
Avon *R* (Hants) 9 E1
Avon *R* (Warw) 9 E3
Avonmouth 9 D2
Avord 25 F3
Avoriaz 27 E4
Avranches 18 B4
Avre 19 D4
Avtovac 76 A2
Awe, L 4 B1
Axams 59 D2
Axat 32 B2
Axiohóri 79 F2
Axiós 79 F3
Axioúpoli 79 F2
Ax-les-Thermes 32 A2
Axminster 9 D3
Axós 91 D3
Ay 20 B3
Ayamonte 42 B2
Aydın 115 F4
Ayedo 36 B3
Ayerbe 37 D3
Aylesbury 9 F2
Ayllón 36 A4
Ayllón, Sa de 36 A4
Aylsham 7 F3
Ayna 44 C1
Ayora 41 D4
Ayr 4 C3
Ayre, Pt of 6 A1
Ayvacık 115 E4
Ayvalık 115 E4
Aywaille 51 D4
Azáceta, Pto de 36 B2
Azaila 37 D4
Azambuja 38 A3
Azanja 73 D3
Azaruja 38 B4
Azay-le-Ferron 25 E3
Azay-le-Rideau 25 D2
Azinheira dos Barros 42 A1
Azkoitia 36 B1
Aznalcázar 43 D3
Aznalcóllar 43 D2
Azpeitia 36 B1
Azuaga 43 E1
Azuara 37 D4
Azuer, R 40 A4
Azuqueca de Henares 40 B2
Azután, Emb de 39 F3
Azzano Decimo 59 E3

B

Barcelona

Map of Barcelona (scale 0 – 2 km). Labels include: STA COLOMA DE GRAMENET, S. ANDREU, S. ADRIA DE BESOS, BADALONA, TIBIDABO (532), VALLVIDRERA, Parque Güell, Pl. de Lesseps, SAGRADA FAMILIA, Monasterio de Pedralbes, Pl. Francesc Macià, DIAGONAL, Pl. de Joan Carles I, Pl. de les Glòries Catalanes, PLAZA DE TOROS MONUMENTAL, Pl. de Tetuán, PARQUE DE LA CIUDADELA, Pl. de Catalunya, CATEDRAL, BARRIO GÓTICO, Barcelona-Termino, Ciudad Universitaria, Estación Barcelona Sants, Pl. de Toros Las Arenas, Pl. d'Espanya, ESTACIÓN MARITIMA, PUERTO, Parque de Atracciones, MONTJUIC, CASTILLO DE MONTJUIC, S. JUST DESVERN, ESPLUGUES DE LLOBREGAT, L'HOSPITALET DE LLOBREGAT, CORNELLA DE LLOBREGAT, MICHELIN, MAR MEDITERRÁNEO.

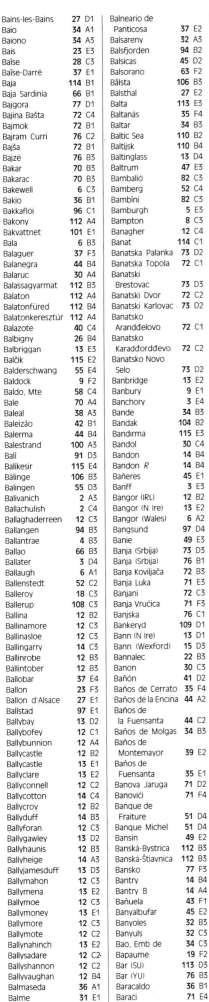

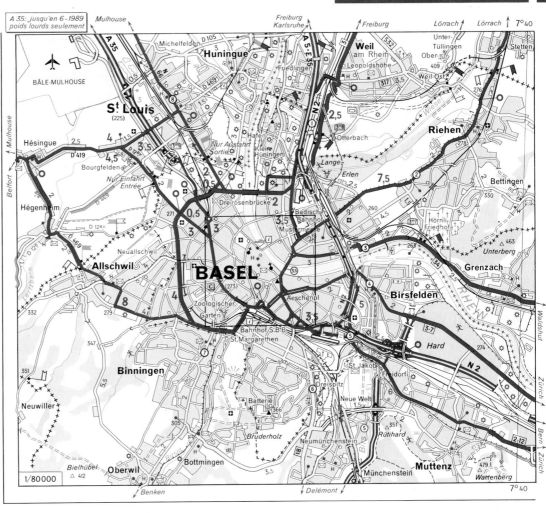

A 35: jusqu'en 6 - 1989 poids lourds seulement · Mulhouse · Freiburg Karlsruhe · Freiburg · Lörrach Lörrach 7°40

Huningue · Weil am Rhein · Unter-Tüllingen · Stetten

St Louis (225) · Riehen

Hésingue · Bourgfelden · Otterbach · Lange · Erlen 7,5 · Bettingen

Hégenheim · Neuallschwil · BASEL · Badischer Bahnhof · Hörnli Friedhof · Grenzach

Allschwil · (273) · Zoologischer Garten · Aeschenpl · Birsfelden · Unterberg

Binningen · Bahnhof S.B.B. · St. Margarethen · St. Jakob · Hard

Neuwiller · Batterie · Neue Welt · Freidorf · N 2

Bielhübel · Dreispitz · Rütihard

1/80000 · Oberwil · Bottmingen · Neumünchenstein · Münchenstein · Muttenz · Wartenberg

Bruderholz

Benken · Delémont · 7° 40

Bains-les-Bains	27 D1	Balneario de Panticosa	37 E2			
Baio	34 A1	Balsareny	32 A3			
Baiono	34 A3	Balsfjorden	94 B2			
Bais	23 E3	Balsicas	45 D2			
Baîse	28 C3	Balsorano	63 F2			
Baîse-Darré	37 E1	Bålsta	106 B3			
Baja	114 B1	Balsthal	27 E2			
Baja Sardinia	66 B1	Balta	113 E3			
Bajgora	77 D1	Baltanás	35 F4			
Bajina Bašta	72 C4	Baltar	34 B3			
Bajmok	72 B1	Baltic Sea	110 B2			
Bajram Curri	76 C2	Baltijsk	110 B4			
Bajša	72 B1	Baltinglass	13 D4			
Bajzë	76 B3	Baltrum	47 E3			
Bakar	70 B3	Bambalió	82 C3			
Bakarac	70 B3	Bamberg	52 C4			
Bakewell	6 C3	Bambíni	82 C3			
Bakio	36 B1	Bamburgh	5 E3			
Bakkaflói	96 C1	Bampton	8 C3			
Bakony	112 A4	Banagher	12 C4			
Bakvattnet	101 E1	Banat	114 C1			
Bala	6 B3	Banatska Palanka	73 D2			
Balaguer	37 F3	Banatska Topola	72 C1			
Balanegra	44 B4	Banatski Brestovac	73 D3			
Balaruc	30 A4	Banatski Dvor	72 C2			
Balassagyarmat	112 B3	Banatski Karlovac	73 D2			
Balaton	112 A4	Banatsko Aranđelovo	72 C1			
Balatonfüred	112 B4	Banatsko Karađorđevo	72 C2			
Balatonkeresztúr	112 A4	Banatsko Novo Selo	73 D2			
Balazote	40 C4	Banbridge	13 E2			
Balbigny	26 B4	Banbury	9 E1			
Balbriggan	13 E3	Banchory	3 E4			
Balčik	115 E2	Bande	34 B3			
Balderschwang	55 E4	Bandak	104 B2			
Baldock	9 F2	Bandirma	115 E3			
Baldo, Mte	58 C4	Bandol	30 C4			
Bale	70 A4	Bandon	14 B4			
Baleal	38 A3	Bandon R	14 B4			
Baleizão	42 B1	Bañeres	45 E1			
Balerma	44 B4	Banff	3 E3			
Balestrand	100 A3	Bangor (IRL)	12 B2			
Bali	91 D3	Bangor (N Ire)	13 E2			
Balikesir	115 E4	Bangor (Wales)	6 A2			
Bälinge	106 B3	Bangsund	97 D4			
Balingen	55 D3	Banie	49 E3			
Balivanich	2 A3	Banja (Srbija)	73 D3			
Ballachulish	2 C4	Banja (Srbija)	76 B1			
Ballaghaderreen	12 C3	Banja Koviljača	72 B3			
Ballangen	94 B3	Banja Luka	71 E3			
Ballantrae	4 B3	Banjani	72 C3			
Ballao	66 B3	Banja Vrućica	71 F3			
Ballater	3 D4	Banjska	76 C1			
Ballaugh	6 A1	Bankeryd	109 D1			
Ballenstedt	52 C2	Bann (N Ire)	13 D1			
Balleroy	18 C3	Bann (Wexford)	15 D3			
Ballerup	108 C3	Bannalec	22 B3			
Ballina	12 B2	Banon	30 C3			
Ballinamore	12 C3	Bañón	41 D2			
Ballinasloe	12 C3	Baños de Cerrato	35 F4			
Ballingarry	14 C3	Baños de la Encina	44 A2			
Ballinrobe	12 B3	Baños de la Fuensanta	44 C2			
Ballintober	12 B3	Baños de Molgas	34 B3			
Ballobar	37 E4	Baños de Montemayor	39 E2			
Ballon	23 F3	Baños de Fuensanta	35 E1			
Ballon d'Alsace	27 E1	Banova Jaruga	71 D2			
Ballstad	97 E1	Banovići	71 F4			
Ballybay	13 D2	Banque de Fraiture	51 D4			
Ballybofey	12 C1	Banque Michel	51 D4			
Ballybunnion	12 A4	Bansin	49 E2			
Ballycastle	18 B2	Banská-Bystrica	112 B3			
Ballycastle	13 E1	Banská-Štiavnica	112 B3			
Ballyclare	13 E2	Bansko	77 F3			
Ballyconnell	12 C2	Bantry	14 B4			
Ballycotton	14 C4	Bantry B	14 A4			
Ballycroy	12 B2	Bañuela	43 F1			
Ballyduff	14 B3	Banyalbufar	45 E2			
Ballyforan	12 C3	Banyoles	32 B3			
Ballygawley	13 D2	Banyuls	32 C3			
Ballyhaunis	12 B3	Bao, Emb de	34 C3			
Ballyheige	14 A3	Bapaume	19 F2			
Ballyjamesduff	13 D3	Bar (SU)	113 D3			
Ballymahon	12 C3	Bar (YU)	76 B3			
Ballymena	13 E2	Baracaldo	36 B1			
Ballymoe	12 C3	Baraći	71 E4			
Ballymoney	13 E1	Baradla	112 B3			
Ballymore	12 C3					
Ballymote	12 C2					
Ballynahinch	13 E2					
Ballysadare	12 C2					
Ballyshannon	12 C2					
Ballyvaughan	12 B4					
Balmaseda	36 A1					
Balme	31 E1					
Balmoral Castle	3 D4					

Barahona	36 B4	Bare	76 B1	Barre-des-Cévennes	29 F3	Bassano del Grappa	59 D4	Baux, les 30 B3
Barajas	40 B2	Barèges	37 E2	Barreiro	38 A4	Bassée, la	19 F1	Bavanište 73 D2
Barajas de Melo	40 B3	Barentin	19 D3	Barrême	31 D3	Bassella	37 F3	Bavay 20 B1
Barajevo	73 D3	Barenton	18 C4	Barrhead	4 C2	Bassens	28 B2	Bavella, Col de 33 F4
Baralla	34 C2	Bares, Estaca de	34 B1	Barrhill	4 C3	Bassum	17 F1	Båven 106 B4
Barane	76 C2	Barfleur	18 B2	Barri	9 D2	Båstad	108 C3	Baveno 58 A4
Baranoviči	111 D4	Barfleur, Pte de	18 B2	Barrow-in-Furness	6 B1	Bastasi	71 D4	Bawtry 7 D2
Baraqueville	29 E3	Bargas	40 A3	Barrow, R	15 D3	Bastelica	33 F3	Bayard, Col 31 D2
Barasona, Emb de	37 E3	Bargoed	9 D2	Barruecopardo	39 D1	Bas'tevarri	95 D3	Bayerisch Eisenstein 56 C1
Barbadillo del Mercado	36 A3	Bargteheide	48 B2	Barruelo de Santullán	35 F2	Bastia	33 F2	Bayerischer Wald 56 B2
Barban	70 A3	Bari	65 D3	Barry	9 D2	Bastide-de-Sérou, la	37 F2	Bayern 55 F2
Barbarano Vicentino	61 D1	Barić Draga	70 C4	Barsinghausen	52 A1	Bastogne	20 C2	Bayeux 18 C3
Barbarušince	77 E2	Barisciano	63 F2	Bar-sur-Aube	26 B1	Bastunäsfjället	97 E4	Bayhirivagh 2 A4
Barbastro	37 E3	Barjac	30 B3	Bar-sur-Seine	26 B1	Bastuträsk	98 B4	Bayındır 115 F4
Barbat	70 B4	Barjols	31 D4	Barth	49 D1	Bataille, Col de la	30 C2	Bayon 21 D4
Barbate de Franco	43 D4	Barlby	7 D2	Barthe-de-Neste, la	37 E1	Batajnica	72 C3	Bayonne 28 A4
Barbate, Emb de	43 D4	Bar, le	31 E3	Barton-upon-Humber	7 D2	Batak	115 D3	Bayreuth 52 C4
Barbazan	37 F2	Bar-le-Duc	20 C4	Baruth	53 E1	Batalha	38 B3	Bayrischzell 56 B4
Barberino di Mugello	60 C3	Barletta	65 D3	Barvas	2 B2	Batea	41 F1	Baza 44 B3
Barbezieux	28 B1	Barlinek	49 F3	Barycz	112 A2	Bath	9 D2	Bazas 28 B3
Barbizon	19 F4	Barlovento	42 A4	Barzio	58 B4	Bathgate	5 D2	Baza, Sa de 44 B3
Barbotan	28 B3	Barmouth	6 A3	Bàscara	32 B3	Bâtie-Neuve, la	31 D2	Bazoches-sur-Hoëne 19 D4
Barby	52 C1	Barmstedt	48 A2	Baschi	63 E1	Batina	72 B1	Bazzano 60 C2
Barca de Alva	39 D1	Barna	12 B3	Basconcillos del Tozo	35 F2	Batlava	77 D1	Beachy Head 10 C3
Barca, Emb de la	35 D1	Barnard Castle	5 E4	Basel	27 E2	Batočina	73 D3	Beaconsfield 9 F2
Barcarrota	42 C1	Bärnau	53 D4	Baselga di Pinè	59 D3	Batsi	88 B1	Béal an Átha 12 B2
Barcellona Pozzo di Gotto	69 D2	Barneveld	16 C3	Bas-en-Basset	30 B1	Battaglia Terme	61 D1	Béal Átha na Sluaighe 12 C3
Barcelona	32 B4	Barneville	18 B3	Basento	65 D4	Battenberg	17 F4	Beaminster 9 D3
Barcelonnette	31 D2	Barnsley	7 D2	Basildon	11 D2	Battice	51 D3	Beanntraí 14 B4
Barcelos	34 A4	Barnstaple	8 C3	Basilicata	65 D4	Battipaglia	64 B4	Beara 14 A4
Barcena, Emb de	34 C2	Barnstorf	17 F1	Basingstoke	9 E3	Battle	11 D3	Beariz 34 B2
Barchfeld	52 B3	Barntrup	52 A1	Baška	70 B3	Batz (Finistère)	22 B2	Beas 42 C2
Barcis	59 E3	Barovo	77 E3	Baška Voda	75 E2	Batz (Loire-Atlantique)	24 A2	Beasain 36 C1
Barcones	36 B4	Barquinha	38 B2	Baške Oštarije	70 C4	Baud	22 C3	Beas de Segura 44 B2
Barcs	114 A1	Barr	21 E4	Baslow	6 C3	Baugé	23 E4	Beattock 5 D3
Bardal	101 D1	Barra	2 A4	Basovizza	59 F4	Baugy	26 A2	Beaucaire 30 B3
Bardejov	112 B3	Barracas	41 E3	Bas-Rhin	21 E4	Baule, la	24 A2	Beaufort (Jura) 26 C3
Bardi	60 B2	Barrachina	41 D2			Baumholder	54 B1	Beaufort (Savoie) 27 E4
Bardineto	31 F3	Barraco	39 F2			Bauska	110 C3	Beaufort-en-Vallée 23 E4
Bardolino	60 C1	Barrafranca	68 C4			Bautzen	53 F2	Beaugency 25 E2
Bardonecchia	31 D1	Barra Head	2 A4					Beaujeu 26 C4
Bardu	94 B3	Barranco Velho	42 B2					Beaulieu (Alpes-Maritime) 31 E3
Bardufoss	94 B3	Barranda	44 C2					
		Barra, Sd of	2 A4					
		Barrax	40 C4					
		Barrea	64 A2					

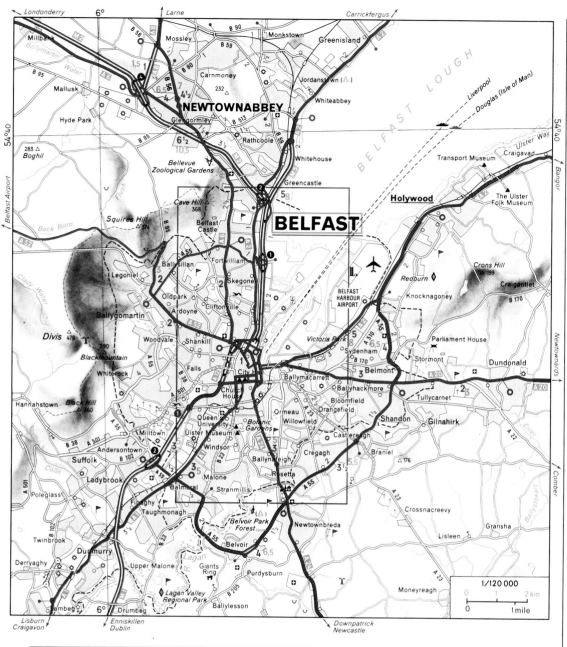

1/120 000

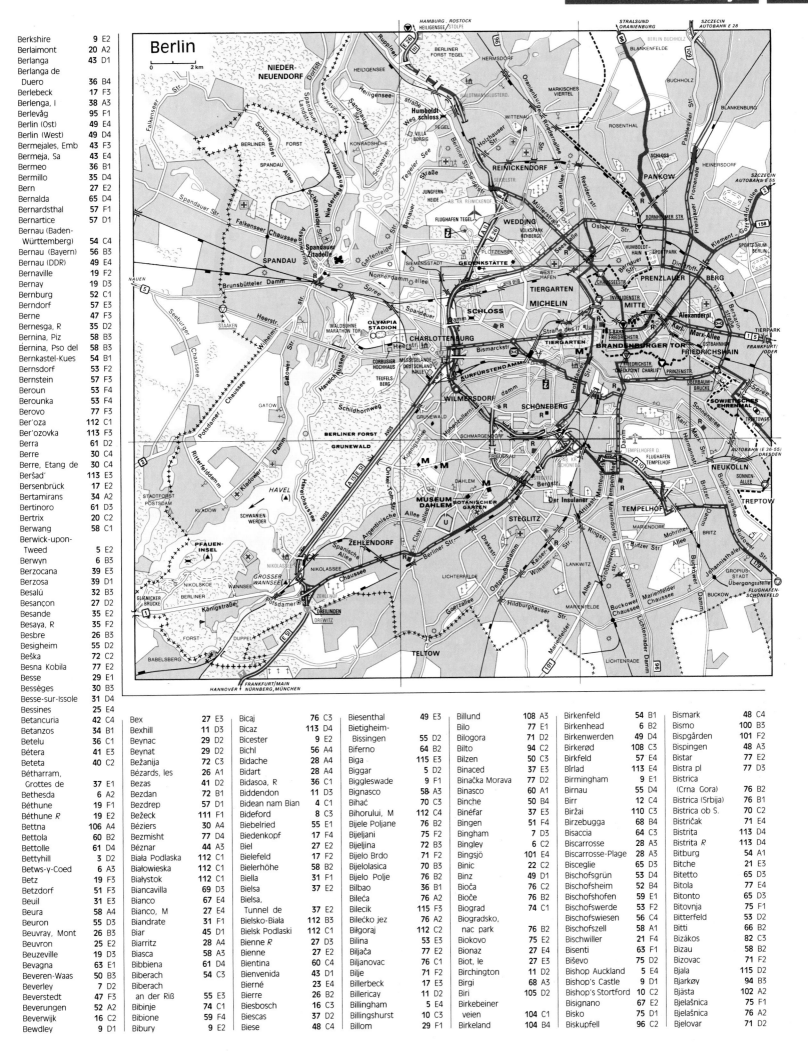

Berlin

0   2 km

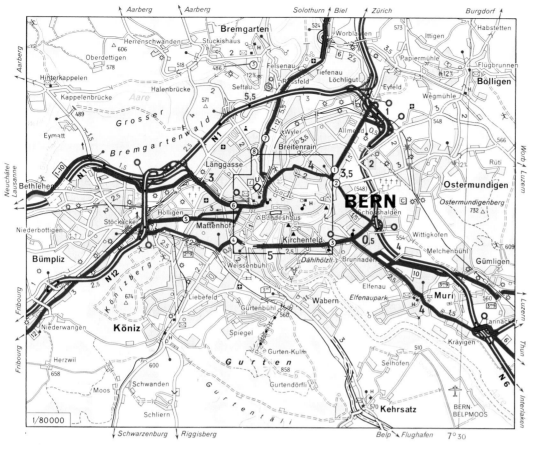

Map of Bern region. Scale 1/80000. 7°30

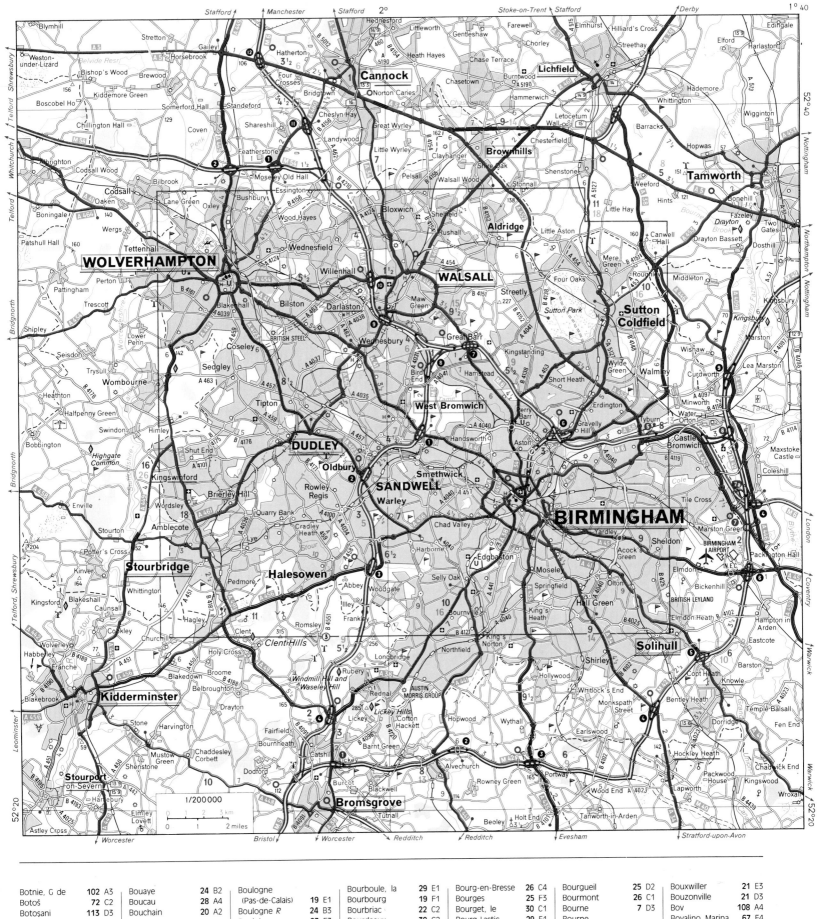

Bologna

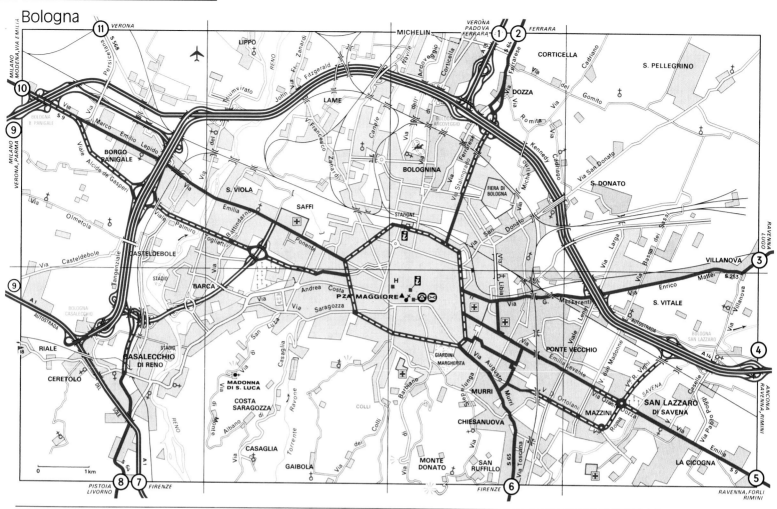

Bonn

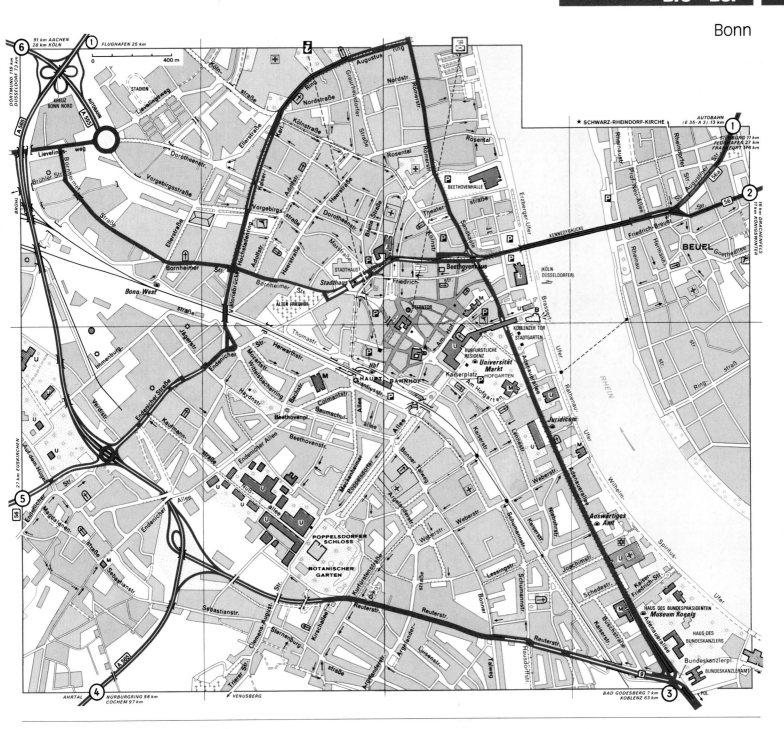

Bordeaux

Brugge

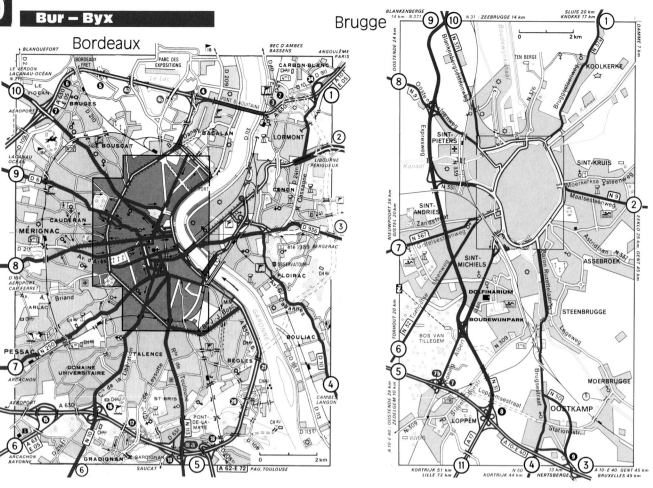

BUDAPEST

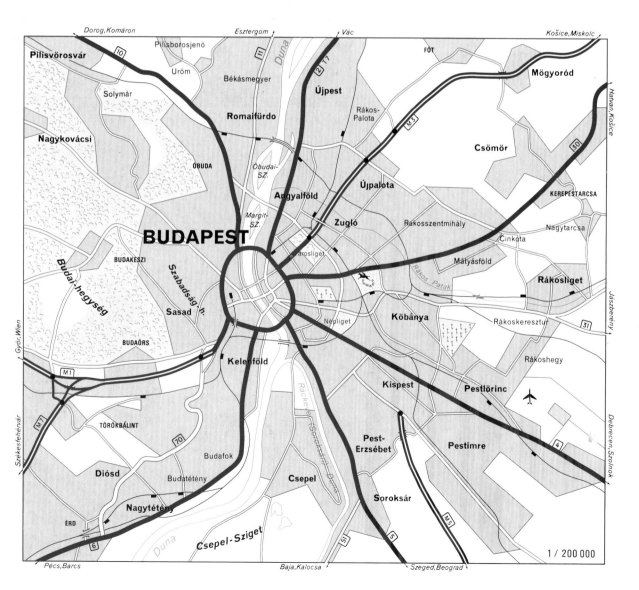

1 / 200 000

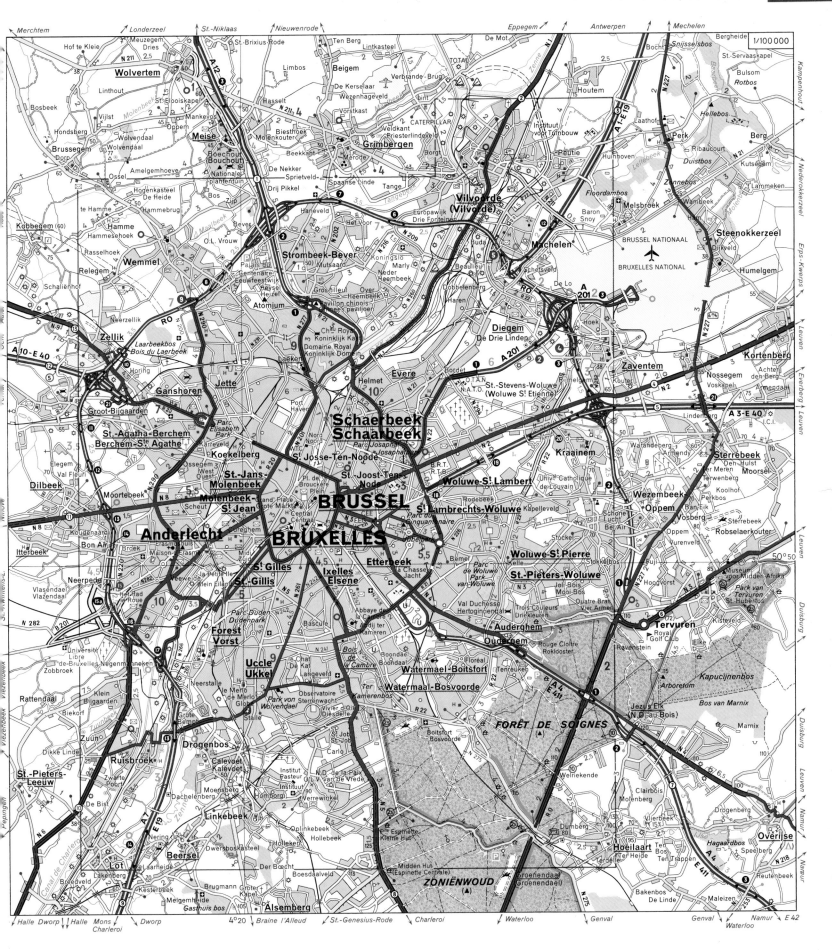

C

Cabañaquinta 35 D2
Cabañas 44 B2
Cabanes 41 F3
Cabannes, les 32 A2
Čabar 70 B3
Cabeceiras 34 B4
Cabeço de Vide 38 C3
Cabella Ligure 60 A2
Cabeza del Buey 39 E4
Cabezas Rubias 42 C2
Cabezo Gordo 42 C2
Cabezón 35 E4
Cabezón de la Sal 35 F2
Cabezuela del Valle 39 E2
Cabo de Gata 44 C4
Cabourg 18 C3
Cabra 43 F2
Cabra del Santo Cristo 44 A2
Cabras 66 A3
Cabre, Col de 30 C2
Cabreira, Sa da 34 B4
Cabreiros 34 B1
Cabrejas, Pto de 40 C3
Cabrejas, Sa de 36 A3
Cabréra 36 C4
Cabrera, I de 45 F3
Cabrera, Sa de la 34 C3
Cabrerets 29 D3
Cabriel, R 41 D3
Cabril, Bgem do 38 B2
Cabrillas 39 E1
Cabrito, Pto del 43 D4
Cabuérniga 35 F2
Čabulja 75 E1
Cacabelos 34 C2
Čačak 73 D4
Caccamo 68 B3
Cacela 42 B3
Cáceres 39 D3
Cachafeiro 34 A2
Cachopo 42 B2
Čačinci 71 E2
Cadabo 34 C2
Cadalso de los Vidrios 40 A2
Cadaqués 32 C3
Cadarache 30 C3
Cadaval 38 A3
Čađavica 71 E4
Čadca 112 B3
Cadelbosco di Sopra 60 C2
Cadenabbia 58 B4
Cadena, Pto de la 45 D2
Cadenberge 47 F2
Cadenet 30 C3
Cader Idris 6 A3
Cádiar 44 A3
Cadillac 28 B2
Cadipietra 59 D2
Cadi, Serra del 32 A3
Cádiz 43 D4
Cádiz, B de 43 D4
Cádiz, G de 42 C3
Cadouin 28 C2
Čadyr-Lunga 113 E4
Caen 18 C3
Caerdydd 9 D2
Caerfyrddin 8 C2
Caergybi 6 A2
Caernarfon 6 A3
Caernarfon B 6 A3
Caerphilly 9 D2
Caersws 9 D1
Cafasan 77 D4
Cagli 61 E4
Cagliari 66 B4
Cagliari, G di 66 B4
Čaglin 71 E2
Cagnano Varano 64 C2
Cagnes 31 E3
Caha Mts 14 A4
Caher 14 C3
Cahersiveen 14 A4
Cahore Pt 15 E3
Cahors 29 D3
Caia, Bgem do 38 C4
Caianello 64 A3
Caión 34 A1
Cairn Gorm 3 D4
Cairngorm Mts 3 D4
Cairnryan 4 B3
Cairo Montenotte 31 F2
Caiseal 14 C3
Caisleán an Bharraigh 12 B3
Caistor 7 D2
Caivano 64 B4
Cajarc 29 D3
Čajetina 72 C4
Čajniče 76 B1
Čakor 76 C2
Čakovec 70 C1
Čakovice 53 F3
Çal 115 F4
Calabor 34 C3
Calabria 67 E2
Calaceite 41 F1
Calacuccia 33 F3
Cala d'Or 45 F3
Cala, Emb de la 43 D2
Calaf 37 F3
Calafat 114 C2
Calafell 37 F4
Calafort Ros Láir 15 D4
Cala Gonone 66 C2
Calahonda 44 A4
Calahorra 36 C2
Calais 19 E1
Calamocha 41 D1
Calañas 42 C2
Calanche, les 33 E3
Calanda 41 E1
Calanda, Emb de 41 E2
Calangianus 66 B1
Cala'n Porter 45 F2
Calar Alto 44 B3
Călărași 115 E1
Cala Ratjada 45 F2
Calasetta 66 A4
Calasparra 44 C2
Calatafimi 68 B3
Calatañazor 36 B3
Calatayud 36 C4
Calatorao 36 C4
Calau 53 E1
Calazzo 64 B3
Calbe 52 C1
Calcena 36 C3
Caldaro 59 D3
Caldarola 61 F4
Caldas da Rainha 38 A3
Caldas das Taipas 34 A4
Caldas de Reis 34 A2
Caldas de Vizela 34 A4
Caldeirão, Sa do 42 B2
Caldelas 34 A3
Caldera de Taburiente, Pque Nac de la 42 A4
Calderina 40 A4
Caldes de Boí 37 F2
Caldes de Malavella 32 B3
Caldes de Montbui 32 A4
Caldirola 60 A2
Caledonian Canal 2 C4
Calella (Palamós) 32 C3
Calella (Pinedo de Mar) 32 B4
Calenzana 33 F3
Calera de León 43 D1
Calera y Chozas 39 F3
Caleruega 36 A3
Caletta, la 66 C2
Càlig 41 F2
Călimănești 115 D1
Călimani, M 113 D4
Calitri 64 C3
Calizzano 31 F3
Callac 22 B3
Callan 15 D3
Callander 4 C1
Calla, Pso della 61 D3
Callington 8 C4
Callosa de Ensarria 45 E1
Callosa de Segura 45 D2
Calmazzo 61 E3
Calmbach 54 C2
Calne 9 E2
Calolziocorte 58 B4
Calonge 32 B3
Calpe 45 E1
Caltabellotta 68 B3
Caltagirone 69 D4
Caltanissetta 68 C3
Caltavuturo 68 C3
Caluso 31 E1
Calvados 18 C3
Calvi 33 E3
Calvitero 39 E2
Calvörde 48 C4
Calw 54 C2
Calzada de Calatrava 44 A1
Calzada de Valdunciel 39 E1
Cam 9 F1
Camacho, Pto 44 A3
Camaiore 60 C3
Camaldoli 61 D3
Camaleño 35 E2
Camarasa 37 F3
Camarasa, Emb de 37 F3
Camarat, Cap 31 D4
Camarena 40 A2
Camarès 32 B1
Camaret 22 A3
Camarillas 41 E2
Camarillas, Emb de 44 C1
Camariñas 34 A1
Camarzana 35 D3
Camas 43 D2
Cambados 34 A2
Cambas 38 C2
Camberley 9 F2
Cambil 44 A2
Cambo-les-Bains 28 A4
Camborne 8 B4
Cambrai 20 A2
Cambre 34 B1
Cambremer 19 D3
Cambrian Mts 8 C1
Cambridge 10 C1
Cambridgeshire 10 C1
Cambrils de Mar 37 F4
Camburg 52 C3
Camelford 8 B3
Camerino 61 E4
Camigliatello Silano 67 E2
Caminha 34 A3
Caminomorisco 39 D2
Caminreal 41 D2
Camogli 60 A3
Campagna 64 C4
Campagne-lès-Hesdin 19 E2
Campan 37 E1
Campana 67 F2
Campanario 39 E4
Campania 64 B4
Campaspero 35 F4
Campbeltown 4 B3
Campello 45 E1
Campi Bisenzio 60 C3
Campiglia Marittima 62 C1
Campilhas, Bgem de 42 A1
Campillo de Altobuey 41 D3
Campillo de Aragón 36 C4
Campillo de Arenas 44 A2
Campillo de Llerena 43 D1
Campillos 43 E3
Campione 58 A4
Campi Salentina 65 F4
Campitello M 64 B3
Campli 63 F1
Campo 37 E2
Campobasso 64 B3
Campobello di Licata 68 C4
Campobello di Mazara 68 A3
Campo Carlo Magno 58 C3
Campo de Beisteros 38 B1
Campo de Caso 35 E2
Campo de Criptana 40 B4
Campo di Fiori 58 A4
Campo di Giove 64 A2
Campodonico 61 E4
Campoformido 59 F3
Campogalliano 60 C2
Campo Imperatore 63 F1
Campo Ligure 60 A3
Campo Maior 38 C4
Campomanes 35 D2
Campomarino 64 B2
Campora San Giovanni 67 E3
Camporredondo, Emb de 35 E2
Camporrobles 41 D3
Campos 45 F3
Camposampiero 59 D4
Campos, Canal de 35 E4
Campotosto, L di 63 F1
Campo Tures 59 D2
Camprodon 32 B3
Camucia 61 D4
Camuñas 40 B3
Cañada de Benatanduz 41 E2
Cañadas, Pto 43 D1
Çanakkale 115 E3
Çanakkale Boğazı 115 E3
Canal du Nord 19 F2
Canal du Rhône au Rhin 27 E2
Canales de la Sierra 36 A3
Canals 41 E4
Canal San Bovo 59 D3
Cañamero 39 E3
Canarias, Is 42 B4
Canas de Senhorim 38 C1
Cañaveral 39 D3
Cañaveral de León 43 D2
Cañaveras 40 C2
Canazei 59 D3
Cancale 18 B4
Cancárix 45 D1
Canche 19 E1
Cancon 28 C2
Candanchu 37 D2
Candas 35 D1
Candasnos 37 E4
Candé 23 E4
Candeeiros, Sa dos 38 A3
Candela 64 C3
Candelaria, Sa 39 E2
Candelario 39 E2
Candelaro 64 C2
Candeleda 39 F2
Candes 25 D2
Canelles, Emb de 37 F3
Canelli 31 F2
Canero 35 D1
Canet de Mar 32 B4
Cañete 41 D3
Cañete de las Torres 43 F2
Cañete la Real 43 E3
Canet-Plage 32 B2
Canfranc-Estación 37 D2
Cangas 34 A3
Cangas de Narcea 34 C2
Cangas de Onís 35 E1
Canha 38 B4
Canicatti 68 C4
Canicattini Bagni 69 D4
Canigou, Pic du 32 B2
Cañigral 41 D3
Caniles 44 B3
Canin, M 59 F3
Canino 63 D2
Canis 18 B3
Cañizál 39 E1
Canjáyar 44 B3
Canna 2 B4
Cannero Riviera 58 A4
Cannes 31 E4
Canneto 60 C4
Cannich 2 C3
Cannobio 58 A4
Cannock 9 E1
Canonbie 5 D3
Canosa di Puglia 64 C3
Canourgue, la 29 F3
Cansano 64 A2
Cansiglio 59 E3
Cantabria 35 F2
Cantal (Dépt) 29 E2
Cantal, Mts du 29 E2
Cantalapiedra 39 F1
Cantalejo 40 A1
Cantalpino 39 E1
Cantanhede 38 B2
Cantavieja 41 E2
Čantavir 72 B1
Canterbury 11 D3
Cantillana 43 D2
Cantoira 31 E1
Cantoral 35 E2
Cantoria 44 C3
Cantù 60 A1
Canvey I 11 D2
Cany-Barville 19 D2
Caorle 59 E4
Caorso 60 B2
Capaccio 64 C4
Capaci 68 B3
Capalbio 63 D2
Capannelle, Pso delle 63 F1
Caparde 72 B4
Caparroso 36 C2
Capbreton 28 A4
Cap Corse 33 F2
Cap-d'Agde, le 30 A4
Cap d'Antibes 31 E4
Capdenac-Gare 29 E2
Capel Curig 6 A3
Capelle, la 20 B2
Capendu 32 B2
Capestang 30 A4
Capestrano 64 A2
Capileira 44 A3
Capistrello 63 F2
Čapljina 75 F2
Capmany 32 B3
Cappelle sul Tavo 64 A1
Cappoquin 14 C4
Capracotta 64 A2
Capraia, I di 62 B1
Caprera, I 66 B1
Capri 64 B4
Capriati a Volturno 64 A3
Capri, I di 64 B4
Captieux 28 B3
Capua 64 B3
Capurso 65 D3
Capvern 37 E1
Caracal 115 D2
Caracuel 40 A4
Caragh, L 14 A4
Caraman 29 D4
Caramanico Terme 64 A2
Caramulo 38 B1
Caramulo, Sa do 38 B1
Caransebeș 114 C1
Carantec 22 B2
Caravaca de la Cruz 44 C2
Caravai, Pso di 66 B3
Caravius, M. is 66 B4
Carbajales de Alba 35 D4
Carballiño 34 B2
Carballo 34 A1
Carbayo 35 D2
Carbonara, C 66 C4
Carbonara, Pzo 68 C3
Carbon-Blanc 28 B2
Carboneras 44 C3
Carboneras de Guadazaón 41 D3
Carbonero el Mayor 40 A1
Carbonia 66 B4
Carbonin 59 E2
Carbonne 37 F1
Carcaboso 39 D2
Carcabuey 43 F3
Carcaixent 41 E4
Carcans 28 A2
Carcans-Plage 28 A2
Carcare 31 F2
Carcassonne 32 B1
Carcastillo 36 C2
Carcès 31 D4
Carche 45 D1
Čardak 71 F4
Çardak 115 F4
Cardedeu 32 B4
Cardeña 43 F1
Cardener, R 32 A4
Cardenete 41 D3
Cardiff 9 D2
Cardigan 8 B1
Cardigan B 8 B1
Cardona 32 A3
Carei 112 C3
Carentan 18 B3
Cares, R 35 E2
Carevdar 71 D2
Carev Dvor 77 D4
Cargèse 33 E3
Carhaix-Plouguer 22 B3
Caria 38 C2
Cariati 67 F2
Caričin Grad 77 D1
Carignan 20 C2
Carignano 31 E2
Carina 77 D4
Cariñena 36 C4
Carini 68 B3
Cariño 34 B1
Carinola 64 A3
Carisio 31 F1
Carlet 41 E4
Carling 21 D3
Carlingford 13 E3
Carlingford L 13 E3
Carlisle 5 D3
Carlit, Pic 32 A2
Carloforte 66 A4
Carlow 13 D4
Carlow (Co) 13 D4
Carloway 2 B2
Carluke 4 C2
Carmagnola 31 E2
Carmarthen 8 C2
Carmarthen B 8 B2
Carmaux 29 E3
Carmona 43 E2
Carna 12 A3
Carnac 22 C4
Carnaio, Pso del 61 D3
Carn Ban 2 C4
Carndonagh 13 D1
Carnedd Llewelyn 6 A3
Carn Eige 2 C3
Carneros, Pto de los 39 F4
Carnew 15 D3
Carnforth 6 B1
Carnia 59 F3
Carnia (Reg) 59 E3
Carnlough 13 E1
Carnon 30 B4
Carnota 34 A2
Carnoustie 5 D1
Carnsore Pt 15 D4
Carnwath 5 D2
Caroch 41 D4
Carolles 18 B4
Carovigno 65 E3
Carpaneto Piacentino 60 B2
Carpații Meridionali 114 C1
Carpenedolo 60 B1
Carpentras 30 C3
Carpi 60 C2
Carpignano Sesia 58 A4
Carpineti 60 C3
Carpineto Romano 63 F3
Carpinone 64 A3
Carquefou 24 B2
Carqueiranne 31 D4
Carracedelo 34 C2
Carradale 4 B2
Carraig na Siúire 14 C3
Carral 34 B1
Carrantuohill 14 A4
Carranza 36 A1
Carrara 60 B3
Carrascal 41 E2
Carrascosa del Campo 40 C3
Carrascoy 45 D2
Carrasqueta, Pto de la 45 E1
Carrazeda de Ansiães 34 B4
Carrazedo de Montenegro 34 B4
Carrbridge 3 D4
Carregado 38 A3
Carregal do Sal 38 B2
Carreña de Cabrales 35 E1
Carrickfergus 13 E2
Carrickmacross 13 D3
Carrick-on-Shannon 12 C3
Carrick-on-Suir 14 C3
Carrigart 12 C1
Carrio 34 B1
Carrión de Calatrava 40 A4
Carrión de los Condes 35 E3
Carrión, R 35 E3
Carrizo de la Ribera 35 D2
Carro 30 C4
Carrouges 18 C4
Carrù 31 F2
Carry-le-Rouet 30 C4
Carsoli 63 F2
Cartagena 45 D3
Cártama 43 F4
Cartaxo 38 A3
Cartaya 42 C2
Carter Bar 5 D3
Carteret 18 B3
Carvajal 43 F4
Carviçais 39 D1
Carvin 19 F1
Carvoeira 42 A3
Carvoeiro, C 38 A3
Casabermeja 43 F3
Casa Branca (Alentejo) 42 A1
Casa Branca (Ribatejo) 38 B4
Casacalenda 64 B2
Casalárreina 36 B2
Casalbordino 64 B2
Casalbuttano 60 B1
Casal di Principe 64 A4
Casalecchio di Reno 60 C2
Casale Monferrato 31 F1
Casale sul Sile 59 E4
Casalmaggiore 60 B2
Casalpusterlengo 60 B2
Casamassima 65 D3
Casamicciola Terme 64 A4
Casa Nuevas 44 C2
Casarabonela 43 E3
Casarano 65 F4
Casar de Cáceres 39 D3
Casares 43 E4
Casares de las Hurdes 39 D2
Casariche 43 E3
Casarsa 59 E3
Casas de Don Pedro 39 E4
Casas de Fernando Alonso 40 C4
Casas de Juan Núñez 41 D4
Casas del Puerto 45 D1
Casas de Luján 40 B3
Casas de Miravete 39 E3
Casas Ibáñez 41 D4
Casasimarro 40 C4
Casatejada 39 E3
Casavieja 39 F2
Cascais 38 A4
Cascante 36 C3
Cascia 63 E1
Casciana Terme 60 C4
Cascina 60 C4
Casei Gerola 60 A2
Caselle in Pittari 67 D1
Caselle Torinese 31 E1
Caserio del Puente 35 D3
Caserta 64 B3

D

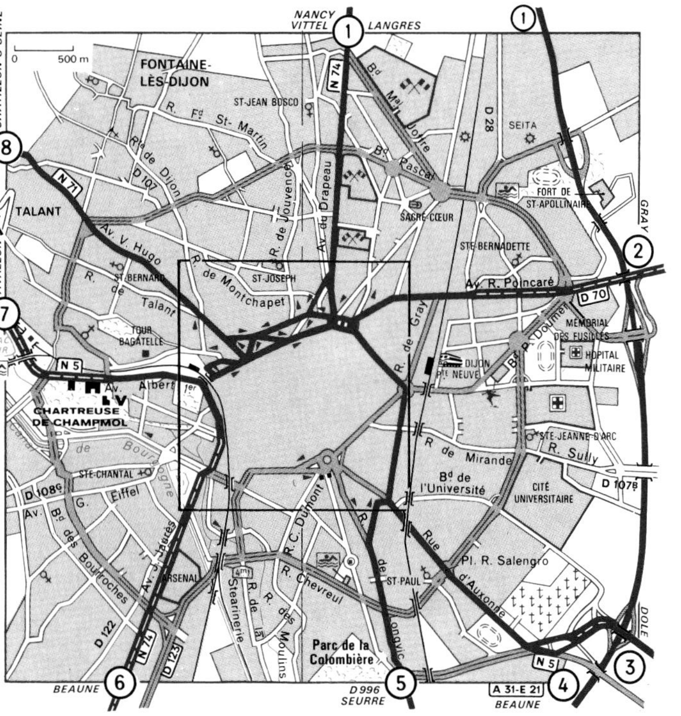
NANCY
VITTEL
LANGRES
TROYES
CHÂTILLON-S-SEINE
500 m
FONTAINE-LÈS-DIJON
TALANT
A 38 : MOULINS
AVALLON
GRAY
DOLE
BEAUNE
D 996
SEURRE
A 31-E 21
BEAUNE
SAINT-JOSEPH
SACRÉ-CŒUR
STE-BERNADETTE
FORT DE ST-APOLLINAIRE
TOUR BAGATELLE
CHARTREUSE DE CHAMPMOL
MÉMORIAL DES FUSILLÉS
HÔPITAL MILITAIRE
DIJON VILLE
STE-JEANNE D'ARC
CITÉ UNIVERSITAIRE
STE-CHANTAL
ST-PAUL
ARSENAL
Parc de la Colombière
Bd de l'Université
Pl. R. Salengro
Av. R. Poincaré
N 5
N 71
N 74
D 70
D 107
D 122
D 108
D 28

Dijon

Desborough 9 F1
Descartes 25 D3
Desenzano 60 B1
Desertas 42 A3
Desfiladero de Despeñaperros 44 A1
Desfiladero de la Hermida 35 F2
Desfiladero de los Beyos 35 E2
Desfiladero del Teverga 35 D2
Desfina 83 E4
Desimirovac 73 D4
Desio 60 A1
Deskáti 83 D1
Desna 111 F3
Despotikó, N 88 B3
Despotovac 73 E3
Despotovo 72 B2
Dessau 53 D1
Destriana 35 D3
Desulo 66 B3
Desvres 19 E1
Deta 114 C1
Đetinja 72 C4
Detmold 52 A1
Dettelbach 55 E1
Dettifoss 96 C1
Deurne 17 D3
Deutsche Alpenstraße 55 E4
Deutsche Bucht 47 E2
Deutschkreutz 57 F3
Deutschlandsberg 70 B1
Deutsch-Wagram 57 F2
Deux-Alpes, les 31 D2
Deux-Sèvres 24 C3
Deva 114 C1
Deve Bair 77 E2
Deventer 17 D2
Deveron 3 E3
Devetak 72 B4
Devil's Bridge 8 C1
Devil's Elbow 3 D4
Devizes 9 E2
Devnja 115 E2
Dewsbury 6 C2
Deza 36 C4
Diablerets, les 27 E3
Diablerets, les *Mt* 27 E3
Diafáni 93 D2
Diakoftó 86 C1
Diamante 67 E2
Día, N 91 E3
Diano Marina 31 F3
Diápora Nissiá 87 E1
Diavatá 79 F3
Díavlos Alonissou 84 B2
Díavlos Oreón 83 F3
Díavlos Pelagonissou 84 B2
Díavlos Skiáthou 84 A2
Díavlos Skopélou 84 A2
Díavlos Trikeriou 83 F3
Díavlos Zákinthou 86 A1
Diavolítsi 86 C3
Diavolo, Pso del 64 A2
Diavolórema 81 E2
Dibbersen 48 A3
Dicmo 75 D1
Dicomano 61 D3
Dídima 87 E2
Dídimo, Óros 87 E2
Didimótiho 81 F1
Die 30 C2
Dieburg 52 A4
Diedorf 52 B2
Diego Alvaro 39 E2
Diekirch 21 D2
Diemel 52 A2
Diemelstadt 52 A2
Diepholz 17 F2
Dieppe 19 E2
Dierdorf 51 E4
Dieren 17 D3
Diesdorf 48 B4
Dießen 56 A3
Diest 50 C3
Dietenheim 55 E3
Dietfurt 55 F2
Dietikon 27 F2
Dietmannsried 55 E4
Dieulefit 30 C2
Dieulouard 21 D4
Dieuze 21 D4
Diez 51 F4
Diezma 44 A3
Differdange 21 D3
Digerkampen 100 B3
Digermulen 94 A4
Dignano 59 E3
Digne 31 D3
Digoin 26 B3
Dijle 50 C3
Dijon 26 C2
Dikanäs 97 F3
Díkea 81 F1
Díkela 81 E2
Diksmuide 50 A3
Diktéo Ándro 91 E4
Diktinéon 90 B3
Dikti, Óros 91 E4
Dilessi 84 B4
Dilináta 82 B4
Dilj 71 E2
Dillenburg 51 F3
Dillingen (Bayern) 55 E2
Dillingen (Saarland) 54 A2
Dílofos 81 F1
Dílos 88 C2
Dílos, N 88 C2
Dímena 87 E2
Dimitra 83 E1
Dimitritsi 80 B2
Dimitrovgrad (BG) 115 D3
Dimitrovgrad (YU) 77 F1
Dimitsána 86 C2
Dinami 67 E4
Dinan 18 B4
Dinant 50 C4
Dinar 115 F4
Dinara *Mt* 75 D1
Dinara (Reg) 75 D1
Dinard 18 B4
Dinbych 6 B3
Dinbych-y-pysgod 8 B2
Dingelstädt 52 B2
Dingle 14 A3
Dingle 105 D4
Dingle (Reg) 14 A3
Dingle B 14 A3
Dingli 68 B4
Dinglingen 54 C3
Dingolfing 56 B2
Dingwall 2 C3
Dinjiška 70 C4
Dinkelsbühl 55 E2
Dinklage 17 F2
Dinslaken 17 D3
Dío 79 F4
Diónissos 87 F1
Dióriga Korínthou 87 E1
Dipótama 80 C1
Dippoldiswalde 53 E2
Diráhio 86 C3
Dirfis, Óros 84 B3
Disentis 58 A3
Disgrazia, Mte 58 B3
Dispilio 79 D3
Diss 11 D1
Dissen 17 F2
Distomo 83 E4
Dístos 84 B4
Ditiki Rodópi 80 C1
Dittaino 69 D3
Ditzingen 55 D2
Divača 70 A3
Divaráta 82 B4
Divčibare 72 C4
Dives 18 C3
Dives *R* 18 C3
Divič 72 B4
Divjakë 76 C4
Divljana 77 E1
Divonne 27 D3
Divor, Bgem do 38 B4
Divor, Rib de 38 B4
Divoúnia, Ni 92 C2
Dívri 83 E3
Divuša 71 D3
Djupini 96 A3
Djupvik 94 C2
Djurås 105 F2
Djursland 108 B2
Dmitrov 111 F2
Dnepr 111 E3
Dneprodzeržinskoje Vodochranilišče 113 F2
Dneprovskij Liman 113 F3
Dnestr 112 C3
Dnestrovskij Liman 113 F4
Dno 111 D2
Dobanovci 72 C3
Dobbiaco 59 E2
Dobel 54 C2
Dobele 110 C3
Döbeln 53 E2
Doberlug-Kirchhain 53 E1
Döbern 53 F1
Dobersberg 57 E1
Dobieszczyn 49 E2
Doboj 71 F3
Dobošnica 71 F3
Dobra (PL) 49 F2
Dobra (YU) 73 E3
Dobra *R* 70 C3
Dobra Voda 73 D4
Dobra Voda *Mt* 77 D3
Dobrašinci 77 F3
Dobratsch 59 F2
Dobrčane 77 D2
Döbriach 59 F2
Dobrica 73 D2
Dobričevo 73 D2
Dobri Do 77 D1
Dobrinj 70 B3
Dobříš 53 F4
Dobrljin 71 D3
Dobrna 70 B1
Dobromani 75 F2
Dobro Polje 76 A1
Dobrovnik 70 C1
Dobrun 72 C4
Dobruš 111 E4
Dobruševo 77 E4
Dobrzany 49 F2
Dobšiná 112 B3
Docksta 102 A2
Doc Penfro 8 B2
Dodekánissa 89 E3
Dodóni 82 B1
Doesburg 17 D3
Doetinchem 17 D3
Doganović 77 D2
Dogliani 31 F2
Doïráni 79 F2
Doïránis, L 79 F2
Doiras, Emb de 34 C1
Dojransko Ez 77 F3
Dokanj 72 B3
Dokka 104 C2
Dokkum 47 D3
Dokós, N 87 E3
Doksy 53 F3
Dolac 76 C2
Dol-de-Bretagne 18 B4
Dole 26 C2
Dôle, la 27 D3
Dølemo 104 B4
Dolenci 77 D4
Dolenja Vas 70 B2
Dolenjske Toplice 70 B2
Dolga Vas 71 D1
Dolgellau 6 A3
Doliana 78 C4
Dolianova 66 B4
Dolihi 79 E4
Dolina 112 C3
Doljani 71 D4
Doljevac 77 D1
Dolla 12 C4
Döllach 59 E2
Dollar 5 D2
Dolle 48 C4
Dolní Dvořiště 57 D2
Dolno Kosovrasti 77 D3
Dolo 61 D1
Dolomiti 59 D3
Dolores 45 D2
Dolovo 73 D2
Dol Poustevna 53 F2
Domaševo 75 F2
Domažlice 56 B1
Dombås 100 B3
Dombasle 21 D4
Dombóvár 114 B1
Domburg 16 B3
Domène 30 C1
Doméniko 83 E1
Domèvre-en-Haye 21 D4
Domfront 18 C4
Dömitz 48 C3
Domme 29 D2
Dommitzsch 53 D2
Domnista 83 D3
Domodossola 58 A4
Domokós 83 E2
Dompaire 27 D1
Dompierre 26 B3
Domrémy 20 C4
Domusnovas 66 B4
Domžale 70 B2
Don (England) 7 D2
Don (Scotland) 3 E4
Donaghadee 13 E2
Doña María Ocaña 44 B3
Doña Mencia 43 F2
Doñana, Parque Nac de 43 D3
Donau 56 C2
Donaueschingen 54 C4
Donauwörth 55 E2
Donawitz 57 E4
Don Benito 39 E4
Doncaster 7 D2
Donegal 12 C2
Donegal B 12 C2
Donegal (Co) 12 C1
Dongen 16 C3
Donges 23 D4
Donington 7 E3
Donja Bebrina 71 F3
Donja Brela 75 E2
Donja Brezna 76 B2
Donja Bukovica 76 B2
Donja Kamenica 72 C3
Donja Šatornja 73 D3
Donje Crniljevo 72 C3
Donje Dragovlje 77 E1
Donje Ljupče 77 D2
Donji Andrijevci 71 F3
Donji Barbeš 77 E1
Donji Kanzanci 75 D1
Donji Lapac 71 D4
Donji Malovan 75 E1
Donji Miholjac 71 E2
Donji Milanovac 73 E3
Donji Ruzani 75 D1
Donji Seget 75 D2
Donji Vakuf 71 E4
Donji Vijačani 71 E3
Donji Zemunik 74 C1
Donjon, le 26 B3
Dønna 97 D3
Donnemarie-Dontilly 20 A4
Donnersbachwald 57 D4
Dønnes 97 D2
Donon 21 E4
Donon, Col du 21 E4
Donostia-San Sebastián 36 C1
Donoússa, N 89 D3
Donzenac 29 D2
Donzère 30 B2
Donzy 26 A2
Doorn 16 C3
Doornik 50 A4
Dora Baltéa 27 E4
Dora Riparia 31 E1
Dorat, le 25 D4
Đorče Petrov 77 D3
Dorchester 9 D3
Dordives 25 F1
Dordogne 29 E1
Dordogne (Dépt) 28 C2
Dordogne *R* 28 B2
Dordrecht 16 C3
Dore 29 F1
Dorfen 56 B3
Dorfmark 48 A4
Dorgali 66 C2
Dório 86 C3
Dorkáda 80 A2
Dorking 10 C3
Dormagen 17 E4
Dormans 20 A3
Dornbirn 58 B2
Dornburg 52 C3
Dorndorf 52 B3
Dornes 26 A3
Dornie 2 B3
Dornoch 3 D3
Dornoch Firth 3 D3
Dornstetten 54 C3
Dornum 47 E3
Dorog 112 B4
Dorogobuž 111 E3
Dorohoi 113 D3
Dorotea 101 F1
Dörpstedt 48 A1
Dorset 9 D3
Dorsten 17 E3
Dortan 27 D3
Dortmund 17 E3
Dortmund-Ems-Kanal 17 E2
Dorum 47 F3
Dörzbach 55 D1
Dosbarrios 40 B3
Dos Hermanas 43 D3
Dosse 49 D3
Douai 19 F2
Douarnenez 22 A3
Doubs 26 C3
Doubs (Dépt) 27 D2
Doucier 27 D3
Doudeville 19 D2
Doué 24 C2
Douglas (I of Man) 6 A1
Douglas (Scotland) 4 C2
Doukáto, Akr 82 B3
Doulaincourt 20 C4
Doulevant-le-Château 20 C4
Doullens 19 F2
Doulus Head 14 A4
Doune 4 C2
Doupov 53 E3
Dourdan 19 E4
Dourgne 32 A1
Douro 34 A4
Douro, R 34 A4
Douvaine 27 D3
Douve 18 B3
Douvres 18 C3
Dover 11 D3
Dover, Str of 11 D3
Dovre 100 C3
Dovrefjell 100 C3
Dovsk 111 E4
Down 13 E2
Downham Market 10 C1
Downpatrick 13 E2
Dowra 12 C2
Doxarás 83 E2
Doxáto 80 C2
Dozulé 19 D3
Drac 30 C2
Dračevo 77 E3
Drachten 17 D1
Drag 94 A4
Dragalovci 71 E3
Dragaš 77 D3
Drăgășani 115 D1
Dragaši 76 B1
Draginac 72 C3
Draginje 72 C3
Dragočaj 71 E3
Dragocvet 73 D4
Dragoevo 77 E3
Dragoman 114 C2
Dragonera, I 45 E3
Dragoni 64 B3
Dragør 108 C3
Dragoš 77 E4
Dragotiná 82 A2
Dragović 71 E2
Dragovića Polje 76 B2
Dragozetići 70 B3
Dragsfjärd 107 D3
Dragsvik 100 A3
Draguignan 31 D4
Dráma 80 C2
Dráma (Nomos) 80 C1
Drammen 104 C3
Drammen selva 104 C3
Drangajökull 96 A1
Drangedal 104 C3
Dranske 49 D1
Drápano, Akr 90 C3
Drasenhofen 57 F1
Drau 59 F2
Dráva 71 E2
Dravograd 70 B1
Drawno 49 F2
Drawsko Pomorskie 112 A1
Draženov 56 B1
Draževac 72 C3
Drebkau 53 F1
Drenewydd 9 D1
Drenovac 77 E2
Drenovci 72 B3
Drenovo 77 E3
Drenthe 17 D1
Drépano (Makedonía) 79 E3
Drépano (Pelopónissos) 87 E2
Drépano, Akr (Anáfi) 91 E1
Drépano, Akr (Makedonía) 80 B4
Dresden 53 E2
Dreux 19 E4
Drežnik-Grad 70 C3
Driebergen 16 C3
Driebes 40 B2
Driméa 83 E3
Drimós 79 F3
Drin 76 C3
Drina 76 A1
Drini i Zi 77 D3
Drinit, Gjiri i 76 B3
Drinjača 72 B4
Drinjača *R* 72 B4
Drinovci 75 E2
Driopída 88 A2
Driós 88 C3
Drisht 76 C3
Driva 100 B2
Drlače 72 C4
Drnholec 57 F1
Drniš 75 D1
Drnje 71 D1
Drnovo 70 C2
Drøbak 105 D3
Drobeta-Turnu Severin 114 C1
Drochtersen 48 A2
Drogheda 13 D3
Drogobyč 112 C3
Droichead Átha 13 D3
Droichead Nua 13 D4
Droitwich 9 E1
Drokija 113 E3
Dromcolliher 14 B3
Drôme (Dépt) 30 C2
Drôme *R* 30 C2
Dromore (Down) 13 E2
Dromore (Tyrone) 13 D2
Dronero 31 E2
Dronfield 7 D2
Drongaráti 82 B4
Dronne 28 C1
Dronninglund 108 B2
Dronten 16 C2
Drosendorf Stadt 57 E1
Drossáto 79 F2
Drosseró 79 E2
Drossiá 84 A4
Drossohóri 83 E4
Drossopigí (Árta) 82 C2
Drossopigí (Ioánina) 78 C4
Drossopigí (Makedonía) 79 D3
Drottningholm 106 B4
Droué 25 E1
Drulingen 21 E3

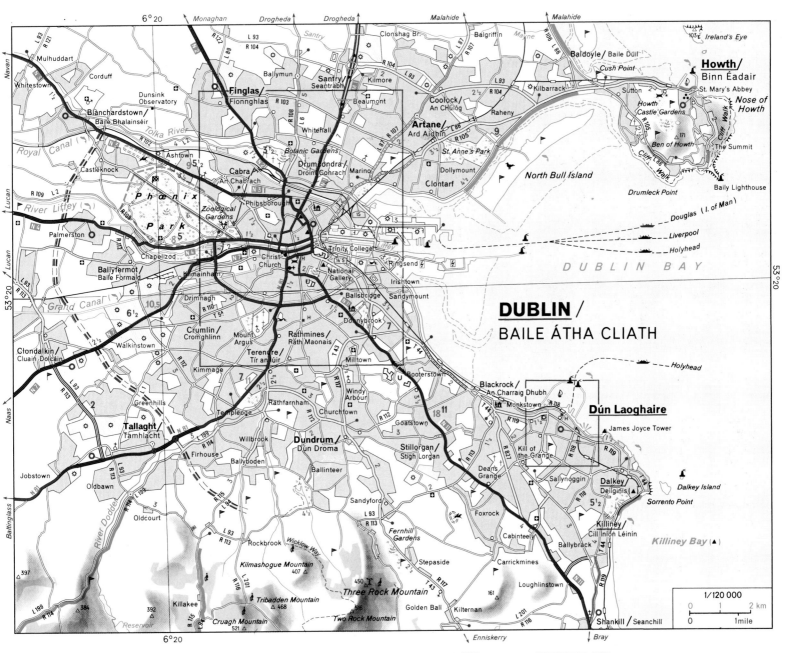

DUBLIN /
BAILE ÁTHA CLIATH

1/120 000

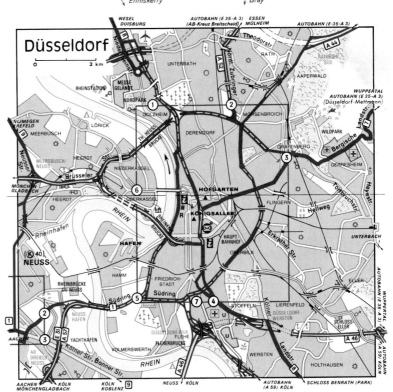

Düsseldorf

Essen

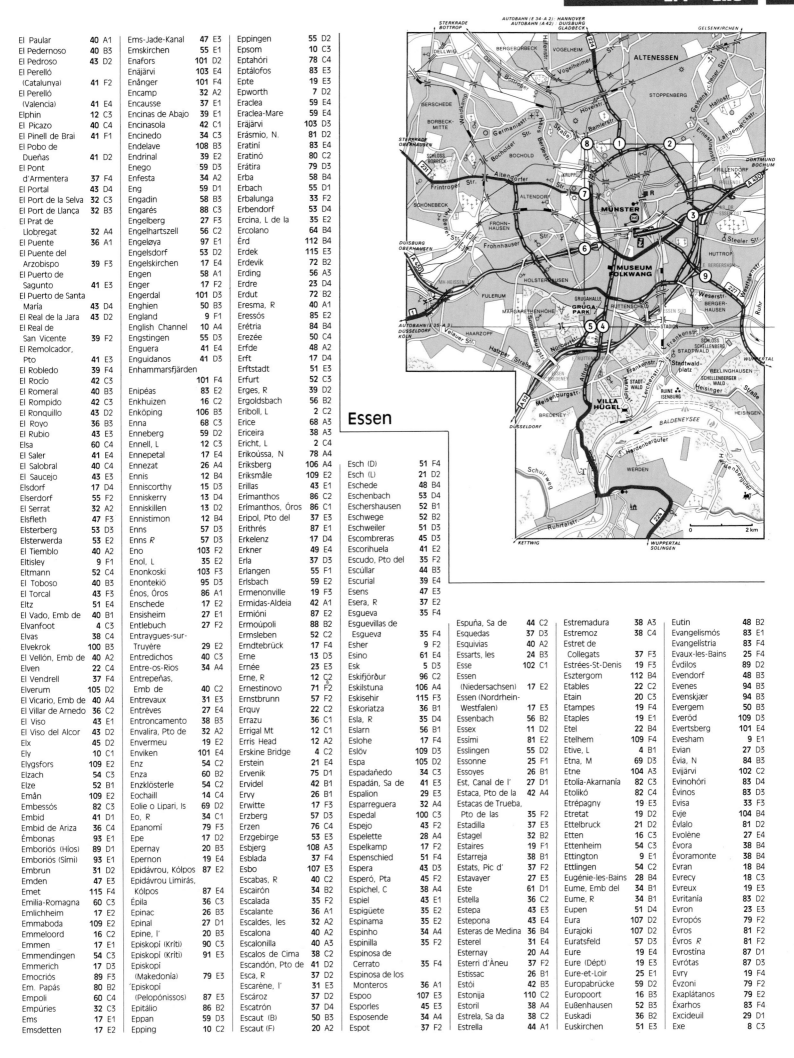

Exeter	8 C3		
Exmes	19 D4		
Exmoor Nat Pk	8 C3		
Exmouth	8 C3		
Exohí (Ípiros)	78 C4		
Exohí (Makedonía)	79 E3		
Exohí (Makedonía)	80 B1		
Exómvourgo	88 C2		
Exter	17 F2		
Extremadura	39 E4		
Eydehavn	104 C4		
Eye	9 F1		
Eyemouth	5 E2		
Eye Pen	2 B2		
Eygues	30 C2		
Eyguières	30 C4		
Eygurande	29 E1		
Eyjafjördur	96 A1		
Eymet	28 C2		
Eymoutiers	29 D1		
Eyre	28 B3		
Eyrieux	30 B2		
Eysturoy	96 A3		
Eyzies, les	29 D2		
Ezcaray	36 B2		
Eze	31 E3		
Ezine	115 E4		

F

Place	Ref	Place	Ref
Faak	59 F2	Falces	36 C2
Fabara	37 E4	Falconara Marittima	61 F3
Fåberg	105 D2	Falcone	69 D2
Fabero	34 C2	Falcone, C del	66 A1
Fåborg	108 B4	Falerna	67 E3
Fabriano	61 E4	Faliráki	93 F1
Fábricas de Riópar	44 C1	Falkefjellet	95 F1
Fabro	63 D1	Falkenberg (D)	53 E2
Facinas	43 D4	Falkenberg (S)	108 C2
Facture	28 A2	Falkensee	49 D4
Faenza	61 D3	Falkenstein	53 D3
Færøerne	96 A3	Falkirk	4 C2
Faeto	64 B3	Falkland	5 D2
Fafe	34 A4	Falkonéra, N	87 F3
Fågåras	113 D4	Falköping	109 D1
Fågărașului, M	113 D4	Fallersleben	48 B4
Fågelfors	109 E2	Fällfors	98 A1
Fagernes (Oppland)	104 C2	Fallingbostel	48 A4
Fagernes (Troms)	94 C2	Falmouth	8 B4
Fagersta	105 F3	Falset	37 F4
Fairford	9 E2	Falster	108 C4
Fair Head	13 E1	Falterona Mte	61 D3
Fair I	3 F3	Fålticeni	113 D3
Fakenham	7 E3	Falun	105 F2
Fakovići	72 C4	Falzarego, Pso	59 D3
Fakse	108 C4	Fámjin	96 A4
Fakse Ladeplads	108 C4	Fanad Head	13 D1
Falaise	18 C4	Fanári (Pelopónissos)	87 E2
Falakró, Óros	80 C1	Fanári (Pelopónissos)	86 C2
Falássarna	90 B3	Fanári (Thessalía)	83 D2
Falcade	59 D3	Fanári (Thráki)	81 D2

Place	Ref	Place	Ref
Fanári, Akr	89 D2	Fårösund	109 F3
Fanefjord	108 C4	Farra d'Alpago	59 E3
Fani i Madh	76 C3	Fársala	83 E2
Fani i Vogël	76 C3	Farsø	108 A2
Fanjeaux	32 A1	Farsund	104 A4
Fannich, L	2 C3	Farum	108 C3
Fano	61 E3	Fasano	65 E3
Fanø	108 A3	Fašku Vaskojoki	95 E3
Fanø Bugt	108 A3	Fastov	113 E2
Fanós	79 F2	Fátima	38 B3
Faouët, le	22 B3	Fatmomakke	97 E4
Faou, le	22 B3	Faucille, Col de la	27 D3
Farángi Samariás	90 B4	Faucogney	27 D1
Farángi Víkou	78 C4	Faulquemont	21 D3
Fara Novarese	58 A4	Fauquembergues	19 E1
Fårbo	109 E2	Fauske	97 F2
Fardes, R	44 A3	Fauville	19 D3
Fareham	9 E3	Fåvang	100 C3
Fårevejle	108 B3	Favara	68 C4
Färgelanda	105 D4	Favareta	41 E4
Färila	101 F3	Faverges	27 D4
Farindola	63 F1	Faverney	27 D1
Faringdon	9 E2	Faversham	11 D3
Farini d'Olmo	60 B2	Favignana, I	68 A3
Färjestaden	109 E2	Fawley	9 E3
Farkadóna	83 E1	Faxaflói	96 A2
Farkaždin	72 C2	Fayence	31 D4
Farlete	37 D3	Fayl-Billot	26 C1
Farmakoníssi	89 F2	Fayón	37 E4
Farnborough	9 F3	Fay-sur-Lignon	30 B2
Farnese	63 D2	Fažana	70 A4
Farnham	9 F3	Feale	14 B3
Faro	42 B3	Fécamp	19 D2
Fårö	109 F3	Féclaz, la	31 D1

Place	Ref	Place	Ref
Feda	104 B4	Fervenza, Emb de	34 A1
Feggesund	108 A2	Festós	91 D4
Fehmarn	48 B1	Festre, Col du	30 C2
Fehmarnbelt	48 B1	Festvåg	97 E1
Fehmarnsund	48 B1	Fethard	14 C3
Fehrbellin	49 D3	Fetlar	3 F1
Fehring	57 F4	Fetsund	105 D3
Fejø	108 B4	Feucht	55 F1
Feketić	72 B2	Feuchtwangen	55 E2
Felanitx	45 F3	Feunte Dé	35 E2
Felbertauern-tunnel	59 E2	Feurs	26 B4
Feld	59 F2	Feyzin	30 B1
Feldafing	56 A3	Ffestiniog	6 A3
Feldbach	57 F4	Fflint	6 B2
Feldberg (D)	54 C4	Fiano R.	63 E2
Feldberg (DDR)	49 D3	Fiastra	61 F4
Feldkirch	58 B2	Ficarolo	60 C2
Feldkirchen	59 F2	Fichtel-gebirge	53 D4
Felgueiras	34 A4	Fidenza	60 B2
Felixstowe	11 D2	Fieberbrunn	59 E1
Fellbach	55 D2	Fier	114 B3
Felletin	25 F4	Fiera di Primiero	59 D3
Fellingsbro	105 F3	Fierzës, Liq i	76 C3
Felton	5 E3	Fiesole	61 D3
Feltre	59 D3	Fife	5 D2
Femer Bælt	108 B4	Fife Ness	5 D1
Femundsmarka	101 D3	Figália	86 C2
Fene	34 B1	Figeac	29 E2
Fener	59 D3	Figline Valdarno	61 D4
Fenestrelle	31 E1	Figueira da Foz	38 B2
Fénétrange	21 E3	Figueira de Castelo Rodrigo	39 D1
Feolin Ferry	4 B2	Figueiró dos Vinhos	38 B2
Fer à Cheval, Cirque du	27 E4	Figueras	32 B3
Feraklós	93 F2	Figueres	32 B3
Ferbane	12 C4	Figueruela de Arriba	34 C3
Ferdinandovac	71 D1	Fíhtio	87 D2
Ferdinandshof	49 E2	Filabres, Sa de los	44 B3
Fère-Champenoise	20 B4	Filadélfi	80 B1
Fère-en-Tardenois	20 A3	Filadelfia	67 F3
Fère, la	20 A2	Filáki	83 E2
Ferentino	63 F3	Filákio	81 F1
Féres	81 E2	Filakopí	88 A4
Feria	43 D1	Filérimos	93 F1
Feričanci	71 E2	Filey	7 E1
Ferlach	70 A1	Filfola	68 B4
Fermanagh	12 C2	Filí	87 F1
Fermo	61 F4	Fília (Lésvos)	85 F2
Fermoselle	34 C4	Fília (Pelopónissos)	86 C1
Fermoy	14 C4	Filiátes	82 B1
Fernancaballero	40 A4	Filiatrá	86 B3
Fernán Núñez	43 F2	Filicudi, I	68 C2
Ferney-Voltaire	27 D4	Filiouri	81 E2
Fernpaß	58 C1	Filipi	80 C2
Ferrandina	65 D4	Filipiáda	82 C2
Ferrara	61 D2	Filipjakov	74 C1
Ferreira	34 C1	Filipos, Akr	88 B3
Ferreira do Alentejo	42 B1	Filipstad	105 E3
Ferreira do Zêzere	38 B3	Fílira	81 E2
Ferreiras	42 A3	Fillan	100 C1
Ferreras de Abajo	35 D3	Fille-fjell	104 B1
Ferreries	45 F2	Fílo	83 E2
Ferreruela de Huerva	41 D1	Filótas	79 D3
Ferret, Cap	28 A2	Filottrano	61 F4
Ferrette	27 E2	Finale Emilia	60 C2
Ferriere	60 B2	Finale Ligure	31 F3
Ferrières	25 F1	Fiñana	44 B3
Ferrol	34 B1	Finca de la Concepción	43 F3
Ferru, M	66 B3	Finchingfield	11 D2
Ferté-Alais, la	19 f4	Findhorn	3 D3
Ferté-Bernard, la	23 F3	Fínikas	88 B2
Ferté-Frênel, la	19 D4	Finikoúndas	86 C4
Ferté-Gaucher, la	20 A4	Finistère	22 B3
Ferté-Macé, la	18 C4	Finisterre, Emb de	40 A3
Ferté-Milon, la	20 A3	Finja	109 D3
Ferté-St-Aubin, la	25 E2	Finn	13 D1
Ferté-sous-Jouarre, la	20 A3	Finneidfjord	97 E3
Ferté-Vidame, la	19 D4	Finnentrop	17 F4
Fertilia	66 A2	Finnmark	95 D2
		Finnmark	95 E1
		Finnmarksvidda	95 D3

Place	Ref
Finnøy	104 A3
Finnsnes	94 B3
Finow	49 E3
Finowfurt	49 E3
Finskij Zaliv	110 C1
Finspång	105 F4
Finsteraarhorn	27 F3
Finsterau	56 C2
Finsterwalde	53 E1
Finström	106 C3
Fintona	13 D2
Fintown	12 C1
Fionnphort	4 A1
Fiorenzuola d'Arda	60 B2
Firenze	60 C3
Firenzuola	61 D3
Firminy	30 B1
Firmo	67 E2
Fischamend Markt	57 F2
Fischbach	55 F1
Fischbeck	48 C4
Fischen	55 E4
Fishbourne	9 E3
Fishguard	8 B1
Fiskárdo	82 B4
Fiskari	107 E3
Fiskebøl	94 A3
Fismes	20 A3
Fissíni	85 D1
Fisterra	34 A2
Fitero	36 C3
Fitíes	82 C3
Fitjar	104 A2
Fiuggi	63 F3
Fiumicino	63 E3
Fivemiletown	13 D2
Fivizzano	60 B3
Fjällåsen	94 C4
Fjällbacka	105 D4
Fjällnäs	101 D2
Fjärdhundra	106 B3
Fjærland	100 A3
Fjätervålen	101 D3
Fjelie	108 C3
Fjellerup	108 B2
Fjerritslev	108 A2
Fjerze	76 C3
Flå	104 C2
Fladså	108 A3
Fladungen	52 B3
Flaine	27 E4
Flakk	100 C2
Flåm	104 B2
Flamborough Head	7 E1
Flambourári	82 C1
Flámbouro (Makedonía)	79 D3
Flámbouro (Makedonía)	80 B2
Flamignano	63 F2
Flamouriá	79 E3
Flannan I	2 A2
Flåsjön	101 F1
Flåten	94 C2
Flatey	96 A1
Flatråker	104 A2
Flattnitz	59 F2
Flatval	100 C1
Flèche, la	23 E4
Fleetwood	6 B1
Flekkefjord	104 A4
Flen	106 A4
Flensborg Fjord	108 A4
Flensburg	48 A1
Flers	18 C4
Flesberg	104 C3
Flesnes	94 A3
Fleurance	28 C4
Fleurier	27 D3
Fleurus	50 C4
Fleury	19 F4
Fleury-sur-Andelle	19 E3
Fléves, N	87 F2

FIRENZE
PIANTA D'INSIEME

0   2 km

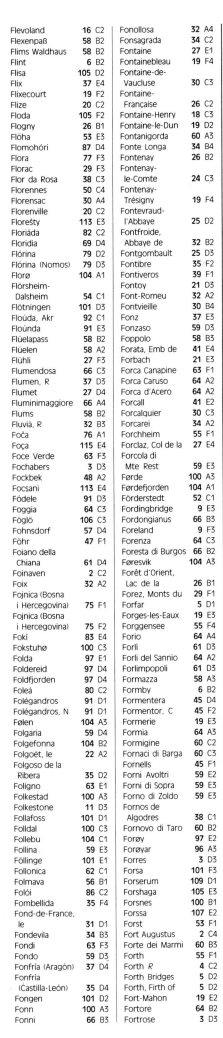

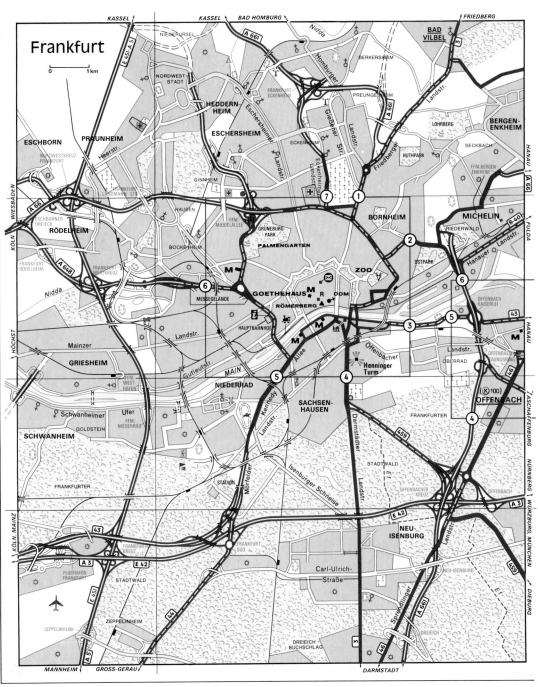

Frankfurt

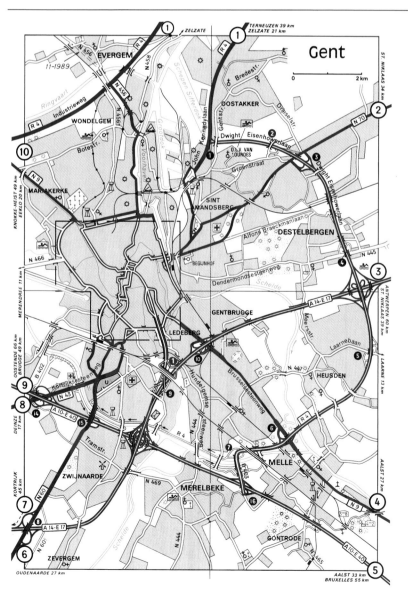

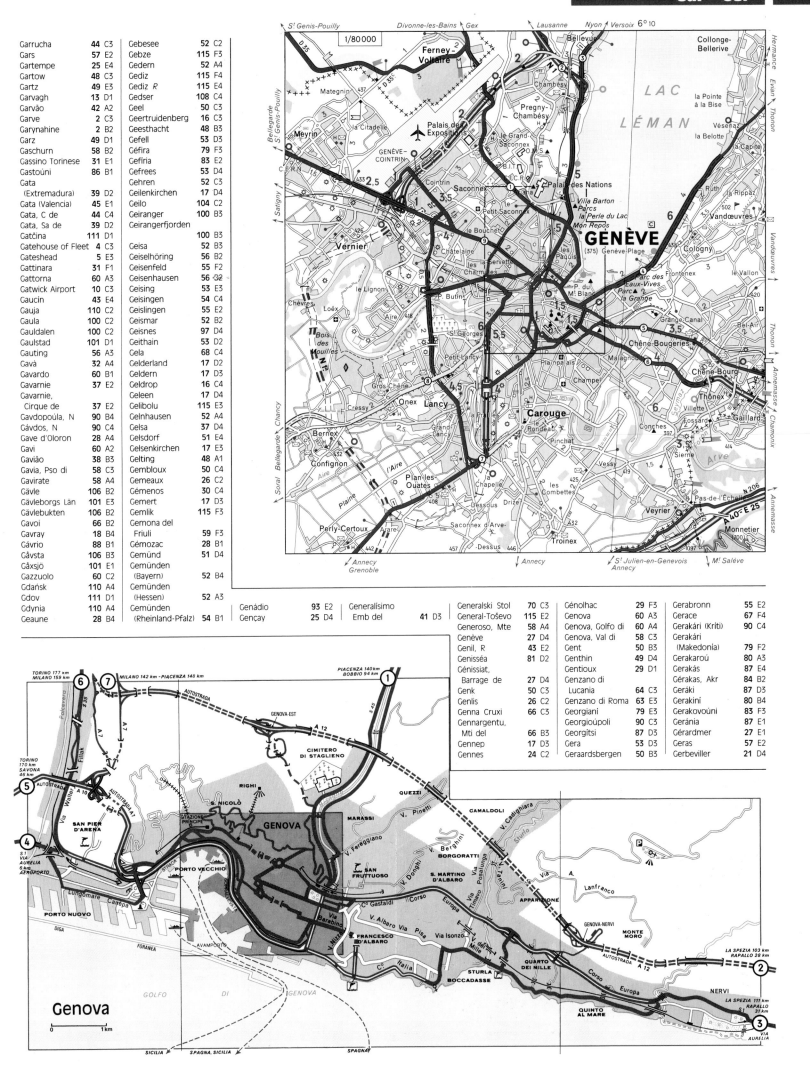

Genova

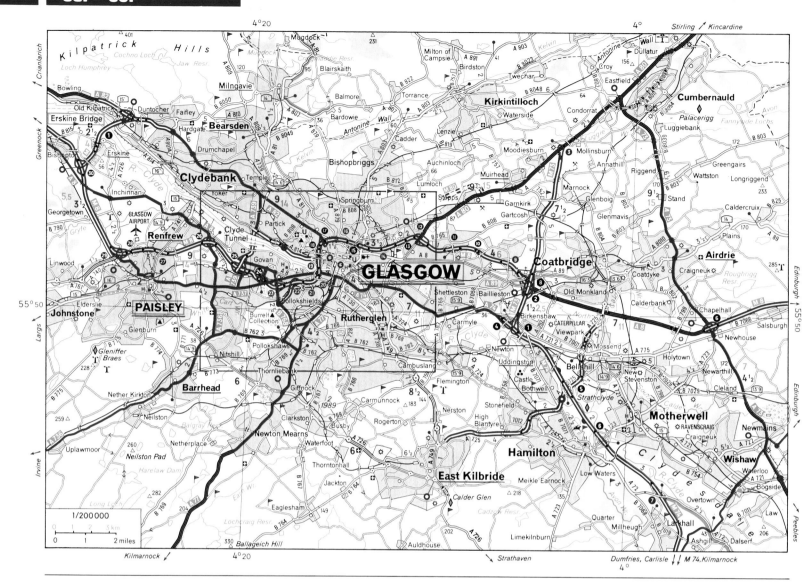

Goljam Perelik 115 D3
Göllersdorf 57 E2
Golling 59 E1
Golo 33 F3
Golpejas 39 E1
Golßen 53 E1
Golspie 3 D3
Golubac 73 E3
Golubovci 76 B3
Golubovec 70 C2
Golzow 49 D4
Gómara 36 B3
Gomáti 80 B3
Gombrèn 32 A3
Gomecello 39 E1
Gomel' 111 E4
Gomera 42 A4
Gómfi 83 D2
Gommern 52 C1
Goncelin 31 D1
Gondomar 34 A4
Gondomar (E) 34 A3
Gondrecourt 20 C4
Gönen 115 E3
Góni 83 E1
Goniá 90 B3
Goniés 91 D3
Gonnesa 66 B4
Gonnosfanadiga 66 B4
Goole 7 D2
Goor 17 D2
Goppenstein 27 F3
Göppingen 55 D2
Gora 70 C3
Goražde 76 A1
Gördalen 101 D3
Gordes 30 C3
Gorenja Vas 70 A2
Gorey (GB) 18 B3
Gorey (IRL) 15 D3
Gorgona, I di 60 B4
Gorgonzola 60 A1
Gorgopótamos 78 C4
Gorica (Bosna i Hercegovina) 75 E2
Gorica (Makedonija) 77 D4
Goričan 71 D1
Gorice 70 B3
Gorinchem 16 C3
Goritsá 87 D3
Gorizia 59 F3
Gorjanci 70 C2
Gorki 111 E3
Gorleston-on-Sea 7 F4
Gorlice 112 B3
Görlitz 53 F2
Gorna Orjahovica 115 D2
Gornja Dobrinja 72 C4
Gornja Grabovica 75 F1
Gornja Kamenica 73 F4
Gornja Klina 77 D2
Gornja Ljubovidđa 72 C4
Gornja Ljuta 75 F1
Gornja Ploča 70 C4
Gornja Radgona 70 C1
Gornja Sabanta 73 D4
Gornja Sanica 71 D4
Gornja Slatina 71 F3
Gornja Toplica 72 C4
Gornja Toponica 73 E4
Gornja Tuzla 72 B3
Gornje Dubočke 76 A2
Gornje Ratkovo 71 E4
Gornje Selo 75 D2
Gornji Grad 70 B2
Gornji Kokoti 76 B3
Gornji Kosinj 70 C4
Gornji Lapac 71 D4
Gornji Lukavac 76 A2
Gornji Milanovac 73 D4
Gornji Petrovci 70 C1
Gornji Podgradci 71 D3
Gornji Rajić 71 E3
Gornji Stepoš 73 E4
Gornji Vakuf 75 E1
Gornji Zabar 71 F3
Gorno Orizari 77 E3
Goro 61 D2
Gorodišče 113 F2
Gorodn'a 111 E4
Gorodok (Belorussija) 111 D3
Gorodok (Ukraina) 112 C2
Gorredijk 17 D1
Gorron 23 E3
Gort 12 B4
Gorteen 12 C3
Gortin 13 D2
Górtis 91 D4
Gortmore 12 B3
Gorumna I 12 B3
Goryn' 113 D2
Góry Świętokrzyskie 112 B2
Görzke 53 D1
Gorzów Wielkopolski 49 F3
Gosaldo 59 D3
Gosau 59 F1
Gosausee 59 F1
Göschenen 58 A3
Gościno 49 F1
Gosforth 5 D4
Gößl 56 C3
Goslar 52 B1
Gößnitz 53 D3
Gospić 70 C4
Gospođinci 72 C2
Gosport 9 E3
Gossau 58 B2
Gosselies 50 B4
Gossensass 59 D2
Gössweinstein 52 C4
Gostivar 77 D3
Göstling 57 D3
Gostyń 112 A2
Götaälv 108 C1
Göta Kanal 105 E4
Göteborg 108 C1
Göteborgs och Bohus Län 108 C1
Götene 105 E4
Gotha 52 C3
Gothem 109 F4
Gotland 109 F4
Gotlands Län 109 F4
Gotska Sandön 106 C4
Göttingen 52 B2
Gottwaldov 112 A3
Götzis 58 B2
Gouarec 22 C3
Gouda 16 C3
Gouménissa 79 F2
Goumois 27 E2
Goúra 87 D1
Gourdon 29 D2
Gourin 22 B3
Gournay-en-Bray 19 E3
Goúrnes 91 E3
Gourniá 91 E4
Gourock 4 C2
Gouveja 38 C2
Goúves 91 E3
Gouviá 82 A1
Gouzon 25 F4
Goveđari 75 E2
Goverla 113 D3
Gowienica 49 F2
Göynük 115 F3
Gozd 70 A1
Gozo 68 B4
Gozzano 58 A4
Graal-Müritz 48 C1
Graben-Neudorf 54 C2
Grabenstätt 56 B3
Grabovac 75 E2
Grabovci 72 C3
Grabow 48 C3
Gračac 70 C4
Gračanica (Bosna i Hercegovina) 71 F3
Gračanica (Crna Gora) 76 B2
Gračanica (Kosovo) 77 D2
Gračanica (Srbija) 72 C4
Graçay 25 E2
Grächen 27 F4
Gradac (Crna Gora) 76 B1
Gradac (Hrvatska) 75 E2
Gradac (Srbija) 76 C1
Gradačac 71 F3
Gradara 61 E3
Gradče, Ez 77 F2
Gradec 71 D2
Gradefes 35 E2
Gradeška pl 77 F3
Gradina 77 F1
Gradisca d'Isonzo 59 F3
Gradište (Hrvatska) 71 E2
Gradište (Makedonija) 77 E2
Grado (E) 35 D1
Grado (I) 59 F4
Gradsko 77 E3
Gradskovo 73 F3
Grafelfing 56 A3
Grafenau 56 C2
Gräfenberg 55 F1
Gräfenhainichen 53 D1
Grafenwöhr 55 F1
Grafing 56 B3
Gragnano 64 B4
Grahovo (Bosna i Hercegovina) 76 A2
Grahovo (Slovenija) 70 A2
Graiguenamanagh 15 D3
Grain 11 D2
Grainau 55 F4
Grajewo 110 C4
Gram 108 A3
Gramat 29 D2
Gramatikó 83 E2
Gramatikoú 83 D4
Graméni 80 B2
Graméno 82 B1
Grametten 57 D1
Grammichele 69 D4
Grámos, Óros 78 C3
Grampian 3 E4
Grampian Mts 4 C1
Gramsh 77 D4
Gramzow 49 E3
Gran 105 D2
Granada 44 A3
Granadella 37 E4
Granadilla de Abona 42 B4
Granard 12 C3
Gran Canaria 42 B4
Grancey-le-Château 26 C2
Grandas 34 C1
Grand Ballon 27 E1
Grand Bois, Col du 30 B1
Grand-Bornand, le 27 D4
Grand-Bourg 25 E4
Grandcamp-Maisy 18 C3
Grand Canal d'Alsace 27 E1
Grand Canyon du Verdon 31 D3
Grand-Champ 22 C4
Grand-Colombier 27 D4
Grand-Combe, la 30 B3
Grand Combin 27 E4
Grand-Couronne 19 D3
Grand-Croix 30 B1
Grande Casse 31 D1
Grande de Europa, Punta 43 E4
Grande Dixence, Bge de la 27 E4
Grande-Motte, la 30 B4
Grande Sassière 31 E1
Grandes Rousses 31 D1
Grand-Fougeray 23 D4
Grand-Lemps, le 30 C1
Grand Lieu, L de 24 B3
Grand-Lucé, le 23 F4
Grand Morin 20 A4
Grândola 42 A1
Grandpré 20 C3
Grand-Pressigny, le 25 D3
Grand Rhône 30 B4
Grandrieu 29 F2
Grand-Serre, le 30 C1
Grands Goulets 30 C2
Grandval, Bge de 29 F2
Grandvilliers 19 E3
Grañén 37 D3
Grangärde 105 F3
Grangemouth 5 D2
Grange-Over-Sands 6 B1
Grängesberg 105 F3

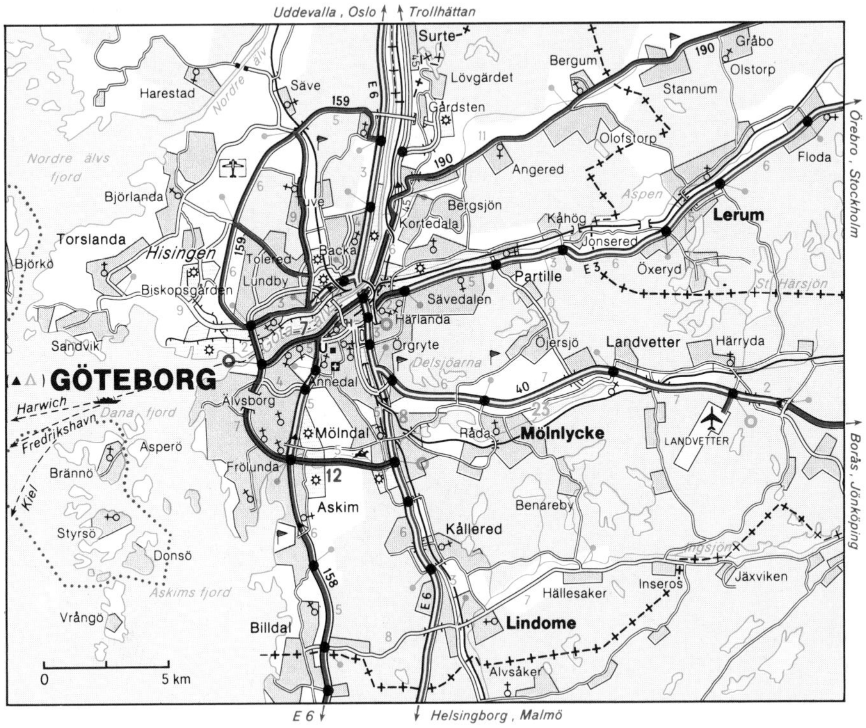
Uddevalla, Oslo
Trollhättan
Surte
Gråbo
Olstorp
Bergum
Lövgärdet
Stannum
Harestad
Säve
Gårdsten
Nordre älvs fjord
Olofstorp
Floda
Örebro, Stockholm
Angered
Björlanda
Bergsjön
Lerum
Kortedala
Kåhög
Jonsered
Torslanda
Hisingen
Tolered
Backa
Björkö
Lundby
Partille
Öxeryd
Biskopsgården
Sävedalen
Härlanda
Sandvik
Örgryte
Öjersjö
Landvetter
Härryda
GÖTEBORG
Delsjöarna
Annedal
Harwich
Älvsborg
Fredrikshavn
Dana fjord
Mölndal
Råda
Mölnlycke
LANDVETTER
Borås, Jönköping
Asperö
Frölunda
Brännö
Kiel
Askim
Benareby
Styrsö
Kållered
Donsö
Askims fjord
Jäxviken
Inserös
Hällesaker
Vrångö
Billdal
Lindome
Alvsåker
0
5 km
E 6
Helsingborg, Malmö

Granges-sur-Vologne 27 E1
Granier, Col du 30 C1
Granítis 80 B1
Granítsa 83 D2
Granja (Alentejo) 42 C1
Granja (Douro) 34 A4
Granja de Torrehermosa 43 E1
Granja, Pto de la 43 D1
Gränna 109 D1
Granollers 32 A4
Granön 102 A1
Gran Paradiso 31 E1
Gran San Bernardo, Colle del 27 E4
Gran San Bernardo, Traforo del 27 E4
Gran Sasso d'Italia 63 F1
Gransee 49 D3
Gran Tarajal 42 C4
Grantham 7 D3
Grantown-on-Spey 3 D3
Granville 18 B4
Granvin 104 B2
Grappa, Mte 59 D3
Grasleben 52 C1
Grasmere 5 D4
Grassano 65 D4
Grasse 31 E3
Gråsten 108 A4
Grästorp 108 C1
Gratangen 94 B3
Gratiní 81 E2
Gratkorn 57 E4
Graubünden 58 B2
Grau-du-Roi, le 30 B4
Graulhet 29 D4
Graus 37 E3
Gravalos 36 C3
Gravdal 97 E1
Grave 17 D3
Gravedona 58 B3
Grave, la 31 D1
Gravelines 19 F1
Gravellona-Toce 58 A4
Grave, Pointe de 28 A1
Gravesend 11 D2
Graviá 83 E3
Gravina in Puglia 65 D3
Gravona 33 F3
Gravoúna 80 C2
Gray 26 C2
Grays Thurrock 10 C2
Graz 57 E4
Grazalema 43 E3
Grazzanise 64 A3
Grdelica 77 E1
Great Blasket I. 14 A3
Great Driffield 7 D1
Great Dunmow 11 D2
Great Grimsby 7 E2
Great Malvern 9 D1
Great Ormes Head 6 A2
Great Ouse 7 E3
Great Torrington 8 C3
Great Yarmouth 7 F4
Grebbestad 105 D4
Greccio 63 E2
Greding 55 F2
Gredos 39 F2
Gredos, Sa de 39 F2
Greenhead 5 D3
Greenlaw 5 E2
Greenock 4 C2
Greenodd 6 B1
Greggio 31 F1
Gregolimano 83 F3
Greifenburg 59 E2
Greiffenberg 49 E3
Greifswald 49 D1
Greifswalder Bodden 49 D1
Grein 57 D2
Greiz 53 D3
Grenå 108 B2
Grenade (Haute-Garonne) 29 D4
Grenade (Landes) 28 B4
Grenchen 27 E2
Grenoble 30 C1
Grense Jakobselv 95 F2
Gréoux-les-Bains 31 D3
Gressåmoen 101 E1
Gresse 30 C2
Gressoney-la-Trinite 27 F4
Gressoney-St-Jean 27 F4
Gresten 57 D3
Grésy 31 D1
Greußen 52 C2
Greve 61 D4
Greven 17 E2
Grevená 79 D4
Grevená (Nomos) 79 D4
Grevenbroich 17 D4
Grevenbrück 17 F4
Grevenítio 82 C1
Grevesmühlen 48 B2
Greve Strand 108 C3
Greyabbey 13 E2
Greystones 13 E4
Grez-en-Bouère 23 E3
Grezzana 60 C1
Grgur 70 B4
Griá, Akr 88 B1
Grianan of Aileach 13 D1
Griebenow 49 D2
Gries 59 D2
Gries im Sellrain 58 C2
Grieskirchen 56 C3
Griffen 70 B1
Grignan 30 B2
Grigno 59 D3
Grignols 28 B3
Grimaldi 67 E3
Grimaud 31 D4
Grimma 53 D2
Grimmen 49 D2
Grimone, Col de 30 C2
Grimsbu 100 C3
Grimselpass 27 F3
Grimsey 96 B1
Grimstad 104 B4
Grindaheim 104 C2
Grindavík 96 A2
Grindelwald 27 F3
Grindsted 108 A3
Griñón 40 A2
Grintavec 70 B2
Gripsholm 106 B4
Grisignano 61 D1
Gris Nez, Cap 19 E1
Grisolles 29 D4
Grisslehamn 106 B3
Griva 79 E2
Grizáno 83 D1
Grk 71 F3
Grljan 73 F3
Grmec 71 D4
Grøa 100 B2
Gröbming 59 F1
Grocka 73 D3
Gröditz 53 E2
Grodno 110 C4
Groenlo 17 D3
Gröer Arber 56 B1
Groitzsch 53 D2
Groix 22 B4
Groix, I de 22 B4
Grömitz 48 B2
Gronau 17 E2
Grönenbach 55 E4
Grong 97 D4
Grönhögen 109 E3
Groningen 47 D3
Groningen (Prov) 47 D3
Gröningen 52 C1
Grönskåra 109 E2
Grønsund 108 C4
Gropello Cairoli 60 A2
Großbreitenbach 52 C3
Großburgwedel 48 A4
Groscavallo 31 E1
Großenbrode 48 B1
Großenhain 53 E2
Großenzersdorf 57 F2
Groß Gerungs 57 D2
Großglockner 59 E2
Großglockner Hochalpenstraße 59 E2
Großhabersdorf 55 E1
Grosio 58 C3
Grosne 26 C3
Groß Ötscher 57 E3
Großpetersdorf 57 F4
Großraming 57 D3
Großraschen 53 E1
Groß Reken 17 E3
Großröhrsdorf 53 F2
Groß Rosennock 59 F2
Gross Beerberg 52 C3
Gross Bösenstein 57 D4
Groß-Schönebeck 49 E3
Grosse Pierre 27 E1
Grosse Röder 53 E2
Grosser Plöner See 48 B2
Grosseto 62 C1
Gross Feldberg 51 F4
Gross-Gerau 54 C1
Groß Siegharts 57 E2
Gross Priel 57 D3
Gross Rachel 56 C2
Grossschönau 53 F2
Gross-Umstadt 55 D1
Grostenquin 21 D3
Grosuplje 70 B2
Großvenediger 59 E2
Großweil 56 A4
Grötlingbo 109 F4
Grøtsundet 94 C2
Grotta di Nettuno 66 A2
Grottaglie 65 E4
Grottaminarda 64 B3
Grottammare 61 F4
Grotte di Pertosa 64 C4
Grotteria 67 F4
Grouin, Pte du 18 B4
Grove 34 A2
Grövelsjön 101 D3
Grovfjord 94 B3
Grubišno Polje 71 D2
Gruda 76 A3

H

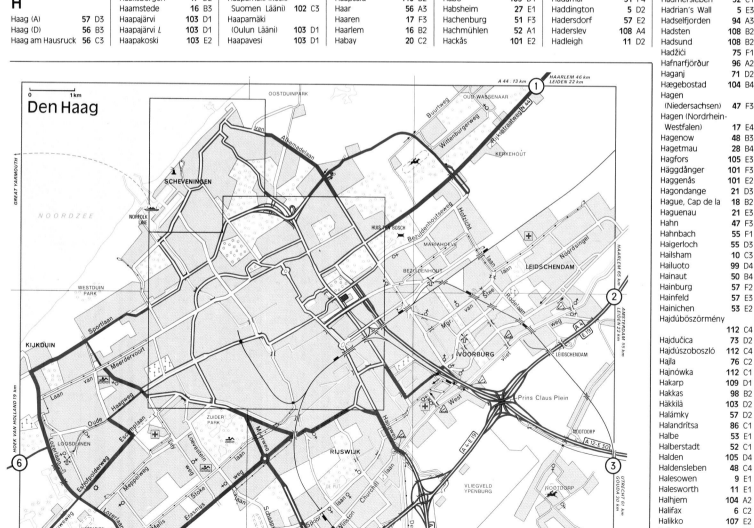

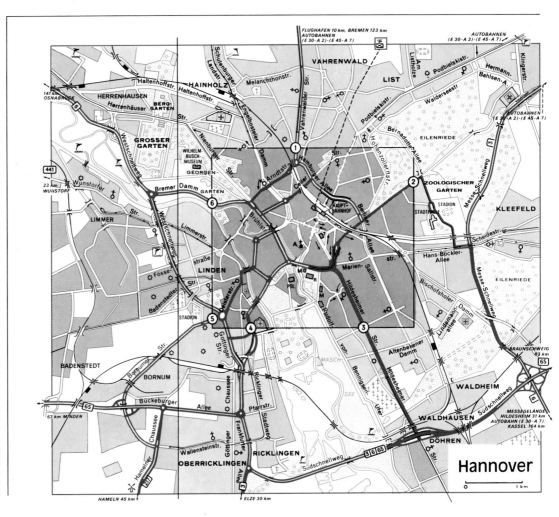

Hannover

Herma Ness 3 F1
Hermannsburg 48 B4
Hermansverk 104 B1
Hermenault, l' 24 C3
Herment 29 E1
Hermeskeil 54 B1
Hermigua 42 A4
Hermsdorf 53 D3
Hernani 36 C1
Hernansancho 39 F1
Herne 17 E3
Herne Bay 11 D3
Herning 108 A3
Heroldsberg 55 F1
Herónia 83 F4
Herøy 100 A2
Herrala 107 F2
Herre 104 C3
Herrenberg 55 D3
Herrenchiemsee 56 B3
Herrera (Andalucía) 43 E3
Herrera (Aragón) 37 D4
Herrera *Mt* 37 D4
Herrera de Alcántara 38 C3
Herrera del Duque 39 F4
Herrera de Pisuerga 35 F3
Herrera, Pto de 36 B2
Herreruela 39 D3
Herrestad 108 C1
Herrieden 55 E2
Herrljunga 109 D1
Herrnburg 48 B2
Herrnhut 53 F2
Herrsching 56 A3
Herrskog 102 A2
Hersbruck 55 F1
Herselt 50 C3
Hérso 79 F2
Hersónissos Akrotíri 90 C3
Hersónissos Methánon 87 E2
Hersónissos Spinalónga 91 E3
Herstal 51 D3
Herten 17 E3
Hertford 9 F2
Hertfordshire 9 F2
Hervás 39 E2
Herzberg (D) 52 B2
Herzberg (DDR) 53 E1
Herzogenaurach 55 F1
Herzogenburg 57 E2
Herzsprung 49 D3
Hesdin 19 E2
Hesel 47 E3
Hessen 52 A3
Hesseng 95 F2
Hessisch-Lichtenau 52 B2
Hessisch Oldendorf 52 A1
Hestfjørður 96 A4
Hetekylä 99 E3
Hetin 72 C1
Hettange 21 D3
Hettstedt 52 C2
Heubach 55 E2
Heuchin 19 F1
Heukuppe 57 E3
Hevlin 57 F1
Hexham 5 E3
Heyrieux 30 C1
Heysham 6 B1
Hiddensee 49 D1
Hieflau 57 D3
Hiekkasarkät 102 C1
Hierbas 41 E3
Hierro 42 A4
Hiersac 28 C1
Hietaniemi 95 F4
Higham Ferrers 9 F1
Highland 2 C3
High Peak 6 C2
High Willhays 8 C3
High Wycombe 9 F2
Higuera de Arjona 44 A2
Higuera de la Serena 43 E1
Higuera de la Sierra 43 D2
Higuera de Vargas 42 C1
Higuera la Real 42 C1
Higueruela 41 D4
Hiidenportti 103 E1
Hiiumaa 110 B1
Híjar 37 D4
Hilchenbach 17 F4
Hildburghausen 52 C3
Hilden 17 E4
Hilders 52 B3
Hildesheim 52 B1
Hiliomódi 87 E1
Hillegom 16 B2
Hillerød 108 C3
Hillesøy 94 B2
Hillswick 3 F1
Hiloús, Akr 92 C1
Hilpoltstein 55 F2
Hiltula 103 E3
Hilvarenbeek 16 C4
Hilversum 16 C2
Himanka 102 C1
Hímaros 80 A2
Himmerland 108 B2
Hinckley 9 E1
Hindelang 55 E4
Hindhead 9 F3
Hindsholm 108 B3
Hinnøya 94 A3
Hinodejo 36 B3
Hinojares 44 B2
Hinojosa de Duero 39 D1
Hinojosa del Duque 43 E1
Hinterrhein 58 B3
Hintersee (D) 56 B4
Hintersee (DDR) 49 E2
Hinterstoder 57 D3
Hintertux 59 D2
Hinterweidenthal 54 B2
Híos 85 F4
Híos, N 85 E4
Hirschau 55 F1
Hirschberg 53 D3
Hirschegg 58 B2
Hirsingue 27 E2
Hirson 20 B2
Hirşova 115 E1
Hirtshals 108 B1
Hirvasvaara 99 E2
Hirvensalmi 103 E3
Hirvilahti 103 E2
Hirwaun 8 C2
Hisarja 115 D2
Histria 115 E1
Hitchin 9 F2
Hitra 100 C1
Hitzacker 48 B3
Hjälmaren 105 F4
Hjartdal 104 C3
Hjellestad 104 A2
Hjelmeland 104 A3
Hjelmsøya 95 D1
Hjo 109 D1
Hjørring 108 B1
Hjørundfjorden 100 A2
Hlebine 71 D1
Hlemoútsi 86 B1
Hlomó, Óros 83 F3
Hluboká 57 D1
Hobro 108 B2
Höchberg 55 D1
Hochdorf 27 F2
Hochfeiler 59 D2
Hochfelden 21 E4
Hochgolling 59 F1
Hochgrabe 59 E2
Hochosterwitz 70 B1
Hochreichart 57 D4
Hochschober 59 E2
Hochschwab 57 D3
Hochspeyer 54 C1
Höchst 55 D1
Höchstadt 55 E1
Höchstädt 55 E2
Hochtannbergpaß 58 B2
Hochtor (Osttirol) 59 E2
Hochtor (Steiermark) 57 D3
Hockenheim 54 C2
Hoddesdon 9 F2
Hodenhagen 48 A4
Hœdic 22 C4
Hódmezővásárhely 114 B1
Hodnet 6 B3
Hodonín 57 F1
Hodoš 70 C1
Hodovo 75 F2
Hoedekenskerke 16 B4
Hoek van Holland 16 B3
Hoemsbu 100 B2
Hof 53 D4
Hofgeismar 52 A2
Hofheim 52 B4
Hofles 97 D4
Höfn 96 C2
Hofolding 56 A3
Hofors 105 F2
Hofsjökull 96 B2
Höganäs 108 C3
Høgebru 100 A3
Höglekardalen 101 E2
Högsäter 105 D4
Högsby 109 E2
Høgset 100 B2
Hohe Acht 51 E4
Hohenau 57 F2
Hohenberg 57 E3
Hohenems 58 B2
Hohengandern 52 B2
Hohenlimburg 17 E4
Hohenlinden 56 B3
Hohenlockstedt 48 A2
Hohenmölsen 53 D2
Hohenpeißenberg 56 A4
Hohenseeden 48 C4
Hohenstein 53 D3
Hohentauern 57 D4
Hohenwestedt 48 A2
Hohenzollern 55 D3
Hoher Zinken 56 C3
Hohe Tauern 59 E2
Hohe Tauern, Nat Pk 59 E2
Hohlakas 93 E2
Hohneck 27 E1
Hohwachter Bucht 48 B1
Hohwald, le 21 E4
Højer 108 A4
Hokksund 104 C3
Hol 104 C2
Holbæk 108 C3
Holbeach 7 E3
Holdorf 17 F2
Holič 57 F1
Höljäkkä 103 E1
Höljes 101 D4
Hollabrunn 57 E2
Høllen 104 B4
Hollenstedt 48 A3
Höllental 57 E3
Holles 97 D4
Hollfeld 52 C4
Hollingsholm 100 B2
Hollola 107 F2
Hollum 16 C1
Hollywood 13 D4
Holm (N) 97 D3
Holm (S) 101 F2
Hólmavík 96 A1
Holmec 70 B1
Holmen 105 D2
Holmestrand 104 C3
Holmfirth 6 C2
Holmön 102 B1
Holmsjön 101 E3
Holmslands Klit 108 A3
Holmsund 102 B1
Holomóndas, Óros 80 B3
Holstebro 108 A2
Holsted 108 A3
Holsworthy 8 C3
Holt 7 F3
Holwerd 47 D3
Holycross Abbey 14 C3
Holyhead 6 A2
Holy I (Anglesey) 6 A2
Holy I (Northumberland) 5 E2
Holywell 6 B2
Holywood 13 E2
Holzappel 51 F4
Holzgau 58 C2
Holzkirchen 56 A3
Holzleitner Sattel 58 C2
Holzminden 52 A2
Homberg (Hessen) 52 A3
Homberg (Nordrhein-Westfalen) 17 D3
Homburg 54 B2
Hommelstø 97 D3
Hommelvik 100 C2
Hommersåk 104 A3
Homoljske planine 73 E3
Hondarribia Fuenterrabia 36 C1
Hondón de las Nieves 45 D2
Hönebach 52 B3
Hønefoss 104 C3
Honfleur 19 D3
Høng 108 B3
Hónikas 87 D2
Honiton 9 D3
Honkajoki 102 B3
Honningsvåg 95 E1
Honrubia 40 C3
Honrubia de la Cuesta 36 A3
Hontalbilla 40 A1
Hontoria del Pinar 36 A3
Hooge 47 F1
Hoogeveen 17 D2
Hoogezand 47 D3
Hoogstraten 50 C2
Hook Head 15 D4
Höör 109 D3
Hoorn 16 C2
Hopetoun House 5 D2
Hopfgarten 59 D1
Hopperstad 104 B1
Hóra (Dodekánissa) 89 E2
Hóra (Pelopónissos) 86 C3
Hora Svatého Šebestiána 53 E3
Horažďovice 56 C1
Horb 54 C3
Hörby 109 D3
Horcajo de los Montes 39 F4
Horcajo de Santiago 40 B3
Horcajo de Trevélez 44 A3
Horcajo-Medianero 39 E2
Horche 40 B2
Hordaland 104 B2
Horden 5 E4
Horeftó 83 F2
Horezu 115 D1
Horgen 58 A2
Horgoš 72 C1
Horley 10 C3
Horn (A) 57 E2
Horn (Baden-Württemberg) 55 D4
Horn (N) 97 D3
Horn (Nordrhein-Westfalen) 52 A2
Hornachos 43 D1
Hornachuelos 43 E2
Hornavan 98 A2
Hornberg 54 C3
Hornburg 52 B1
Horncastle 7 E3
Horndal 106 A3
Horneburg 48 A3
Hörnefors 102 A2
Hörnerkirchen 48 A2
Hornet 100 C2
Hornindal 100 A3
Hornindalsvatn 100 A3
Hørning 108 B3
Horni Počernice 53 F3
Hornisgrinde 54 C3
Horni Slavkov 53 E4
Hornos 44 B2
Hornoy 19 E2
Hornsea 7 E2
Hörnum 47 F1
Hořovice 53 F4
Horsens 108 B3
Horsham 10 C3
Hørsholm 108 C3
Horšovský Týn 56 B1
Horst 48 B3
Horstmar 17 E2
Hortafjorden 97 D3
Horten 104 C3
Hortezuela 36 B4
Hortiátis 80 A3
Hospental 58 A3
Hospital 14 C3
Hospital de Orbigo 35 D3
Hossa 99 F3
Hossegor 28 A4
Hostalric 32 B4
Hotagen 101 E1
Hotagen *L* 101 E1
Hotton 50 C4
Houat 22 C4
Houches, les 27 E4
Houdain 19 F1
Houdan 19 E4
Houeillès 28 B3
Houffalize 51 D4
Houghton-le-Spring 5 E4
Houlgate 18 C3
Houmnikó 80 B2
Hoúni 83 D3
Hourtin 28 A2
Houtskår 107 D3
Hov 108 B3
Hovärken 101 D3
Hovden 104 B3
Hove 10 C3
Hovet 104 B2
Hovmantorp 109 E2
Høvringen 100 C3
Howden 7 D2
Howth 13 E4
Höxter 52 A2
Hoy 3 D1
Hoya 17 F1
Høyanger 100 A3
Hoyerswerda 53 F2
Hoylake 6 B2
Høylandet 97 D4
Hoym 52 C1
Hoyos 39 D2
Höytiainen 103 F2
Hoz de Beteta 40 C2
Hozoviótissa 89 D3
Hracholuská přehr nádrž 53 E4
Hradec-Králove 112 A2
Hrádek 57 E1
Hrádek nad Nisou 53 F2
Hranice (Severomoravský) 112 A3
Hranice (Západočeský) 53 D4
Hrasnica 75 F1
Hrastnik 70 B2
Hrastovlje 70 A3
Hřensko 53 F2
Hríssafa 87 D3
Hrissí, N 91 E4
Hrissó 80 B2
Hrissoskalítissa 90 B3
Hrissoúpoli 80 C2
Hrissovítsi 86 C2
Hristianí, N 91 D1
Hristianó 86 C3
Hristós 89 D2
Hrómio 79 D4
Hrtkovci 72 C3
Hrušovany 57 F1
Hrvace 75 D1
Hrvatska 70 C2
Hückeswagen 17 E4
Hucknall 7 D3
Hucqueliers 19 E1
Huddersfield 6 C2
Hude 47 F3
Hudiksvall 101 F3
Huebra, R 39 E1
Huedin 112 C4
Huélago 44 A3
Huélamo 40 C2
Huelgoat 22 B3
Huelma 44 A2
Huelva 42 C2
Huelva, Riv. de 43 D2
Huércal-Overa 44 C3
Huérguina 41 D3
Huerta del Rey 36 A3
Huerta de Valdecarábanos 40 A3
Huertahernando 40 C2
Huerto 37 E3
Huerva, R 37 D4
Huesa 44 B2
Huesca 37 D3
Huéscar 44 B2
Huesna, Emb de 43 D2
Huete 40 B3
Huétor-Santillán 44 A3
Huétor-Tájar 43 F3
Hüfingen 54 C4
Huftarøy 104 A2
Huisne 23 F3
Huittinen 107 D2
Huizen 16 C2
Hulst 16 B4
Hultsfred 109 E2
Humada 35 F3
Humanes 40 B1
Humber Bridge 7 D2
Humber, R 7 E2
Humberside 7 D2
Humberside (Airport) 7 D2
Humenné 112 C3
Humppila 107 E2
Hundested 108 C3
Hundorp 100 C3
Hunedoara 114 C1
Hünfeld 52 B3
Hungerford 9 E2
Hunnebostrand 105 D4
Húnsflói 96 A1
Hunspach 21 F3
Hunsrück 54 B1
Hunstanton 7 E3
Hunte 17 F1
Huntingdon 9 F1
Huntly 3 E3
Hurdal 105 D2
Huriel 25 F4
Hurones, Emb de los 43 D3
Hurskaala 103 E3
Hürth 17 E4
Hurum 104 C1
Hurup 108 A2
Húsavík 96 B1
Husavik 104 A2
Husbands Bosworth 9 F1
Hushinish 2 A2
Huşi 113 E4
Huskvarna 109 D1
Husnes 104 A2
Hustadvika 100 B2
Hustopeče 57 F1
Husum (D) 47 F1
Husum (S) 102 A2
Hutovo 75 F2
Hutovo Blato 75 F2
Hüttenberg 57 D4
Hüttschlag 59 E1
Huttula 103 D3
Huttwil 27 F2
Huy 50 C4
Hvalba 96 A4
Hvalfjörður 96 A2
Hvalpsund 108 A2
Hvalvik 96 A3
Hvar 75 D2
Hvar *I* 75 E2
Hvarski kan 75 D2
Hveragerði 96 A2
Hveravellir 96 B2
Hvidbjerg 108 A2
Hvide Sande 108 A3
Hvítá 96 A2
Hvittingfoss 104 C3
Hvitträsk 107 E3
Hvolsvöllur 96 B3
Hwlffordd 8 B2
Hyde 6 C2
Hyen 100 A3
Hyères 31 D4
Hyères, Iles d' 31 D4
Hylsfjorden 104 A3
Hyltebruk 108 C2
Hyrynsalmi 99 E4
Hythe 11 D3
Hyvinkää 107 E2
Hyypiö 99 D2

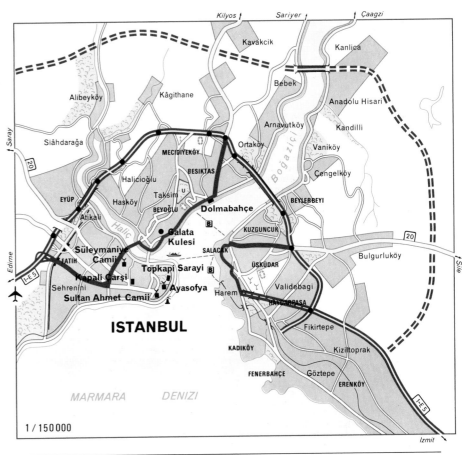

ISTANBUL

1 / 150 000

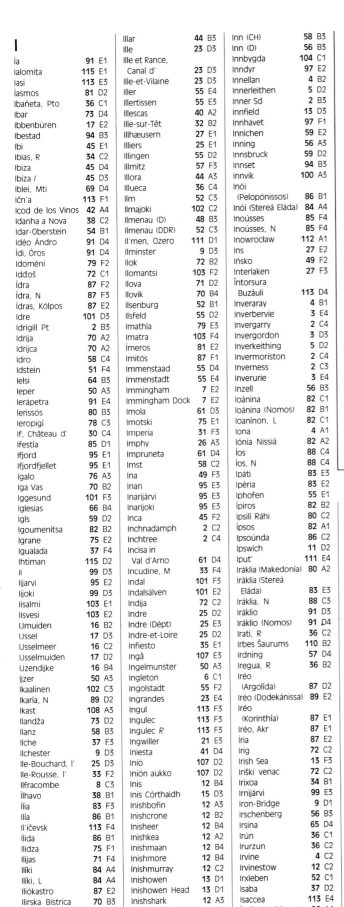

J

Jaala 107 F2
Jääsjärvi 103 D3
Jabalón, R 44 A1
Jabbeke 50 A3
Jablanac 70 B4
Jablan Do 76 A2
Jablanica 75 F1
Jablanica (Reg) 77 D4
Jablanica *R* 77 D1
Jablaničko jez 75 F1
Jablonec nad Nisou 112 A2
Jablonné v Podještědí 53 F3
Jabugo 42 C2
Jabuka (Bosna i Hercegovina) 76 A1
Jabuka (Srbija) 76 B1
Jabuka (Vojvodina) 73 D2
Jabuka, I 74 C2
Jabukovac (Hrvatska) 71 D3
Jabukovac (Srbija) 73 F3
Jabukovik 77 E1
Jaca 37 D2
Jáchymov 53 E3
Jadar (Bosna i Hercegovina) 72 C4
Jadar (Srbija) 72 B3
Jäder 106 A3
Jaderberg 47 F3
Jadovik 76 B1
Jadovnik 71 D4
Jadranska Lešnica 72 B3
Jadransko More 74 B2
Jadraque 40 B1
Jaén 44 A2
Jagodnjac 71 F2
Jagotin 113 F2
Jagst 55 E2
Jagsthausen 55 D2
Jahorina 76 A1
Jahorina (Reg) 76 A1
Jajce 71 E4
Jäkkvik 97 F2
Jakobselv 95 F2
Jakobstad 102 C1
Jakšić 71 E2
Jakupica 77 E3
Jalasjärvi 102 C3
Jaligny 26 A3
Jalón, R 36 C3
Jalovik Izvor 73 F4
Jambol 115 E2
Jamena 72 B3
Jämijärvi 102 C3
Jäminkipohja 102 C3
Jämjö 109 E3
Jammerbugten 108 A2
Jamnička Kiselica 70 C2
Jämsä 103 D3
Jämsänkoski 103 D3
Jämtlands Län 101 E2
Janakkala 107 E2
Janče 77 D3
Jandía, Pta de 42 C4
Jándula, Emb del 44 A1
Jandula, R 44 A1
Jänisselkä 103 F2
Janja 72 B3
Janjevo 77 D2
Janjina 75 E2
Jankov kamen 76 C1
Jañona 39 D2
Jantra 115 D2
Janville 25 E1
Janzé 23 D3
Japetić 70 C2
Jäppilä 103 E2
Jaraba 36 C4
Jarafuel 41 D4
Jaraicejo 39 E3
Jaráiz 39 E2
Jarak 72 C3
Jarama, R 40 B2
Jarandilla de la Vera 39 E2
Järbo 106 A2
Jarcevo 111 E3
Jard 24 B3
Jæren 104 A4
Jaren 105 D2
Jargeau 25 E1
Jarkovac 73 D2
Jarmen 49 D2
Jarmenovci 73 D3
Jarnac 28 B1
Jarnages 25 E4
Järna (Kopparbergs Län) 105 E2
Järna (Stockholms Län) 106 B4
Jarny 21 D3
Jarocin 112 A2
Jaroměřice 57 E1
Jarosław 112 C2
Järpen 101 E2
Jarrow 5 E3
Jarvelä 107 F2
Järvenpää 107 E2
Järvsö 101 F3
Jaša Tomić 73 D2
Jasenak 70 B3
Jasenica (Bosna i Hercegovina) 71 D3
Jasenica (Srbija) 73 D3
Jasenovac 71 D3
Jasenovo (Crna Gora) 76 B2
Jasenovo (Srbija) 76 B1
Jasenovo (Vojvodina) 73 D2
Jasień 53 F1
Jasika 73 E4
Jasikovo 73 E3
Jasło 112 C3
Jasmund 49 D1
Jastrebarsko 70 C2
Jastrowie 112 A1
Jászberény 112 B4
Jau, Col de 32 B2
Jaufenpass 59 D2
Jaunay-Clan 25 D3
Jaunpass 27 E3
Jausiers 31 D2
Javalambre 41 D3
Javalambre, Sa de 41 E3
Javalón 41 D2
Javea 45 E1
Jävenitz 48 C4
Javie, la 31 D3
Javor 76 C1
Javořice 57 D1
Javornjača 71 D4
Javorov 112 C2
Jävre 98 B4
Javron 23 E3
Jedburgh 5 D3
Jedincy 113 D3
Jędrzejów 112 B2
Jeesiö 95 E4
Jeetze 48 B3
Jegun 28 C4
Jegunovce 77 D3
Jēkabpils 110 C3
Jektevik 104 A2
Jelah 71 E3
Jelašca 76 A1
Jelenia Góra 112 A2
Jelenje 70 B3
Jelgava 110 C3
Jelling 108 A3
Jel'n'a 111 E3
Jelsa (N) 104 A3
Jelsa (YU) 75 E2
Jemnice 57 E1
Jena 52 C3
Jenbach 59 D1
Jengejetneme 97 E4
Jennersdorf 57 F4
Jeppo 102 C2
Jerez de la Frontera 43 D3
Jerez de los Caballeros 42 C1
Jérica 41 E3
Jerichow 49 D4
Jerisjärvi 95 D4
Jerpoint Abbey 15 D3
Jersey 18 A3
Jerte 39 E2
Jerte, R 39 E2
Jerxheim 52 B1
Jerzu 66 C3
Jesenice (CS) 53 E4
Jesenice (YU) 70 A1
Jeseník 112 A2
Jesi 61 F4
Jeßnitz 53 D2
Jesolo 59 E4
Jessen 53 D1
Jessheim 105 D3
Jetzelsdorf 57 E2
Jeumont 20 B1
Jevenstedt 48 A2
Jever 47 E3
Jevišovice 57 E1
Jevnaker 105 D2
Jezerane 70 C3
Jezerce 77 D2
Jezercë, M 76 C2
Jezero 71 E4
Jezero Šćit 75 E1
Jezersko 70 B1
Ježevica 72 C4
Jičín 112 A2
Jiekkevarre 94 C2
Jihlava 57 E1
Jihlava *R* 57 E1
Jijona 45 E1
Jiloca, R 41 D2
Jílové u Prahy 53 F4
Jimbolia 114 C1
Jimena 44 A2
Jimena de la Frontera 43 E4
Jindřichovice 53 D3
Jindřichův Hradec 57 D1
Jirkov 53 E3
Jiu 115 D2
Jizera 53 F3
Joachimsthal 49 E3
Jockfall 98 C2
Jódar 44 A2
Jodoigne 50 C3
Joensuu 103 F2
Jõgeva 110 C1
Johanngeorgenstadt 53 D3
John o'Groats 3 D2
Johnstone 4 C2
Johovac 71 F3
Joigny 26 A1
Joinville 20 C4
Jokela 107 E2
Jokijärvi 99 E3
Jokikylä 99 E4
Jokioinen 107 E2
Jokkmokk 98 B2
Jökulsá-á Fjöllum 96 C1
Joloskylä 99 D3
Jølstravatnet 100 A3
Jomala 106 C3
Jönåker 106 A4
Jondal 104 B2
Jongunjärvi 99 E3
Joniškis 110 C3
Jönköping 109 D1
Jönköpings Län 109 D2
Jonzac 28 B1
Jordbro 106 B4
Jordbruksveien 95 D2
Jormlien 97 E4
Jörn 98 B4
Joroinen 103 E3
Jørpeland 104 A3
Jørstadmoen 105 D2
Jošanica 73 E4
Jošanička Banja 76 C1
Jošavka 71 E3
Josenfjorden 104 A3
Josipdol 70 C3
Josipovac 71 F2
Josselin 22 C3
Jostedalsbreen 100 A3
Jotunheimen 100 B3
Jou, Coll de 32 A3
Joué 25 D2
Jougne 27 D3
Joutjärvi 107 F2
Joutsa 103 D3
Joutseno 103 E4
Joutsijärvi 99 E2
Joyeuse 30 B2
Juankoski 103 E2
Juan-les-Pins 31 E4
Júcar, R 41 E4
Jüchen 17 D4
Juchnov 111 F3
Judaberg 104 A3
Judenau 57 E2
Judenburg 57 D4
Judio 43 F1
Juelsminde 108 B3
Jugenheim 54 C1
Jugon 22 C3
Jugorje 70 B2
Juillac 29 D1
Juist 47 E3
Jukkasjärvi 94 C4
Jülich 17 D4
Julierpass 58 B3
Jullouville 18 B4
Jumaliskylä 99 F4
Jumeaux 29 F1
Jumièges 19 D3
Jumilhac-le-Grand 29 D1
Jumilla 45 D1
Jumilla, Pto de 45 D1
Juminen 103 E1
Jumisko 99 E2
Juneda 37 F4
Jungfrau 27 F3
Junik 76 C2
Juniville 20 B3
Junkeren 97 E2
Junosuando 95 D4
Junsele 101 F2
Juntusranta 99 F3
Juojärvi 103 E2
Juoksenki 98 C2
Juorkuna 99 E4
Jura 4 B2
Jura (Canton) 27 E2
Jura (Dépt) 27 D3
Jura, Sd of 4 B2
Jurbarkas 110 C3
Jurjevo 70 B4
Jūrmala 110 C2
Jurmofjärden 107 D3
Jurmu 99 E3
Juromenha 38 C4
Jurva 102 B2
Jussey 27 D1
Justel 34 D3
Jüterbog 53 E1
Juuka 103 E2
Juupajoki 103 D3
Juurusvesi 103 E2
Juva (Mikkelin Lääni) 103 E3
Juva (Turun ja Porin Lääni) 107 D2
Juvigny-le-Tertre 18 C4
Juvigny-sous-Andaine 18 C4
Juvola 103 E3
Juzennecourt 26 C1
Južna Morava 73 E4
Južnyj Bug 113 E2
Jyderup 108 B3
Jylland 108 A3
Jyrkkä 103 E1
Jyväskylä 103 D3

K

Kaamanen 95 E3
Kaamaskoki 95 E2
Kaaresuvanto 95 D3
Kaarina 107 D2
Kaatsheuvel 16 C3
Kaavi 103 E2
Kaavinjärvi 103 E2
Kåbdalis 98 B3
Kablart 72 C4
Kać 72 C2
Kačanik 77 D2
Kačarevo 73 D2
Kačikol 77 D2
Kadaň 53 E3
Kadi Bogaz 73 F4
Kadrifakovo 77 E3
Kafiréas, Akr 84 C4
Kafiréa, Stenó 88 B1
Kåfjord 95 E1
Kåfjorden 94 C2
Kaga 106 A4
Kagarlyk 113 E2
Kagul 113 E4
Kahla 52 C3
Kaiáfas 86 B2
Kailbach 55 D1
Kaïmaktsalán 79 E2
Kainasto 102 B3
Kaindorf 57 E4
Kaipola 103 D3
Kairala 95 F4
Kaisergebirge 59 D1
Kaiserslautern 54 B1
Kaisheim 55 E2
Kaitumälven 94 C4
Kaiuđerovo 73 E2
Kajaani 99 E4
Kakan 74 C1
Kakanj 71 F4
Kakí Thálassa 88 A1
Kakí Vígla 87 F1
Kakslauttanen 95 E3
Kalajoki 102 C1
Kalajoki *R* 102 C1
Kalak 95 E1
Kalamáki (Lárissa) 83 F2
Kalamáki (Magnissía) 84 A2
Kalamáki, Akr 85 D2
Kalamáta 86 C3
Kalambáka 83 D1
Kalambáki 80 C2
Kalámi 89 E1
Kalamiótissa 91 F1
Kalamítsi (Makedonía) 80 B4
Kalamitsi (Stereá Eláda) 82 B3
Kálamos, N 82 C3
Kalamotí 85 F4
Kalamotó 80 A3
Kalándra 80 A4
Kalá Nerá 83 F2
Kalá Nissiá 87 E1
Kalanti 107 D2
Kalapódi 83 F3
Kalaraš 113 E3
Kalarne 101 F2
Kalavárda 93 E1
Kalávrita 86 C1
Kal'azin 111 F1
Kalbe 48 C4
Kalce 70 A2
Kaldakvísl 96 B2
Kaléndzi (Ípiros) 82 C2
Kaléndzi (Pelopónissos) 86 C1
Kalenić 73 D4
Kalérgo 84 C4
Kalesija 72 B3
Kali 74 C1
Kaliakoúda 83 D3
Kaliáni 87 D1
Kalídromo, Óros 83 E3
Kalifitos 80 C2
Kalí Liménes 91 D4
Kalí Límni 93 D3
Kalimassiá 85 F4
Kalimenci, Ez 77 F2
Kálimnos 89 F3
Kálimnos, N 89 E3
Kalinin 111 F2
Kaliningrad 110 B4
Kalinkoviči 113 E1
Kalinovik 75 F1
Kalipéfki 79 E4
Kalirráhi 79 D4
Kalithéa (Dodekánissa) 93 F1
Kalithéa (Ilía) 86 C2
Kalithéa (Makedonía) 80 B2
Kalithéa (Messinía) 86 C3
Kalithéa (Stereá Eláda) 83 D3
Kalithéa (Thessalía) 80 B4
Kalithiés 93 F1
Kalithiro 83 D2
Kalivári 88 B1
Kalíves (Kríti) 90 C3
Kalíves (Thássos) 80 C3
Kalívia (Ahaïa) 86 C1
Kalívia (Atikí-Piréas) 87 F1
Kalívia (Etolía-Akarnanía) 82 C3
Kalívia (Korinthía) 87 D1
Kalívia Varikoú 79 F4
Kalix 98 C3
Kalixälven 98 C2
Kaljord 94 A3
Kalkar 17 D3
Kalkkinen 107 F1
Kall 101 D2
Kallaktjåkkå 94 B4
Kallavesi 103 E2
Kållby 102 C1
Kållby 105 E4
Kallinge 109 E3
Kallio 102 C3
Kalliojoki 99 F4
Kallislahti 103 E3
Kallmünz 55 F2
Kallsjön 101 D1
Kalmar 109 E2
Kalmar Län 109 E2
Kalmar sund 109 E2
Kalmit 54 C2
Kalna 73 F4
Kalnik 71 D2
Kalnik *Mt* 71 D2
Kalocsa 112 B4
Kalogerikoú 87 D2
Kalogriá 86 B1
Kalohóri 83 D1
Kaló Horió 91 E4
Kalókastro 80 A2
Kaló Neró 86 C3
Kaloní (Lésvos) 85 F2
Kaloní (Pelopónissos) 87 E2
Kalonís, Kólpos 85 F2
Kaloskopí 83 E3
Kalotássi, Akr 89 D4
Kalø Vig 108 B3
Kalpáki 78 C4
Kals 59 E2
Kalsdorf 57 E4
Kaltbrunn 58 A2
Kaltenkirchen 48 A2
Kaltennordheim 52 B3
Kaltern 59 D3
Kaltezés 87 D2
Kaluga 111 F3
Kalundborg 108 B3
Kaluš 112 C3
Kalvåg 104 A1
Kalvehave 108 C4
Kälviä 102 C1
Kalvola 107 E2
Kalvträsk 98 B4
Kamáres (Kríti) 91 D4
Kamarés (Páros) 88 C3
Kamáres (Pelopónissos) 83 D4
Kamáres (Sífnos) 88 B3
Kamári 91 E1
Kamariótissa 81 E3
Kambanós, Akr 88 B1
Kambiá 85 E4
Kámbos (Kríti) 90 B3
Kámbos (Pelopónissos) 86 C3
Kámbos (Stereá Eláda) 83 D4
Kamčija 115 E2
Kamen 17 E3
Kamenari 76 A3
Kaména Voúria 83 F3
Kamenec-Podol'skij 113 D3
Kamenica 77 F2
Kamenice 57 D1
Kaméni, N 91 E1
Kamenjak, Rt 70 A4
Kamenka 113 F2
Kamensko (Hrvatska) 71 E2
Kamensko (Hrvatska) 75 E1
Kamenz 53 F2
Kamień Pomorski 49 E2
Kamieński, Zalew 49 E2
Kamilári 91 D4
Kaminia 86 B1
Kámiros 93 E1
Kamnik 70 B2
Kamp 57 E2
Kamp-Bornhofen 51 E4
Kampen (D) 47 F1
Kampen (NL) 17 D2
Kamp-Lintfort 17 D3
Kanal 70 A2
Kanála 88 A2
Kanal Dunav-Tisa-Dunav 73 D2
Kanália 55 D4
Kanatádika 83 F3
Kánava 88 A4
Kándanos 90 B3
Kandel 54 C2
Kandel *Mt* 54 C3
Kandern 54 C4
Kandersteg 27 F3
Kándia 87 E2
Kandíla (Pelopónissos) 87 D2
Kandíla (Stereá Eláda) 82 C3
Kandíli 84 A3
Kandíra 115 F3
Kandrše 70 B2
Kanestraum 100 B2
Kanev 113 F2
Kanfanar 70 A3
Kangádio 86 B1
Kangasala 107 E1
Kangaslampi 103 E2
Kangasniemi 103 D3
Kangosjärvi 95 D4
Kanjiža 72 C1
Kankaanpää 102 C3
Kannonkoski 103 D2
Kannus 102 C1
Kannusjärvi 103 E4

Kanturk 14 B3
Kaona 73 D4
Kaonik (Bosna i Hercegovina) 71 F4
Kaonik (Srbija) 73 E4
Kapandriti 87 F1
Kaparéli 83 F4
Kapariá 88 B2
Kapele, Vrh 70 C3
Kapellskär 106 C3
Kapélo, Akr 90 A2
Kapfenberg 57 E3
Kaplice 57 D2
Kaposvár 114 B1
Kapp 105 D2
Kappel 51 E4
Kappeln 48 A1
Kappelshamnsviken 109 F3
Kaprije 74 C1
Kaprun 59 E1
Kapsáli 90 A2
Kápsas 87 D2
Kapsoúri 88 B1
Kapsukas 110 C4
Kapuvár 112 A4
Karabiga 115 E3
Karaburun 115 E4
Karačev 111 F4
Karadeniz Boğazı 115 F3
Karan 72 C4
Karasjåkka 95 E2
Karasjok 95 E2
Karasu 115 F3
Karats 98 A2
Karavás 90 A1
Karavómilos 83 F3
Karavónissia 92 C2
Karavostássis 91 D1
Kårböle 101 E3
Karcag 112 B4
Kardámena 89 F3
Kardámila 85 E4
Kardamíli 86 C3
Kardeljevo 75 E2
Kärdla 110 B1
Kardítsa 55 D4
Kardítsa (Nomos) 55 D4
Kărdžali 115 D3
Karerpass 59 D3
Karesuando 95 D3
Karfás 85 F4
Karhukangas 99 D4
Karhula 103 F4
Karhunkierros 99 F2
Karhutunturi 95 F4
Kariá (Pelopónissos) 87 D2
Kariá (Stereá Eláda) 83 F3
Kariés (Makedonía) 80 C4
Kariés (Pelopónissos) 87 D3
Karigasniemi 95 E2
Karijoki 102 B3
Karinainen 107 D2
Kariótisa 79 E3
Karis 107 E3
Káristos 88 A1
Karítena 86 C2
Karjaa 107 E3
Karjalohja 107 E3
Karkaloú 86 C2
Karkinágri 89 D2
Karkku 107 D1
Kärkölä 107 E2
Karleby 102 C1
Karlevi 109 E3
Karlino 49 F1
Karl-Marx-Stadt 53 E3
Karlobag 70 C4
Karlovac 70 C3
Karlovássi 89 E1
Karlovo 115 D2
Karlovy Vary 53 E4
Karlsborg 105 E4
Karlsburg 49 D2
Karlsfeld 55 F3
Karlshamn 109 D3
Karlshuld 55 F2
Karlskoga 105 E4
Karlskrona 109 E3
Karlsøy 94 C2
Karlsruhe 54 C2
Karlstad 105 E3
Karlstadt 52 B4
Karlštejn 53 F4
Karlstift 57 D2
Karmøy 104 A3
Karnezéika 87 E2
Karnobat 115 E2
Kärnten 59 F2
Karolinerleden 101 E2
Karow 48 C2
Kärpankylä 99 F2
Kárpathos 93 D3
Kárpathos, N 93 D3
Karpeníssi 83 D3
Karperí 80 A2
Karperó 79 D4
Kärsämäki 103 D1
Kårsatjåkka 94 B4
Kärsava 111 D2
Karstädt 48 C3
Karstula 103 D2
Kartal 115 F3
Kartéri (Ípiros) 82 B2
Kartéri (Pelopónissos) 87 D1
Karterós 91 D3
Kártsino, Akr 84 C3
Karttula 103 E2
Kartuzy 110 A4
Karungi 98 C3
Karunki 98 C3
Karup 108 A2
Karvala 102 C2
Kärväskylä 103 D2
Karvia 102 C3
Karviná 112 B3
Karvoskylä 103 D1
Karvounári 82 B2
Karwendelgebirge 59 D1
Kašalj 76 C1
Kašin 111 F1
Kašina 70 C2
Kaskinen 102 B3
Kasko 102 B3
Káspakas 85 D1
Kašperské Hory 56 C1
Kassándra 80 B4
Kassándras, Kólpos 80 B4
Kassándria 80 A4
Kassel 52 A2
Kassiópi 82 A1
Kassópi 82 B2
Kássos, N 93 D3
Kastaniá (Makedonía) 79 E3
Kastaniá (Pelopónissos) 87 D1
Kastaniá (Thessalía) 82 C1
Kastaniá (Thessalía) 83 D2
Kastaniés 81 F1
Kastaniótissa 83 F3
Kastéla 84 B4
Kastelhoms 106 C3
Kastéli (Kriti) 90 B3
Kastéli (Kriti) 91 E4
Kastellaun 51 E4
Kastelórizo 93 F2
Kastélou, Akr 93 D3
Kastelruth 59 D3
Kaštel Stari 75 D1
Kaštel Žegarski 75 D1
Kasterlee 50 C3
Kastl 55 F1
Kastorf 48 B2
Kastóri 87 D3
Kastoriá 79 D3
Kastoriá (Nomos) 78 C3
Kastoriás, L 79 D3
Kastós, N 82 C4
Kastráki (Kikládes) 88 C3
Kastráki (Stereá Eláda) 82 C3
Kastráki (Thessalía) 83 D1
Kastrakiou, Teh L 82 C3
Kastrí (Pelopónissos) 87 D2
Kastrí (Stereá Eláda) 83 E3
Kastrí (Thessalía) 83 F1
Kástro (Pelopónissos) 86 B1
Kástro (Skíathos) 84 A2
Kástro (Stereá Eláda) 83 F4
Kastrossikiá 82 B2
Katafígio 79 E4
Katáfito 80 B1
Katáfourko 82 C3
Katahás 79 F3
Katákolo 86 B2
Katálako 85 D1
Kátano, Akr 88 A3
Katápola 89 D3
Katára 82 C1
Katastári 86 A1
Katavía 93 E2
Katelimátsa 91 F1
Kateliós 86 A1
Kateríni 79 F4
Katerloch 57 E4
Katharó 91 E4
Katheni 84 B4
Katići 76 C1
Kätkäsuvanto 95 D4
Katlanovo 77 E3
Katlanovska Banja 77 E3
Katlenburg-Duhm 52 B2
Káto Ahaía 86 B1
Káto Alissós 86 B1
Káto Asséa 87 D2
Káto Dolianá 87 D2
Káto Figália 86 C2
Káto Gadzéa 83 F2
Katohí 82 C4
Káto Kamíla 80 B2
Káto Klinés 79 D2
Káto Makrinoú 83 D4
Katoméri, Akr 88 C3
Káto Moussounítsa 83 E3
Káto Nevrokópi 80 B1
Káto Ólimbos 83 E1
Káto Tithoréa 83 E4
Katoúna (Lefkáda) 82 B3
Katoúna (Stereá Eláda) 82 C3
Káto Vassilikí 83 D4
Káto Vérga 86 C3
Káto Vérmio 79 E3
Káto Vlassia 86 C1
Katowice 112 B2
Káto Zahlorou 86 C1
Káto Zákros 91 F4
Katrineholm 106 A4
Katschberg 59 F2
Katschberg-Tunnel 59 F2
Kattegat 108 C2
Katwijk aan Zee 16 B2
Kaub 51 F4
Kaufbeuren 55 E3
Kauhajärvi 102 C2
Kauhajoki 102 B3
Kauhaneva-Pohjankangas 102 C3
Kauhava 102 C2
Kaukonen 95 E4
Kaunas 110 C3
Kaupanger 104 B1
Kaušany 113 E4
Kaustinen 102 C2
Kautokeino 95 D3
Kautokeinoelva 95 D3
Kauttua 107 D2
Kavadarci 77 E3
Kavajë 76 C4
Kavála 80 C2
Kavála (Nomos) 80 C2
Kaválas, Kólpos 80 C2
Kavarna 115 E2
Kavíli 81 F1
Kävlinge 108 C3
Kávos 82 A2
Kavoússi 91 F4
Käylä 99 E2
Kaysersberg 27 E1
Kazan 73 E2
Kažani 77 E4
Kazanlăk 115 D2
Kazárma 86 C3
Kazatin 113 E2
Kazimierz Dolny 112 C2
Kazincbarcika 112 B3
Kdyně 56 B1
Kéa 88 A2
Keadew 12 C2
Keady 13 D2
Keähkkiljohka 95 D3
Keal, L na 4 B1
Kéa Meriá 88 A2
Kéa, N 88 A2
Kéas, Stenó 88 A2
Kebnekaise 94 B4
Kebnekaise *Mt* 94 B4
Kebock Head 2 B2
Kecskemét 112 B4
Kėdainiai 110 C3
Kédros 83 D2
Kędzierzyn-Koźle 112 B2
Keel 12 A2
Keerbergen 50 C3
Kefalári 87 D2
Kefálas, Akr 80 C3
Kefáli, Akr 90 A2
Kefaloniá, N 82 B4
Kéfalos 89 F4
Kéfalos, Akr 88 A2
Kefalóvrisso (Ípiros) 78 C4
Kefalóvrisso (Pelopónissos) 86 C3
Kefalóvrisso (Stereá Eláda) 82 C4
Kefalóvrisso (Thessalía) 83 D1
Keflavík 96 A2
Kehl 54 C3
Kehlstein 56 C4
Kehrókambos 80 C2
Kéhros 81 E2
Keighley 6 C2
Keimaneigh, Pass of 14 B4
Keitele 103 D2
Keitele *L* 103 D2
Keith 3 D3
Kéla 79 D2
Kelankylä 99 E3
Kelberg 51 E4
Kelbra 52 C2
Këlcyrë 114 C4
Kelebija 72 B1
Kelefá 87 D4
Kelheim 55 F2
Kellinghusen 48 A2
Kellojärvi 99 F4
Kellokoski 107 E2
Kells 13 D3
Kelso 5 E2
Kelujärvi 95 E4
Kemberg 53 D1
Kembs 27 E1
Kemi 99 D3
Kemihaara 95 F4
Kemijärvi 99 E2
Kemijärvi *L* 99 E2
Kemijoki 99 D2
Keminmaa 99 D3
Kemiö 107 D3
Kemnath 53 D4
Kempele 99 D4
Kempen 17 D4
Kempenich 51 E4
Kempten 55 E4
Kendal 6 B1
Kéndras, Akr 88 B3
Kendrikó 79 F2
Kenilworth 9 E1
Kenmare 14 A4
Kenmare River 14 A4
Kennacraig 4 B2
Kenoúrgio 83 D3
Kent 11 D3
Kentallen 4 B1
Kenzingen 54 C3
Keramía 85 F2
Keramídi 83 F2
Keramitsa 82 B1
Kéramos 85 E4
Keramotí 81 D2
Kerassiá (Évia) 84 A3
Kerassiá (Thessalía) 83 F2
Kerassiés 79 E2
Kerassohóri 83 D3
Kerassóna 82 C2
Kérata, Akr 83 F3
Keratéa 87 F2
Kerava 107 E2
Kerdília, N. 80 B3
Kérēs 72 C1
Kerí 86 A2
Kerimäki 103 F3
Kerken 17 D3
Kerketéas, Óros 89 E1
Kerkétio, Óri 83 D2
Kerkíni, Óros 80 A1
Kerkínis, L 80 A2
Kérkira 82 A1
Kérkira, N 82 A1
Kerkonkoski 103 D2
Kerkrade 51 D3
Kernascléden 22 B3
Kéros, N 88 C3
Kerpen 17 D4
Kerrera 4 B1
Kerry 14 B3
Kerry Head 14 A3
Kerteminde 108 B3
Kértezi 86 C1
Kerzers 27 E2
Kesälahti 103 F3
Keşan 115 E3
Kesch, Piz 58 B3
Kesh 12 C2
Keski-Suomen Lääni 103 D2
Kessariani 87 F1
Kestilä 99 D4
Keswick 5 D4
Keszthely 112 A4
Kętrzyn 110 B4
Kettering 9 F1
Kettletoft 3 E1
Kettwig 17 E4
Ketzin 49 D4
Keukenhof 16 B2
Keurusselkä 103 D3
Keuruu 102 C3
Kevelaer 17 D3
Kevo 95 E2
Kevo (Nat Pk) 95 E2
Key, L 12 C3
Keynsham 9 D2
Kežmarok 112 B3
Kiani 81 F1
Kiantajärvi 99 F3
Kiáto 87 D1
Kiberg 95 F1
Kičevo 77 D3
Kidderminster 9 D1
Kidlington 9 E2
Kidsgrove 6 C3
Kidwelly 8 C2
Kiefersfelden 56 B4
Kiekinkoski 99 F4
Kiel 48 A1
Kielce 112 B2
Kielder Reservoir 5 E3
Kieler Bucht 48 A1
Kiental 27 F3
Kierinki 99 D1
Kietz 49 F4
Kifissiá 87 F1
Kifissós 83 F4
Kifjord 95 E1
Kihlanki 95 D4
Kihniö 102 C3
Kihti Skiftet 107 D3
Kiihtelysvaara 103 F2
Kiikala 107 E2
Kiikka 107 D2
Kiikoinen 107 D1
Kiimanen 99 E4
Kiiminginjoki 99 D3
Kiiminki 99 D3
Kiiskilä 102 C1
Kiistala 95 E4
Kijev 113 E2
Kijevo (Hrvatska) 75 D1
Kijevo (Kosovo) 77 D2
Kijevskoje Vodochranilišče 113 E2
Kikinda 72 C1
Kiklådes 88 B2
Kil 105 E3
Kila 79 D3
Kiláda (Makedonía) 79 E3
Kiláda (Pelopónissos) 87 E2
Kilafors 101 F4
Kilbaha 12 A4
Kilbeggan 12 C4
Kilbirnie 4 C2
Kilboghamn 97 E2
Kilbotn 94 B3
Kilbrannan Sd 4 B2
Kilchoan 2 B4
Kilcock 13 D4
Kilcormac 12 C4
Kilcreggan 4 C2
Kilcullen 13 D4
Kildare 13 D4
Kildare (Co) 13 D4
Kildorrery 14 C3
Kilfenora 12 B4
Kilgarvan 14 B4
Kilija 113 E4
Kilingi-Nõmme 110 C2
Kilíni 86 B1
Kilíni, Óros 87 D1
Kilkee 12 A4
Kilkeel 13 E3
Kilkenny 15 D3
Kilkenny (Co) 15 D3
Kilkhampton 8 B3
Kilkieran B 12 A3
Kilkís 79 F2
Kilkís (Nomos) 79 F2
Killadysert 12 B4
Killala B 12 B2
Killaloe 12 B4
Killarney 14 B4
Killary Harbour 12 A3
Killashandra 12 C3
Killenaule 14 C3
Killimer 12 B4
Killin 4 C1
Killinkoski 102 C3
Killorglin 14 A3
Killybegs 12 C2
Killyleagh 13 E2
Kilmaing 12 B3
Kilmallock 14 B3
Kilmarnock 4 C2
Kilmartin 4 B2
Kilmore Quay 15 D4
Kilmurry 12 B4
Kilninver 4 B1
Kilnsea 7 E2
Kilpisjärvi 94 C3
Kilpisjärvi *L* 94 C3
Kilrea 13 D1
Kilronan 12 B4
Kilrush 12 B4
Kilsyth 4 C2
Kiltamagh 12 B3
Kiltealy 15 D3
Kilwinning 4 C2
Kilyos 115 F3
Kimássi 84 A3
Kiméria 81 D2
Kimi 84 B3
Kimina 79 F3
Kimis, Órmos 84 B4
Kimísseos Theotókou 87 D2
Kimito 107 D3
Kimolos 88 B4
Kímolos, N 88 B4
Kimólou Sífnou, Stenó 88 B3
Kimry 111 F2
Kimstad 105 F4
Kínaros, N 89 D3
Kinbrace 3 D2
Kincardine 5 D2
Kindberg 57 E3
Kindelbrück 52 C2
Kinéta 87 E1
Kingisepp 111 D1
Kingissepp 110 B2
Kingsbridge 8 C4
Kingscourt 13 D3
King's Lynn 7 E3
Kingston 9 F2
Kingston-upon-Hull 7 E2
Kingswear 8 C4
Kington 9 D1
Kingussie 3 D4
Kínira 81 D3
Kinlochbervie 2 C2
Kinlochewe 2 C3
Kinloch Rannoch 4 C1
Kinna 108 C1
Kinnairds Head 3 E3
Kinnasniemi 103 F2
Kinnegad 13 D3
Kinnitty 12 C4
Kinnula 103 D2
Kinross 5 D2
Kinsale 14 B4
Kinsarvik 104 B2
Kintaus 103 D3
Kintore 3 E4
Kintyre 4 B2
Kinvarra 12 B4
Kinzig 54 C3
Kióni 82 B4
Kiparissí 87 E3
Kiparissía 86 C3
Kiparissiakós Kólpos 86 B2
Kiparissías, Óri 86 C3
Kipárissos 83 E2
Kípi (Ípiros) 78 C4
Kípi (Thráki) 81 F2
Kipinä 99 D3
Kipos, Akr 81 E3
Kipourío 79 D4
Kippure 13 D4
Kipséli 83 E2
Kir 76 C3
Kirá Panagiá, N 84 B2
Kirchbach 57 E4
Kirchberg (D) 54 B1
Kirchberg (DDR) 53 D3
Kirchberg (Nieder österreich) 57 E2
Kirchberg (Tirol) 59 E1
Kirchberg an der Pielach 57 E3
Kirchdorf 57 D3
Kirchenlamitz 53 D4
Kirchenthumbach 53 D4
Kirchhain 52 A3
Kirchheim (Baden-Württemberg) 55 D2
Kirchheim (Hessen) 52 B3
Kirchheimbolanden 54 C1
Kirchheim unter Teck 55 D2
Kirchhundem 17 F4
Kirchlengern 17 F2
Kirchmöser 49 D4
Kirchschlag 57 F3
Kiriakí 81 F1
Kiriáki 83 F4
Kiriši 111 E1
Kırkağaç 115 E4
Kirkby Lonsdale 6 C1
Kirkby Stephen 5 E4
Kirkcaldy 5 D2
Kirkcolm 4 B3
Kirkcudbright 4 C3
Kirkenær 105 D2
Kirkenes 95 F2
Kirkeøy 105 D4
Kirkestinden 94 B3
Kirkham 6 B2
Kirki 81 E2
Kirkintilloch 4 C2
Kirkjubøur 96 A4
Kirkkonummi 107 E3
Kirklareli 115 E3
Kirkonmaanselkä 103 F4
Kirkwall 3 E1
Kirn 54 B1
Kirov 111 F3
Kirovograd 113 F2
Kirovsk 111 D1
Kirriemuir 5 D1
Kirtorf 52 A3
Kiruna 94 C4
Kisa 109 E1
Kisac 72 C2
Kiseljak (Loznica) 72 B3
Kiseljak (Sarajevo) 75 F1
Kiseljak (Tuzla) 71 F3
Kišin'ov 113 E3
Kisko 107 E3
Kiskőrös 112 B4
Kiskunfélegyháza 112 B4
Kiskunhalas 114 B1
Kißlegg 55 E4

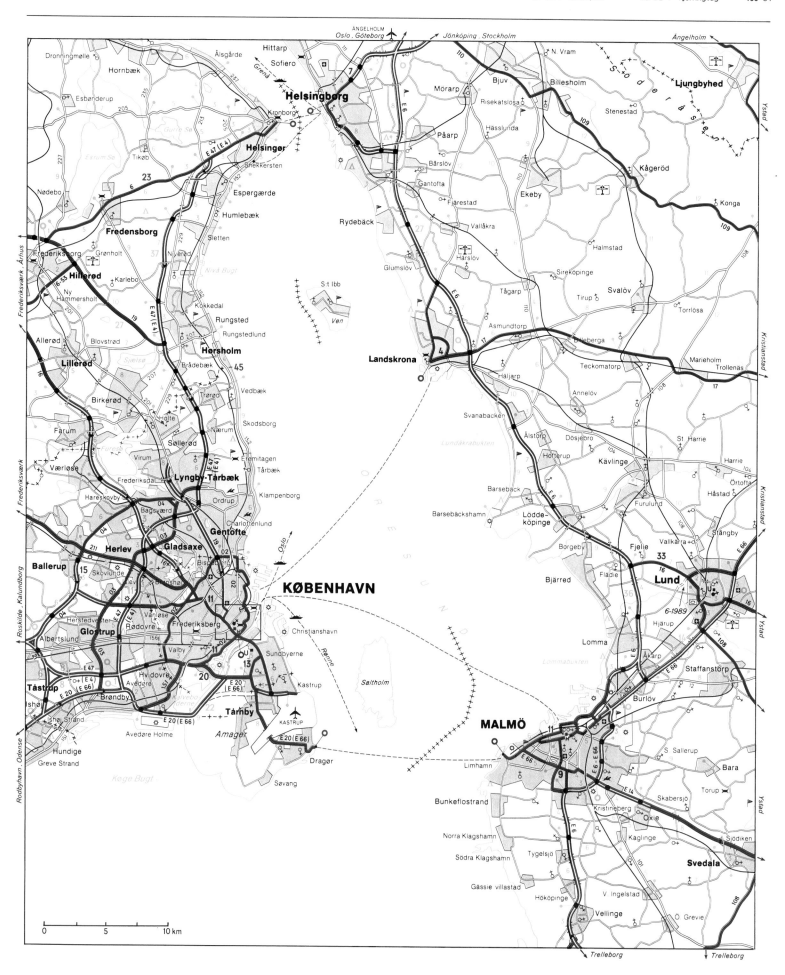

Kjerringvik 101 D1
Kjølifjell 101 D2
Kjøllefjord 95 E1
Kjøpsvik 94 B4
Kjustendil 114 C3
Klæbu 100 C2
Kladanj 72 B4
Kladnica 76 C1
Kladnice 75 D1
Kladno 53 F4
Kladovo 73 F2
Klagenfurt 70 A1
Klaipėda 110 B3
Klaksvik 96 A3
Klana 70 B3
Klanac 70 C4
Klanxbüll 47 F1
Klarälven 105 E2
Klašnice 71 E3
Klässbol 105 E3
Klášterec 53 E3
Klasvík 96 A3
Klatovy 56 C1
Klaukkala 107 E2
Klausen 59 D2
Klausenpass 58 A2
Klazienaveen 17 E2
Kleinhaugsdorf 57 E2
Kleinheubach 55 D1
Kleinwalsertal 55 E4
Klekovača 71 D4
Klenike 77 E2
Klenovica 70 B3
Kleppe 104 A3
Kleppestø 104 A2
Kleve 17 D3
Kličevac 73 D2
Klimoviči 111 E4
Klimpfjäll 97 E4
Klin 111 F2
Klina 76 C2
Klinča Selo 70 C2
Klincy 111 E4
Klingenbach 57 F3
Klingenthal 53 D3
Klinovec 53 E3
Klintehamn 109 F4
Klippan 108 C3
Klippen 97 E3
Klippitztörl 57 D4
Klis 75 D1
Klissoúra 79 D3
Klisura (Makedonija) 77 F3
Klisura (Srbija) 77 E1
Klitoría 86 C1
Klitten 53 F2
Klixbüll 47 F1
Kljajićevo 72 B2
Ključ 71 D4
Kłodzko 112 A2
Kløfta 105 D3
Klokkarvik 104 A2
Klokočevac 73 F3
Klos 76 C4
Kloštar 71 D2
Kloštar Ivanić 71 D2
Klösterle 58 B2
Klosterneuburg 57 F2
Klosters 58 B2
Kloten 58 A2
Klötze 48 C4
Klöverträsk 98 B3
Klövsjö 101 E3
Kluczbork 112 A2
Klupe 71 E3
Klütz 48 B2
Knapdale 4 B2
Knappogue Castle 12 B4
Knäred 109 D2
Knaresborough 6 C1
Knarvik 104 A2
Kneginec 71 D1
Kneža 115 D2
Knežak 70 B3
Kneževi Vinogradi 71 F2
Kneževo 71 F2
Knežica 71 D3
Knežina 72 B4
Knić 73 D4
Knídi 79 D4
Knighton 9 D1
Knight's Town 14 A4
Knin 75 D1

Knittelfeld 57 D4
Knivskjellodden 95 D1
Knivsta 106 B3
Knjaževac 73 F4
Knockmealdown Mts 14 C3
Knokke-Heist 50 A3
Knole House 10 C3
Knossós 91 D3
Knutsford 6 C2
Koarvikodds 95 E3
Kobarid 70 A2
Kobbfjorden 95 D1
Kobel'aki 113 F2
København 108 C3
Kobern-Gondorf 51 E4
Kobišnica 73 F3
Koblenz 51 E4
Kobrin 112 C1
Koca D 115 F3
Kočani 77 F2
Koceljevo 72 C3
Kočerin 75 E2
Kočevje 70 B2
Kočevski rog 70 B2
Kochel 56 A4
ocher 55 E2
Kodiksami 107 D2
Kodisjoki 107 D2
Köflach 57 E4
Køge 108 C3
Køge Bugt 108 C3
Kohtla-Järve 110 C1
Koikkala 103 E3
Koirakoski 103 E1
Koitajoki 103 F2
Koitelainen 95 E4
Koitere 103 F2
Koivujärvi 103 D1
Koi vusuo 103 F2
Kokála 87 D4
Kökar 106 C3
Kokári 89 E1
Kökarsfjärden 106 C3
Kokemäenjoki 107 D1
Kokemäki 107 D2
Kokin Brod 76 B1
Kókino Neró 83 F1
Kokkola 102 C1
Kokoti 83 F3
Koksijde-Bad 50 A3
Kola 71 E3
Koláka 83 F4
Kolari (SF) 98 C1
Kolari (YU) 73 D3
Kolåsen 101 D1
Kolašin 76 B2
Kolbäck 105 F3
Kołbacz 49 F2
Kołbaskowo 49 E2
Kolbermoor 56 B3
Kolby Kås 108 B3
Kolding 108 A3
Kolho 103 D3
Koli 103 F2
Kolima 103 D2
Kolimvári 90 B3
Kolín 112 A3
Kolindrós 79 F3
Kolínes 87 D3
Kolka 110 B2
Kolkanlahti 103 D2
Kolkasrags 110 B2
Kölleda 52 C2
Kolmården 106 A4
Köln 17 E4
Koło 112 B1
Kołobrzeg 49 F1
Koločep 75 F2
Kolomyja 113 D3
Koloveč 56 B1
Kolovrat 76 B1
Kolpino 111 D1
Kolsva 105 F3
Kolubara 72 C3
Kolvereid 97 D4
Komagfjord 95 D2
Kómanos 79 D3
Komar 71 E4
Komára 81 F1
Komárno 112 B4
Kombóti 82 C2
Koméno 82 C3
Kómi (Kikládes) 88 B2

Kómi (Híos) 89 D1
Komílio 82 B3
Komin 70 C2
Kómito 88 B1
Komiža 75 D2
Komló 114 B1
Komninádes 78 C3
Komniná (Makedonía) 79 D3
Komniná (Thráki) 81 D2
Komorane 77 D2
Komotiní 81 E2
Komovi 76 B2
Komrat 113 E4
Komulanköngäs 99 E4
Konak 73 D2
Konakovo 111 F2
Končanica 71 D2
Kondiás 85 D1
Kondopoúli 85 D1
Kondós, Akr 88 B3
Kondovázena 86 C1
Kondrić 71 F2
Konečka pl 77 E3
Køng 108 C4
Köngernheim 54 C1
Konginkangas 103 D2
Kongsberg 104 C3
Kongselva 94 A3
Kongsfjord 95 F1
Kongsvinger 105 D3
Kœnigsbourg 27 E1
Königsbrück 53 E2
Königsbrunn 55 F3
Königsee 52 C3
Königsfeld 54 C3
Königslutter 52 B1
Königsschlösser 55 F4
Königssee 56 C4
Königssee L 56 C4
Königstein (D) 51 F4
Königstein (DDR) 53 F2
Königswiesen 57 D2
Königswinter 51 E3
Königs-Wusterhausen 49 E4
Konin 112 A1
Koniskós 83 D1
Konístres 84 B4
Kónitsa 78 C4
Konj 75 E1
Konjevrate 75 D1
Konjic 75 F1
Konjsko 76 A2
Konjsko 73 F3
Konjuh 71 F4
Konkämäälven 94 C3
Könnern 52 C2
Konnevesi 103 D2
Konnevesi L 103 D2
Könönpelto 103 E3
Konopište 77 E3
Konotop 113 F1
Konsko 77 F4
Konsmo 104 B4
Konstantinovy Lázně 53 E4
Konstanz 55 D4
Kontich 50 B3
Kontiolahti 103 F2
Kontiomäki 99 E4
Konttajärvi 98 C2
Konz 54 A1
Kopaída 83 F4
Kopáník 82 C2
Kopaída 83 F4
Kopanós 79 E3
Kopaonik 77 D1
Koparnes 100 A2
Kópasker 96 C1
Kopavogur 96 A2
Köpenick 49 E4
Koper 70 A3
Kopervik 104 A3
Köping 105 F3
Köpingsvik 109 E2
Koplik 76 B3
Köpmanholmen 102 A2
Koporiće 77 D1
Koppang 100 C3
Kopparberg 105 F3
Kopparbergs Län 105 E2
Kopparleden 101 E2
Kopperby 48 A1
Kopperveien 100 D3
Koprivna 71 F3

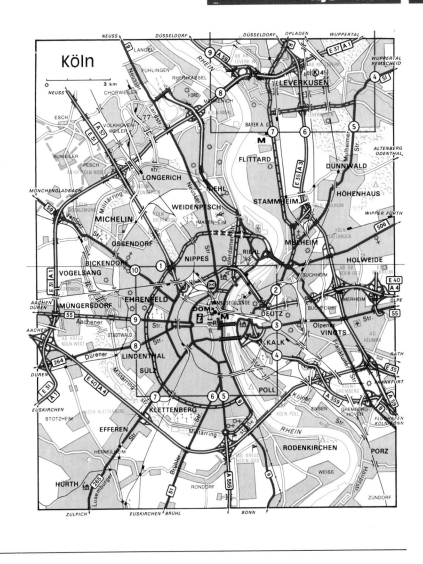

Köln

Koprivnica (Bosna i Hercegovina) 71 D1
Koprivnica (Srbija) 73 F3
Korab 77 D3
Kórakas, Akr 88 C3
Koralpe 70 B1
Korana 70 C3
Korbach 52 A2
Korbevac 77 E2
Korbovo 73 F2
Korçë 114 C3
Korčula 75 E2
Korčula I 75 E2
Korčulanski kan 75 E2
Korenovsk 113 E2
Korensko sedlo 70 A1
Kórfos 87 E2
Korgåsen 95 F2
Korgen 97 E3
Koria 107 F2
Korifássi 86 C3
Korikío Ándro 83 E4
Kórimvos 81 F1
Koríni 83 F4
Korinós 79 F4
Korinthía 87 D1
Korinthiakós Kólpos 87 D1
Kórinthos 87 E1
Korissía 88 A2
Korissós 79 D3
Korita (Bosna i Hercegovina) 76 A2
Korita (Crna Gora) 76 B2
Korita (Mljet) 75 F2
Koríthi 86 A1
Koritnik 76 C1
Koritnik, M. 77 D3
Korkeakangas 103 F3
Korkeakoski 103 D2
Körmend 112 A4
Kornat 74 C1
K ornati 74 C1
Korneuburg 57 F2

Kornofoléa 81 F2
Kornwestheim 55 D2
Koromacno 70 B4
Koróna 79 F2
Koróni 86 C4
Koronía 83 F4
Koronía, L 80 A3
Koronída 88 C3
Koronissía 82 C3
Kóronos 88 C3
Koronoúda 80 A2
Koropí 87 F1
Körös 112 B4
Korosten' 113 E2
Korostyšev 113 E2
Kórouma 99 E2
Korpilahti 103 D3
Korpilombolo 98 C2
Korpo 107 D3
Korppoo 107 D3
Korsberga 109 E2
Korsfjorden 104 A2
Korsholm 102 B2
Korsnäs 102 B2
Korsør 108 B4
Korsun-Ševčenkovskij 113 F2
Kortesjärvi 102 C2
Kórthio 88 B2
Kortrijk 50 A3
Kortteenperä 99 D2
Korvala 99 D2
Korvaluoma 102 C3
Korvatunturi 95 F3
Kos 89 F3
Kosančić 77 D1
Kosanica 76 B1
Kościan 112 A1
Kościerzyna 110 A4
Kosel 77 D4
Koserow 49 E1
Košice 112 C1
Kosjerić 72 C4

Koška 71 F2
Koskenkorva 102 B2
Koskenpää 103 D3
Koski (Hameen Lääni) 107 E2
Koski (Turun ja Porin Lääni) 107 D2
Kóskina 84 B4
Koskue 102 C3
Kosmaj 73 D3
Kosmás 87 D3
Kósmio 81 E2
Kos, N 89 F3
Kosovo 77 D2
Kosovo Polje 77 D2
Kosovska Kamenica 77 D2
Kössen 59 E1
Kósta 87 E3
Kostajnica 71 D3
Kostanjevac 70 C2
Kostanjevica 70 C2
Kostenec 115 D3
Koster 105 D4
Kostolac 73 D3
Kostonjärvi 99 E3
Kostopol' 113 D2
Kóstos 88 C3
Kostrzyn 49 F4
Kosturino 77 F3
Kosula 103 E2
Koszalin 110 A4
Kőszeg 112 A4
Kotala (Keski-Suomen Lääni) 102 C3
Kotala (Lapin Lääni) 99 E1
Kotel 115 E2
Köthen 53 D1
Kotka 103 F4
Kotor 76 B3
Kotoriba 71 D1

Kotorsko 71 F3
Kotor Varoš 71 E4
Kotovsk (Moldavija) 113 E4
Kotovsk (Ukraina) 113 E3
Kotraža 73 D4
Kótronas 87 D4
Kotroniá 81 F2
Kötschach-Mauthen 59 E2
Köttsjön 101 F2
Kötzting 56 B1
Koufália 79 F3
Koufoníssi (Kikládes) 88 C3
Koufoníssi (Kríti) 91 F4
Koufós 80 B4
Kouklii 82 B1
Koukounariés 84 A2
Koúla 81 D1
Kouméika 89 E2
Koúndouros 88 A2
Kounoupéli 86 B1
Koura 102 C2
Koúrenda 82 B1
Kourkoulí 84 A3
Kournás 90 C3
Kouroúta 86 B2
Koutselió 82 C1
Koutsó 81 D2
Koutsóhero 83 E1
Kouvola 107 F2
Kovačica 72 C2
Kovel' 112 C2
Kovero 103 F2
Kovin 73 D3
Köyliö 107 D2
Kozáni 79 D3
Kozáni 79 D3
Kozara 71 D3
Kozarac (Bosna i Hercegovina) 71 D3
Kozarac (Hrvatska) 71 F2

L

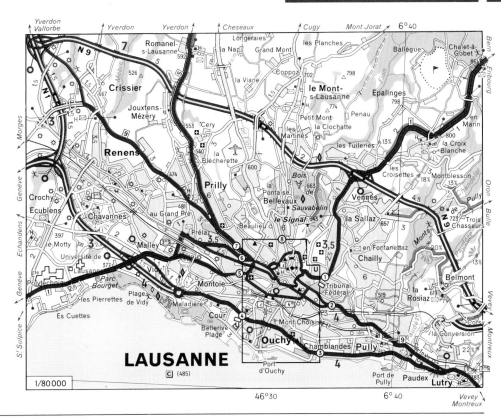

LAUSANNE
C (485)
1/80 000

La Muela	37 D4	Langrune	18 C3	Lärbro	109 F3	La Selva del Camp 37 F4

La Muela 37 D4
Lamure 26 B4
Lana 58 C3
Lanaja 37 D3
Lanaken 51 D3
Lanark 4 C2
La Nava de
 Ricomalillo 39 F3
La Nava de
 Santiago 39 D4
Lancashire 6 B2
Lancaster 6 B1
Lanchester 5 E4
Lanciano 64 A2
Landau (Bayern) 56 B2
Landau (Rheinland-
 Pfalz) 54 C2
Landeck 58 C2
Landerneau 22 B2
Landes 28 B3
Landes de
 Lanvaux 22 C3
Landete 41 D3
Landévennec 22 A3
Landivisiau 22 B2
Landivy 18 C4
Landmannalaugar 96 B2
Landquart 58 B2
Landrecies 20 A2
Landriano 60 A1
Landsberg 53 D2
Landsberg 56 A3
Land's End 8 A4
Landshut 56 B2
Landskapet
 Åland 106 C2
Landskrona 108 C3
Landstuhl 54 B2
Landverk 101 D2
Lanersbach 59 D2
Lanesborough 12 C3
Langáda (Híos) 85 F4
Langáda
 (Pelopónissos) 87 D4
Langadás 79 F3
Langadás 87 D3
Langa de Duero 36 A3
Langádia 86 C2
Langadíkia 80 A3
Langangen 104 C4
Langeac 29 F2
Langeais 25 D2
Langeland 108 B4
Langelandsbælt 108 B4
Langelmäki 103 D3
Langelmävesi 103 D3
Langelsheim 52 B1
Langenargen 55 D4
Langenau 55 E3
Langenberg 53 D3
Langenbruck 55 F2
Langenburg 55 D2
Langeneß 47 F1
Langenfeld 17 E4
Längenfeld 58 C2
Langenhagen 48 A4
Langenhahn 51 F3
Langen (Hessen) 52 A4
Langen
 (Niedersachsen) 47 F3
Langenlois 57 E2
Langenthal 27 F2
Langenwang 57 E3
Langenzenn 55 E1
Langeoog 47 E3
Långeserud 105 E3
Langeskov 108 B3
Langesund 104 C4
Langevåg 100 A2
Langevåg 104 A3
Långfjället 101 D3
Langfjord 95 D2
Langfjorden 95 E1
Langfjordjøkelen 94 C2
Langforden 100 B2
Langhirano 60 B2
Langholm 5 D3
Langjökull 96 B2
Langnau 27 F2
Langogne 29 F2
Langon 28 B2
Langøya 94 A3
Langport 9 D3
Langres 26 C1

Langrune 18 C3
Långsele 101 F2
Långshyttan 105 F2
Långträsk 98 B3
Lanjarón 44 A3
Lanke 49 E3
Länkipohja 103 D3
Lanmeur 22 B2
Lannemezan 37 E1
Lannilis 22 A2
Lannion 22 B2
Lanouaille 29 D1
Lans-en-Vercors 30 C1
Lanslebourg 31 E1
Lanta 29 D4
Lantosque 31 E3
La Nuez de Arriba 35 F3
Lanusei 66 C3
Lanvollon 22 C2
Lanzahita 39 F2
Lanzarote 42 C3
Lanzo Torinese 31 E1
Laois 12 C4
La Oliva
 (Is Canarias) 42 C4
La Oliva (Navarra) 36 C2
Laon 20 A3
La Orotava 42 B4
La Paca 44 C2
Lapalisse 26 B4
La Palma 42 A4
La Palma del
 Condado 42 C2
La Panadella 37 F4
Lápas 86 B1
Lapa, Sa da 38 C1
Laperdiguera 37 E3
La Pinilla 36 A4
Lapinjärvi 107 F2
Lapin Lääni 95 E4
Lapinlahti 103 E2
La Platja d'Aro 32 B4
La Plaza 35 D2
Lapleau 29 E1
Laplume 28 C3
La Pobla de Lillet 32 A3
La Pobla de
 Massaluca 37 E4
La Pobla de Segur 37 F3
La Pobla de
 Vallbona 41 E3
Lapoutroie 27 E1
Lapovo 73 D3
Lappajärvi 102 C2
Lappajärvi L 102 C2
Lappea 98 C2
Lappeenranta 103 F4
Lappfjärd 102 B3
Lappfors 102 C2
Lappi 107 D2
Lappoå 102 C2
Lappohja 107 E3
Lappträsk 98 C3
Lappträsk 107 F2
Lappvesi 106 C3
Lapua 102 C2
Lapuanjoki 102 C2
La Puebla de
 Almoradiel 40 B3
La Puebla de
 Cazalla 43 E3
La Puebla de Híjar 37 D4
La Puebla de
 los Infantes 43 E2
La Puebla del Río 43 D3
La Puebla de
 Montalbán 39 F3
La Puebla de
 Valverde 41 D2
La Pueblanueva 39 F3
La Puerta de
 Segura 44 B1
Lapväärtti 102 B3
L'Aquila 63 F2
La Rábida 42 C3
La Rábita 44 B4
Laracha 34 A1
Laragh 13 D4
Laragne-
 Montéglin 30 C3
La Rambla 43 F2

Lärbro 109 F3
Larche (Alpes-de-
 Haute-Provence) 31 E2
Larche (Corrèze) 29 D2
Larche, Col de 31 E2
Lærdalsøyri 104 B1
Lardarello 60 C4
Lárdos 93 F2
Lárdos, Akr 93 F2
Laredo 36 A1
Laren 16 C2
Largentière 30 B2
Largs 4 C2
Lárimna 84 A4
La Rinconada 43 D2
Larino 64 B2
La Rioja 36 B2
Lárissa 83 E1
Lárissa (Nomos) 83 E2
Larmor 22 B4
Larne 13 E2
La Robla 35 D2
La Roca 32 B4
La Roca de la
 Sierra 39 D4
Larochette 21 D2
La Roda
 (Andalucía) 43 E3
La Roda (Castilla-la-
 Mancha) 40 C4
Laroles 44 B3
Laroquebrou 29 E2
Laroque-d'Olmes 32 A2
Laroque-Timbaut 28 C3
Larouco 34 B3
Larraga 36 C2
Larrau, Pto de 37 D2
Larseng 94 B2
Larsmo 102 C1
Laruns 37 D2
Larv 109 D1
Larvik 104 C4
Lasalle 29 F3
Las Alpujarras 44 A3
Las Arenas 36 B1
Lasarte 36 C1
Las Batuecas 39 E2
Las Cabezas de
 San Juan 43 D3
Las Cabrillas,
 Pto de 41 E2
Las Caldas de
 Besaya 35 F2
Las Campanas 36 C2
Lascaux, Grotte de 29 D2
La Seca 35 E4

La Selva del Camp 37 F4
La Sénia 41 F2
La Seu d'Urgell 32 A3
Las Huelgas Reales 35 F3
Lasinjski Sjeničak 70 C3
Laško 70 B2
Las Mesas 40 B4
Las Mestas 39 E2
Las Minas 44 C1
Las Navas de la
 Concepción 43 E2
Las Navas del
 Marqués 40 A2
Las Negras 44 C4
Læsø 108 B2
La Solana 40 B4
Las Pajanosas 43 D2
Las Palmas de Gran
 Canaria 42 B4
Las Pedroñeras 40 C4
Las Pedrosas 37 D3
La Spezia 60 B3
Las Portas,
 Emb de 34 B3
Las Rozas 40 A2
Lassan 49 E2
Lassay 23 E3
Lassigny 19 F3
Lassíthi 91 E4
Lassíthi
 (Nomos) 91 F4
Lastovo 75 E3
Lastovo I 75 E3
Lastovski kan 75 E3
Lastra a Signa 60 C3
Lastres 35 E1
Lastrup 17 E1
Lastva 76 A2
Lašva 71 F4
Las Veguillas 39 E1
Las Ventas con Peña
 Aguilera 40 A3
Las Vertientes 44 B3
Las Viñas 28 C3
Lätäseno 95 D3
Laterza 65 D4
Lathen 17 E1
Latheron 3 D2
Latiano 65 E3
Latikberg 97 F4
Latina 63 F3
Latisana 59 F3
Lató 91 E4
La Torre del Valle 35 D3
Latour-de-France 32 B2
Latronico 65 D4

Latronquière 29 E2
Latvija 110 C3
Lauchhammer 53 E2
Lauder 5 D2
Lauenau 52 A1
Lauenburg 48 B3
Lauenstein 53 E3
Lauf 55 F1
Laufen (CH) 27 E2
Laufen (D) 56 B3
Laufenburg 54 C4
Lauffen 55 D2
Laugarvatn 96 B2
Lauhanvuori 102 B3
Laujar de Andarax 44 B3
Laukaa 103 D3
Lauksundskaret B3
Launceston 8 B3
La Unión 45 D3
Laupheim 55 E3
Lauragh 14 A4
Laureana di
 Borrello 67 E4
Laurencekirk 3 E4
Laurenzana 65 D4
Lauria 67 E1
Laurière 25 E4
Lausanne 27 D3
Lauta 53 E2
Lautaret, Col du 31 D2
Lautenthal 52 B1
Lauter 54 C2
Lauterbach 52 A3
Lauterbourg 21 F3
Lauterbrunnen 27 F3
Lauterecken 54 B1
Lautrec 32 A1
Lauttakylä 107 D2
Lauvstad 100 A2
Lauvvik 104 A3
Lauzerte 29 D3
Lauzet-Ubaye, le 31 D2
Lavagna 60 A3
Laval 23 E3
Lavamünd 70 B1
Lavandou, le 31 D4
Lavangen 94 B3
Lavant 70 B1
Lávara 81 F2
Lavardac 28 C3
La Vecilla 35 D2
Lavelanet 32 A2
La Vellés 39 E1
Lavello 64 C3

Lavelsloh 17 F2
Lavenham 11 D1
Laveno 58 A4
Lavéra 30 C4
Lavia 102 C3
Laviano 64 C4
Lavik 104 A1
La Villa de Don
 Fadrique 40 B3
Lavinio Lido
 di Enea 63 E3
La Virgen del
 Camino 35 D2
Lavis 59 D3
Lavit 28 C3
Låvong 97 E3
Lavour 29 D4
Lavoûte-Chilhac 29 F2
Lavre 38 B4
Lávrio 88 A2
Lavvuoai'vi 95 D3
Laxå 105 E4
Laxe 34 A1
Laxford Bridge 2 C2
Laxo 3 F1
Lay 24 B3
La Yesa 41 D3
Layos 40 A3
Laza 34 B3
Lazarevac 72 C3
Lazarev Krst 76 B2
Lazarevo 72 C2
Lazaropole 77 D3
Lazio 63 E2
Lazise 60 C1
Lázně Kynžvart 53 D4
Laznica 73 E3
Leadenham 7 D2
Leamington Spa,
 Royal 9 E1
Leane, L 14 B4
Łeba 110 A4
Lebach 54 B2
Lebane 77 E1
Lebedin 113 F1
Lebesby 95 E1
Łebork 110 A4
Lebrija 43 D3
Lebus 49 F4
Lecce 65 F4
Lecco 58 B4
Lécera 37 D4
Lećevica 75 D1
Lech (A) 58 B2
Lech (D) 55 E2

Léchère, la 31 D1
Lechlade 9 E2
Leciñena 37 D3
Leck 47 F1
Lecques, les 30 C4
Lectoure 28 C3
Lecumberri 36 C1
Ledaña 41 D4
Ledanca 40 B1
Ledbury 9 D1
Ledesma 39 E1
Lédignan 30 B3
Ledmore 2 C2
Lee 14 B4
Leeds 6 C2
Leek 6 C3
Leenane 12 B3
Leer 47 E3
Leerdam 16 C3
Leese 48 A4
Leeuwarden 16 C1
Lefkáda 82 B3
Lefkáda, N 82 B3
Lefkádia 79 E3
Lefkadíti 83 E3
Lefkandi 84 B4
Lefká Óri 90 B3
Léfkara 79 E4
Léfkes 88 C3
Lefkími 81 F2
Lefkími, Akr 82 A2
Lefkógia 80 B1
Lefkopigí 79 D4
Léfktra 83 F4
Legan 48 A2
Leganés 40 A2
Legé 24 B3
Legnago 60 C1
Legnano 60 A1
Legnica 112 A2
Legrad 71 D1
Legrená 87 F2
Léguevin 29 D4
Legutiano 36 B1
Le Havre 19 D3
Lehená 86 B1
Lehnin 49 D4
Léhovo 79 D3
Lehrberg 55 E1
Lehre 52 B1
Lehrte 52 B1
Lehtimäki 102 C2
Lehtovaara (Lapin
 Lääni) 99 D1
Lehtovaara (Oulun
 Lääni) 103 E1

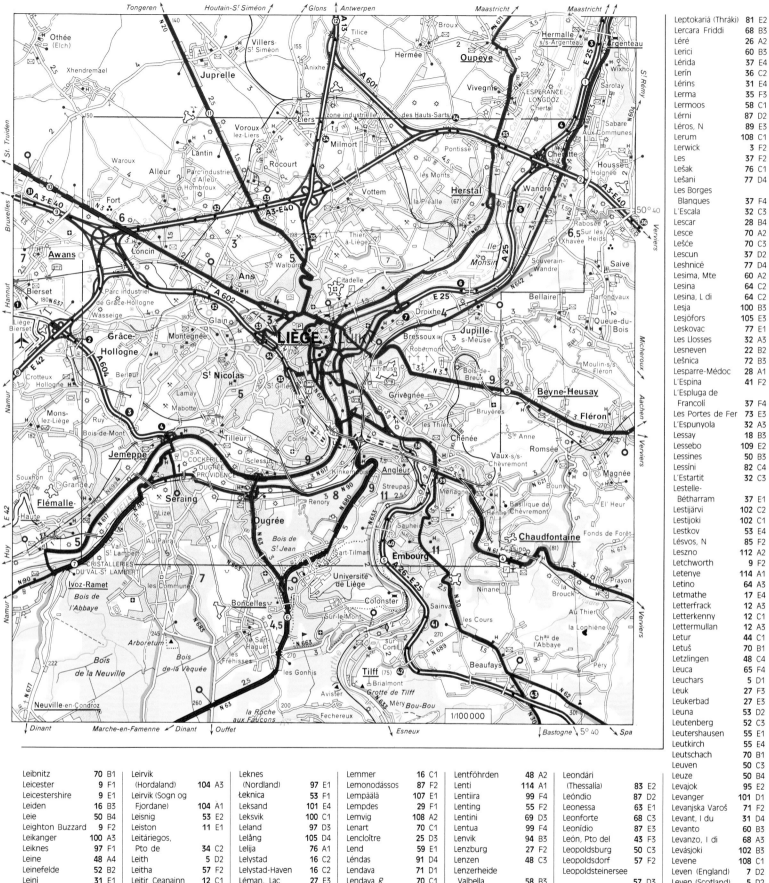

Lille

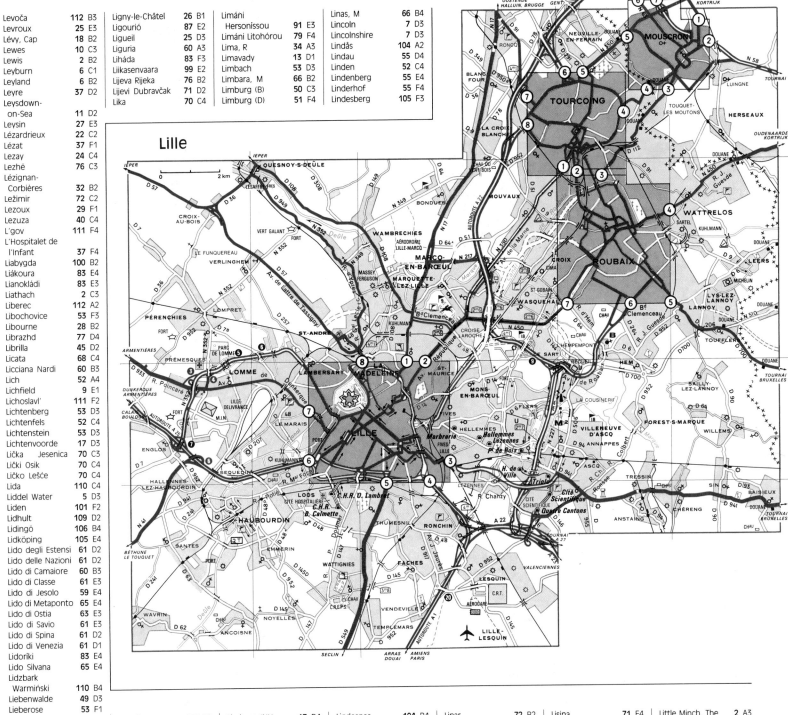

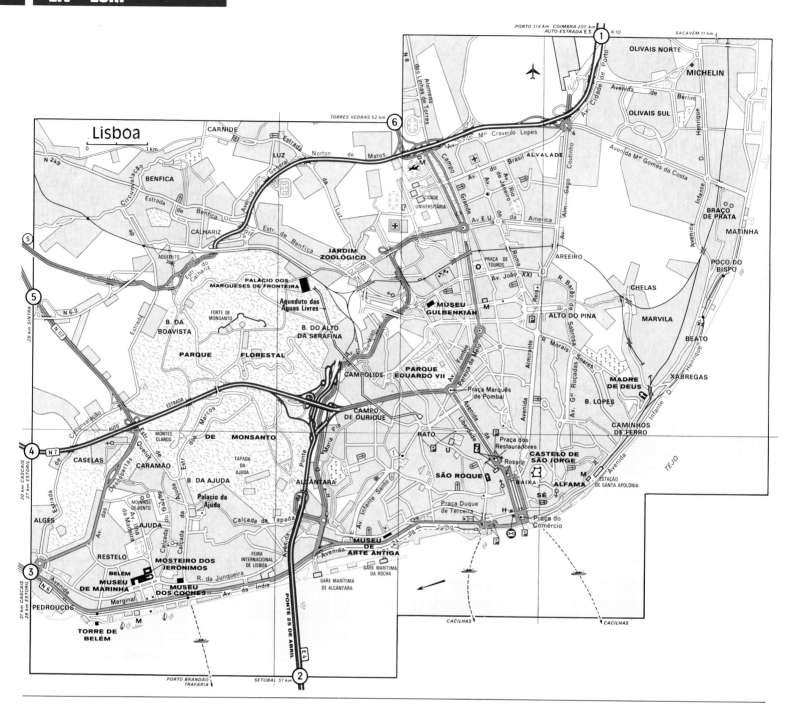

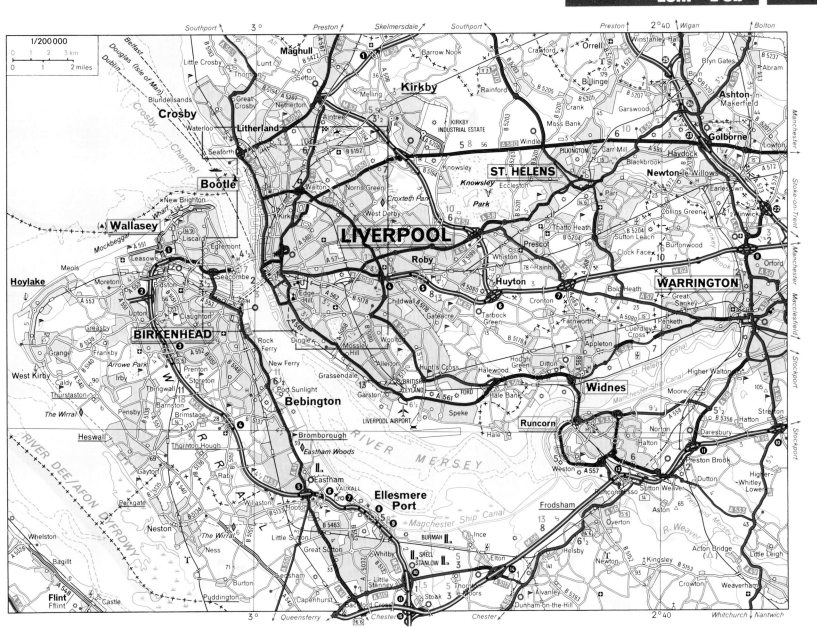

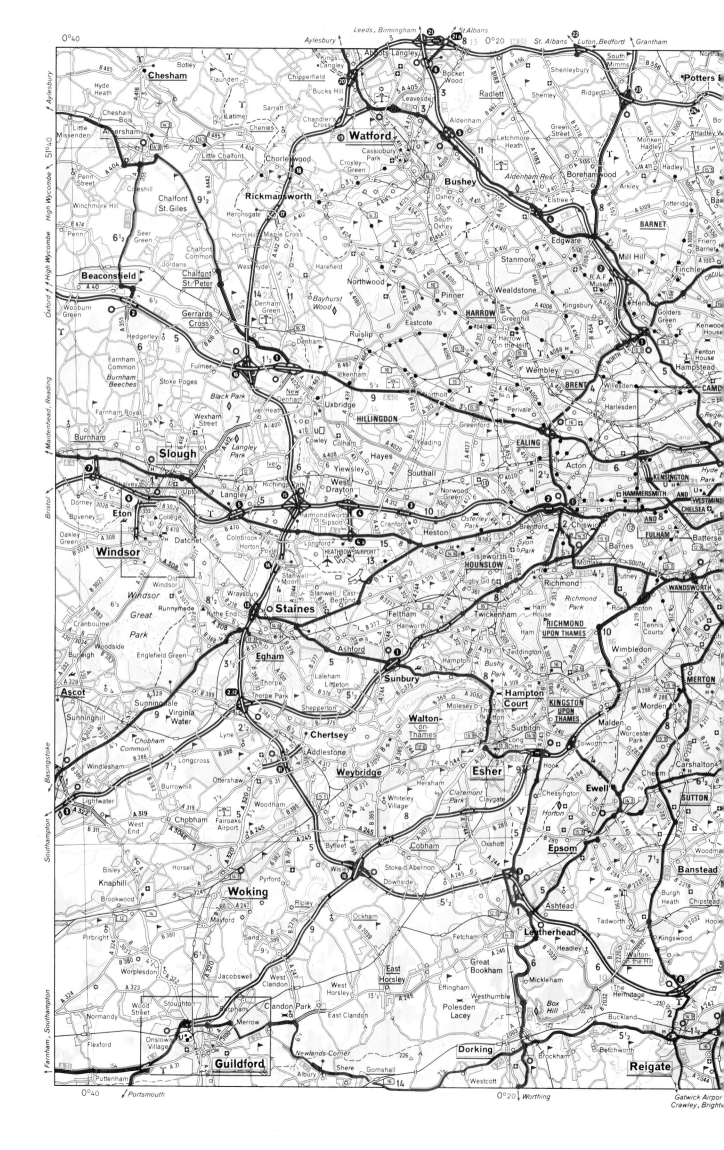

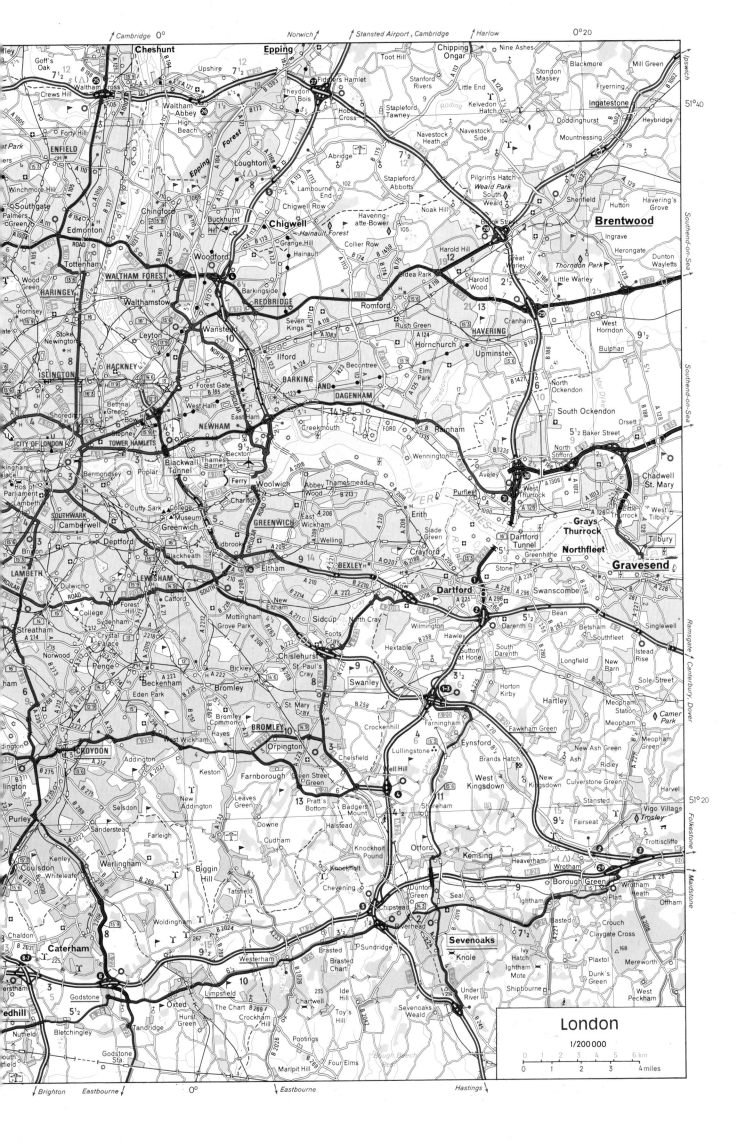

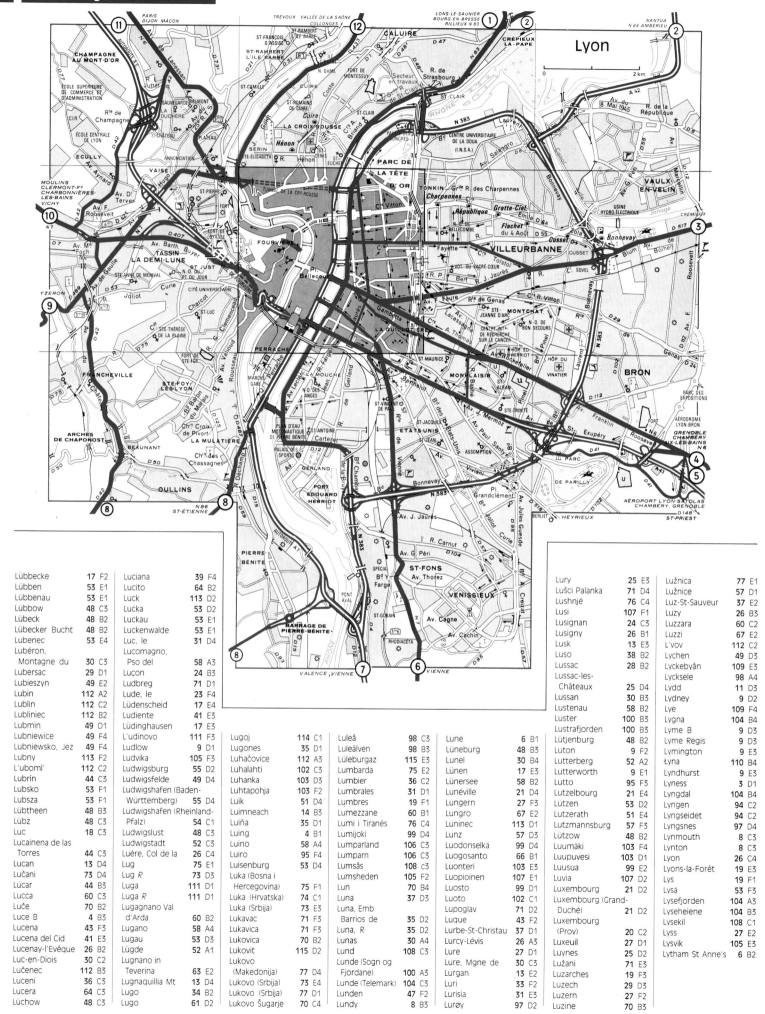

Lyon

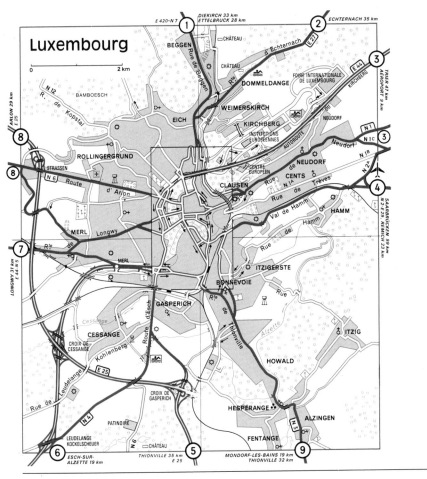

Luxembourg

0   2 km

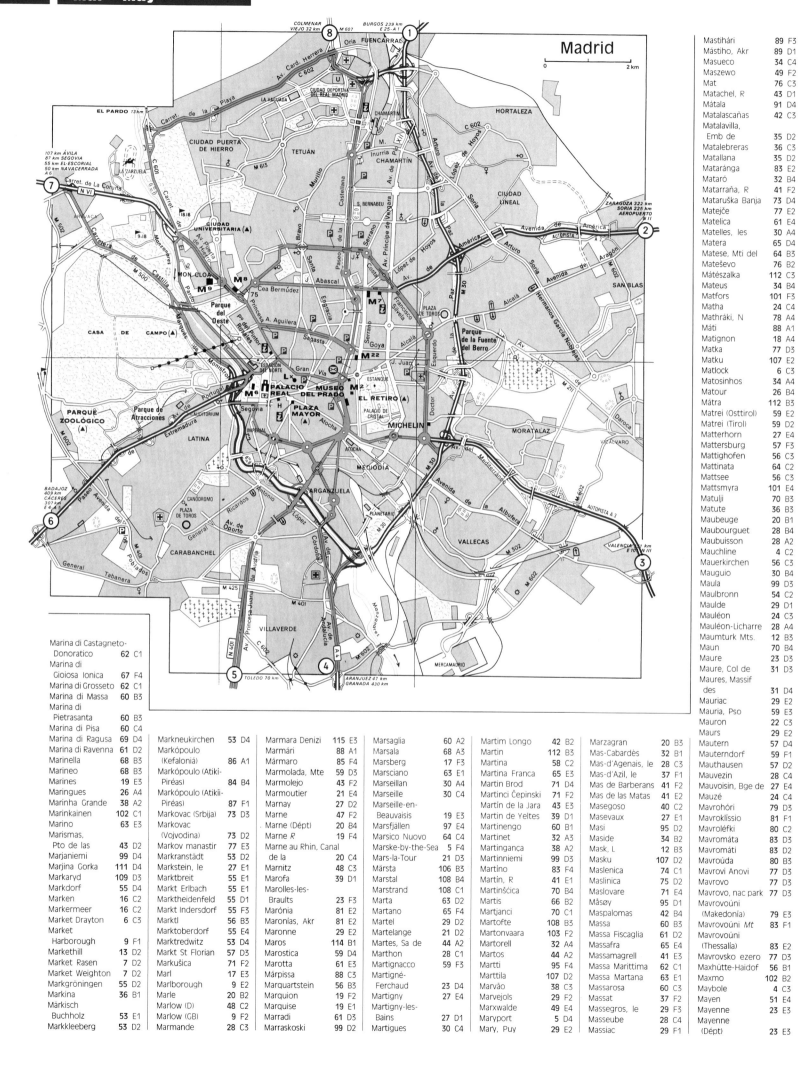

Madrid

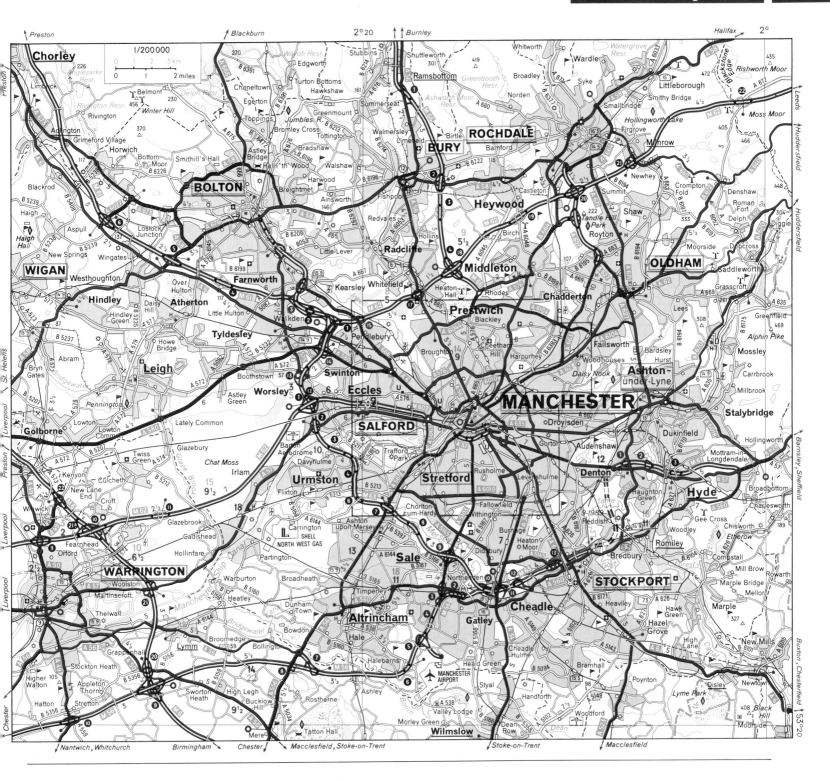

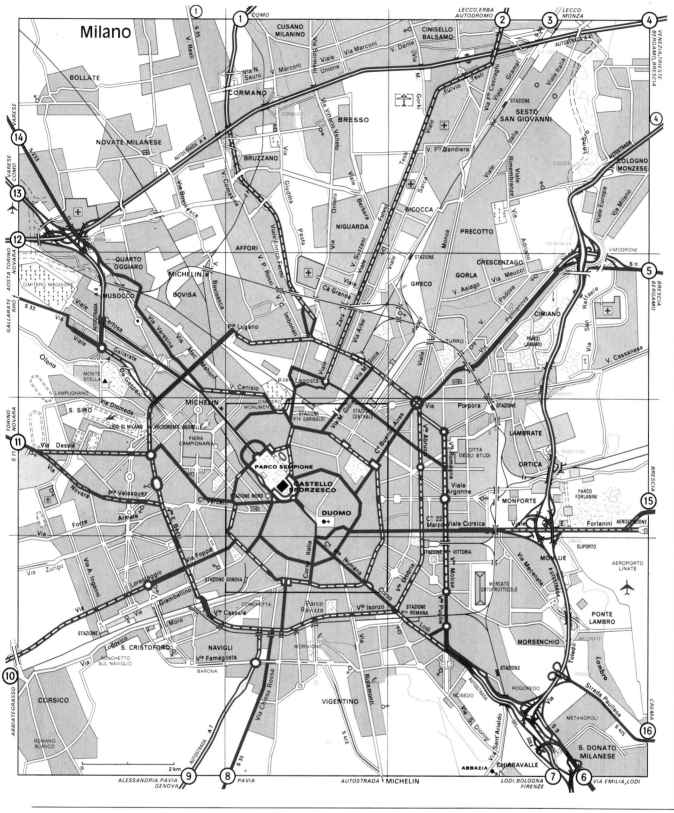

Milano

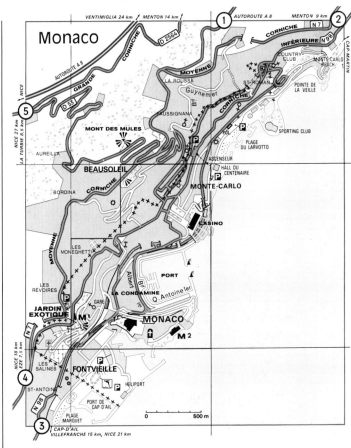

Monaco

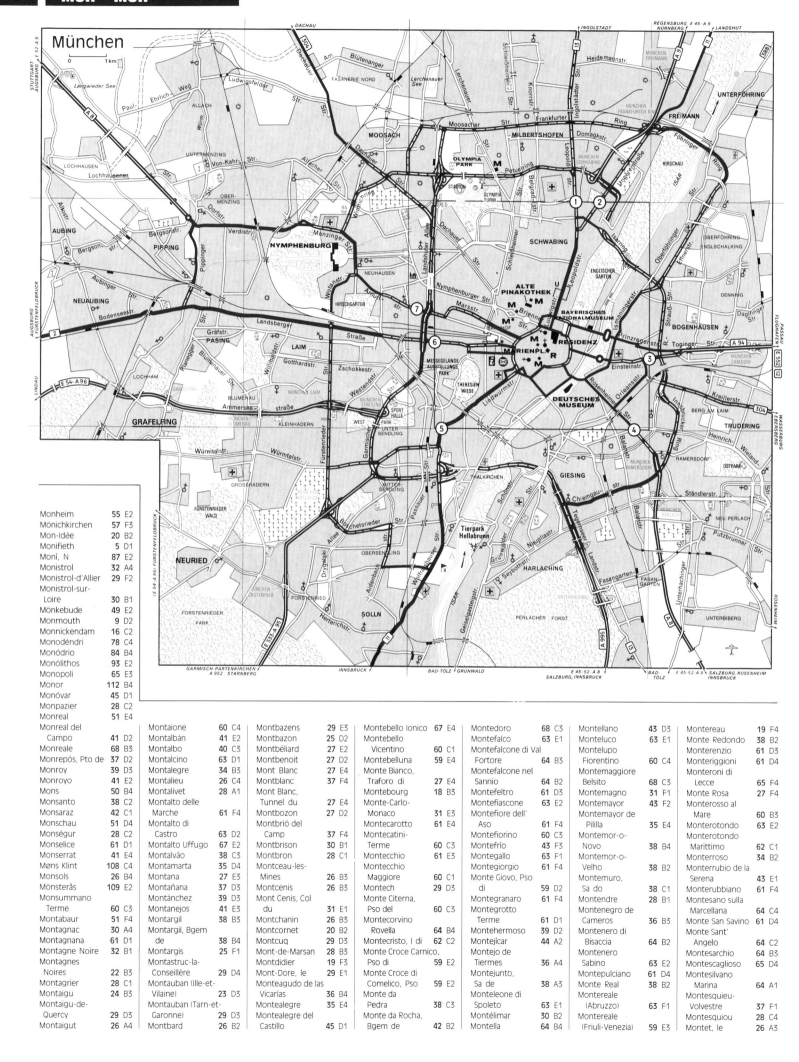

München

Montets, Col des 27 E4
Montevarchi 61 D4
Monteviejo, Pto de 35 E2
Montfaucon-en-Velay 30 B1
Montfaucon (Maine-et-Loire) 24 B2
Montfaucon (Meuse) 20 C3
Montfort 23 D3
Montfort-en-Chalosse 28 B4
Montfort-l'Amaury 19 E4
Montfort-sur-Risle 19 D3
Montgaillard 32 A2
Montgenèvre 31 D2
Montgenèvre, Col de 31 D2
Montgiscard 29 D4
Montgomery 9 D1
Montguyon 28 B1
Monthermé 20 C2
Monthey 27 E4
Monthois 20 C3
Monthureux 27 D1
Monti 66 B2
Montichiari 60 B1
Monticiano 61 D4
Montiel 44 B1
Montier-en-Der 20 C4
Montignac 29 D2
Montigny-le-Roi 26 C1
Montigny-sur-Aube 26 C1
Montijo (E) 39 D4
Montijo (P) 38 A4
Montilla 43 F2
Montioni 62 C1
Montivilliers 19 D3
Montjean 23 E4
Montlhéry 19 f4
Montlieu 28 B1
Montlouis 25 D2
Mont-Louis 32 A3
Montluçon 25 F4
Montluel 26 C4
Montmarault 26 A4
Montmartin 18 B3
Montmédy 20 C3
Montmélian 31 D1
Montmirail (Marne) 20 A4
Montmirail (Sarthe) 23 F3
Montmirey-le-Château 26 C2
Montmoreau 28 C1
Montmorillon 25 D4
Montmort 20 B3
Montoggio 60 A3
Montoire 23 F4
Montoito 38 C4
Montone 61 D3
Montorio al Vomano 63 F1
Montoro 43 F2
Montòro, Emb de 43 F1
Montpellier 30 A4
Montpellier-le-Vieux, Chaos de 29 F3
Montpezat-de-Quercy 29 D3
Montpezat-sous-Bauzon 30 B2
Montpon-Ménestérol 28 C2
Montpont 26 C3
Montréal (Aude) 32 A2
Montréal (Gers) 28 C3
Montréal-la-Cluse 26 C4
Montredon-Labessonnie 32 B1
Montréjeau 37 E1
Montrésor 25 E2
Montresta 66 A2
Montreuil 19 E1
Montreuil-Bellay 24 C2
Montreux 27 E3
Montrevault 24 B2
Montrevel 26 C3
Montrichard 25 E2
Mont-roig del Camp 37 F4
Montrond-les-Bains 30 B1
Montrose 5 E1
Mont-St-Michel, le 18 B4
Mont-St-Vincent 26 B3
Montsalvy 29 E2
Montsant, Sa del 37 F4
Montsauche 26 B2
Montsec, Serra de 37 F3
Montseny 32 B4
Montseny, Sa de 32 B4
Montserrat 32 A4
Mont-sous-Vaudrey 26 C3
Monts-sur-Guesnes 25 D3
Montsûrs 23 E3
Montuenga 39 F1
Montuiri 45 F3
Monviso 31 E2
Monza 60 A1
Monzón 37 E3
Monzón de Campos 35 F3
Moordorf 47 E3
Moorfoot Hills 5 D2
Moosburg 56 B2
Mór 112 B4
Mora (E) 40 A3
Mora (P) 38 B4
Mora (S) 101 E4
Morača 76 B2
Morača *R* 76 B2
Morača klisura 76 B2
Móra d'Ebre 37 E4
Mora de Rubielos 41 E2
Moraira 45 E1
Moraira, Pta de 45 E1
Morais 34 C4
Moraïtika 82 A2
Morakovo, G. 76 B2
Móra la Nova 41 F1
Moral de Calatrava 40 A4
Moraleda de Zafayona 44 A3
Moraleja 39 D2
Moraleja de Sayago 39 E1
Morales de Rey 35 D3
Morales de Toro 35 E4
Morano Calabro 67 E2
Mora, Pto de la 44 A3
Morar, L 2 B4
Mörarp 108 C3
Morasverdes 39 D2
Morata de Jalón 36 C4
Morata de Tajuña 40 B2
Moratalla 44 C2
Morata, Pto de 36 C4
Morava 57 E1
Morava *R* 112 A3
Moravče 70 B2
Moravci 70 C1
Moravica 73 D4
Moravské Budějovice 57 E1
Moravske Toplice 70 C1
Moravský Krumlov 57 E1
Moray Firth 3 D3
Morbach 54 B1
Morbegno 58 B3
Morbihan 22 C3
Mörbisch 57 F3
Mörbylånga 109 E3
Morcenx 28 A3
Morciano di Romagna 61 E3
Morcone 64 B3
Morcote 58 A4
Morcuera, Pto de la 40 A1
Mordelles 23 D3
Morecambe 6 B1
Morecambe Bay 6 B1
Moreda 44 A3
Morée 25 E1
Moreleja del Vino 35 D4
Morella 41 E2
Møre og Romsdal 100 B2
Mores 66 B2
Morestel 30 C1
Moret 19 F4
Moreton 9 E2
Moretonhampstead 8 C3
Moreuil 19 F2
Morez 27 D3
Morfasso 60 B2
Mórfio 82 B2
Morgat 22 A3
Morges 27 D3
Morgex 27 E4
Morgins, Pas de 27 E4
Morhange 21 D3
Mori 58 C4
Morina 76 C2
Moritzurg 53 E2
Morjärv 98 C3
Morlaàs 37 E1
Morlaix 22 B2
Mormanno 67 E2
Mormant 19 F4
Mormoiron 30 C3
Mornant 30 B1
Mórnou, Teh L 83 E4
Morón de Almazán 36 B4
Morón de la Frontera 43 E3
Morosaglia 33 F3
Morović 72 B3
Morpeth 5 E3
Morrón 44 B3
Mörrum 109 D3
Mors 108 A2
Morsbach 17 E4
Mörsil 101 E2
Morsleben 52 C1
Mortagne 28 B1
Mortagne-au-Perche 19 D4
Mortagne-sur-Sèvre 24 C3
Mortágua 38 B2
Mortain 18 C4
Mortara 60 A2
Morteau 27 D2
Mortrée 19 D4
Morven 3 D2
Moryń 49 E3
Morzine 27 E4
Morzyczyn 49 F2
Mosbach 55 D2
Mosby 104 B4
Moščenice 70 B3
Moščenička Draga 70 B3
Moschendorf 57 F4
Mosel 51 E4
Moselle (Dépt) 21 D3
Moselle *R* 27 D4
Moshokariá 83 E3
Moshopótamos 79 E3
Mosjøen 97 E3
Moskenesøya 97 E1
Moskenstraumen 97 E1
Mosko 76 A2
Moskosel 98 B3
Moskva 111 F2
Moskva *R* 111 F2
Moslavačka gora 71 D2
Mosonmagyaróvár 112 A4
Mosor 75 E2
Mosqueruela 41 E2
Moss 105 D3
Mossala 107 D3
Mossat 3 D4
Mosses, Col des 27 E3
Mössingen 55 D3
Most (CS) 53 E3
Most (YU) 70 A2
Mosta 68 B4
Mostar 75 F2
Mosteiro 34 A2
Mosterhamn 104 A3
Mostiska 112 C2
Móstoles 40 A2
Mostonga 72 B2
Mostrim 12 C3
Mosty 110 C4
Møsvatn 104 B3
Mosvik 101 D1
Mota del Cuervo 40 B3
Mota del Marqués 35 E4
Motajica 71 E3
Motala 105 F4
Motala S 106 A4
Mothe-Achard, la 24 B3
Motherwell 4 C2
Mothe-St-Héray, la 24 C4
Motilla del Palancar 40 C3
Motovun 70 A3
Motril 44 A4
Motta di Livenza 59 E4
Motta S.A. 69 D3
Motta Visconti 60 A1
Motte-Chalancon, la 30 C2
Motte, la 31 D3
Mottola 65 E4
Mouchard 27 D3
Moudon 27 E3
Moúdros 85 D1
Mougins 31 E4
Mouhijärvi 107 D1
Mouilleron-en-Pareds 24 C3
Moulins 26 A3
Moulins-Engilbert 26 B3
Moulins-la-Marche 19 D4
Moult 18 C3
Moúnda, Akr 86 A1
Mountain Ash 8 C2
Mount Bellew 12 C3
Mountmellick 13 D4
Mountrath 12 C4
Mount's B 8 B4
Mountsoúna 88 C3
Moura 42 B1
Mourão 42 C1
Moúrdzeflos, Akr 85 D1
Mourenx 28 B4
Mouríki 84 A4
Mourmelon-le-Grand 20 B3
Mourne 13 D2
Mourne Mts 13 E3
Mourniés 90 B3
Mourujärvi 99 E2
Mouscron 50 A3
Moustiers-Ste-Marie 31 D3
Mouthe 27 D3
Mouthier 27 D2
Mouthoumet 32 B2
Moutier 27 E2
Moûtiers 31 D1
Moutiers-les-Mauxfaits 24 B3
Mouy 19 F3
Mouzakéi 82 C1
Mouzáki 83 D2
Mouzon 20 C2
Moville 13 D1
Moy 12 B2
Moyenneville 19 E2
Moyeuvre 21 D3
Moyuela 37 D4
Možajsk 111 F2
Mozirje 70 B1
Mozyr' 113 E1
Mrągowo 110 B4
Mrakovica 71 D3
Mramorak 73 D2
Mratinje 76 A1
Mrazovac 70 C3
Mrčajevci 73 D4
Mrežičko 77 E4
Mrkonjić Grad 71 E4
Mrkopalj 70 B3
Mrzeżyno 49 F1
Mšeno 53 F3
Msta 111 E1
Mstislavl' 111 E3
Mú 42 B2
Muć 75 D1
Muccia 61 E4
Much 17 E4
Mücheln 52 C2
Much Wenlock 9 D1
Mucientes 35 E4
Muck 2 B4
Muckle Roe 3 F1
Muckross House 14 B4
Mudanya 115 F3
Mudau 55 D1
Muddus 98 B2
Muel 37 D4
Muelas del Pan 35 D4
Muff 13 D1
Muge 38 B3
Mügeln 53 E2
Muggia 59 F4
Mugron 28 B4
Mugueimes 34 B3
Mühlbach 59 E1
Mühlberg 53 E2
Mühldorf 56 B3
Mühlen-Eichsen 48 B2
Mühlhausen 52 B2
Mühltroff 53 D3
Muhniemi 107 F2
Muhos 99 D4
Muhu 110 B2
Muineachán 13 D2
Muine Bheag 15 D3
Muirkirk 4 C3
Muir of Ord 2 C3
Mukačevo 112 C3
Mukos 77 E3
Mula 45 D2
Mülacker 54 C2
Mula, R 45 D2
Mulargia, L 66 B3
Mulhacén 44 A3
Mülheim 17 E3
Mulhouse 27 E1
Mull 4 B1
Müllheim 54 C4
Mullingar 13 D3
Mull of Galloway 4 B4
Mull of Kintyre 4 B3
Mull of Oa 4 A2
Müllrose 49 F4
Mull, Sd of 4 B1
Mullsjö 109 D1
Mulrany 12 B2
Multia 103 D3
Mumbles, The 8 C2
Muñana 39 F2
Münchberg 53 D4
Müncheberg 49 E4
München 56 A3
Münchhausen 17 F4
Münden 52 B2
Mundesley 7 F3
Mundford 11 D1
Mundo, R 44 C1
Munera 40 C4
Mungia 36 B1
Muñico 39 F2
Muniesa 37 D4
Munkebo 108 B3
Munkedal 105 D4
Munkfors 105 E3
Münnerstadt 52 B4
Muñogalindo 39 F2
Munsala 102 B2
Munsfjället 101 E1
Münsingen (CH) 27 E3
Münsingen (D) 55 D3
Munster (F) 27 E1
Münster (CH) 27 F3
Münster (Niedersachsen) 48 B3
Münster (Nordrhein-Westfalen) 17 E3
Münstertal 54 C4
Münzenberg 52 A4
Münzkirchen 56 C2
Muodoslompolo 95 D4
Muojärvi 99 F2
Muonio 95 D4
Muonioälven 95 D4
Muotkatonturit 95 E2
Mur 57 E4
Mura 70 C1
Muraglione, Pso del 61 D3
Murano 61 D1
Murat 29 E2
Murato 33 F3
Murat-sur-Vèbre 32 B1
Murau 57 D4
Muravera 66 C4
Murça 34 B4
Murchante 36 C3
Murcia 45 D2
Murcia (Reg) 44 C2
Mur-de-Barrez 29 E2
Mur-de-Bretagne 22 C3
Mureck 57 E4
Mure, la 30 C2
Mureș 112 C4
Muret 29 D4
Murg 54 C2
Murguía 36 B1
Muri 27 F2
Murias de Paredes 35 D2
Murino 76 C2
Muriqan 76 B3
Müritz See 49 D3
Murjek 98 B2
Murnau 56 A4
Muro 33 F3
Muro de Alcoy 45 E1
Murol 29 E1
Murole 102 C3
Muro Lucano 64 C4
Muros 34 A2
Mürren 27 F3
Murrhardt 55 D2
Murska Sobota 70 C1
Mursko Središće 70 C1
Murten 27 E3
Murter 74 C1
Murter *I* 74 C1
Murtosa 38 B1
Murtovaara 99 F3
Murvica 74 C1
Murviel 30 A4
Mürz 57 E3
Mürzsteg 57 E3
Mürzzuschlag 57 E3
Musala 115 D3
Mussalo 103 F4
Musselburgh 5 D2
Musselkanaal 17 E1
Mussidan 28 C2
Mussomeli 68 C3
Mussy 26 B1
Mustair 58 C3
Mustasaari 102 B2
Mustèr 58 A3
Mustion as 107 E3
Mustvee 110 C1
Muta 70 B1
Mutala 102 C3
Mutterstadt 54 C1
Mutzschen 53 E2
Muurame 103 D3
Muurasjärvi 103 D1
Muuratjärvi 103 D3
Muurla 107 E2
Muurola 99 D2
Muuruvesi 103 E2
Muxía 34 A1
Muy, le 31 D4
Muzillac 22 C4
Muzzana del Turgnano 59 F3
Mweelrea Mts. 12 B3
Myckegensjö 101 F2
Mykines 96 A3
Myllykoski 107 F2
Myllykylä 102 C3
Myllymäki 102 C2
Mynämäki 107 D2
Mýrdalsjökull 96 B3
Myre 94 A3
Myrlandshaugen 94 B3
Myrskylä 107 F2
Myrviken 101 E2
Mysen 105 D3
Mysingen 106 B4
Myśla 49 F3
Myślibórskie, Jez 49 F3
Myślibórz 49 F3
Mývatn 96 B1
Mže 53 E4

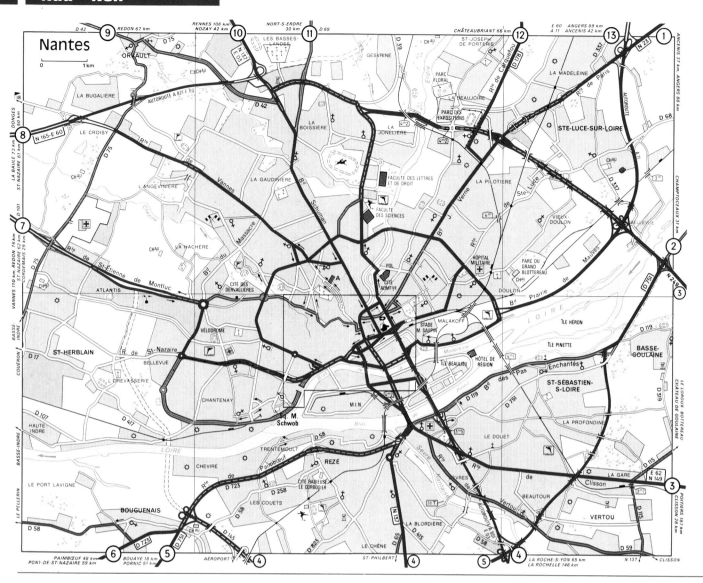

Nantes

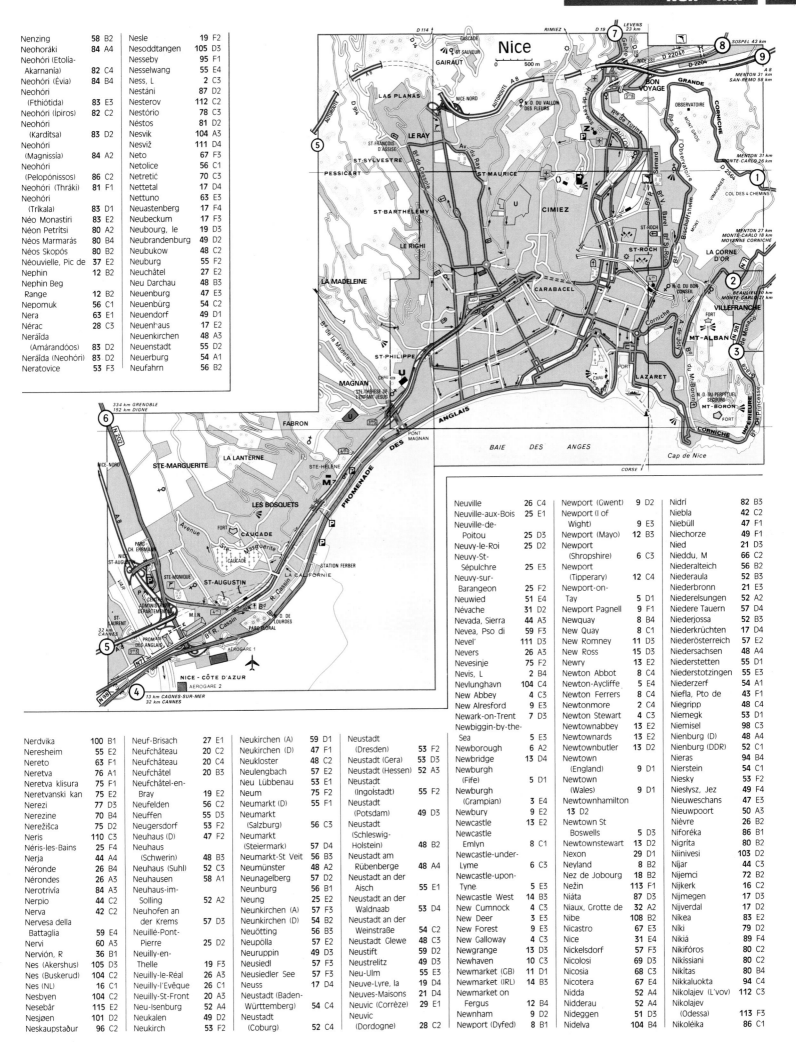

Nice

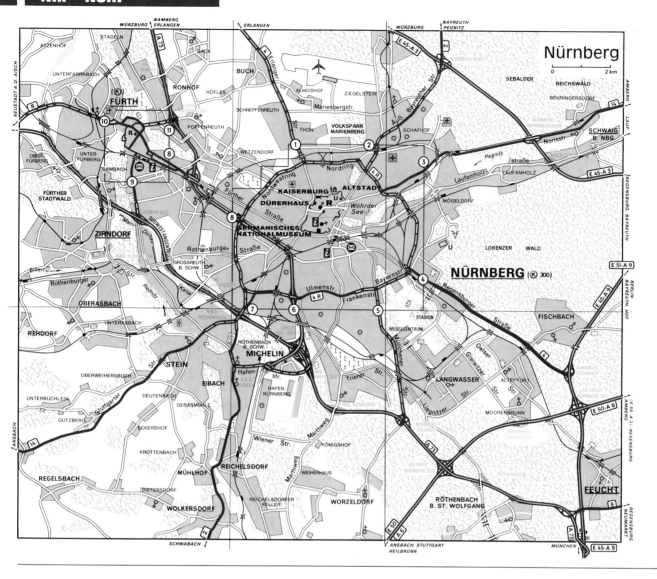

Nürnberg

Nummi 107 E2
Nuneaton 9 E1
Nunnanen 95 D3
Nuñomoral 39 D2
Nunspeet 17 D2
Nuorajärvi 103 F2
Nuorgam 95 E2
Nuoro 66 B2
Nurallao 66 B3
Nürburg 51 E4
Núria 32 B3
Nurmes 103 E1
Nurmijärvi (Pohjois-Karjalan Lääni) 103 F1
Nurmijärvi (Uudenmaan Lääni) 107 E2
Nurmo 102 C2
Nürnberg 55 F1
Nürtingen 55 D3
Nus 27 E4
Nusse 48 B2
Nuštar 71 F2
Nuthe 49 D4
Nuttlar 17 F3
Nuttupera 103 D1
Nuutajärvi 107 E2
Nuvvos-Ailigas 95 E2
Nyåker 102 A1
Nybergsund 105 E2
Nyborg 108 B4
Nybro 109 E2
Nyírbátor 112 C3
Nyíregyháza 112 C3
Nykarleby 102 B2
Nykøbing F (Storstrøm) 108 C4
Nykøbing M (Viborg) 108 A2
Nykøbing S (Vestsjælland) 108 C3
Nyköping 106 B4
Nykvarn 106 B4
Nynäshamn 106 B4
Nyon 27 D3
Nyons 30 C3
Nýřany 53 E4
Nyrdalur 96 B2
Nyrsko 56 B1
Nyrud 95 F2
Nysa 112 A2
Nysa Łużycka 53 F1
Nysäter 105 E3
Nyseter 100 B3
Nysted 108 C4
Nyvoll 95 D2

O

Oadby 9 F1
Oakham 9 F1
Oanes 104 A3
Óassi 87 D1
Oban 4 B1
O Barco 34 C3
Obbola 102 B1
Obdach 57 D4
Obdacher Sattel 57 D4
Obedska bara 72 C3
Obejo 43 F2
Oberalppass 58 A3
Oberammergau 55 F4
Oberau 56 A4
Oberaudorf 56 B4
Oberdrauburg 59 E2
Oberessfeld 52 C4
Obergeis 52 B3
Obergrafendorf 57 E2
Obergrünzburg 55 E4
Obergurgl 58 C2
Oberhaslach 21 E4
Oberhausen 17 E3
Oberhof 52 C3
OberjochPaß 58 C1
Oberkirch 54 C3
Oberkirchen 17 F4
Oberkochen 55 E2
Obermarchtal 55 D3
Obernai 21 E4
Obernberg 56 C3
Obernburg 55 D1
Oberndorf (A) 56 C3
Oberndorf (D) 54 C3
Obernzell 56 C2
Oberölsbach 55 F1
Oberösterreich 56 C2
Oberprechtal 54 C3
Oberpullendorf 57 F3
Oberseebach 21 F3
Obersontheim 55 E2
Oberstaufen 55 E4
Oberstdorf 55 E4
Oberstein 54 B1
Obertauern 59 F1
Obertraun 59 F1
Oberursel 51 F4
Obervellach 59 E2
Oberviechtach 56 B1
Oberwart 57 F4
Oberwesel 51 E4
Oberwiesenthal 53 E3
Oberwölz 57 D4
Oberzeiring 57 D4
Óbidos 38 A3
Obilić 77 D2
Obing 56 B3
Obiou, l' 30 C2
Objat 29 D1
Obninsk 111 F3
O Bolo 34 C3
Obón 41 E1
Oborniki 112 A1
Obornjača 72 C1
Oborovo 70 C2
Obrenovac 72 C3
Obrež 72 C3
Obrov 70 A3
Obrovac (Split) 75 D1
Obrovac (Zadar) 74 C1
Obršani 77 E4
Obsteig 58 C2
Obudovac 71 F3
Obzor 115 E2
Obzova 70 B3
Očakov 113 F3
Oca, Mtes de 36 A2
Ocaña 40 B3
Oca, R 36 A2
Očauš 71 E4
Occhiobello 61 D2
Occhito, L di 64 B3
Očevlje 71 F4
Ochagavia 37 D2
Ochil Hills 5 D1
Ochsenfurt 55 E1
Ochsenhausen 55 E3
Ochtrup 17 E2
Ockelbo 106 A2
Öckerö 108 C1
Ocreza, R 38 C3
Ocrkavlje 76 A1
Ödåkra 108 C3
Odda 104 B2
Odden Færgehavn 108 B3
Odder 108 B3
Oddesund 108 A2
Odeceixe 42 A2
Odeleite 42 B2
Odelzhausen 55 F3
Odemira 42 A2
Ödemiş 115 F4
Odense 108 B3
Odenthal 17 E4
Oder 49 E3
Oderberg 49 E3
Oderbruch 49 E3
Oderbucht 49 E1
Oderhaff 49 E2
Oderzo 59 E4
Ödeshög 109 D1
Odessa 113 F4
Odet 22 B3
Odiel, R 42 C2
Odivelas 42 B1
Odivelas, Bgem de 42 B1
Odolo 60 B1
Odorheiu Secuiesc 113 D4
Odra 112 A2
Odžaci 72 B2
Odžak (Bosna i Hercegovina) 71 F3
Odžak (Crna Gora) 76 B1
Oebisfelde 48 B4
Öebro 105 F4
Oederan 53 E3
Oeiras 38 A4
Oelde 17 F3
Oelsnitz (Plauen) 53 D3
Oelsnitz (Zwickau) 53 D3
Oettingen 55 E2
Oetz 58 C2
Ofanto 64 C3
Ofenpass 58 C3
Offaly 12 C4
Offenbach 52 A4
Offenburg 54 C3
Offida 63 F1
Offranville 19 E2
Ofir 34 A4
Ofotfjorden 94 B3
Oggiono 60 A1
Ogliastro Cilento 67 D1
Oglio 58 C4
Ognon 27 D2
Ogošte 77 E2
Ograđen 77 F3
Ogre 110 C2
Ogulin 70 C3
Ohanes 44 B3
Óhi, Óros 88 A1
Ohiró 80 B1
Ohlstadt 56 A4
Ohorn 53 F2
Ohrdruf 52 C3
Ohre 48 B4
Ohře 53 E3
Ohrid 77 D4
Ohridsko Ez 77 D4
Ohringen 55 D2
Ohrit, Liq i 77 D4
Óhthia 82 C3
Ohthoniá 84 B4
Oijärvi 99 D3
Oijärvi L 99 D3
Oikarainen 99 D2
Oirschot 16 C3
Oise 20 B2
Oise (Dépt) 19 F3
Oisemont 19 E2
Oisterwijk 16 C3
Oitti 107 E2
Oituz 113 D4
Ojakylä 99 D4
Öje 101 E4
Öjebyn 98 B3
Ojén 43 E4
Ojos Negros 41 D2
Ojuelos Altos 43 E1
Öjung 101 E4
Okehampton 8 C3
Oker 48 B4
Oklaj 75 D1
Oknö 109 E2
Okol 76 C2
Oksbøl 108 A3
Oksby 108 A3
Øksfjord 95 D2
Øksfjorden 94 A3
Øksfjordjøkelen 94 C2
Øksnes 94 A3
Okstindan 97 E3
Okučani 71 E3
Okulovka 111 E1
Olafsfjörður 96 B1
Olafsvík 96 A2
Öland 109 E2
Olan, Pic d' 31 D2
Olargues 32 B1
Olazagutía 36 B2
Olbernhau 53 E3
Olbia 66 B1
Oldcastle 13 D3
Oldebroek 17 D2
Oldeide 100 A3
Olden 100 A3
Oldenburg (Niedersachsen) 47 F3
Oldenburg (Schleswig Holstein) 48 B1
Oldenzaal 17 E2
Olderdalen 94 C2
Oldervik 94 C2
Oldfjällen 101 E1
Oldham 6 C2
Old Head of Kinsale 14 B4
Oldmeldrum 3 E4
Oldsum 47 F1
Oleggio 60 A1
Oleiros 34 B1
Oleiros 38 C2
Ølen 104 A3
Oléron, Ile d' 24 B4
Olesa 32 A4
Oleśnica 112 A2
Oletta 33 F2
Olette 32 B2
Olevsk 113 D2
Ølgod 108 A3
Olhão 42 B3
Olhava 99 D3
Oliana 32 A3
Oliana, Emb d' 32 A3
Olib 70 B4
Olib I 70 B4
Oliena 66 B2
Oliete 37 D4
Olimbía 86 C2
Olimbiáda (Makedonía) 80 B3
Olimbiáda (Thessalía) 79 E4
Ólimbos 93 D2
Ólimbos, Óros (Évia) 84 B4
Ólimbos, Óros (Pieriá) 79 E4
Ólinthos 80 A4
Olite 36 C2
Oliva 45 E1
Oliva de la Frontera 42 C1
Oliva de Mérida 39 D4
Olivares 40 C3
Oliveira de Azeméis 38 B1
Oliveira de Frades 38 B1
Oliveira do Bairro 38 B1
Oliveira do Douro 34 B4
Oliveira do Hospital 38 C2
Olivenza 38 C4
Olivenza, R de 38 C4
Olivet 25 E1
Olivone 58 A3
Olleria, Pto de l' 41 E4
Ollerton 7 D3
Ollières, les 30 B2
Olliergues 29 F1
Ollioules 31 D4
Ollöla 103 F2
Olmedillo de Roa 35 F4
Olmedo (E) 35 E4
Olmedo (I) 66 A2
Olmeto 33 F4
Olocau del Rey 41 E2
Olofström 109 D3
Olombrada 35 F4
Olomouc 112 A3
Olonzac 32 B1
Oloron Ste Marie 37 D1
Olost 32 A3
Olot 32 B3
Olovo 71 F4
Olpe 17 F4
Olsberg 17 F3
Olshammar 105 F4
Olst 17 D2
Ølstykke 108 C3
Olsztyn 110 B4
Olszyna 53 F1
Olt 115 D2
Oltedal 104 A3
Olten 27 F2
Oltenia 115 D1
Oltenita 115 E1
Olula del Río 44 C3
Olvega 36 C3
Olvera 43 E3
Omagh 13 D2
Omalí 79 D4
Omalós 90 B3
Omarska 71 D3
Ombrone 63 D1
Omegna 58 A4
Omiš 75 E2
Omišalj 70 B3
Omme Å 108 A3
Ommen 17 D2
Omodeo, L 66 B3
Omoljica 73 D3
Omorfohóri 83 E1
Ömossa 102 B3
Oña 36 A2
Oñati 36 B1
Oncala, Pto de 36 B3
Onda 41 E3
Ondara 45 E1
Ondárroa 36 B1
Oneglia 31 F3
OnesseetLaharie 28 A3
Onich 2 C4
Onkamo (Lapin Lääni) 99 E2
Onkamo (Pohjois Karjalan Lääni) 103 F2
Onkivesi 103 E2
Ons, I de 34 A2
Ontaneda 35 F2
Ontiñena 37 E3
Ontinyent 45 E1
Ontojärvi 99 F4
Ontur 45 D1
Onzain 25 E2
Oostburg 16 B4
OostelijkFlevoland 16 C2
Oostende 50 A3
Oosterbeek 17 D3
Oosterend 16 C1
Oosterhout 16 C3
Oostkamp 50 A3
Oostmalle 50 C3
OostVlaanderen 50 B3
OostVlieland 16 C1
Ootmarsum 17 E2
Opatija 70 B3
Opatovac 72 B2
Opava 112 A3
Opladen 17 E4
Oplenac 73 D3
Opočka 111 D2
Opole 112 A2
Opovo 72 C2
Oppach 53 F2
Oppdal 100 C2
Oppenau 54 C3
Oppenheim 54 C1
Opphaug 100 C1
Oppido Lucano 64 C4
Oppido Mamertina 67 E4
Oppland 104 C1
Oputten 16 C2
Opuzen 75 F2
Ora 59 D3
Oradea 112 C4
Oradour-sur-Glane 25 D4
Oradour-sur-Vayres 28 C1
Orahova 71 D3
Orahovac 77 D2
Orahovica 71 E2
Oraison 31 D3
Orajärvi 98 C2
Orange 30 B3
Orani 66 B2
Oranienbaum 53 D1
Oranienburg 49 D3
Oranmore 12 B3
Orašac (Hrvatska) 75 F2
Orašac (Srbija) 73 D3
Orasi 76 B3
Orašje 71 F3
Orăştie 114 C1
Oravainen 102 B2
Oravais 102 B2
Oravikoski 103 E2
Oraviţa 114 C1
Orb 30 A4
Orba 45 E1
Ørbæk 108 B4
Orbassano 31 E2
Orbe 27 D3
Orbec 19 D3
Orbetello 63 D2
Orbey 27 E1
Orbigo, R 35 D2
Orce 44 B2
Orce, R 44 B2
Orcera 44 B1
Orchies 20 A1
Orcières 31 D2
Orcival 29 E1
Orco 31 E1
Ordes 34 A1
Ordesa, Parque Nac. de 37 E2
Ordino 32 A2
Ordizia 36 C1
Orduña 36 B1
Orduña, Pto de 36 B1
Ore 101 E4
Orea 41 D2
Oreälven 102 A1
Orebić 75 E2
Örebro Län 105 F3
Öregrund 106 B3
Öregrundsgrepen 106 B2
Orei 83 F3
Orellana de la Sierra 39 E4
Orellana, Emb de 39 E4
Orellana la Vieja 39 E4
Orense 34 B3
Oréo 81 D2
Oreókastro 79 F3
Orestiáda 81 F1
Oresund 108 C3
Orfós, Akr 89 F4
Orgáni 81 E2
Organyà 32 A3
Orgañyà 37 F3
Orgaz 40 A3
Orgejev 113 E3
Orgelet 26 C3
Orgères-en-Beauce 25 E1
Orgon 30 C3
Orgosolo 66 B2
Orhi, Pic d' 37 D1
Orhomenós 83 F4
Oria 44 C3
Oria 65 E4
Oria, R 36 C1
Origny-Sainte-Benoîte 20 A2
Orihuela 45 D2
Orihuela del Tremedal 41 D2
Orimattila 107 F2
Oriní 80 B2
Oriolo 65 D4
Oripää 187 D2
Orissaare 110 B2
Oristano 66 B3
Oristano, G di 66 A3
Orivesi 102 C3
Orivesi L 103 F2
Orjahovo 115 D2
Ørjavik 100 B2
Ørje 105 D3
Orjen 76 A2
Orjiva 44 A3
Orkanger 100 C2
Orkelljunga 109 D3
Orkla 100 C2
Orkney Is 3 E1
Ørlandet 100 C1
Orlando, C d' 69 D2
Orlane 77 D1
Orlate 77 D2
Orléans 25 E1
Orlická přehr nádrž 56 C1
Orlovat 72 C2
Orly 19 F4
Orménio 81 F1
Ormília 80 B4
Órmos 79 F3
Órmos Korthiou 88 B1
Órmos Panagías 80 B4
Órmos Prinou 80 C3
Ormož 70 C1
Ormsjö 97 F4
Ormsjön 101 F1
Ormskirk 6 B2
Ormtjernkampen 104 C1
Ornain 20 C4
Ornans 27 D2
Orne (Calvados) 18 C4
Orne (Dépt) 20 B3
Orne (Meuse) 21 D3
Ørnes 97 E2
Ornós 88 C2
Örnsköldsvik 102 A2
Or'ol 111 F4
Orolik 72 B2
Orom 72 B1
Oron-la-Ville 27 E3
Oropesa (Castilla la Mancha) 39 F3
Oropesa (Valencia) 41 F3
Orosei 66 C2
Orosei, G di 66 C2
Orosháza 112 B4
Orpierre 30 C3
Orpington 10 C2
Orra 100 C3
Orsa 101 E4
Orša 111 E3
Orsajön 101 E4
Orsay 19 F4
Orsières 27 E4
Orsogna 64 A2
Orşova 114 C1
Ørsta 100 A2
Örsundsbro 106 B3
Orta Nova 64 C3
Orta San Giulio 58 A4
Orte 63 E2
Ortegal, C 34 B1
Orth 57 F2
Orthez 28 B4
Ortigueira 34 B1
Ortisei 59 D3
Ortles 58 C3
Ortnevik 104 B1
Orton 5 D4
Ortona 64 A2
Ortrand 53 E2
Örträsk 102 A1
Orubica 71 E3
Orune 66 B2
Orusco 40 B2
Orvalho 38 C2
Orvieto 63 E1
Órvilos, Óros 80 B1
Orvinio 63 F2
Orzinuovi 60 B1
Os 100 D3

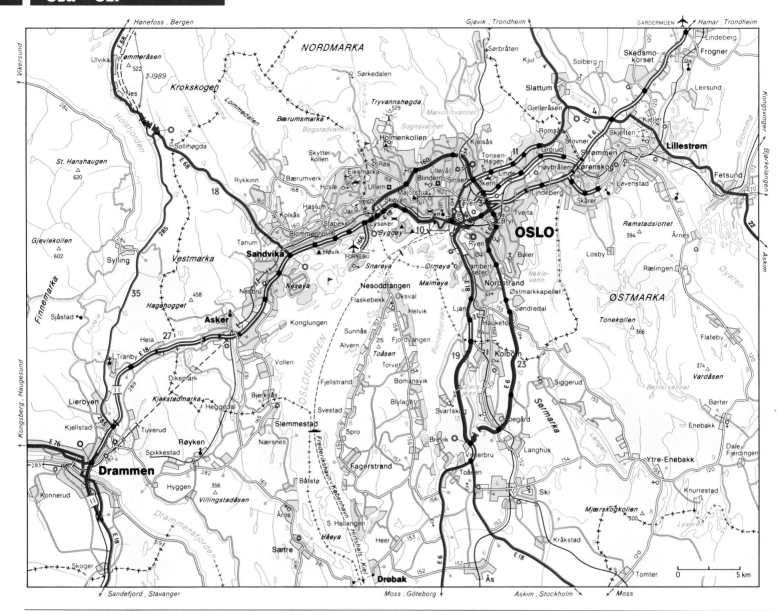

P

Paakkila 103 E2
Paalasmaa 103 E1
Páamo de Masa, Pto de 35 F3
Paar 55 F3
Paasselkä 103 F3
Paavola 99 D4
Pabianice 112 B2
Pacaudière, la 26 B4
Paceco 68 A3
Pachino 69 D4
Packsattel 57 E4
Paço de Sousa 34 A4
Paços de Ferreira 34 A4
Pacov 57 D1
Pacy 19 E4
Padasjoki 107 E1
Padej 72 C1
Pađene 75 D1
Paderborn 17 F3
Paderne 42 B2
Padiham 6 C2
Padina 72 C2
Padinska Skela 72 C2
Padirac, Gouffre de 29 D2
Padjelanta 97 F1
Padornelo 34 C3
Padova 61 D1
Padrela, Sa da 34 B4
Padrón 34 A2
Padru 66 B2
Padstow 8 B3
Padul 44 A3
Paesana 31 E2
Paestum 64 B4
Pag 70 C4
Pag *I* 70 B4
Paganico 63 D1
Pagassés, N 83 F2
Pagassitikós Kólpos 83 F2
Paglia 63 D1
Pagny 21 D3
Pagóndas (Évia) 84 A3
Pagóndas (Sámos) 89 E2
Pagoúria 81 D2
Paguera 45 E3
Páhi 87 E1
Pahiá Ámos 91 F4
Pahís, Akr 80 C3
Paide 110 C1
Paignton 8 C4
Päijänne 103 D3
Païko, Óros 79 E2
Paimbœuf 23 D4
Paimio 107 D2
Paimpol 22 C2
Painswick 9 E2
Paisley 4 C2
Paistunturit 95 E2
País Vasco 36 B1
Paittasjärvi 94 C4
Paiva, R 38 B1
Pajala 98 C1
Pájara 42 C4
Pajares, Pto de 35 D2
Paklenica Nac Park 70 C4
Pakoštane 74 C1
Pakrac 71 E2
Pakračka Poljana 71 D2
Paks 112 B4
Palacios de la Sierra 36 A3
Palacios del Sil 34 C2
Palacios de Sanabria 34 C3
Palade, Pso del 58 C3
Paládio 81 D2
Paladru 30 C1
Palafrugell 32 C3
Palagía 81 E2
Palagiano 65 E4
Palagonia 69 D3
Palagruža 75 D3
Palaia 60 C4
Palaiseau 19 F4
Palais, le 22 C4
Palamás 83 E2
Palamós 32 C3
Palancia, R 41 E3
Palanga 110 B3
Pala, Pto del 34 C1
Palas de Rei 34 B2
Palata 64 B2
Palatitsia 79 E3
Palatna 77 D1
Palau 66 B1
Palavas 30 B4
Palazzo del Pero 61 D4
Palazzolo Acreide 69 D4
Palazzolo sull' Oglio 60 B1
Palazzo San Gervasio 64 C3
Palazzuolo sul Senio 61 D3
Paldiski 110 C1
Pale 76 A1
Paléa Epídavros 87 E2
Palékastro 91 F4
Palena 64 A2
Palencia 35 E3
Paleohóra (Égina) 87 F2
Paleohóra (Kríti) 90 B4
Paleohóri (Grevená) 79 D4
Paleohóri (Halkidikí) 80 B3
Paleohóri (Ípiros) 82 B2
Paleohóri (Lésvos) 85 F3
Paleohóri (Pelopónissos) 87 D3
Paleohóri (Thessalía) 83 D1
Paleokastrítsa 82 A1
Paleókastro (Halkidikí) 80 A3
Paleókastro (Kozáni) 79 D4
Paleókastro (Sámos) 89 F2
Paleókastro (Séres) 80 B2
Paleókastro (Stereá Eláda) 83 D3
Paleokómi 80 B2
Paleópirgos (Stereá Eláda) 83 D4
Paleópirgos (Thessalía) 83 F1
Paleópoli (Ándros) 88 B1
Paleópoli (Samothráki) 81 E3
Paleós Kavála 80 C2
Paleós Xánthis 81 D2
Palermo 68 B3
Páleros 82 C3
Palérou, Órm 82 B3
Palestrina 63 F2
Palež 72 B4
Páli 89 F4
Paliano 63 F3
Palić 72 B1
Palidoro 63 E2
Palinges 26 B3
Palinuro 67 D2
Palioúri 80 B4
Paliouriá 79 D4
Paliseul 20 C2
Pälkäne 107 E1
Pålkem 98 B2
Pallas Ounastunturi 95 D3
Pallastunturi 95 D4
Pallice, la 24 B4
Palluau 24 B3
Palma 45 E3
Palmaces, Emb de 36 B4
Palma del Río 43 E2
Palma di Montechiaro 68 C4
Palmadula 66 A2
Palmanova 59 F3
Palmela 38 A4
Palmi 67 E4
Palo del Colle 65 D3
Palojoensuu 95 D3
Palojoki 95 D3
Palokki 103 E2
Palomäki 103 E1
Palomares del Campo 40 C3
Palomas 39 D4
Palomas, Pto de las 44 B2
Palombara Sabina 63 E2
Palombera, Pto de 35 F2
Palomera 41 D2
Pálos, Akr 88 B2
Palos, C de 45 D3
Palos de la Frontera 42 C3
Pals 32 C3
Pålsboda 105 F4
Paltamo 99 E4
Paltaselkä 99 E4
Paluzza 59 E2
Pámfila 85 F2
Pamhagen 57 F3
Pamiers 32 A2
Pampilhosa 38 B2
Pampilhosa da Serra 38 C2
Pampliega 35 F3
Pamplona 36 C2
Pamporovo 115 D3
Pamukkale 115 F4
Panagía (Ípiros) 82 C2
Panagía (Límnos) 85 D1
Panagía (Makedonía) 79 D4
Panagía (Thássos) 81 D3
Panagía (Thessalía) 82 C1
Panagjurište 115 D2
Panahaïkó, Óros 83 D4
Panarea, I 69 D2
Panaro 60 C3
Pancalieri 31 E2
Pančevo 73 D2
Pančićev vrh 77 D1
Pancorbo 36 A2
Pandánassa 87 E4
Pandeleimónas 79 F4
Pandino 60 B1
Pandokrátor 82 A1
Pandrup 108 B2
Panes 35 F2
Panetolikó, Óros 83 D3
Panetólio 82 C4
Panevėžys 110 C3
Pangbourne 9 E2
Pangéo, Óros 80 B2
Paniza, Pto de 36 C4
Pankajärvi 103 F1
Pankakoski 103 F1
Pankow 49 E4
Panórama (Dráma) 80 B2
Panórama (Thessaloníki) 80 A3
Panormítis 93 E1
Pánormos (Kikládes) 88 B2
Pánormos (Kríti) 91 D3
Päntäne 102 B3
Pantelleria 68 A4
Pantelleria, I di 68 A4
Paola 67 E2
Pápa 112 A4
Papádes 84 A3
Papádos 85 F3
Páparis 86 C2
Pápas, Akr 89 D2
Papasidero 67 E2
Papa Stour 3 F1
Papenburg 47 E3
Papíkio 81 D2
Pápingo 78 C4
Pappenheim 55 F2
Papuk *Mt* 71 E2
Papuk (Reg) 71 E2
Parabita 65 F4
Paracin 73 E4
Paracuellos de Jiloca 36 C4
Parada de Cunhos 34 B4
Paradas 43 E3
Paradela 34 B3
Paradíssia 86 C2
Parádissos 81 D2
Parainen 107 D3
Parajes 34 C1
Parakálamos 78 C4
Parákila 85 F2
Paralía (Ahaïa) 86 C1
Paralía (Lakonía) 87 E3
Paralía (Makedonía) 79 F4
Paralía (Stereá Eláda) 83 F4
Paralía Akrátas 87 D1
Paralía Ástros 87 D2
Paralía Kímis 84 B3
Paralía Kotsikiás 84 A3
Paralía Skotínas 79 F4
Paralía Tiroú 87 E3
Paralímni 84 A4
Paralovo 77 D2
Paramé 18 B4
Paramera, Pto de 39 F2
Paramithía 82 B2
Páramo del Sil 34 C2
Paranésti 80 C2
Parapanda 43 F3
Parapótamos 82 B1
Paraspóri, Akr 93 D2
Paray-le-Monial 26 B3
Parchim 48 C3
Pardubice 112 A3
Paredes 34 A4
Paredes de Coura 34 A3
Paredes de Nava 35 E3
Pareja 40 C2
Pareloup, Lac de 29 E3
Parentis-en-Born 28 A3
Párga 82 B2
Pargas 107 D3
Parikkala 103 F3
Parîngului, M 114 C1
Paris 19 F4
Parkalompolo 95 D4
Parkano 102 C3
Parla 40 A2
Parlavà 32 B3
Parma 60 B2
Parnassós, Óros 83 E4
Parndorf 57 F2
Párnitha, Óros 87 F1
Párnonas, Óros 87 D3
Pärnu 110 C2
Parola 107 E2
Páros 88 C3
Páros, N 88 B3
Parrett 9 D3
Parsberg 55 F2
Parsdorf 56 A3
Parseierspitze 58 C2
Parsęta 49 F1
Parsteiner See 49 E3
Partakko 95 F2
Partanna 68 B3
Partenen 58 B2
Partenkirchen 55 F4
Parthenay 24 C3
Parthéni 89 E3
Partille 108 C1
Partinico 68 B3
Partizani 73 D3
Partizanske Vode 72 C4
Partney 7 E3
Partry Mountains 12 B3
Pasaia-Pasajes 36 C1
Pas de Calais 11 E3
Pas-de-Calais (Dépt) 19 E1
Pas de la Case 32 A2
Pas-en-Artois 19 F2
Pasewalk 49 E2
Pashalítsa 83 E2
Pasikovci 71 E2
Pašman 74 C1
Pašman *I* 74 C1
Passais 18 C4
Passá-Limáni 85 E4
Passás, N 85 F4
Passau 56 C2
Passavás 87 D4
Passero, C 69 D4
Passignano sul Trasimeno 61 D4
Passwang 27 E2
Pastrana 40 B2
Paštrik 76 C3
Pásztó 112 B4
Patay 25 E1
Pateley Bridge 6 C1
Patéras, Óros 87 E1
Paterna del Campo 43 D2
Paterna de Rivera 43 D4
Paternion 59 F2
Paternò 69 D3
Paternopoli 64 B3
Patersdorf 56 B2
P'atichatki 113 F2
Patiópoulo 82 C2
Patitíri 84 B2
Pátmos 89 E2
Pátmos, N 89 E2
Pátra 83 D4
Patraïkós Kólpos 82 C4
Patreksfjördur 96 A1
Patrington 7 E2
Pattada 66 B2
Patterdale 5 D4
Patti 69 D2
Pattijoki 99 D4
Patvinsuo 103 F2
Pau 37 D1
Pauillac 28 B2
Paúl 38 C2
Paularo 59 F2
Paulhaguet 29 F2
Paullo 60 A1
Pavia (I) 60 A2
Pavia (P) 38 B4
Pavilly 19 D3
Pavino Polje 76 B1
Pávliani 83 E3
Pávlos 83 F4
Pavullo nel Frignano 60 C3
Paxí 82 A2
Paxí, N 82 A2
Payerne 27 E3
Paymogo 42 C2
Payrac 29 D2
Pazardžik 115 D3
Pazin 70 A3
Pčinja 77 E2
Péage-de-Roussillon, le 30 B1
Peak District Nat Pk 6 C2
Peal de Becerro 44 B2
Peania 87 F1
Peares, Emb de los 34 B2
Peć 76 C2
Peča 70 B1
Peccioli 60 C4
Pečenjevce 77 E1
Pech-Merle, Grotte du 29 D3
Pečigrad 70 C3
Pećinci 72 C3
Pecka 72 C4
Peckelsheim 52 A2
Pécs 114 B1
Pećka Banja 76 C2
Pečurice 76 B3
Pedaso 61 F4
Pedersker 109 D4
Pedersöre 102 C2
Pédi 93 E1
Pedrafita do Cebreiro 34 C2
Pedrafita do Cebreiro, Pto de 34 C2
Pedrajas de San Esteban 35 E4
Pedralba (Castilla-León) 34 C3
Pedralba (Valencia) 41 E3
Pedras Salgadas 34 B4
Pedraza de la Sierra 40 A1
Pedrera 43 E3
Pedrizas, Pto de las 43 F3
Pedro Abad 43 F2
Pedro Bernardo 39 F2
Pedrógão (Alentejo) 42 B1
Pedrógão (Estremadura) 38 A2
Pedrógão Grande 38 B2
Pedrola 36 C3
Pedro Muñoz 40 B4
Peebles 5 D2
Peel 6 A1
Peene 49 D2
Peenemünde 49 E1
Peer Gynt veien 100 C3
Pefkári 80 C3
Pefkí 83 F3
Péfkos 78 C3
Pega 38 C2
Pegalajar 44 A2
Pegau 53 D2
Pegli 60 A3
Pegnitz 55 F1
Pego 45 E1
Pego do Altar, Bgem de 38 B4
Pegognaga 60 C2
Pegolotte 61 D1
Pehčevo 77 F3
Peine 52 B1
Peio Terme 58 C3
Peïra-Cava 31 E3
Peißenberg 56 A4
Peiting 56 A4
Peitz 53 F1
Pek 73 D3
Péla 79 E2
Péla (Nomos) 79 F3
Pelado 41 D3
Pelagie, Is 68 A4
Pelasgía 83 F3
Pelat, Mt 31 D3
Pełczyce 49 F3
Pelekános 79 D3
Pélekas 82 A1
Peletá 87 E3
Pelhřimov 57 D1
Pelinéo 85 E4
Pelister 77 E4
Pelješac 75 E2
Pelkosenniemi 99 E1
Pellegrino, M 68 B2
Pellegrino Parmense 60 B2
Pellegrue 28 C2
Pellerin, le 24 B2
Pellesmäki 103 E2
Pello 98 C2
Pellworm 47 F1
Pelopónissos 86 C2
Peloritani, M 69 D2
Peltosalmi 103 E1
Peltovuoma 95 D3
Pélussin 30 B1
Pelvoux, Mt 31 D2
Pembroke 8 B2
Pembroke Dock 8 B2
Pembrokeshire Coast Nat Pk 8 B1
Penacova 38 B2
Peña de Francia 39 D2
Peña, de Francia, Sade 39 D2
Peña de Oroel 37 D2
Penafiel 34 A4
Peñafiel 35 F4
Peñaflor 43 E2
Peñagolosa 41 E3
Peña Gorbea 36 B1
Peñalara 40 A1
Penalva do Castelo 38 C1
Penamacor 38 C2
Peña Mira 34 C3
Peña Nofre 34 B3
Peña Prieta 35 E2
Peñaranda de Bracamonte 39 F1
Peñaranda de Duero 36 A3
Peñarroya 41 E2
Peñarroya, Emb de 40 B4
Peñarroya-Pueblonuevo 43 E1
Penarth 9 D2
Peña, Sa de la 37 D2
Peña Sagra 35 F2
Peñas, C de 35 D1
Peñascosa 44 C1
Peñas de Cervera 36 A3
Peñas de San Pedro 44 C1
Peña Trevinca 34 C3
Peña Ubiña 35 D2
Peñausende 35 D4
Pendagií 83 D4
Pendálofo 82 C4
Pendálofos 78 C4
Pendéli 87 F1
Pendéli *Mt* 87 F1
Pendeória 83 E4
Pénde Vrísses 80 A2
Pendine 8 B2
Peneda-Gerês, Pque Nac da 34 A3
Peneda, Sa da 34 A3
Penedono 38 C1
Penela 38 B2
Pénestin 22 C4
Penha 34 A4
Penhas da Saude 38 C2
Penhas Juntas 34 C4
Penhir, Pte de 22 A3
Penice, Pso del 60 A2
Peniche 38 A3
Penicuik 5 D2
Penig 53 D3
Peñíscola 41 F2
Penkun 49 E3
Penmaenmawr 6 A2
Penmarch, Pte de 22 A3
Pennabilli 61 E3
Penne 63 F1
Penne-d'Agenais 28 C3
Pennes, Pso di 59 D2
Pennines, The 6 C1
Peñón de Ifach 45 E1
Penrhyndeudraeth 6 A3
Penrith 5 D4
Penryn 8 B4
Penserjoch 59 D2
Pentland Firth 3 D2
Pentland Hills 5 D2
Pentrefoelas 6 B3
Pen-y-bont 8 C2
Penzance 8 A4
Penzberg 56 A4
Penzlin 49 D2
Peqin 76 C4
Perahóra 87 E1
Peraleda de Zaucejo 43 E1
Peralejos de las Truchas 40 C2
Perales del Alfambra 41 D2
Perales del Puerto 39 D2
Perales de Tajuña 40 B2
Perales, Pto de 39 D2
Peralta 36 C2
Peralta de Alcofea 37 E3
Peralva 42 B2
Pérama (Ípiros) 82 C1
Pérama (Kérkira) 82 A1
Pérama (Kríti) 91 D3
Pérama (Lésvos) 85 F3
Pérama (Stereá Eláda) 87 F1
Perämeri 98 C3
Perä-Posio 99 E2
Peräseinäjoki 102 C2
Perast 76 B3
Peratáta 86 A1
Percy 18 B4
Perdido, M 37 E2
Pérdika (Égina) 87 F2
Pérdika (Ioánina) 82 C2
Pérdika (Thesprotía) 82 B2
Perdikáki 82 C3
Perdíkas 79 D3
Peréa (Péla) 79 E3
Peréa (Thessaloníki) 79 F3
Perejaslav-Chmel'nickij 113 F2
Pereruela 35 D4
Pereval Jablonickij 113 D3
Pereval Srednij Vereckij 112 C3
Pereval Užokskij 112 C3
Perg 57 D2
Pergine Valsugana 59 D3
Pergola 61 E4
Perho 102 C2
Perhonjoki 102 C1
Periana 43 F3
Périers 18 B3
Périgueux 28 C2

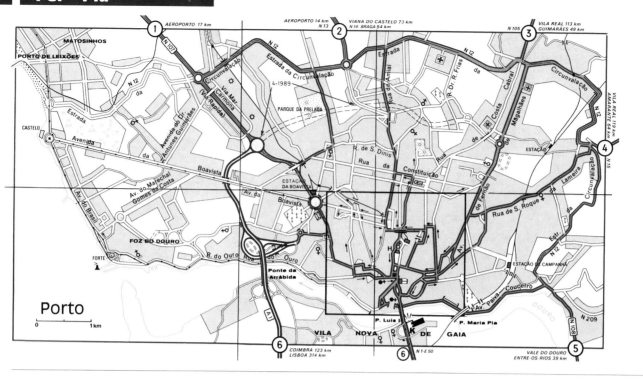

Porto

0   1km

Plataniá (Makedonía) 80 C2
Platánia (Pelopónissos) 86 C2
Plataniá (Thessalía) 84 A2
Platanistós 88 A1
Platanítis 83 D4
Plátanos (Kríti) 90 B3
Plátanos (Pelopónissos) 87 D3
Plátanos (Thessalía) 83 F2
Platariá 82 B2
Plateau-d'Assy 27 E4
Plateés 87 E1
Pláti 81 F1
Platiána 86 C2
Platičevo 72 C3
Platíkambos 83 E1
Platís Gialós (Kefaloniá) 86 A1
Platís Gialós (Míkonos) 88 C2
Platís Gialós (Sífnos) 88 B3
Platístomo 83 E3
Plattling 56 B2
Plau 48 C3
Plaue 49 D4
Plauen 53 D3
Plauer See (Potsdam) 49 D4
Plauer See (Schwerin) 48 C3
Plav 76 C2
Plavča 70 C3
Plavna 73 E3
Plavnica 76 B3
Plavnik *I* 70 B4
Plavnik *Mt* 70 B3
Playa de Gandía 41 E4
Playa de San Juan 45 E1
Pleaux 29 E2
Pleine-Fougères 18 B4
Pleinfeld 55 F2
Pleiße 53 D2
Plélan-le-Grand 23 D3
Plélan-le-Petit 22 C3
Pléneuf 22 C2
Plentzia 36 B1
Plépi 87 E2
Plešin 76 C1
Plestin 22 B2
Pleternica 71 E2
Plettenberg 17 F4
Pletvar 77 E3
Pleumartin 25 D3
Pleumeur-Bodou 22 B2
Pleven 115 D2
Pleyben 22 B3
Pliego 44 C2
Plítra 87 D4
Plitvice 70 C3
Plitvička jezera 70 C3
Plitvički Ljeskovac 70 C4
Plješevica 70 C4
Pljevlja 76 B1
Ploaghe 66 B2
Ploče 75 E2
Plochingen 55 D2
Płock 112 B1
Plöckenpaß 59 E2
Plöckenstein 56 C2
Pločno 75 E1
Ploërmel 22 C3
Ploiești 115 D1
Plomári 85 F3
Plomb du Cantal 29 E2
Plombières 27 D1
Plomin 70 B3
Plön 48 B2
Plonéour-Lanvern 22 A3
Płoń, Jez 49 F3
Płońsk 112 B1
Płoty 49 F2
Plouagat 22 C2
Plouaret 22 B2
Plouay 22 B3
Ploubalay 18 A4
Plœuc 22 C3
Ploudalmézeau 22 A2
Plouescat 22 B2
Plougasnou 22 B2
Plougastel-Daoulas 22 A3
Plougonven 22 B2
Plouguenast 22 C3
Plouha 22 C2
Plouigneau 22 B2
Ploumanach 22 B2
Plouzévédé 22 B2
Plovdiv 115 D3
Plumbridge 13 D2
Plungė 110 B3
Pľussa 111 D1
Pluvigner 22 C3
Plužine 76 A1
Plympton 8 C4
Plymstock 8 C4
Plzeň 53 E4
Po 60 C2
Poarta de Fier 114 C1
Pobierowo 49 F1
Poblet 37 F4
Pobrdđe 76 C1
Počep 111 F4
Pöchlarn 57 E2
Počinok 111 E3
Počitelj 75 F2
Pocking 56 C2
Poćuta 72 C4
Pódareš 77 F3
Podbořany 53 E3
Podčetrtek 70 C2
Podensac 28 B2
Podersdorf 57 F3
Podgajci Posavski 72 B3
Podgarič 71 D2
Podgora 75 E2
Podgorač (Hrvatska) 71 F2
Podgorac (Srbija) 73 E3
Podgrad 70 A3
Podhum 75 E1
Podjuchy 49 E2
Podkoren 70 A1
Podlugovi 71 F4
Podnovlje 71 F3
Podogorá 82 C3
Podohóri 80 B2
Podol'sk 111 F2
Podol'skaja Vozvyšennost' 113 D3
Podpec 70 B2
Podrašnica 71 E4
Podravska Slatina 71 E2
Podromanija 72 B4
Podsreda 70 C2
Podsused 70 C2
Podturen 71 D1
Podujevo 77 D1
Podunavci 73 D4
Poel 48 C2
Poganovo 77 E1
Poggibonsi 60 C4
Poggio Imperiale 64 C2
Poggio Mirteto 63 E2
Poggio Renatico 61 D2
Poggio Rusco 60 C2
Pöggstall 57 E2
Pogoniani 78 B4
Pogradec 77 D4
Pohja 107 E3
Pohja-Lankila 103 F3
Pohjaslahti (Keski-Suomen Lääni) 102 C3
Pohjaslahti (Lapin Lääni) 99 D2
Pohjois-Karjalan Lääni 103 F2
Pohořelice 57 F1
Pohorje 70 B1
Poiana Brașov 113 D4
Poio 34 A2
Poiré, le 24 B3
Poirino 31 F2
Poissons 20 C4
Poitiers 25 D3
Pöitsamaa 110 C2
Poix 19 E2
Poix-Terron 20 B2
Pojate 73 E4
Pojo 107 E3
Pokka 95 E3
Poklečani 75 E1
Pokljuka 70 A2
Pokupsko 70 C3
Polače 75 E2
Polacra, Pta de la 44 C4
Pola de Allande 34 C1
Pola de Gordón, la 35 D2
Pola de Laviana 35 E2
Pola de Lena 35 D2
Pola de Siero 35 D1
Polán 40 A3
Polcenigo 59 E3
Połczyn-Zdrój 110 A4
Polegate 10 C3
Poles 113 D1
Polesella 61 D2
Polessk 110 B4
Polhov Gradec 70 A2
Policastro 67 D1
Policastro, Golfo di 67 D2
Police 49 E2
Poličnik 74 C1
Policoro 65 D4
Polidéndri 84 B4
Polidrossos 83 E3
Poliegos, N 88 B4
Poliégou Folegándrou, Stenó 88 B4
Polígiros 80 A3
Polignano a Mare 65 E3
Poligny 27 D3
Polihnitos 85 F3
Polikárpi 79 E2
Polikástano 78 C3
Polikastro 79 F2
Polímilos 79 E3
Polinéri (Makedonía) 79 D4
Polinéri (Thessalía) 82 C2
Polipótamo 79 D3
Polipótamos 84 C4
Políraho 79 E4
Polirinía 90 B3
Polis, M 77 D4
Polissito 81 D2
Polistena 67 E4
Polithéa 82 C1
Politiká 84 A4
Poljana (Slovenija) 70 B1
Poljana (Srbija) 73 D3
Poljčane 70 C1
Polje 71 E3
Poljica 75 E2
Poljice 71 F4
Polla 64 C4
Pölläkkä 103 E2
Pöllau 57 E4
Polle 52 A1
Pollença 45 F2
Pollfoss 100 B3
Pollino, Mte 67 E2
Pollos 35 E4
Polmak 95 E2
Polock 111 D3
Polonnoje 113 D2
Polperro 8 B4
Poltava 113 F2
Polvijärvi 103 F2
Polzela 70 B2
Pomar 37 E3
Pomarance 60 C4
Pomarkku 102 B3
Pombal 38 B2
Pómbia 91 D4
Pomellen 49 E2
Pomezi 53 D4
Pomezia 63 E3
Pomigliano d'Arco 64 B4
Pommersfelden 55 E1
Pomokaira 95 E4
Pomorie 115 E2
Pomorze 110 A4
Pomovaara 95 E4
Pompei 64 B4
Pomposa 61 D2
Poncin 26 C4
Pondoiráklia 79 F2
Pondokómi 79 D3
Ponferrada 34 C2
Ponikovica 72 C4
Pons 28 B1
Ponsacco 60 C4
Pontacq 37 E1
Pontailler 26 C2
Pont-á-Marcq 19 F1
Pont-à-Mousson 21 D3
Pontão 38 B2
Pontardawe 8 C2
Pontarddulais 8 C2
Pontarion 25 E4
Pontarlier 27 D3
Pontassieve 61 D3
Pontaubault 18 B4
Pont-Audemer 19 D3
Pontaumur 26 A4
Pont-Aven 22 B3
Pont Canavese 31 E1
Pontcharra 31 D1
Pontchartrain 19 E4
Pontchâteau 23 D4
Pont-Croix 22 A3
Pont-d'Ain 26 C4
Pont-de-Beauvoisin, le 30 C1
Pont-de-Chéruy 26 C4
Pont-de-Claix, le 30 C2
Pont-de-Dore 26 A4
Pont-de-l'Arche 19 E3
Pont-de-Montvert, le 29 F3
Pont-de-Roide 27 E2
Pont-de-Salars 29 E3
Pont-d'Espagne 37 E2
Pont de Suert 37 F2
Pont-de-Vaux 26 C3
Pont-de-Veyle 26 C4
Pont-d'Oléron 28 A1
Pont-d'Ouilly 18 C4
Pont-du-Château 26 A4
Pont-du-Gard 30 B3
Ponte Arche 58 C3
Ponteareas 34 A3
Pontebba 59 F2
Pontecagnano 64 B4
Ponte Caldelas 34 A2
Ponteceno 60 B2
Ponte Ceso 34 A1
Pontecorvo 64 A3
Ponte da Barca 34 A3
Pontedecimo 60 A3
Ponte de Lima 34 A3
Pontedera 60 C4
Ponte de Sor 38 B3
Pontedeume 34 B1
Ponte di Legno 58 C3
Ponte di Piave 59 E4
Pontefract 7 D2
Pontelandolfo 64 B3
Ponte-Leccia 33 F3
Pontenelle Alpi 59 E3
Pont-en-Royans 30 C1
Ponte San Pietro 60 B1
Pontet, le 30 C3
Ponte Tresa 58 A4
Pontevico 60 B1
Pontfaverger-Moronvilliers 20 B3
Pontgibaud 29 E1
Pontigny 26 B1
Pontinia 63 F3
Pontinvrea 31 F2
Pontivy 22 C3
Pont-l'Abbé 22 A3
Pont-l'Evêque 19 D3
Pontlevoy 25 E2
Pontoise 19 E3
Pontones 44 B2
Pontón, Pto del 35 E2
Pontoon 12 B2
Pontorson 18 B4
Pontremoli 60 B3
Pontresina 58 B3
Pontrieux 22 C2
Pontrilas 9 D2
Ponts 37 F3
Pont-Ste-Maxence 19 F3
Pont-St-Esprit 30 B3
Pont St-Martin 31 E1
Pont-St-Vincent 21 D4
Pont-Scorff 22 B3
Ponts-de-Cé, les 23 E4
Pontsenni 8 C1
Pont-sur-Yonne 26 A1
Pontvallain 23 F4
Pontypool 9 D2
Pontypridd 8 C2
Ponza, I 63 F4
Ponziane, I 63 F4
Poole 9 E3
Poperinge 50 A3
Popinci 72 C3
Popoli 64 A2
Popovac 73 E4
Popovača 71 D2
Popova Šapka 77 D3
Popov Most 76 A1
Popovo 115 E2
Poppenhausen 52 B4
Poppi 61 D3
Poprad 112 B3
Porcari 60 C3
Porchov 111 D2
Porcuna 43 F2
Pordenone 59 E3
Poreč 70 A3
Pori 107 D1
Porjus 98 B2
Porkkalanselkä 107 E3
Porma, Emb del 35 E2
Porma, R 35 E2
Pornainen 107 F2
Pörnbach 55 F2
Pornic 24 A2
Pornichet 24 A2
Póros (Kefaloniá) 86 A1
Póros (Lefkáda) 82 B3
Póros (Póros) 87 F2
Póros, N 87 F2
Porozina 70 B3
Pórpi 81 D2
Porquerolles 31 D4
Porrentruy 27 E2
Porretta Terme 60 C3
Porriño 34 A3
Porsangen 95 E1
Porsangerhalvøya 95 D1
Porsgrunn 104 C3
Pórshöfn 96 C1
Portadown 13 D2
Portaferry 13 E2
Portaje, Emb de 39 D3
Porta, la 33 F3
Portalegre 38 C3
Portalé, Pto del 37 D2
Portalrubio 41 D2
Portariá 83 F2
Portarlington 13 D4
Port Askaig 4 B2
Portavogie 13 E2
Port-Bacarès 32 B2
Portbail 18 B3
Portbou 32 C3
Port Charlotte 4 A2
Port, Col de 37 F2
Port-Cros 31 D4
Port-de-Bouc 30 C4
Porte, Col de 30 C1
Port-Einon 8 C2
Portella Femmina Morta 69 D3
Port Ellen 4 A2
Portelo 34 C3
Port-en-Bessin 18 C3
Port Erin 6 A1
Pórtes 87 F2
Portet-d'Aspet, Col de 37 F2
Portezuelo 39 D3
Port Glasgow 4 C2
Portglenone 13 E1
Porthcawl 8 C2
Porthmadog 6 A3
Porthmós Elafonissou 90 A1
Portici 64 B4
Portile de Fier 114 C1
Portilla de la Reina 35 E2
Portillo 35 E4
Portillo de la Canda 34 C3
Portillo de Padornelo 34 C3
Portillo, Pto del 39 E2
Portimão 42 A2
Portimo 99 D2
Portinatx, Cala de 45 D3
Portishead 9 D2
Port-Joinville 24 A3
Port Láirge 15 D4
Portland, Bill of 9 D4
Port-la-Nouvelle 32 B2
Portlaoise 13 D4
Port-Leucate 32 B2
Port-Louis 22 B4
Portman 45 D3
Port-Manech 22 B3
Portmarnock 13 E4
Portnacroish 4 B1
Portnaguran 2 B2
Portnahaven 4 A2
Port-Navalo 22 C4
Porto (F) 33 E3
Porto (P) 34 A4
Porto Azzurro 62 C1
Pórto Carrás 80 B4
Porto Ceresio 58 A4
Porto Cervo 66 B1
Porto Cesareo 65 F4
Porto Cristo 45 F3
Porto de Envalira 32 A2
Porto de Lagos 42 A2
Porto de Mós 38 A3
Portodemouros, Emb de 34 B2
Porto do Barqueiro 34 B1
Porto do Son 34 A2
Porto Empedocle 68 B4
Portoferraio 62 C1
Portofino 60 A3
Port of Ness 2 B2
Porto Garibaldi 61 D2
Porto, G de 33 E3
Pórto Germenó 87 E1
Portogruaro 59 E4
Portohéli 87 E2
Pórto Kágio 87 D4
Pörtom 102 B2
Portomaggiore 61 D2
Portomarín 34 B2
Porto-Maurizio 31 F3
Porto Moniz 42 A3
Portomouro 34 A2
Portonovo 34 A2
Porto Petro 45 F3
Porto Pino 66 B4
Pórto Ráfti 88 A1
Porto Recanati 61 F4
Porto Rotondo 66 C1
Portorož 70 A3
Porto San Giorgio 61 F4
Porto Sant' Elpidio 61 F4
Porto Santo 42 A3
Porto Santo, I de 42 A3
Porto Santo Stefano 63 D2
Portoscuso 66 A4
Porto Tolle 61 D2
Porto Torres 66 A2
Porto-Vecchio 33 F4
Portovenere 60 B3
Portpatrick 4 B3
Portree 2 B3
Portrush 13 D1
Port-Ste-Marie 28 C3
Port-St-Louis 30 B4
Port St Mary 6 A1
Portsalon 13 D1
Pörtschach 70 A1
Portsmouth 9 F3
Portstewart 13 D1
Port-sur-Saône 27 D1
Port Talbot 8 C2
Porttipahdan tekojärvi 95 E4
Portugalete 36 B1
Portumna 12 C4
Port-Vendres 32 B2
Port William 4 C4
Porvoo 107 F2
Porvoonjoki 107 F2
Porzuna 40 A4
Posada 66 C2
Posadas 43 E2
Pöschenhöhe 56 C3
Pošechonje-Volodarsk 111 F1
Posedarje 74 C1
Posets, Pico 37 E2
Posio 99 E2
Positano 64 B4
Poßneck 52 C3
Possídi 80 A4
Possidonía 88 B2
Posta 63 F1
Postavy 111 D3
Postira 75 D2
Postojna 70 B2
Postojnska jama 70 A2
Poštorná 57 F1
Posušje 75 E1
Potamí 80 C1
Potamiá 87 D3
Potamiés 91 E4
Potamós (Andikíthira) 90 A2
Potamós (Kíthira) 90 A1
Potamoúla 82 C3
Potenza 64 C4
Potenza *R* 61 E4
Potenza Picenza 61 F4
Potes 35 E2
Potídea, N. 80 A4
Potigny 18 C3
Potoci 75 F1
Potok 71 D2
Potós 80 C3
Potpećko jez 76 B1
Potsdam 49 D4
Pottenstein 57 E3
Potters Bar 9 F2
Pöttmes 55 F2
Potton 9 F1
Pouancé 23 D4
Pougues-les-Eaux 26 A2
Pouilly (Nièvre) 26 A2
Pouilly (Rhône) 26 B4
Pouilly-en-Auxois 26 C2
Poulaphouca Reservoir 13 D4
Poúlari, Akr 92 C1
Pouldu, le 22 B3
Pouliguen, le 24 A2
Poúlithra 87 E3
Poúnda 88 C3
Poúnda, Akr 84 B4
Pournári 83 E2
Pournári, Teh L 82 C2
Pourniás, Kólpos 85 D1
Pourri, Mt 31 D1
Poussu 99 F3
Pouyastruc 37 E1
Pouzauges 24 C3
Pouzin, le 30 B2
Považská Bystrica 112 B3
Poveda 40 C2
Povlja 75 E2
Povljana 70 C4
Povljen 72 C4
Povoa de Lanhoso 34 A4
Póvoa de Varzim 34 A4
Powerscourt 13 D4
Powys 9 D1
Poysdorf 57 F2
Pöytyä 107 D2
Poza de la Sal 36 A2
Požarevac 73 D3
Požega 72 C4
Požeranje 77 D2
Poznań 112 A1
Pozo Alcón 44 B2
Pozoblanco 43 F1
Pozo Cañada 44 C1
Pozo de Guadalajara 40 B2
Pozo Higuera 44 C3
Pozohondo 44 C1
Pozondón 41 D2
Pozozal, Pto 35 F2
Pozuelo (Castilla-la-Mancha) 44 C1
Pozuelo (Extremadura) 39 D2
Pozuelo de Calatrava 40 A4
Pozzallo 69 D4
Pozzomaggiore 66 B2
Pozzuoli 64 A4
Pozzuolo 59 F3
Präbichl 57 D3
Prača 76 A1
Prachatice 56 C1
Prada, Emb de 34 C3
Pradairo 34 C2
Pradarena, Pso di 60 B3
Pradelles 29 F2
Prádena 36 A4

R

Raab 56 C2
Raab R 57 E4
Raabs 57 E1
Raahe 99 D4
Raajärvi 99 D2
Rääkkylä 103 F2
Raalte 17 D2
Raanujärvi 99 D2
Raasay 2 B3
Raasay, Sd of 2 B3
Raattama 95 D4
Rab 70 B4
Rab 70 B4
Rába 112 A4
Rabac 70 B3
Rábade 34 B1
Rabastens 29 D4
Rabastens-de-
  Bigorre 37 E1
Rabat 68 B4
Rabe 72 C1
Rabka 112 B3
Rabrovo
  (Makedonija) 77 F3
Rabrovo (Srbija) 73 E3
Rača (Kragujevac) 73 D3
Rača (Radan) 77 D1
Racconigi 31 E2
Rače 70 C1
Rachov 112 C3
Racibórz 112 A2
Račinovci 72 B3
Račišće 75 E2
Radalj 72 B3
Radan 77 D1
Rădăuti 113 D3
Radbuza 56 B1
Rade 48 A3
Råde 105 D3
Radeberg 53 E2
Radebeul 53 E2
Radeburg 53 E2
Radeče 70 B2
Radechov 112 C2
Radenci 70 C1
Radenthein 59 F2
Radevowald 17 E4
Radici, Pso delle 60 C3
Radicondoli 60 C4
Radika 77 D3
Radimlje 75 F2
Radiovce 77 D3
Radlje 70 B1
Radljevo 72 C3
Radnice 53 E4
Radohinës, Maj'e 76 C2
Radojevo 73 D1
Radom 112 B2
Radomsko 112 B2
Radomyšl' 113 E2
Radotin 53 F4
Radovče 76 B2
Radovići 76 B3
Radoviš 77 F3
Radovljica 70 A2
Radovnica 77 E2
Radøy 104 A2
Radstadt 59 F1
Radstädter
  Tauernpaß 59 F1
Radstock 9 D2
Raduša 75 E1
Radusa 77 D3
Radviliškis 110 C3
Radzyn' Podlaski 112 C2
Raesfeld 17 E3
Raffadali 68 B4
Rafina 88 A1
Ragama 39 F1
Raglan 9 D2
Rago 97 F1
Ragua, Pto de la 44 B3
Raguhn 53 D1
Ragunda 101 F2
Ragusa 69 D4
Rahden 17 F2
Ráhes 83 F3
Rahlstedt 48 B3
Raia, Rib de 38 B4
Rain 55 F2
Räisälä 99 E2
Raisduoddarhal'di 94 C2

Raisio 107 D2
Raittijärvi 94 C3
Rajac 73 F3
Raja-Jooseppi 95 F3
Rajamäki 107 E2
Rajince 77 E2
Raka 70 C2
Rakalj 70 A4
Rakitna 70 B2
Rakitnica 71 D2
Rakkestad 105 D3
Rakova Bara 73 E3
Rakovac 71 E3
Rakovica 70 C3
Rakovnik 53 E4
Rakvere 110 C1
Ralja 73 D3
Ram 73 D2
Ramacca 69 D3
Ramales de la
  Victoria 36 A1
Ramallosa 34 A2
Ramberg 97 E1
Rambervillers 21 D4
Rambouillet 19 E4
Rambucourt 20 C4
Ramno 77 D2
Ramnoús 84 B4
Ramor, L 13 D3
Ramsau 56 B4
Ramsau 59 F1
Ramsele 101 F2
Ramsey
  (Cambridge) 9 F1
Ramsey (I of Man) 6 A1
Ramsgate 11 D3
Ramsjö 101 E3
Ramstein 54 B1
Ramsund 94 B3
Ramundberget 101 D2
Ramvik 101 F2
Rana 97 D3
Ranalt 59 D2
Rance 22 C3
Randaberg 104 A3
Randak 104 B3
Randalstown 13 E2
Randan 26 A4
Randanne 29 E1
Randazzo 69 D3
Randers 108 B2
Randijaure 98 A2
Randow 49 E2
Randsfjorden 105 D2
Rånéâ 98 C3
Rånëälven 98 B2
Rangsdorf 49 E4
Rankweil 58 B2
Rannoch, L 4 C1
Ranovac 73 E3
Rantasalmi 103 E3
Rantsila 99 D4
Ranua 99 D3
Raon-l'Etape 21 E4
Rapallo 60 A3
Rapolano Terme 61 D4
Rapolla 64 C3
Rapperswil 58 A2
Rapsáni 83 E1
Raptópoulo 86 C3
Raša 70 A3
Räsälä 103 E2
Raša R 70 A3
Rasbo 106 B3
Rascafría 40 A1
Rasdorf 52 B3
Raseiniai 110 C3
Rasimbegov Most 77 E4
Rasina 73 E4
Raška 76 C1
Rasno 75 E2
Raso, C 38 A4
Rasquera 41 F1
Rastatt 54 C2
Rastede 47 F3
Rastegai'sa 95 E2
Rastenberg 52 C2
Rastenfeld 57 E2
Rasueros 39 F1
Rätan 101 E3
Rateče 70 A1
Ratekau 48 B2
Rates 34 A4
Rathdowney 12 C4

Rathdrum 13 D4
Rathenow 49 D4
Rathfriland 13 E2
Rathkeale 14 B3
Rathlin I 13 E1
Rath Luirc 14 B3
Rathmelton 13 D1
Rathmore 14 B4
Rathmullan 13 D1
Raticosa, Pso della 61 D3
Ratingen 17 E4
Ratkovac 76 C2
Ratkovo 72 B2
Ratten 57 E3
Rattenberg 59 D1
Rattersdorf 57 F3
Rattray 5 D1
Rattray Head 3 E3
Rättvik 101 E4
Ratzeburg 48 B2
Raubling 56 B3
Raucourt-et-Flaba 20 C2
Raudanjoki 99 D2
Raudaskylä 102 C1
Raufarhöfn 96 C1
Raufoss 105 D2
Rauha 103 E4
Rauhamäki 103 D3
Rauland 104 B3
Rauma (N) 100 B3
Rauma (SF) 107 D2
Rauris 59 E1
Rautalampi 103 D2
Rautas 94 C4
Rautavaara 103 E1
Rautio 102 C1
Rautjärvi 103 F3
Ravan 71 F4
Ravanica 73 E4
Ravanjska 70 C4
Ravanusa 68 C4
Ravello 64 B4
Raven 71 D2
Ravenna 61 D2
Ravensbrück 49 D3
Ravensburg 55 D4
Ravna Dubrava 77 E1
Ravna Gora 70 B3
Ravna Reka 73 E3
Ravne na
  Koroškem 70 B1
Ravnište 77 D2
Ravnje 72 B3
Ravno 75 F2
Ravno Bučje 73 F4
Ravno, G. 75 E1
Rawicz 112 A2
Rawtenstall 6 C2
Rayleigh 11 D2
Rayol 31 D4
Räyrinki 102 C2
Razboj 71 E3
Razbojna 77 D1
Raždaginja 76 C1
Razelm 113 E4
Razgrad 115 E2
Razlog 115 D3
Razlovci 77 F2
Raz, Pte du 22 A3
Reading 9 F2
Reales 43 E4
Réalmont 32 B1
Rebais 20 A4
Rebbenesøy 94 B2
Rebordelo 34 C3
Reç 76 C3
Recanati 61 F4
Recco 60 A3
Recey 26 C1
Rechnitz 57 F4
Rečica (SU) 111 E4
Rečica (YU) 70 C3
Recke 17 E2
Recklinghausen 17 E3
Recknitz 48 C2
Recoaro Terme 59 D4
Recuerda 36 A4
Recz 49 F2
Redange 21 D2
Red B 13 E1
Redcar 5 F4
Redditch 9 E1

Redhill 10 C3
Redon 23 D4
Redondela 34 A3
Redondo 38 C4
Redruth 8 B4
Ree, L 12 C3
Rees 17 D3
Reeth 6 C1
Refsnes 94 A3
Reftele 109 D2
Rega 49 F2
Regalbuto 69 D3
Regen 56 B2
Regensburg 56 B2
Regenstauf 56 B2
Reggello 61 D4
Reggio di Calabria 67 E4
Reggiolo 60 C2
Reggio nell' Emilia 60 C2
Reghin 113 D4
Regnitz 55 E1
Reguengos de
  Monsaraz 42 B1
Rehau 53 D4
Rehburg-
  Loccum 48 A4
Rehden 17 F2
Rehna 48 B2
Reichenau (A) 57 E3
Reichenau (CH) 58 B2
Reichenbach
  (Dresden) 53 F2
Reichenbach
  (Karl-Marx-Stadt) 53 D3
Reichertshofen 55 F2
Reichshoffen 21 E3
Reigate 10 C3
Reignier 27 D4
Ré, Ile de 24 B4
Reillanne 30 C3
Reims 20 B3
Reinach 27 F2
Reinbek 48 B3
Reinberg 49 D1
Reine 97 E1
Reinfeld 48 B2
Reinheim 54 C1
Reinli 104 C2
Reinosa 35 F2
Reinøy 94 C2
Reisaelva 94 C2
Reischenhart 56 B3
Reisjärvi 103 D1
Reiss 3 D2
Reit im Winkl 56 B4
Reitzenhain 53 E3
Reka 70 A3
Rekovac 73 E4
Remagen 51 E4
Rémalard 23 F3
Remeskylä 103 D1
Remich 21 D2
Remiremont 27 D1
Remolinos 36 C3
Remouchamps 51 D4
Remoulins 30 B3
Rempstone 7 D2
Remscheid 17 E4
Rémuzat 30 C2
Rena 105 D2
Renaix 50 B3
Renazé 23 E4
Renchen 54 C3
Rende 67 E2
Rendina
  (Makedonía) 80 B3
Rendína
  (Thessalía) 83 D3
Rendsburg 48 A2
Renginio 83 F3
Rengsdorf 51 E4
Reni 113 E4
Renish Pt 2 A3
Renko 107 E2
Renkum 17 D3
Rennebu 100 C2
Rennerod 51 F3
Rennes-les-Bains 32 B2
Rennesøy 104 A3
Rennweg 59 F2
Reno 61 D2
Rensjön 94 C4
Renwez 20 B2

Réole, la 28 B2
Replot 102 B2
Replotfjärden 102 B2
Repojoki 95 E3
Reposaari 102 B3
République, Col de
  la 30 B1
Repvag 95 E1
Requena 41 D4
Réquista 29 E3
Rerik 48 C2
Resanovci 71 D4
Resavica 73 E3
Reschenpaß 58 C2
Resen
  (Makedonija) 77 D4
Resen (Srbija) 77 D1
Resende 34 B4
Resia, Pso di 58 C2
Resita 114 C1
Resko 49 F2
Resmo 109 E3
Resna 76 B3
Resnik 73 D3
Ressons 19 F3
Restafjorden 94 C2
Restelica 77 D3
Resuttano 68 C3
Retezatului, M 114 C1
Rethel 20 B3
Rethem 48 A4
Rethen 52 B1
Réthimno 90 C3
Réthimno
  (Nomos) 90 C3
Retiers 23 D3
Retortillo, Emb de 43 E2
Retuerta 41 D1
Retuerta del
  Bullaque 39 F3
Retuerta, Emb de 36 A3
Retz 57 E2
Reuilly 25 E3
Reus 37 F4
Reusel 16 C4
Reuss 27 F2
Reuterstadt-
  Stavenhagen 49 D2
Reutlingen 55 D3
Reutte 58 C1
Revard, Mt 27 D4
Revel 29 D4
Revesbotn 95 D1
Revigny 20 C4
Revin 20 B2
Řevnikov 53 F3
Revolcadores 44 C2
Revonlahti 99 D4
Revsnes 104 B1
Rewal 49 F1
Reyðarfjörður 96 C2
Reykjavik 96 A2
Rêzekne 111 D2
Rezzato 60 B1
Rezzoaglio 60 A3
Rgotina 73 F3
Rhaeadr 8 C1
Rhayader 8 C1
Rheda-
  Wiedenbrück 17 F3
Rhede 17 D3
Rhein 17 D3
Rheinbach 51 E4
Rheinberg 17 D3
Rheinböllen 54 B1
Rheine 17 E2
Rheinfelden (CH) 27 F2
Rheinfelden (D) 54 C4
Rheinhausen 17 D3
Rheinland-Pfalz 51 E4
Rheinsberg 49 D3
Rheinwaldhorn 58 B3
Rhêmes N.D. 31 E1
Rhenen 16 C3
Rheydt 17 D4
Rhinau 21 E4
Rhinow 49 D4
Rho 60 A1
Rhondda 8 C2
Rhône 26 C4
Rhône (Dépt) 26 B4
Rhône à Sète,
  Canal du 30 B3
Rhosneigr 6 A2

Rhossili 8 C2
Rhüden 52 B1
Rhum 2 B4
Rhum, Sd of 2 B4
Rhune, la 28 A4
Rhuthun 6 B3
Rhyl 6 B2
Rhynern 17 E3
Rhynie 3 E4
Riaillé 23 D4
Riákia 79 E3
Rial 34 A2
Riaño 35 E2
Riaño, Emb de 35 E2
Rians 30 C4
Riansares R 40 B3
Rianxo 34 A2
Riaza 36 A4
Ribadavia 34 B3
Ribadelago 34 C3
Ribadeo 34 C1
Ribadesella 35 E1
Riba de Saelices 40 C1
Riba de Santiuste 36 A4
Riba-roja, Emb de 37 E4
Ribarci 77 E2
Ribariće 76 C1
Ribarska Banja 73 E4
Ribas de Campos 35 E3
Ribas de Sil 34 B2
Ribatejo 38 B3
Ribble 6 C2
Ribe 108 A3
Ribeauvillé 27 E1
Ribécourt 19 F3
Ribeira de Pena 34 B4
Ribeira, Emb de la 34 B1
Ribemont 20 A2
Ribera de Cardós 32 A2
Ribera del Fresno 43 D1
Ribes de Freser 32 B3
Ribiers 30 C3
Ribnica (Bosna i
  Hercegovina) 71 F4
Ribnica (Kočevje) 70 B2
Ribnica (Postojna) 70 A3
Ribnica na
  Pohorju 70 B1
Ribnik 70 C2
Ribnitz-
  Damgarten 48 C1
Ribolla 62 C1
Riccia 64 B3
Riccione 61 E3
Riceys, les 26 B1
Richelieu 25 D3
Richmond
  (London) 9 F2
Richmond (Yorks) 6 C1
Richtenberg 49 D1
Rickling 48 A2
Ricla 36 C4
Ricobayo, Emb de 35 D4
Riddica 72 B1
Riec 22 B3
Ried
  (Oberösterreich) 56 C3
Ried (Tirol) 58 C2
Riedenburg 55 F2
Riedlingen 55 D3
Riegel 54 C3
Riegersburg 57 F4
Riego de la Vega 35 D3
Riesa 53 E2
Riesi 68 C4
Riestedt 52 C2
Rietberg 17 F3
Rieti 63 D2
Rieumes 29 D4
Rieupeyroux 29 E3
Rieux 37 F1
Riez 31 D3
Riezlern 58 B2
Rîga 110 C2
Rigáni 83 D3
Rígeo 83 E2
Rigi 58 A2
Rignac 29 E3
Rignano Flaminio 63 E2
Rihéa 87 E3
Riihimäki 107 E2

Riisitunturi 99 E2
Riistavesi 103 E2
Riječa 72 B4
Rijeka 70 B3
Rijeka Crnojevića 76 B3
Rijssen 17 D2
Riksgränsen 94 B3
Rila 115 D3
Rila Mts 115 D3
Rillo 41 D2
Rillo de Gallo 40 C1
Rimavská-
  Sobota 112 B3
Rimbo 106 B3
Rimini 61 E3
Rîmnicu Sărat 113 E4
Rîmnicu Vîlcea 115 D1
Rîmnio 79 E4
Rimske Toplice 70 B2
Rincón de la
  Victoria 43 F4
Rincón de Soto 36 C2
Rindal 100 C2
Ringaskiddy 14 C4
Ringe 108 B4
Ringebu 100 C3
Ringford 4 C3
Ringkøbing 108 A3
Ringkøbing
  Fjord 108 A3
Ring of Kerry 14 A4
Ringsaker 105 D2
Ringstad 104 A1
Ringsted 108 C3
Ringvassøy 94 B2
Ringwood 9 E3
Rínia, N 88 C2
Rinkaby 109 D3
Rinns Pt 4 A2
Rinteln 52 A1
Rinvyle Pt 12 A3
Río 83 D4
Riocavado de la
  Sierra 36 A3
Riogordo 43 F3
Riola Sardo 66 A3
Riolo Terme 61 D3
Riom 26 A4
Riomaggiore 60 B3
Rio Maior 38 A3
Rio Marina 62 C1
Riom-ès-
  Montagnes 29 E1
Rionero in Vulture 64 C3
Río, Punta del 44 B4
Rioseco de Tapia 35 D2
Rioz 27 D2
Ripač 70 C4
Ripanj 73 D3
Riparbella 60 C4
Ripatransone 61 F4
Ripley 7 D3
Ripoli 32 A3
Ripollet 32 A4
Ripon 6 C1
Riquewihr 27 E1
Risan 76 B2
Risbäck 97 E4
Risca 9 D2
Riscle 28 B4
Risle 19 D4
Risnes 104 B4
Risnjak 70 B3
Risør 104 C4
Risøyhamn 94 B3
Risøysundet 94 A3
Rissa 100 C1
Ristiina 103 E3
Ristijärvi 99 E4
Ristilampi 99 D2
Ristovac 77 E2
Risum-Lindholm 47 F1
Ritíni 79 E4
Ritoniemi 103 E2
Ritsóna 84 A4
Rittmannshausen 52 B3
Riudoms 37 F4
Riva 58 C4
Rivarolo Canavese 31 E1
Rive-de-Gier 30 B1
Rives 30 C1
Rivesaltes 32 B2
Rivière-Thibouville,
  la 19 D3

Rødekro 108 A4
Rodel 2 A3
Rodellar 37 E3
Roden 47 D3
Ródenas 41 D2
Rödermark 52 A4
Rodewisch 53 D3
Rodez 29 E3
Rodiezmo 35 D2
Rodi Garganico 64 C2
Roding 56 B1
Roditis 81 E2
Rodnei, M 113 D3
Rododáfni 83 D4
Rodohóri 79 E3
Rodolívos 80 B2
Rödön 101 E2
Rodonit, Gjiri i 76 C4
Rodópi (Nomos) 81 E2
Rodopi *Mts* 115 D3
Rodópoli 79 F2
Rodopós 90 B3
Ródos 93 F1
Ródos, N 93 F2
Rodováni 90 B3
Rodvattnet 102 A1
Rødven 100 B2
Rødvig 108 C4
Roermond 17 D4
Roeselare 50 A3
Rogač 75 D2
Rogača 73 D3
Rogačica (Kosovo) 77 E2
Rogačica (Srbija) 72 C4
Rogačov 111 E4
Rogaland 104 A3
Rogaška Slatina 70 C1
Rogatec 70 C2
Rogatica 76 A1
Rogatin 113 D3
Rogätz 48 C4
Rogen 101 D3
Rogen *L* 101 D3
Roggendorf 48 B2
Roggiano Gravina 67 E2
Roggosen 53 F1
Rogliano (F) 33 F2
Rogliano (I) 67 E3
Rognan 97 E2
Rogozna 76 C1
Rogoznica 75 D2
Rohan 22 C3
Rohr 52 B3
Rohrbach (A) 56 C2
Rohrbach (F) 21 E3
Rohrbrunn 52 A4
Rohrer Sattel 57 E3
Roignais 27 E4
Roine Mallasvesi 107 E1
Roisel 19 F2
Roissy 19 F4
Rojales 45 D2
Rök 109 D1
Rokiškis 110 C3
Røkland 97 F2
Rokovci 71 F2
Rokua 99 E4
Rokycany 53 E4
Røldal 104 B3
Rolfstorp 108 C2
Rolla 94 B3
Rollag 104 C3
Rolle 27 D3
Rolle, Pso di 59 D3
Rolvsøya 95 D1
Roma 63 E2
Romagnano Sesia 31 F1
Roman 113 D4
Romana 66 B2
Romanche 31 D1
Romangordo 39 E3
România 73 D1
Romanija 71 F4
Romans 30 C2
Romanshorn 58 B1
Romantische straße 55 E3
Rombas 21 D3
Rombo, Pso del 58 C2
Römhild 52 B4
Romilly 20 B4
Romny 113 F1
Rømø 108 A3
Romont 27 E3
Romorantin 25 E2
Romsdalen 100 B2
Romsdalsfjorden 100 B2
Romsey 9 E3
Rona 2 B3
Ronaldsway 6 A1
Roncade 59 E4
Roncal 37 D2
Ronce 28 A1
Roncegno 59 D3
Roncesvalles 36 C1
Ronchamp 27 D1
Ronchi 59 F3
Ronciglione 63 E2
Roncobilaccio 60 C3
Ronda 43 E3
Rondane 100 C3
Ronda, Serr de 43 E4
Rønde 108 B3
Rondeslottet 100 C3
Rondissone 31 F1
Rondvassbu 100 C3
Rönnäng 108 C1
Rønne 109 D4
Ronneburg 53 D3
Ronneby 109 E3
Ronnebyån 109 E3
Rønnede 108 C4
Rönnöfors 101 E1
Ronse 50 B3
Roosendaal 16 B3
Roperuelos del Páramo 35 D3
Ropi 94 C3
Ropinsalmi 94 C3
Ropotovo 77 E3
Roquebillière 31 E3
Roquebrun 30 A4
Roquebrune-Cap-Martin 31 E3
Roquebrussanne, la 31 D4
Roquecourbe 32 B1
Roquefort 28 B3
Roquefort-sur-Soulzon 29 F3
Roque-Gageac, la 29 D2
Roquemaure 30 B3
Roquesteron 31 E3
Roquetas de Mar 44 B4
Roquevaire 30 C4
Rora Head 3 D1
Rore 71 D4
Røros 101 D2
Rørøy 97 D3
Rorschach 58 B1
Rørvig 108 C3
Rørvik (Nord Trøndelag) 97 D4
Rørvik (Sør Trøndelag) 100 C1
Ros' 113 E2
Rosà 59 D4
Rosal de la Frontera 42 C1
Rosans 30 C2
Rosarito, Emb de 39 E2
Rosarno 67 E4
Roscoff 22 B2
Ros Comáin 12 C3
Roscommon 12 C3
Roscommon (Co) 12 C3
Roscrea 12 C4
Rose (I) 67 E2
Rose (YU) 76 A3
Rosegg 70 A1
Roselend, Cormet de 27 E4
Rosell 41 F2
Rosendal 104 A2
Rosenheim 56 B3
Rosenhof 56 B2
Rosenthal 53 F3
Roses 32 C3
Roses, Golfo de 32 C3
Roseto degli Abruzzi 64 A1
Roßhaupten 55 E4
Rosheim 21 E4
Rosice 57 F1
Rosières 19 F2
Rosiers, les 24 C2
Rosignano Marittimo 60 C4
Roşiori de Vede 115 D2
Roskilde 108 C3
Roški slap 75 D1
Roßlau 53 D1
Roslavl' 111 E3
Rosmaninhal 38 C3
Røsnæs 108 B3
Rosolina Mare 61 D1
Rosolini 69 D4
Rosoman 77 E3
Rosova dolina 115 D2
Rosporden 22 B3
Rossano 67 F2
Rossan Pt 12 C1
Rosscarbery 14 B4
Roßdorf 54 C1
Rosses Point 12 C2
Rossija 111 E2
Rossio 38 B3
Rosskreppfjorden 104 B3
Rosslare 15 D4
Rosslare Harbour 15 D4
Rosslea 13 D2
Rossön 101 F1
Ross-on-Wye 9 D2
Røssvatnet 97 E3
Rosthwaite 5 D4
Røstlandet 97 D1
Rostock 48 C2
Rostrenen 22 B3
Rostrevor 13 E3
Rostujávri 94 C3
Røsvik 94 A4
Rosvik 98 C3
Roßwein 53 E2
Rota 43 D3
Rotenburg (Hessen) 52 B3
Rotenburg (Niedersachsen) 48 A3
Roth 55 F1
Rötha 53 D2
Rothbury 5 E3
Röthenbach 55 F1
Rothenburg 53 F2
Rothenburg ob der Tauber 55 E1
Rothéneuf 18 B4
Rotherham 7 D2
Rothes 3 D3
Rothesay 4 B2
Rothwell 9 F1
Rotja, Pta 45 D4
Rotonda 67 E2
Rotondella 65 D4
Rotondo, M 33 F3
Rott (Bayern) 56 A3
Rott (Bayern) 56 B3
Rott *R* 56 B2
Rottach-Egern 56 A4
Rotten 27 F3
Rottenbach 52 C4
Rottenburg (Baden-Württemberg) 55 D3
Rottenburg (Bayern) 56 B2
Rottenmann 57 D4
Rottenmanner Tauern 57 D4
Rotterdam 16 B3
Rottne 109 D2
Rottneros 105 E3
Rottweil 54 C3
Rötz 56 B1
Roubaix 20 A1
Roudnice 53 F3
Rouen 19 E3
Rouffach 27 E1
Rougé 23 D4
Rougemont 27 D2
Rougemont-le-Château 27 E1
Rouillac 28 B1
Roujan 30 A4
Roulans 27 D2
Roulers 50 A3
Roundstone 12 A3
Rousay 3 E1
Roússa 81 E1
Rousses, les 27 D3
Rousset, Col de 30 C2
Rovaniemi 99 D2
Rovato 60 B1
Rovereto 59 D4
Roverud 105 D3
Roviés 83 F3
Rovigo 61 D2
Rovinj 70 A3
Rovišće 71 D2
Rovno 113 D2
Roxen 106 A4
Roxo, Bgem do 42 B1
Royal Canal 12 C3
Royal Leamington Spa 9 E1
Royal Tunbridge Wells 10 C3
Royan 28 A1
Royat 29 E1
Roybon 30 C1
Roye 19 F3
Royère-de-Vassivière 25 E4
Røyrvik 97 E4
Royston 9 F2
Röyttä 98 C3
Rožaje 76 C2
Rožanstvo 72 C4
Rozay-en-Brie 19 F4
Rozier, le 29 F3
Rožmberk 57 D1
Rožmitál 53 F4
Rožňava 112 B3
Rozoy 20 B2
Roztocze 112 C2
Roztoky 53 F3
Rozvadov 56 B1
Rrasë 76 C3
Rrëshen 76 C3
Rrogozhinë 76 C4
Rtanj 73 E4
Rtanj (Reg) 73 E4
Ruabon 6 B3
Rubbestadneset 104 A2
Rubena 35 F3
Rubeži 76 B2
Rubha a'Mhail 4 B2
Rubha Còigeach 2 C2
Rubha Réidh 2 B3
Rubi 32 A4
Rubiães 34 A3
Rubi de Bracamonte 39 F1
Rubielos de Mora 41 E3
Rubiera 60 C2
Rubio 35 F4
Rudare 77 D1
Rüdersdorf 49 E4
Rüdesheim 51 F4
Rudkøbing 108 B4
Rudn'a 111 E3
Rudna Glava 73 E3
Rudnica (Crna Gora) 76 B1
Rudnica (Srbija) 76 C1
Rudnik (Kosovo) 76 C2
Rudnik (Reg) 73 D4
Rudnik (Srbija) 73 D4
Rudo 76 B1
Rudolstadt 52 C3
Rue 19 E2
Ruecas, R 39 E4
Rueda 35 E4
Rueda de Jalón 36 C3
Ruelle 28 C1
Ruffec 25 D4
Ruffieux 27 D4
Rugby 9 E1
Rugeley 6 C3
Rügen 49 D1
Rugles 19 D4
Rugovska klisura 76 C2
Ruhla 52 B3
Ruhland 53 E2
Ruhner Berge 48 C3
Ruhpolding 56 B3
Ruhr 17 E3
Ruidera 40 B4
Rūjiena 110 C2
Ruka 99 E2
Rukatunturi 99 E2
Ruma 72 C2
Rumblar, Emb del 44 A2
Rumboci 75 E1
Rumburk 53 F2
Rumengol 22 B3
Rumenka 72 C2
Rumigny 20 B2
Rumija 76 B3
Rumilly 27 D4
Runcorn 6 B2
Runde 100 A2
Rundvik 102 A2
Runn 105 F2
Runni 103 D1
Runtuna 106 B4
Ruohtir 95 E2
Ruokojärvi 103 F3
Ruokolahti 103 F3
Ruokovesi 103 E2
Ruokto 98 B1
Ruoms 30 B2
Ruotsinpyhtää 107 F2
Ruovesi 102 C3
Rupa 70 B3
Rupea 113 D4
Ruppiner See 49 D3
Rupt 27 D1
Rur 17 D4
Ruše 70 C1
Ruse 115 D2
Ruševo 71 E2
Rush 13 E3
Rushden 9 F1
Ruski Krstur 72 B2
Rusko 107 D2
Rusko Selo 72 C1
Rusksele 98 A4
Rüsselsheim 51 F4
Russenes 95 D1
Russey, le 27 E2
Russi 61 D3
Rust 57 F3
Rustefjelbma 95 E1
Ruswil 27 F2
Rute 43 F3
Rüthen 17 F3
Ruthin 6 B3
Rüti 58 A2
Rutigliano 65 E3
Rutledal 104 A1
Ruuhitunturi 99 E2
Ruukki 99 D4
Ruuponsaari 103 D2
Ruurlo 17 D3
Ruvo di Puglia 65 D3
Ruwer 54 A1
Ruynes-en-Margeride 29 F2
Ružomberok 112 B3
Ry 108 B3
Rybinsk 111 F1
Rybinskoje Vodochranilišče 111 F1
Rybnica 113 E3
Rybnik 112 B3
Rychnov nad Kněžnou 112 A3
Ryd 109 D3
Ryde 9 E3
Rye 11 D3
Ryfylke 104 A3
Rygge 105 D3
Rykene 104 B4
Ryl'sk 113 F1
Rymań 49 F1
Rymättylä 107 D2
Rypefjord 95 D1
Rysjedalsvika 104 A1
Ryttylä 107 E2
Rzepin 49 F4
Rzeszów 112 C2
Ržev 111 F2

S

Sääksjärvi 102 C2
Saal 55 F2
Saalach 59 E1
Saalbach 59 E1
Saale 52 C1
Saaler Bodden 48 C1
Saales 21 E4
Saalfeld 52 C3
Saalfelden 59 E1
Saane 27 E3
Saanen 27 E3
Saar 54 A1
Saarbrücken 54 B2
Saarburg 54 A1
Saaremaa 110 B2
Saarenkylä 99 D2
Saari 103 F3
Saariharju 99 E3
Saarijärvi 103 D2
Saarikoski 94 C3
Saariselkä 95 F3
Saariselkä (Reg) 95 F3
Saaristomeri 107 D3
Saarland 54 A2
Saarlouis 54 B2
Saas- Fee 27 F4
Šabac 72 C3
Sabadell 32 A4
Sabaudia 63 F3
Sabbioneta 60 C2
Sabero 35 E2
Sabiñánigo 37 D2
Sabini, Mti 63 E2
Sabiote 44 B2
Sablé 23 E4
Sables-d'Olonne, les 24 B3
Sables-d'Or 22 C2
Sæbo 100 A2
Sabóia 42 A2
Sabôr, R 34 C4
Sabres 28 B3
Sabrosa 34 B4
Sabugal 39 D2
Sæby 108 B2
Sa Calobra 45 E2
Sacavém 38 A4
Sacedon 40 C2
Saceruela 39 F4
Sacile 59 E3
Sacra di San Michele 31 E1
Sacramenia 35 F4
Sacratif, C 44 A4
Sada 34 B1
Sádaba 36 C2
Sado, R 38 A4
Sadurniño 34 B1
Saelices 40 B3
Safara 42 C1
Säffle 105 E4
Saffron Walden 10 C2
Safonovo 111 E3
Sagard 49 D1
S'Agaró 32 B4
Sagéika 86 B1
Sagfjorden 94 A4
Sagiáda 82 B1
Sagra, Sa de la 44 B2
Sagres 42 A3
Sagres, Pta de 42 A3
Sagunto 41 E3
Sagvåg 104 A3
Sahagún 35 E3
Sahalahti 107 E1
Šahinovići 71 E3
Sahl 108 A2
Sahloinen 103 D3
Saidus 110 B3
Saignelégier 27 E2
Saija 95 F4
Saillagouse 32 A3
Saillans 30 C2
Saimaa 103 E3
Saimaanranta 103 E4
Sains-du-Nord 20 B2
Sains-Richaumont 20 B2
St Abb's Head 5 E2
St Aegyd 57 E3
St-Affrique 29 E3
St-Agnant 24 B4
St-Agrève 30 B2
St-Aignan 25 E2
St-Aignan-sur-Roë 23 E3
St Alban 29 F2
St Albans 9 F2
St Alban's Head 9 E4
St-Amand-en-Puisaye 26 A2
St-Amand-les-Eaux 20 A1

St-A – Sal 187

St-Amand-Longpré 25 D2
St-Amand-Montrond 25 F3
St-Amans-des-Cots 29 E2
St-Amans 29 F2
St-Amans-Soult 32 B1
St-Amant 29 F1
St-Amant-Roche-Savine 29 F1
St-Amarin 27 E1
St-Ambroix 30 B3
St-Amé 27 D1
St-Amour 26 C3
St Andrä 70 B1
St Andreasberg 52 B2
St-André-de-Cubzac 28 B2
St-André-de-l'Eure 19 E4
St-André-de-Vézines 29 F3
St-André-les-Alpes 31 D3
St Andrews 5 D1
St-Anthème 30 B1
St-Antonin-Noble-Val 29 D3
St Anton 58 C2
St-Arnoult 19 E4
St Asaph 6 B2
St-Astier 28 C2
St-Auban 31 D3
St-Aubin-d'Aubigné 23 D3
St-Aubin-du-Cormier 23 D3
St-Aubin 18 C3
St-Aulaye 28 C2
St Austell 8 B4
St-Avold 21 D3
St-Aygulf 31 D4
St-Beauzély 29 E3
St Bees Head 4 C4
St-Benoît-du-Sault 25 E3
St-Benoît 25 F2
St-Bertrand-de-Comminges 37 E1
St-Béat 37 F2
St-Bénin-d'Azy 26 A3
St Blasien 54 C4
St-Blin 26 C1
St-Bonnet 31 D2
St-Bonnet-de-Joux 26 B3
St-Bonnet-le-Château 30 B1
St-Brévin 24 A2
St-Briac 18 A4
St-Brice-en-Coglès 18 B4
St Brides B 8 B2
St-Brieuc 22 C2
St-Calais 23 F3
St-Cast 18 A4
St Catherine's Pt 9 E4
St-Cergue 27 D3
St-Cernin 29 E2
St-Céré 29 D2
St-Chamas 30 C4
St-Chamond 30 B1
St-Chély-d'Apcher 29 F2
St-Chély-d'Aubrac 29 E2
St-Chinian 32 B1
St Christophen 57 E2
St-Ciers 28 B1
St-Cirq-Lapopie 29 D3
St-Clair-sur-l'Elle 18 C3
St-Clar 28 C3
St-Claud 25 D4
St-Claude 27 D3
St Clears 8 C2
St-Cyprien 29 D2
St-Cyprien-Plage 32 B2
St David's 8 B1
St David's Head 8 B1
St-Denis (Charente-Maritime) 24 B4
St-Denis-d'Orques 23 E3
St-Denis (Seine-St-Denis) 19 F4
St-Didier-en-Velay 30 B1
St-Dié 21 E4
St-Dier-d'Auvergne 29 F1
St-Dizier 20 C4
St-Donat-sur-l'Herbasse 30 C1
St-Eloy-les-Mines 26 A4
St-Emilion 28 B2
St-Etienne (Alpes-de-Haute-Provence) 30 C3
St-Etienne-Cantalès, Bge de 29 E2
St-Etienne-de-Baïgorry 28 A4
St-Etienne-de-Lugdarès 29 F2
St-Etienne-de-Montluc 24 B2
St-Etienne-de-St-Geoirs 30 C1
St-Etienne-de-Tinée 31 E3
St-Etienne-en-Dévoluy 31 D2
St-Etienne (Loire) 30 B1
St-Fargeau 26 A2
St-Félicien 30 B2
St Finan's B 14 A4
St-Firmin 31 D2
St-Florent (Cher) 25 F3
St-Florent (Corse) 33 F2
St-Florentin 26 B1
St-Flour 29 F2
St-François-Longchamp 31 D1
St-Fulgent 24 B3
St Gallen (A) 57 D3
St Gallen (CH) 58 B2
St Gallenkirch 58 B2
St-Galmier 30 B1
St-Gaudens 37 F1
St-Gaultier 25 E3
St-Genest-Malifaux 30 B1
St-Gengoux-le-National 26 C3
St-Geniez-d'Olt 29 E3
St-Genis-de-Stonge 28 B1
St-Genis-Laval 30 B1
St-Genix 30 C1
St-Geoire 30 C1
St Georgen (A) 56 C3
St Georgen am Langsee 70 B1
St Georgen (D) 54 C3
St-Georges 23 E4
St Georges Channel 8 A1
St-Georges-de-Didonne 28 A1
St-Georges-en-Couzan 29 F1
St-Germain-de-Calberte 29 F3
St-Germain-des-Fossés 26 A4
St-Germain-du-Bois 26 C3
St-Germain-du-Plain 26 C3
St-Germain-du-Teil 29 F3
St-Germain 19 F4
St-Germain-Laval 26 B4
St-Germain-Lembron 29 F1
St-Germain-les-Belles 29 D1
St-Germain-l'Herm 29 F1
St-Gertraud 58 C3
St-Gervais-d'Auvergne 26 A4
St-Gervais 27 E4
St-Gervais-sur-Mare 30 A4
St-Géry 29 D3
St-Gildas-de-Rhuys 22 C4
St-Gildas-des-Bois 23 D4
St-Gildas, Pte de 24 A2
St Gilgen 56 C3
St-Gilles-Croix-de-Vie 24 A3
St-Gilles 30 B4
St-Gingolph 27 E3
St-Girons 37 F2
St-Girons-Plage 28 A3
St Goar 51 E4
St Goarshausen 51 E4
St-Gobain 20 A3
St Govan's Head 8 B2
St-Guénolé 22 A3
St-Guilhem-le-Désert 29 F4
St-Haon-le-Châtel 26 B4
St Helens 6 B2
St-Hélier 18 B3
St-Hilaire-des-Loges 24 C3
St-Hilaire-de-Villefranche 28 B1
St-Hilaire-du-Harcouet 18 B4
St-Hilaire 32 B2
St-Hippolyte-du-Fort 29 F3
St-Hippolyte 27 E2
St-Honoré 26 B3
St-Hubert 20 C2
St-Imier 27 E2
St Ingbert 54 B2
St Ives (Cambs) 9 F1
St Ives (Cornwall) 8 A4
St-Jacques 23 D3
St-Jacut 18 A4
St Jakob 59 D2
St Jakob im Rosental 70 A1
St James 18 B4
St-Jean-Brévelay 22 C3
St-Jean-Cap-Ferrat 31 E3
St-Jean-d'Angély 24 C4
St-Jean-de-Bournay 30 C1
St-Jean-de-Daye 18 B3
St-Jean-de-Losne 26 C2
St-Jean-de-Luz 28 A4
St-Jean-de-Maurienne 31 D1
St-Jean-de-Monts 24 A3
St-Jean-du-Bruel 29 F3
St-Jean-du-Gard 30 A3
St-Jean-en-Royans 30 C2
St-Jean-Pied-de-Port 28 A4
St-Jeoire 27 D4
St Johann im Pongau 59 E1
St Johann in Tirol 59 E1
St John's Pt 13 E2
St-Jouin-de-Marnes 24 C3
St-Juéry 29 E3
St-Julien-Chapteuil 30 B2
St-Julien-de-Vouvantes 23 D4
St-Julien-du-Sault 26 A1
St-Julien-en-Genevois 27 D4
St-Julien 26 C3
St-Julien-l'Ars 25 D3
St-Junien 25 D4
St Just 8 A4
St-Just-en-Chaussée 19 F3
St-Just-en-Chevalet 26 B4
St-Justin 28 B3
St Keverne 8 B4
St Lambrecht 57 D4
St-Lary-Soulan 37 E2
St-Laurent (Calvados) 18 C3
St-Laurent-de-la-Salanque 32 B2
St-Laurent-du-Pont 30 C1
St-Laurent-en-Grandvaux 27 D3
St-Laurent-les-Bains 29 F2
St-Laurent-Médoc 28 B2
St-Laurent (Vendée) 24 C3
St-Laurent (Vienne) 28 C1
St-Léger 26 B3
St Leonhard (I) 59 D2
St Leonhard (Niederösterreich) 57 E3
St Leonhard (Tirol) 58 C2
St-Léonard-de-Noblat 25 E4
St Lorenzen 59 E2
St-Lô 18 C3
St-Louis 27 E2
St-Loup-Lamairé 24 C3
St-Loup-sur-Semouse 27 D1
St-Luc 27 F3
St-Lunaire 18 B4
St-Lys 29 D4
St-Macaire 28 B2
St Magnus B 3 F1
St-Maixent-l'Ecole 24 C3
St-Malo-de-la-Lande 18 B3
St-Malo 18 B4
St-Mamet-la-Salvetat 29 E2
St-Mandrier 31 D4
St-Marcellin 30 C1
St-Margarethen 48 A2
St Margaret's Hope 3 E1
St-Mars-la-Jaille 23 D4
St-Martin (Charente-Maritime) 24 B4
St-Martin-d'Auxigny 25 F2
St-Martin-de-Belleville 31 D1
St-Martin-de-Londres 29 F4
St-Martin-de-Seignan 28 A4
St-Martin-de-Valamas 30 B2
St-Martin-en-Bresse 26 C3
St-Martin (Pyrénées-Orientales) 32 B2
St Martin's 8 A4
St-Martin-Vésubie 31 E3
St-Martory 37 F1
St Mary's 8 A4
St Märgen 54 C4
St-Mathieu 28 C1
St-Mathieu, Pte de 22 A3
St-Maurice 27 E4
St Mawes 8 B4
St-Maximin-la-Ste Baume 31 D4
St-Médard-en-Jalles 28 B2
St-Méen 22 C3
St Michaelisdonn 48 A2
St Michael (Salzburg) 59 F2
St Michael's Mount 8 A4
St Michael (Steiermark) 57 E4
St-Michel-de-Maurienne 31 D1
St-Michel-en-Grève 22 B2
St-Michel-en-l'Herm 24 B4
St-Michel 20 B2
St-Michel-Mont-Mercure 24 C3
St-Mihiel 20 C3
St Monance 5 D2
St-Moritz 58 B3
St-Nazaire 24 A2
St-Nectaire 29 E1
St Neots 9 F1
St-Nicolas-d'Aliermont 19 E2
St-Nicolas-de-la-Grave 28 C3
St-Nicolas-de-Port 21 D4
St-Nicolas-du-Pélem 22 C3
St-Niklaas 50 B3
St Niklaus 27 F4
St-Oedenrode 16 C3
St-Omer 19 F1
St Oswald 59 F2
St-Pair 18 B4
St-Palais (Charente-Maritime) 28 A1
St-Palais (Pyrénées-Atlantiques) 28 A4
St-Pardoux-la-Rivière 28 C1
St Paul (A) 70 B1
St-Paul (Alpes-de-Haute-Provence) 31 D2
St-Paul (Alpes-Maritimes) 31 E3
St-Paul-Cap-de-Joux 29 D4
St-Paul-de-Fenouillet 32 B2
St-Paulien 29 F2
St-Paul-Trois-Châteaux 30 B3
St-Père-en-Retz 24 A2
St-Pé-de-Bigorre 37 E1
St-Pée 28 A4
St-Péray 30 B2
St Peter in der Au 57 D3
St-Peter-Ording 47 F2
St Peter Port 18 A3
St-Philbert 24 B3
St-Pierre (Charente-Maritime) 24 B4
St-Pierre-d'Albigny 31 D1
St-Pierre-de-Chartreuse 30 C1
St-Pierre-de-Chignac 28 C2
St-Pierre-Eglise 18 B2
St-Pierre-le-Moûtier 26 A3
St-Pierre (Morbihan) 22 C4
St-Pierre-sur-Dives 18 C3
St-Pois 18 C4
St-Pol-de-Léon 22 B2
St-Pol-sur-Ternoise 19 F2
St-Pons-de-Thomières 32 B1
St-Porchaire 28 B1
St Pölten 57 E2
St-Pourçain 26 A4
St-Privat 29 E2
St-Quay-Portrieux 22 C2
St-Quentin 20 A2
St-Rambert 30 B1
St-Rambert-d'Albon 30 B1
St-Rambert-en-Bugey 26 C4
St-Raphaël 31 E4
St-Renan 22 A2
St-Rémy-de-Provence 30 B3
St-Rémy-sur-Durolle 26 B4
St-Riquier 19 E2
St-Romain-de-Colbosc 19 D3
St-Rome-de-Tarn 29 E3
St-Saëns 19 E3
St-Satur 26 A2
St-Saulge 26 A2
St-Sauveur-en-Puisaye 26 A2
St-Sauveur-Lendelin 18 B3
St-Sauveur-le-Vicomte 18 B3
St-Sauveur-sur-Tinée 31 E3
St-Savin (Gironde) 28 B2
St-Savinien 24 C4
St-Savin (Vienne) 25 D3
St-Seine-l'Abbaye 26 C2
St-Sernin-sur-Rance 29 E3
St-Sever (Calvados) 18 C4
St-Sever (Landes) 28 B4
St-Sulpice-les-Feuilles 25 E4
St-Symphorien-de-Lay 26 B4
St-Symphorien-d'Ozon 30 B1
St-Symphorien 28 B3
St-Symphorien-sur-Coise 30 B1
St-Trivier-de-Courtes 26 C3
St-Trivier-sur-Moignans 26 C4
St-Trojan 28 A1
St-Tropez 31 D4
St-Truiden 50 C3
St Ulrich 59 D3
St-Vaast-la-Hougue 18 B3
St Valentin an der Haide 58 C2
St Valentin 57 D3
St-Valery 19 E2
St-Valery-en-Caux 19 D2
St-Valier 30 B1
St-Vallier-de-Thiey 31 D3
St-Varent 24 C3
St-Vaury 25 E4
St Veit 70 A1
St-Véran 31 E2
St-Vincent 27 F4
St-Vincent-de-Tyrosse 28 A4
St Vith 51 D4
St-Vivien-de-Médoc 28 A1
St-Wandrille 19 D3
St Wendel 54 B1
St Wolfgang 56 C3
St-Yorre 26 A4
St-Yrieix-la-Perche 29 D1
Ste-Adresse 19 D3
Ste-Anne-d'Auray 22 C4
Ste-Baume, la 31 D4
Ste-Croix-du-Mont 28 B2
Ste-Croix 27 D3
Ste-Croix, Lac de 31 D3
Ste-Croix-Volvestre 37 F1
Ste-Enimie 29 F3
Ste-Foy-la-Grande 28 C2
Ste-Foy-l'Argentière 30 B1
Ste-Geneviève-sur-Argence 29 E2
Ste-Hélène 28 B2
Ste-Hermine 24 B3
Ste-Livrade 28 C3
Ste-Lucie-de-Tallano 33 F4
Ste-Marie-aux-Mines 21 E4
Ste-Maure-de-Touraine 25 D2
Ste-Maxime 31 D4
Ste-Menehould 20 C3
Ste-Mère-Eglise 18 B3
Ste-Odile, Mt 21 E4
Ste-Sévère 25 F3
Ste-Suzanne 23 E3
Ste-Tulle 30 C3
Saintes 28 B1
Stes-Maries-de-la-Mer 30 B4
Saissac 32 B1
Šajkaš 72 C2
Sakarya 115 F3
Sakskøbing 108 B4
Sakule 72 C2
Säkylä 107 D2
Sala 106 A3
Salacgrīva 110 C2
Sala Consilina 64 C4
Salada 41 E3
Salakovac 73 D3
Salamajärvi 102 C2
Salamajärvi *L* 103 D2
Salamanca 39 E1
Salamina 87 F1
Salamina, N 87 E1
Salándi 87 E2
Salangen 94 B3
Salar 43 F3
Salardú 37 F2
Salas 35 D1
Salaš 73 F3
Salas de los Infantes 36 A3
Salazar, R 37 D2
Salbohed 105 F3
Salbris 25 E2
Salcombe 8 C4
Saldaña 35 E3
Sale 60 A2
Sålekinna 100 D3
Salem 55 D4
Salemi 68 A3
Sälen 101 D4
Salen (Highland) 2 B4
Salen (Mull) 4 B1
Salernes 31 D4
Salerno 64 B4
Salerno, Golfo di 64 B4
Salers 29 E2
Salève, Mt 27 D4
Salgótarján 112 B3
Salgueiro do Campo 38 C2
Sali 74 C1
Salice Terme 60 A2
Salies-de-Béarn 28 A4
Salies-du-Salat 37 F1
Salignac-Eyvigues 29 D2
Salihli 115 F4
Salime, Emb de 34 C1
Salina, I 69 D2
Salinas (Andalucía) 43 F3
Salinas (Asturias) 35 D1
Salinas, C 45 F3
Salindres 30 B3
Sälinkää 107 F2
Salins 27 D3
Salisbury 9 E3
Salla 99 E2
Sallanches 27 E4
Sallent 32 A4
Sallent-de-Gállego 37 D2
Salles 32 A1
Salles-Curan 29 E3
Salling 108 A2
Salling Sund 108 A2
Salmerón 40 C2
Salmoral 39 F1
Salò 60 B1
Salo 107 E2
Salobreña 44 A4
Salona 75 D1
Salon-de-Provence 30 C4
Salonta 112 C4
Salorino 38 C3
Salor, R 39 D3
Salou 37 F4
Salou, C de 37 F4
Salpausselkä 107 F2
Salsbruket 97 D4
Salses-le-Château 32 B2
Salso 68 C3
Salsomaggiore Terme 60 B2
Salsta 106 B3
Saltash 8 C4
Saltburn-by-the-Sea 5 F4
Saltcoats 4 C2
Saltee Is 15 D4
Saltfjellet 97 E2
Saltfjorden 97 E2
Salto 34 B4
Saltoluokta 94 B4
Saltvik 106 C3
Saluggia 31 F1
Saluzzo 31 E2
Salvacañete 41 D3
Salvagnac 29 D3
Salvan 27 E4
Salvaterra de Magos 38 A3
Salvatierra-Agurain 36 B2
Salvatierra de los Barros 42 C1
Salvattera de Miño 34 A3
Salvetat-Peyralès, la 29 E3

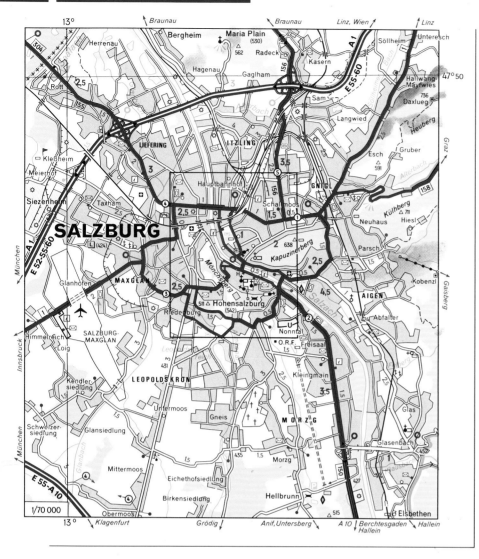

Map: SALZBURG region, scale 1/70 000

Sant Antoni de C. **32** B3
Sant Antoni, Emb de **37** F3
Sant' Apollinare in Classe **61** D3
Sant' Arcangelo di Romagna **61** E3
Sant Boi de Lluçanès **32** A3
Sant Celoni **32** B4
Sant Cugat **32** A4
Sant' Elia a Pianisi **64** B2
Sant' Elpidio a Mare **61** F4
Sant Esteve d'en Bas **32** B3
Sant'Eufemia, Golfodi **67** E3
Sant'Eufemia Lamezia **67** E3
Sant Gervàs **37** F3
Sant Hilari Sacalm **32** B3
Sant Hipòlit de Voltregà **32** A3
Sant Joan de les Abadesses **32** B3
Sant Julià de Lòria **32** A3
Sant Llorenc de Morunys **32** A3
Sant'Onofrio **67** E3
Sant Pau de Seguries **32** B3
Sant Pere de Roda **32** C3
Sant Pol de Mar **32** B4
Sant Ponç, Emb de **32** A3
Sant Quirze de Besora **32** B3
Sant Quirze Safaja **32** A4
Sant Ramon **37** F3
Sant Sadurni d'Anoia **32** A4
Santa Amalia **39** D4
Santa Ana **40** C4
Santa Anna, Emb de **37** E3
Santa Bàrbara (Catalunya) **41** F2
Santa Bárbara (Andalucía) **42** C2
Santa Bárbara *Mt* **44** B3
Santa Catarina **42** B3
Santa Caterina Pittinuri **66** A3
Santa Caterina Valfurva **58** C3
Santa Caterina Villarmosa **68** C3
Santa Cesarea Terme **65** F4
Santa Clara-a-Velha **42** A2
Santa Clara, Bgem de **42** A2
Santa Coloma de Farners **32** B3
Santa Coloma de Queralt **37** F4
Santa Colombo de Somoza **35** D3
Santa Comba Dão **38** B2
Santa Comba de Rossas **34** C4
Santa Comba **34** A1
Santa Cristina de Lena **35** D2
Santa Croce di Magliano **64** B2
Santa Cruz de Campezo **36** B2
Santa Cruz de la Palma **42** A4
Santa Cruz de la Sierra **39** E3
Santa Cruz de la Zarza **40** B3
Santa Cruz del Retamar **40** A2
Santa Cruz de Moya **41** D3
Santa Cruz de Mudela **44** A1
Santa Cruz de Tenerife **42** B4
Santa Cruz **36** C4
Santa Elena **44** A1
Santa Eufemia **43** E1
Santa Eugenia **34** A2
Santa Eulalia del Río **45** D3
Santa Eulalia de Oscos **34** C1
Santa Eulalia **41** D2
Santa Eulália **38** C4
Santa Fe **44** A3
Santa Fé **32** B4
Santa Fiora **63** D1
Santa Galdana, Cala **45** F2
Santa Gertrude **58** C3
Santa Giusta **66** B3
Santa Inés, Pto de **36** B3
Santa Liestra y San Quilez **37** E3
Santa Lucia d. Mela **69** D2
Santa Luz **34** C4
Santa Luzia **42** A2
Santa Magdalena de Pulpis **41** F2
Santa Margarida do Sádão **42** B1
Santa Margarida i Els Monjos **32** A4
Santa Margarita **45** F2
Santa Margherita **66** B4
Santa Margherita di Belice **68** B3
Santa Margherita Ligure **60** A3
Santa Maria Capua Vetere **64** B3
Santa Maria, C de **42** B3
Santa Maria da Feira **38** B1
Santa Maria d'Angeli **63** E1
Santa Maria del Campo Rus **40** C3
Santa Maria della Versa **60** A2
Santa Maria di Leuca,C **65** F4
Santa Maria la Real de Nieva **40** A1
Santa Maria la Real de Oseira **34** B2
Santa Maria Maggiore **58** A3
Santa Marina **35** E2
Santa Marina del Rey **35** D3
Santa Marinella **63** D2
Santa María de Huerta **36** B4
Santa María del Campo **35** F3
Santa María del Páramo **35** D3
Santa María de Nieva **44** C3
Santa María de Valverde **35** D3
Santa-Maria-Siché **33** F4
Santa Marta **39** D4
Santa Marta de Penaguião **34** B4
Santa Marta de Tormes **39** E1
Santa Olalla del Cala **43** D2
Santa Olalla **39** F3
Santa Pau **32** B3
Santa Pola **45** E2
Santa sa **45** E3
Santa Sofia **61** D3
Santa Sofia d'Epiro **67** E2
Santa Susanna **32** B4
Santa Tecla **34** A3
Santa Teresa di Riva **69** D2
Santa Teresa, Emb de **39** E2
Santa Teresa Gallura **66** B1
Santaella **43** E2
Santana (Estremadura) **38** A4
Santana (Madeira) **42** A3
Santana de Serra **42** A2
Santander **35** F1
Santanyí **45** F3
Santarém **38** B3
Santas Martas **35** E3
Santeramo in Colle **65** D3
Santes Creus **37** F4
Santesteban **36** C1
Santhià **31** F1
Santiago de Alcántara **38** C3
Santiago de Compostela **34** A2
Santiago de la Espada **44** B2
Santiago de la Ribera **45** D2
Santiago do Cacém **42** A1
Santiago do Escoural **38** B4
Santibáñez de Béjar **39** E2
Santibáñez de la Peña **35** E2
Santibáñez de la Sierra **39** E2
Santibáñez de Vidriales **35** D3
Santillana del Mar **35** F1
Santiponce **43** D2
Säntis **58** B2
Santisteban del Puerto **44** B1
Santo Domingo de la Calzada **36** B2
Santo Domingo de Silos **36** A3
Santo Domingo, Ptode **43** D1
Santo Estêvão (Beira Baixa) **38** C2
Santo Estêvão (Estremadura) **38** A4
Santo Estêvão, Rib de **38** A4
Santo Pedro da Torre **34** A3
Santo Severa **63** D2
Santo Stefano di Cadore **59** E2
Santo Stefano d'Aveto **60** B2
Santo Stino di Livenza **59** E4
Santo Tirso **34** A4
Santo Tomé **44** B2
Santok **49** F3
Santolea, Emb de **41** E2
Santomera, Emb de **45** D2
Santoña **36** A1
Santo-Pietro-di-Tenda **33** F2
Santorini, N **91** E1
Santuario de San Ignacio de Loyola **36** B1
Santuario d'Oropa **27** F4
Santu Lussurgiu **66** B3
Santurtzi **36** B1
Sanxenxo **34** A2
Sanza **67** D1
São Bartolomeu de Messines **42** A2
São Brás de Alportel **42** B3
São Cristóvão **38** B4
São Domingos **42** A1
São Gregório **34** B3
São Jacinto **38** B1
São João da Pesqueira **34** B4
São João de Madeira **38** B1
São João de Tarouca **38** C1
São João dos Caldeireiros **42** B2
São José da Lamarosa **38** B3
São Leonardo **42** C1
São Mamede, Sa de **38** C3
São Manços **42** B1
São Marcos da Serra **42** A2
São Marcos do Campo **42** B1
São Martinho das Amoreiras **42** A2
São Martinho do Porto **38** A3
São Matias **42** B1
São Miguel de Machede **38** B4
São Pedro de Açor **38** C2
São Pedro de Moel **38** A2
São Pedro do Sul **38** C1
São Romão **38** C2
São Teotónio **42** A2
São Vicente, C de **42** A2
São Vicente da Beira **38** C2
Saône **26** C3
Saône-et-Loire **26** B3
Saorge **31** E3
Sapanca **115** F3
Sapataria **38** A3
Sápes **81** E2
Sapiéndza, N **86** C4
Sa Pobla **45** F2
Sappada **59** E2
Sappee **107** E2
Sapri **67** D1
Säräisniemi **99** E4
Sarajärvi **99** E3
Sarajevo **76** A1
Sarakiní **79** E2
Sarakiniko **84** B3
Saramon **28** C4
Sarandáporo **79** E4
Sarandáporos **78** C4
Sarandë **114** C4
Saraváli **86** C1
Saray **115** E3
Sarayköy **115** F4
Šarbanovac **73** E3
Sarbinowo (Gorzów Wlkp) **49** F3
Sarbinowo (Koszalin) **49** F1
Sárbogárd **112** B4
Sarca **58** C3
Sardara **66** B3
Sardegna **66** A2
Sardínia **82** C3
Sardoal **38** B3
Sardona, Piz **58** B2
Sarek **98** A1
Šarengrad **72** B2
Sarentino **59** D2
Särfjället **101** D2
Sargans **58** B2
Sariá, N **93** D2
Sari-d'Orcino **33** F3
Sarine **27** E3
Sariñena **37** E3
Sark **18** A3
Särkisalmi **103** F3
Särkisalo **107** D3
Sarlat-la-Canéda **29** D2
Sarmitunturi **95** F3
Särna **101** D3
Sarnano **61** F4
Sarnen **27** F2
Sarnico **60** B1
Sarno **64** B4
Sarnthein **59** D2
Sarny **113** D2
Sarö **108** C1
Sarón **35** F2
Sarone **59** E3
Saronída **87** F2
Saronikós Kólpos **87** F1
Saronno **60** A1
Sárospatak **112** C3
Sar Planina **77** D3
Sarpsborg **105** D3
Sarracín **35** F3
Sarral **37** F4
Sarralbe **21** E3
Sarrans, Bge de **29** E2
Sarre **21** E3
Sarrebourg **21** E4
Sarreguemines **21** E3
Sarre-Union **21** E3
Sarriá **34** B2
Sarrión **41** E3
Sarroch **66** B4
Sarsina **61** D3
Sars-Poteries **20** B2
Sarstedt **52** B1
Sarteano **63** D1
Sartène **33** F4
Sarthe **23** E4
Sarthe (Dépt) **23** F3
Sárti **80** B4
Sartilly **18** B4
Sarule **66** B2
Sárvár **112** A4
Sarvsjö **101** D2
Sarzana **60** B3
Sarzeau **22** C4
Sarzedas **38** C2
Sasa **77** F2
Saßnitz **49** D1
Sassari **66** A2
Sassello **60** A3
Sassenage **30** C1
Sassenberg **17** F3
Sassenheim **16** B2
Sassetta **62** C1
Sasso **63** E2
Sassoferrato **61** E4
Sassoleone **61** D3
Sasso Marconi **60** C3
Sassuolo **60** C2
Sástago **37** D4
Sasyk, Ozero **113** E4
Sátão **38** C1
Säter **105** F3
Satillieu **30** B1
Satolas **30** C1
Šator **75** D1
Sátoraljaújhely **112** C3
Šatorina **70** B4
Satov **57** E1
Satow **48** C2
Sátres **81** D2
Satrup **48** A1
Sattel **58** A2
Sattledt **57** D3
Satu Mare **112** C3
Saualpe **70** B1
Sauca **36** B4
Saucelle, Emb de **39** D1
Sauda **104** A3
Sauðárkrókur **96** B1
Sau, Emb de **32** B3
Sauerlach **56** A3
Sauerland **17** F4
Saugues **29** F2
Saujon **28** B1
Saukkovaara **99** E4
Sauland **104** C3
Sauldre **26** A2
Saulgau **55** D3
Saulieu **26** B2
Sault **30** C3
Saulx **27** D1
Saulxures **27** E1
Saumur **24** C2
Saundersfoot **8** B2
Sauris **59** E3
Saut du Doubs **27** E2
Sautet, Bge du **30** C2
Sautusjärvi **94** C4
Sauve **30** B3
Sauveterre-de-Béarn **28** A4
Sauveterre-de-Guyenne **28** B2
Sauveterre-de-Rouergue **29** E3
Sauvo **107** D2
Sauxillanges **29** F1
Sauze d'Oulx **31** E2
Sauze, le **31** D2
Sauze-Vaussais **24** C4
Sauzon **22** B4
Sava (I) **65** E4
Sava (YU) **71** E3
Savália **86** B1
Sävar **102** B1
Savelli **67** F2
Savenay **23** D4
Saverdun **32** A1
Saverne **21** E4
Savigliano **31** E2
Savignac-les-Eglises **28** C1
Savignano Irpino **64** C3
Savignano sul Rubicone **61** E3
Savigny-sur-Braye **23** F4
Saviñán **36** C4
Savine, Col de la **27** D3
Savines-le-Lac **31** D2
Savinja **70** B1
Savino Selo **72** B2
Savitaipale **103** E4
Sävja **106** B3
Šavnik **76** B2
Savognin **58** B3
Savona **60** A3
Savonlinna **103** E3
Savonranta **103** F3
Sævråsvåg **104** A2
Sävsjö **109** D2
Savudrija **70** A3
Savukoski **95** F4
Sawbridgeworth **10** C2
Sawel Mt **13** D1
Sax **45** D1
Saxmundham **11** E1
Saxnäs **97** E4
Sayatón **40** B2
Säynätsalo **103** D3
Säyneinen **103** E2
Sazadón, Pto de **35** D3
Sázava **112** A3
Scaër **22** B3
Scafa **64** A2
Scafati **64** B4
Scafell Pikes **5** D4
Scala di Santa Regina **33** F3
Scalasaig **4** B2
Scalby **7** D1
Scalea **67** E2
Scalloway **3** F2
Scalpay **2** B3
Scandiano **60** C2
Scanno **64** A2
Scansano **63** D1
Scanzano **65** D4
Scapa Flow **3** D1
Scarba **4** B1
Scarborough **7** D1
Scardovari **61** E2
Scarinish **2** A4
Scarpe **20** A1
Scarriff **12** B4
Šćedro **75** E2
Šćepan Polje **76** A1
Scey-sur-Saône **27** D2
Schaalsee **48** B2
Schachendorf **57** F4
Schafberg **56** C3
Schaffhausen **58** A1
Schafstädt **52** C2
Schagen **16** C2
Schaprode **49** D1
Scharbeutz **48** B2
Schärding **56** C2
Scharhörn **47** F2
Scharmützelsee **49** E4
Scharnitz **59** D1
Schauinsland Feldberg **54** C4
Scheeßel **48** A3
Scheggia **61** E4
Scheibbs **57** E3
Scheifling **57** D4
Scheinfeld **55** E1
Schelde **50** B3
Schenefeld (Hamburg) **48** A3
Schenefeld (Itzehoe) **48** A2
Scherfede **52** A2
Schermbeck **17** E3
Scheßlitz **52** C4
Scheveningen **16** B3
Schia **60** B3
Schiedam **16** B3
Schieder-Schwalenberg **52** A1
Schiehallion **4** C1
Schierling **56** B2
Schiermonnikoog **47** D3
Schiermonnikoog *I* **47** D3
Schiers **58** B2
Schifferstadt **54** C2
Schildau **53** D2
Schilpario **58** C4
Schiltach **54** C3
Schio **59** D4
Schirmeck **21** E4
Schirnding **53** D4
Schkeuditz **53** D2
Schkölen **53** D3
Schladming **59** F1
Schlagsdorf **48** B2
Schlanders **58** C3
Schlangenbad **51** F4
Schleching **56** B3
Schlei **48** A1
Schleiden **51** D4
Schleiz **53** D3
Schleswig **48** A1
Schleswig-Holstein **48** A1
Schleusingen **52** C3
Schlieben **53** E1
Schliersee **56** B4
Schlitz **52** B3
Schlotheim **52** B2
Schluchsee **54** C4
Schlucht, Col de la **27** E1
Schlüchtern **52** B4
Schluderbach **59** E2
Schluderns **58** C3
Schlüsselfeld **55** E1
Schlutup **48** B2
Schmalkalden **52** B3
Schmallenberg **17** F4
Schmidmühlen **55** F1
Schmilka **53** F2
Schmölln (Leipzig) **53** D3
Schmölln (Neu-brandenburg) **49** E3
Schnackenburg **48** C3
Schnaittenbach **55** F1
Schneeberg (A) **57** E3
Schneeberg (D) **53** D4
Schneeberg (DDR) **53** D3
Schneverdingen **48** A3
Schoberpaß **57** D4
Schöckl **57** E4
Schönau **54** C4
Schönberg (A) **59** D2
Schönberg (Bayern) **56** C2
Schönberg (Karl-Marx-Stadt) **53** D4
Schönberg (Rostock) **48** B2
Schönberg (Schleswig-Holstein) **48** B1
Schönbrunn **57** F2
Schönebeck **52** C1
Schöneck **53** D3
Schönecken **51** D4
Schönefeld **49** E4
Schönewalde **53** E1
Schongau **55** F4
Schöningen **52** C1
Schönmünzach **54** C3
Schönsee **56** B1
Schönthal **56** B1
Schönwald **54** C3
Schönwalde **48** B2
Schoonhoven **16** C3
Schopfheim **54** C4
Schöppenstedt **52** B1
Schoppernau **58** B2
Schorndorf **55** D2
Schortens **47** E3
Schotten **52** A4
Schouwen Duiveland **16** B3
Schramberg **54** C3
Schrems **57** D2
Schrobenhausen **55** F2
Schröcken **58** B2
Schrozberg **55** E1
Schruns **58** B2
Schuls **58** C2
Schüttorf **17** E2
Schwaan **48** C2

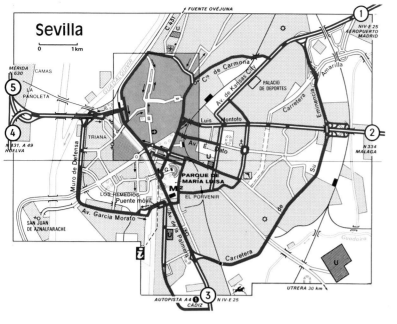

Sevilla

Silloth 5 D4
Šilo 70 B3
Silo 81 E2
Sil, R 34 C2
Sils 32 B4
Sils im Engadin 58 B3
Siltakylä 107 F2
Šilutė 110 B3
Silvalen 97 D3
Silvaplana 58 B3
Silvares 38 C2
Silves 42 A2
Silvi Marina 64 A1
Silvrettagruppe 58 B2
Silz 58 C2
Simancas 35 E4
Símandra 80 A3
Šimanovci 72 C3
Simav 115 F4
Simaxis 66 B3
Simbach (Inn) 56 B3
Simbach (Isar) 56 B2
Simbruini, Mti 63 F2
Simeto 69 D3
Sími 93 E1
Šimići 71 E3
Sími, N 93 E1
Simlångsdalen 108 C2
Simmerath 51 D4
Simmern 54 B1
Simo 99 D3
Simojärvi 99 E2
Simojoki 99 D3
Simola 103 F4
Símonos Pétras 80 C4
Simonsbath 8 C3
Simonswald 54 C3
Simópoulo 86 B1
Simplonpass 27 F3
Simrishamn 109 D3
Sinaia 113 D4
Sinalunga 61 D4
Sinarádes 82 A1
Sinarcas 41 D3
Sindelfingen 55 D2
Sındırgı 115 F4
Síndos 79 F3
Sines 42 A1
Sines, C de 42 A1
Sinettä 99 D2
Sineu 45 F3
Singen 55 D4
Singöfjärden 106 B3
Singra, Pto de 41 D2
Siniscola 66 C2
Sinj 75 D1
Sinjajevina 76 B2
Sinni 65 D4
Sinnicolau Mare 114 C1
Sinopoli 67 E4
Sinsheim 55 D2
Sintra 38 A4
Sinzig 51 E4
Siófok 112 B4
Sion 27 E3
Sioule 26 A4
Šipan 75 F2
Šipanska Luka 75 F2
Šipka 115 D2
Sipoo 107 F2
Sipoonselkä 107 F2
Šipovo 71 E4
Sippola 107 F2
Šiprage 71 E4
Sira 104 A4
Sira R 104 B4
Siracusa 69 D4
Sirdalen 104 B4
Sirdalvatn 104 A4
Siret 113 D3
Siret R 113 E4
Sirevåg 104 A4
Sirig 72 C2
Sirino, Mte 65 D4
Širitovci 75 D1
Sirkka 95 E4
Sirma 95 E2
Sirmione 60 C1
Sírna, N 92 C1
Široko Polje 71 F2
Sirolo 61 F4
Síros, N 88 B2
Siruela 39 F4
Sisak 71 D2
Šišan 70 A4
Sisante 40 C4
Šišljavić 70 C3
Sissa 60 B2
Sissach 27 F2
Sissonne 20 B3
Sisteron 31 D3
Sistiana 59 F3
Sistranda 100 C1
Sitges 32 A4
Sithonía 80 B4
Sitía 91 F4
Sitnica 77 D2
Sittard 17 D4
Sittensen 48 A3
Sittingbourne 11 D3
Siuntio 107 E3
Siuro 107 E1
Siurua 99 D3
Siuruanjoki 99 D3
Siusi 59 D3
Sivac 72 B2
Sıvaslı 115 F4
Síviri 80 A4
Sívota 82 B2
Sívros 82 B3
Siziano 60 A1
Sizun 22 B3
Sjælland 108 C3
Sjællands Odde 108 B3
Sjenica 76 C1
Sjeništa 76 A1
Sjøåsen 97 D4
Sjöbo 109 D3
Sjøholt 100 B2
Sjona 97 E2
Sjötorp 105 E4
Sjoutnäset 97 E4
Sjøvegan 94 B3
Sjulsmark 102 B1
Sjundea 107 E3
Sjusjøen 104 D2
Skåbu 100 C3
Skäckerfjällen 101 D1
Skadarsko jez 76 B3
Skadovsk 113 F4
Skafidiá 86 B2
Skaftá 96 B2
Skagafjörður 96 B1
Skage 97 D4
Skagen 108 B1
Skagern 105 E4
Skagerrak 108 A1
Skaill 3 E1
Skajálfandi 96 B1
Skála (Kefaloniá) 86 A1
Skála (Lésvos) 85 F2
Skála (Pátmos) 89 E2
Skála (Pelopónissos) 87 D3
Skála (Stereá Eláda) 83 F3
Skála Eressoú 85 E2
Skála Kaliráhis 80 C3
Skaland 94 B2
Skála Oropoú 84 B4
Skála Potamiás 81 D3
Skála Rahoníou 80 C3
Skalavík 96 A4
Skála Volissoú 85 E4
Skälderviken 108 C3
Skålevik 104 B4
Skálfandafljót 96 B2
Skalka 98 A2
Skalohóri (Lésvos) 85 E2
Skalohóri (Makedonía) 79 D3
Skaloti 80 C1
Skælskør 108 B4
Skamnéli 78 C4
Skandáli 85 D1
Skandári, Akr 89 F3
Skanderborg 108 B3
Skandzoúra, N 84 B3
Skåne 109 D3
Skånevik 104 A3
Skåningsbukt 94 C2
Skånland 94 B3
Skänninge 106 A4
Skanör Falsterbo 108 C4
Skara 109 D1
Skaraborgs Län 109 D1
Skaramangás 87 F1
Skærbæk 108 A4
Skarberget 94 B4
Škarda 74 B1
Skåre 105 E3
Skárfia 83 F3
Skärgårdshavet 107 D3
Skärhamn 108 C1
Skarnes 105 D3
Skarplinge 106 B2
Skarsvåg 95 E1
Skärvången 101 E1
Skarżysko-Kamienna 112 B2
Skattungbyn 101 E4
Skatval 100 C2
Skaulo 94 C4
Skaun 100 C2
Skee 105 D4
Skegness 7 E3
Skei (Møre og Romsdal) 100 B2
Skei (Sogn og Fjordane) 100 A3
Skeiðarársandur 96 B2
Skela 72 C3
Skellefteå 98 B4
Skellefteälven 98 B4
Skelleftehamn 98 B4
Skellig 14 A4
Skelmersdale 6 B2
Skenderbeut, M i 76 C4
Skender Vakuf 71 E4
Skepastó 80 B2
Skerries 13 E3
Ski 105 D3
Skiathos 84 A2
Skiáthos, N 84 A2
Skibbereen 14 B4
Skibby 108 C3
Skibotn 94 C2
Skiddaw 5 D4
Skídra 79 E3
Skien 104 C3
Skierniewice 112 B2
Skillingaryd 109 D2
Skiloundía 86 C2
Skinári, Akr 86 A1
Skiniás 91 E4
Skinnarbu 104 B3
Skinnskatteberg 105 F3
Skipagurra 95 F1
Skipton 6 C2
Skíros 84 C3
Skíros, N 84 C3
Skiti 83 F1
Skive 108 A2
Skivjane 76 C2
Skjeberg 105 D3
Skjern 108 A3
Skjersholmane 104 A3
Skjerstad 97 E2
Skjerstadfjorden 97 E2
Skjervøy 94 C2
Skjønhaug 105 D3
Sklavopoúla 90 B3
Sklithro 83 F1
Šklov 111 E3
Skočivir 77 E4
Škocjanske jame 70 A3
Skodje 100 B2
Škofja Loka 70 A2
Škofljica 70 B2
Skog (Gävleborgs Län) 101 F4
Skog (Västernorrlands Län) 102 A2
Skógafoss 96 B3
Skogerøya 95 F2
Skoghall 105 E3
Skogstorp 105 F4
Skokloster 106 B3
Skólis 86 B1
Skópelos (Lésvos) 85 F3
Skópelos (Skópelos) 84 B2
Skópelos, N 84 B3
Skopí 91 F4
Skopiá 83 E2
Skopje 77 E3
Skopós 79 D2
Skopun 96 A4
Skorenovac 73 D3
Skorovatn 97 E4
Skorped 101 F2
Skotina 79 F4
Skotterud 105 D3
Skoulikariá 82 C2
Skoúra 87 D3
Skoúrta 87 F1
Skoútari (Makedonía) 80 B2
Skoútari (Pelopónissos) 87 D4
Skoutáros 85 E2
Skövde 109 D1
Skrá 79 E2
Skrad 70 B3
Skradin 75 D1
Skradinski buk 75 D1
Skreia 105 D2
Skrim 104 C3
Skrolsvik 94 B3
Skrydstrup 108 A4
Skudeneshavn 104 A3
Skuleskogen 102 A2
Skull 14 A4
Skultuna 106 A3
Skuodas 110 B3
Skuov'gilraš'ša 95 D2
Skurup 109 D3
Skutskär 106 B2
Skutvik 94 A4
Skvira 113 E2
Skye 2 B3
Slagelse 108 B3
Slagnäs 98 A3
Slănčev Brjag 115 E2
Slancy 111 D1
Slane 13 D3
Slaney 15 D3
Slangerup 108 C3
Slano 75 F2
Slany 53 F3
Šlapanice 57 F1
Slapská přehr nádrž 53 F4
Slapy 53 F4
Śląsk 112 A2
Slatina (Bor) 73 E3
Slatina (Bosna i Hercegovina) 71 E3
Slatina (Kraljevo) 73 D4
Slatina (Makedonija) 77 D3
Slatina (RO) 115 D1
Slatine 75 D2
Slatinski Drenovac 71 E2
Slavgorod 111 E4
Slavinja 77 F1
Slavkovica 72 C4
Slavkov u Brna 57 F1
Slavnik 70 A3
Slavonice 57 E1
Slavonska Požega 71 E2
Slavonski Brod 71 E3
Slavonski Kobaš 71 E3
Slavuta 113 D2
Sławno 110 A4
Sławoborze 49 F2
Sleaford 7 D3
Slea Head 14 A3
Sleat, Sd of 2 B4
Slettfjellet 94 C2
Sliedrecht 16 C3
Sliema 68 B4
Slieve Bloom Mts 12 C4
Slieve Donard 13 E3
Slieve Mish Mts 14 A3
Slievenamon 14 C3
Slieve Snaght 13 D1
Sligachan 2 B3
Sligeach 12 C2
Sligo 12 C2
Sligo (Co) 12 B3
Sligo B 12 C2
Slišane 77 D1
Slite 109 F4
Sliven 115 E2
Sljeme 70 C2
Šljivovica 72 C4
Slobozia 115 E1
Slonim 112 C1
Sloten 16 C1
Slough 9 F2
Slovac 72 C3
Slovenska Bistrica 70 C1
Slovenija 70 A2
Slovenj Gradec 70 B1
Slovenske Konjice 70 C1
Slovenské Rudohorie 112 B3
Slovinci 71 D3
Słubice 49 F4
Sluck 111 D4
Sluderno 58 C3
Sluis 16 A4
Sluknov 53 F2
Slunj 70 C3
Słupsk 110 A4
Slyne Head 12 A3
Småland 109 D2
Smålandsfarvandet 108 B4
Smålands-stenar 109 D2
Šmarje 70 C2
Šmarješke Toplice 70 B2
Šmartin 70 B2
Smedby 109 E2
Smědeč 56 C2
Smederevo 73 D3
Smedjebacken 105 F3
Smederevska Palanka 73 D3
Smela 113 F2
Smigáda 81 E2
Smilčić 74 C1
Smilde 17 D1
Smiltene 110 C2
Smojmirovo 77 F3
Smokovljan 75 F2
Smøla 100 B1
Smolensk 111 E3
Smoleviči 111 D4
Smólikas, Óros 78 C4
Smoljan 115 D3
Smorgon 111 D4
Smørhamn 104 A1
Smygehamn 109 D4
Snaefell 6 A1
Snæfellsnes 96 A2
Snaith 7 D2
Snåsa 101 D1
Snasahögarna 101 D2
Snåsavatnet 101 D1
Sneek 16 C1
Sneem 14 A4
Snežnik 70 B3
Śniardwy, Jez 110 B4
Snigir'ovka 113 F3
Snillfjord 100 C2
Snizort, L 2 B3
Šnjegotina Velika 71 E3
Snøfjord 95 D1
Snøhefta 100 C3
Snøtinden 97 E2
Snowdon 6 A3
Snowdonia Forest and Nat Pk 6 A3
Soave 60 C1
Soběslav 57 D1
Sobra 75 F2
Sobrado 34 B2
Sobral da Adiça 42 C1
Sobral de Monte Agraço 38 A3
Sobreira Formosa 38 C2
Sobrón, Emb de 36 B2
Søby 108 B4
Soča 70 A2
Soča R 70 A2
Sočanica 77 D1
Soccia 33 F3
Sochaczew 112 B1
Sochaux 27 D2
Socol 73 D2
Socovos 44 C1
Socuéllamos 40 B4
Sodankylä 95 E4
Söderåkra 109 E3
Söderbärke 105 F3
Söderfors 106 B3
Söderhamn 101 F4
Söderköping 106 A4
Södermanlands Län 106 A4
Söderskog 109 D3
Södertälje 106 B4
Sodražica 70 B2
Sodupe 36 B1
Soest (D) 17 F3
Soest (NL) 16 C2
Soestdijk 16 C2
Sofádes 83 E2
Sofia 115 D2
Sofiero 108 C3
Sofikó 87 E1
Sofó 83 E2
Sögel 17 E1
Sogliano al Rubicone 61 E3
Soglio 58 B3
Sogndal 100 B3
Søgne 104 B4
Sognefjell 100 B3
Sognefjorden 104 A1
Sognesjøen 104 A1
Sogn og Fjordane 100 A3
Soham 11 D1
Sohós 80 A2
Soignies 50 B4
Soini 102 C2
Soinlahti 103 D1
Soissons 20 A3
Söke 115 E4
Sokna 104 C2
Soko Banja 73 E4
Sokolac 72 B4
Sokolov 53 D4
Sokołow Podlaski 112 C1
Sokosti 95 F3
Sola (Rogaland) 104 A3
Sola (Sogn og Fjordane) 104 A1
Solana de los Barros 39 D4
Solana del Pino 43 F1
Solares 35 F2
Solberg 101 F1
Solbergfjorden 94 B3
Solčava 70 B1
Sol'cy 111 D2
Solda 58 C3
Sölden 58 C2
Soldeu 32 A2
Solent, The 9 E3
Solenzara 33 F4
Solesmes (Nord) 20 A2
Solesmes (Sarthe) 23 E3
Solevåg 100 A2
Solf 102 B2
Solferino 60 C1
Solholmen 100 B2
Solignac (Haute-Loire) 29 F2
Solignac (Haute-Vienne) 29 D1
Soligorsk 111 D4
Solihull 9 E1
Solin 75 D1
Soline 74 B1
Solingen 17 E4
Sölkerpaß 57 D4
Söll 59 D1
Sollana 41 E4
Sollefteå 101 F2
Sollenau 57 F3
Sollentuna 106 B3
Sóller 45 E2
Sollerön 101 E4
Søllested 108 B4
Solliès-Pont 31 D4
Solnečnogorsk 111 F2
Solofra 64 B4
Solosancho 39 F2
Solothurn 27 E2
Solre-le-Château 20 B2
Solrød 108 C3
Solsona 32 A3
Šolta 75 D2
Soltau 48 A3
Solunska Glava 77 E3
Solunto 68 B3
Solvay 60 C4
Sölvesborg 109 D3
Solvorn 100 B3
Solway Firth 4 C4
Solynieve 44 A3
Soma 115 E4
Sombernon 26 C2
Sombor 72 B2
Someren 17 D4
Somero 107 E2
Somerset 9 D3
Somes 112 C4
Somiedo, Pto de 35 D2
Sommarøy 94 B2
Sommatino 68 C4
Somme 19 E2
Somme (Dépt) 19 F2
Sommen 109 E1
Sömmerda 52 C2
Sommesous 20 B4
Sommières 30 B3
Sømna 97 D3
Somolinos 36 A4
Somosierra, Pto de 36 A4
Sompio 95 F3
Somport, Pto de 37 D2
Šomrda 73 E3
Soncillo 35 F2
Soncino 60 B1
Søndeled 104 C4
Sønderborg 108 B4
Sønderby 108 B4
Sønder Felding 108 A3
Sondershausen 52 C2
Søndersø 108 B3
Sondrio 58 B3
Songeons 19 E3
Sonkajärvi 103 E1
Sonnblick 59 E2
Sonneberg 52 C4
Sonnewalde 53 E1
Sonogno 58 A3
Sonsbeck 17 D3
Sonseca 40 A3
Son Servera 45 F3
Sonta 72 B2
Sonthofen 55 E4
Sontra 52 B3
Sopeira 37 F3
Sopilja 76 A1
Sopište 77 D3
Sopoćani 76 C1
Sopot (PL) 110 A4
Sopot (YU) 73 D3
Sopotnica 77 D4
Sopron 112 A4
Sora 64 A3
Soragna 60 B2
Söråker 101 F3
Sørarnøy 97 E2
Sorbas 44 C3
Sorbe, R 40 B1
Sore 28 B3
Soresina 60 B1
Sørfjorden 104 B2
Sør-Flatanger 96 C4
Sørfolda 94 A4
Sörfors 102 A1
Sorga 52 B3
Sorgono 66 B3
Sorgues 30 B3
Sørgutvik 97 D4
Soria 36 B3
Soriano nel Cimino 63 E2
Sørkjosen 94 C2
Sorø 108 B3
Soroki 113 E3
Soro, M 69 D3
Soroní 93 E1
Sørøya 95 D1
Sørøysundet 95 D1
Sorraia, R 38 A4
Sørreisa 94 B3
Sorrento 64 B4
Sor, Rib de 38 B3
Sørrollnes 94 B3
Sorsakoski 103 E2
Sorsele 98 A3
Sorso 66 A2
Sort 37 F2
Sortino 69 D4
Sortland 94 A3
Sortlandsundet 94 A3
Sør Trøndelag 100 C2
Sorunda 106 B4
Sørvågen 97 E1
Sørvágur 96 A4
Sørvær 94 C1
Sørværøy 97 E1
Sörvattnet 101 D3
Sos del Rey Católico 37 D2
Soses 37 E4
Sosnovyj Bor 111 D1
Sosnowiec 112 B2
Sospel 31 E3

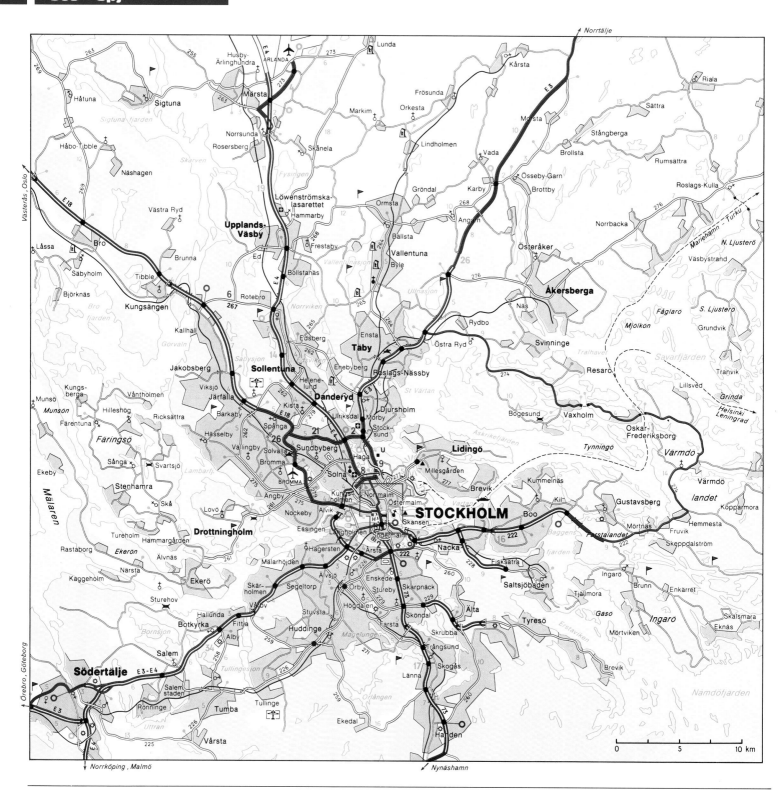

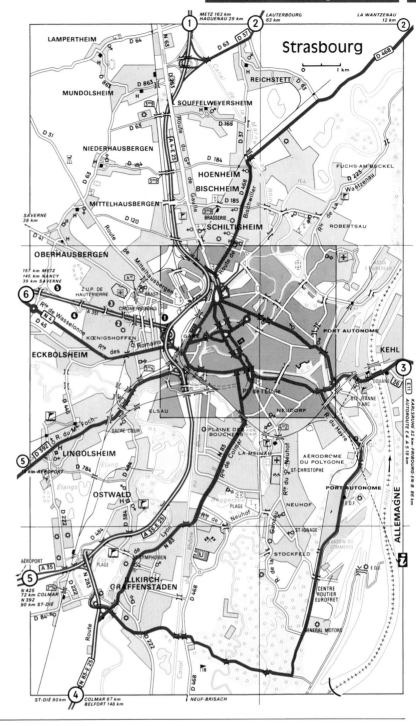

Strasbourg

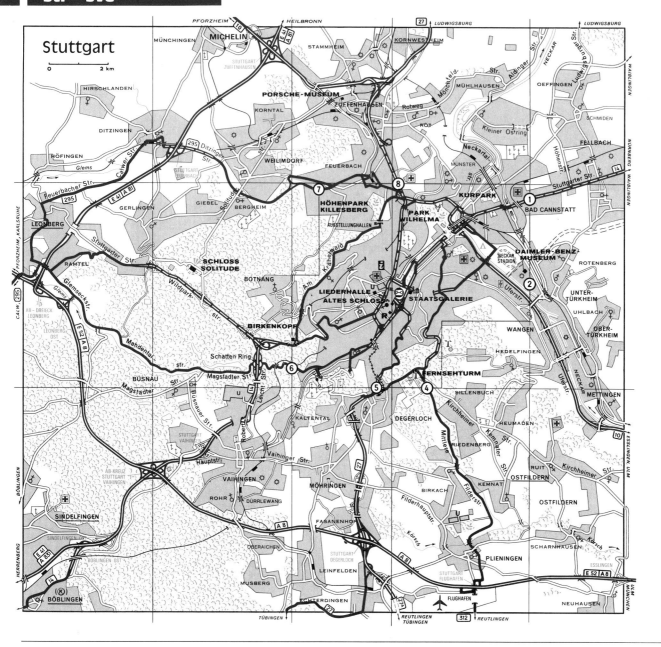

Stuttgart

Name	Page	Ref
Sveti Ilija	75	E2
Sveti Janez	70	A2
Sveti Jovan Bigorski	77	D3
Sveti Naum	77	D4
Sveti Nikita	77	D2
Sveti Nikola	76	B3
Sveti Nikole	77	E3
Sveti Pantelejmon	77	D3
Sveti Rok	70	C4
Sveti Stefan	76	B3
Svetlogorsk (Belorussija)	111	E4
Svetlogorsk (Rossija)	110	B4
Svetlovodsk	113	F2
Svetozarevo	73	D4
Svetozar Miletić	72	B1
Svidník	112	C3
Švihov	56	B1
Svilaja	75	D1
Svilajnac	73	E3
Svilengrad	115	E3
Svingvoll	104	C1
Svinjar	71	E3
Svinoy	96	A3
Svištov	115	D2
Svitavy	112	A3
Svodde	77	E1
Svolvær	94	A4
Svor	53	F3
Svorkmo	100	C2
Svoronáta	86	A1
Svorónos	79	F4
Svrljig	73	F4
Swadlincote	6	C3
Swaffham	11	D1
Swale	6	C1
Swalmen	17	D4
Swanage	9	E4
Swanley	10	C2
Swanlinbar	12	C2
Swansea	8	C2
Świdnica	112	A2
Świdwin	49	F2
Świebodzin	112	A2
Świecie	112	A1
Świecko	49	F4
Świerzno	49	F1
Swilly, L	13	D1
Swindon	9	E2
Swinford	12	B3
Świnoujscie	49	E2
Swords	13	D3
Sybil Head	14	A3
Syčovka	111	F2
Sykäräinen	102	C1
Syke	17	F1
Sykkylven	100	A2
Sylene	101	D2
Sylling	104	C3
Sylt	47	F1
Sylt Ost	47	F1
Sylvenstein-Stausee	56	A4
Synod Inn	8	C1
Syötekylä	99	E3
Syre	3	D2
Sysmä	103	D3
Sysslebäck	101	D4
Syväjärvi	99	D1
Syväri	103	E2
Syvde	100	A3
Syvdsnes	100	A2
Syyspohja	103	E3
Szarvas	112	B4
Szczecin	49	E2
Szczecinek	110	A4
Szczeciński, Zalew	49	E2
Szczytno	110	B4
Szécsény	112	B3
Szeged	114	B1
Székesfehérvár	112	B4
Szekszárd	114	B1
Szentendre	112	B4
Szentes	112	B4
Szigetvár	114	B1
Szolnok	112	B4
Szombathely	112	A4

T

Name	Page	Ref
Tabanovce	77	E2
Tábara	35	D4
Tabarca, I de	45	E2
Taberg	109	D1
Tabernas	44	B3
Tabernes de Valldigna	41	E4
Taboada	34	B2
Tábor	57	D1
Tábua	38	B2
Tabuaço	34	B4
Tabuenca	36	C3
Täby	106	B3
Tachov	53	E4
Tadcaster	7	D2
Tafalla	36	C2
Tafjord	100	B3
Taganheira	42	A1
Taggia	31	F3
Tagliacozzo	63	F2
Tagliamento	59	E3
Taglio di Po	61	D2
Tahal	44	C3
Tahkvuori	103	E2
Taibilla, Sa de	44	C2
Taïgetos, Óros	87	D3
Tain	3	D3
Tain-l'Hermitage	30	B2
Taipadas	38	A4
Taipalsaari	103	E4
Taivalkoski	99	E3
Taivassalo	107	D2
Tajera, Emb de la	40	C1
Tajo, R	40	B2
Tajuña, R	40	B2
Takovo	73	D4
Taktikoúpoli	87	E2
Tálanda	87	E4
Talarrubias	39	E4
Talaván	39	D3
Talave, Emb de	44	C1
Talavera de la Reina	39	F3
Talavera la Real	39	D4
Talayuela	39	E2
Talayuelas	41	D3
Taldom	111	F2
Talgarth	9	D1
Talkkunapää	95	F3
Talla	61	D4
Tallante	45	D3
Tallard	31	D2
Tällberg	101	E4
Tallinn	110	C1
Talloires	27	D4
Tallow	14	C4
Talluskylä	103	D2
Talmont	24	B3
Tal'noje	113	E2
Talsi	110	B2
Talvik	95	D2
Tamames	39	E1
Tamar	8	B3
Támara	35	F3
Tamarite de Litera	37	E3
Tamási	112	B4
Tambre, R	34	A2
Tâmega, R	34	A4
Tâmélos, Akr	88	A2
Tamiš	72	C2
Tammela	107	E2
Tammisaari	107	E3
Tamnava	72	C3
Tampere	107	E1
Tamsweg	56	C4
Tamworth	9	E1
Tana	95	E1
Tana R	95	E1
Tanafjorden	95	E1
Tanágra	84	A4
Tanagro	64	C4
Tanamea, Pso di	59	F3
Tanaro	31	F2
Tancarville, Pont de	19	D3
Tandådalen	101	D4
Tandragee	13	D2
Tandsbyn	101	E2
Tandsjöborg	101	E3
Tangerhütte	48	C4
Tangermünde	48	C4
Tanhua	95	F4
Taninges	27	E4
Tanlay	26	B1
Tann	52	B1
Tännäs	101	D3
Tanndalen	101	D3
Tannheim	58	C1
Tannila	99	D3
Tanumshede	105	D4
Taormina	69	D3
Tapa	110	C1
Tapia de Casariego	34	C1
Tar	70	A3
Tara	72	C4
Tara R	76	B1
Taracena	40	B2
Tara klisura	76	B2
Tarancón	40	B3
Taranto	65	E4
Taranto, Golfo di	65	E4
Tarare	26	B4
Taras	72	C2
Tarašča	113	E2
Tarascon (Ariège)	32	A2
Tarascon (Vaucluse)	30	B3
Taravo	33	F3
Tarayuela	41	E2
Tarazona	36	C3
Tarazona de la Mancha	40	C4
Ťarbát Ness	3	D3
Tarbert (IRL)	14	B3
Tarbert (Strathclyde)	4	B2
Tarbert (Western Is)	2	B2
Tarbes	37	E1
Tarbet	4	C1
Tarcento	59	F3
Tarčin	75	F1
Tardets-Sorholus	37	D1
Tardienta	37	D3
Tärendo	98	C2
Tärendöälven	98	C1
Targon	28	B2
Târgovište	115	E2
Tarifa	43	D4
Tarm	108	A3
Tarmstedt	47	F3
Tarn	29	D3
Tarn (Dépt)	29	E3
Tarna, Pto de	35	E2
Tärnäsjön	97	E3
Tarn-et-Garonne	29	D3
Tarn, Gges du	29	F3
Tarnobrzeg	112	C2
Tarnos	28	A4
Tarnów	112	B2
Taro	60	B2
Tarouca	38	C1
Tarp	48	A1
Tarporley	6	B3
Tarquinia	63	D2
Tarragona	37	F4
Tarrasa	32	A4
Tàrrega	37	F4
Tarrekaise	98	A2
Tårs	108	B4
Tarsia	67	E2
Tartas	28	B3
Tartu	110	C2
Tarvasjoki	107	D2
Tarvisio	59	F2
Täsch	27	F4
Tåsinge	108	B4
Tåsjö	101	F1
Tåsjön	101	F1
Tassin	26	C4
Tåstrup	108	C3
Tata	112	B4
Tatabánya	112	B4
Tatarbunary	113	E4
Tatry	112	B3
Tau	104	A3
Tauber	55	D1
Tauberbischofsheim	55	D1
Taucha	53	D2
Tauerntal	59	E2
Tauerntunnel	59	E2
Taufers i. M.	58	C3
Taufkirchen	56	B3
Taulé	22	B2
Taunton	9	D3
Taunus	51	F4
Taunusstein	51	F4
Tauplitz	57	D4
Tauragė	110	B3
Taurianova	67	E4
Taurion	25	E4
Tauste	36	C3
Tauves	29	E1
Tavankut	72	B1
Tavannes	27	E2
Tavarnelle Val di Pesa	60	C4
Tavastila	103	F4
Tavaux	26	C2
Taverna	67	F3
Tavernelle	63	E1
Tavernes	31	D4
Tavignano	33	F3
Tavira	42	B3
Tavistock	8	C3
Tavolara, I	66	C1
Tavropós	83	D2
Tavropoú, Teh L	83	D2
Tavşanli	115	F3
Taw	8	C3
Taxenbach	59	E1
Taxiárhis	80	B3
Tay	5	D1
Tayinloan	4	B2
Tay, L	4	C1
Taynuilt	4	B1
Tayport	5	D1
Tayside	3	D4
Tazones	35	E1
Tczew	110	A4
Teano	64	A3
Teba	43	E3
Tebay	5	D4
Tech	32	B3
Techendorf	59	F2
Tecklenburg	17	E2
Tecuci	113	E4
Tees	5	E4
Teesside	5	E4
Teféli	91	D4
Tegéa	87	D2
Tegel	49	E4
Tegelen	17	D4
Tegernsee	56	A4
Teggiano	64	C4
Teguise	42	C3
Teide	42	B4
Teide Mt	42	A4
Teide, Pque Nac del	42	B4
Teignmouth	8	C4
Teijo	107	D3
Teil, le	30	B2
Teilleul, le	18	C4
Teisendorf	56	B3
Teisko	102	C3
Teixeiro	34	B1
Teixoso	38	C2
Tejeda, Sa de	43	F3
Tejo, R	38	A3
Tekeriš	72	C3
Tekija	73	E2
Tekirdağ	115	E3
Telč	57	E1
Telde	42	B4
Telemark	104	C3
Télendos, N	89	E3
Teleno	34	C3
Telese	64	B3
Telford	6	C3
Telfs	58	C2
Telgte	17	E3
Tellingstedt	48	A2
Telti	66	B1
Teltow	49	E4
Temerin	72	C2
Temmes	99	D4
Tempelhof	49	E4
Tempio Pausania	66	B1
Templemore	12	C4
Templin	49	D3
Temse	50	B3
Temska	73	F4
Tenala	107	E3
Ténaro, Akr	87	D4
Tenbury Wells	9	D1
Tenby	8	B2
Tence	30	B2
Tende	31	E3
Tende, Col de	31	E3
Tende, Colle di	31	E3
Tendilla	40	B2
Tenerife	42	A4
Tenhola	107	E3
Tenja	71	F2
Tennes	94	B3
Tenniöjoki	95	F4
Teno	95	E2
Tensta	106	B3
Tenterden	11	D3
Tentudia	43	D1
Teolo	61	D1
Teovo	77	E3
Tepelenë	114	C4
Teplá	53	E4
Teplice	53	E3
Tepsa	95	E4
Teramo	63	F1
Ter Apel	17	E1
Tera, R	35	D3
Terebovl'a	113	D3
Terena	38	C4
Terespol	112	C1
Terezino Polje	71	E2
Terges, Rib de	42	B2
Tergnier	20	A2
Terjärv	102	C2
Terlizzi	65	D3
Termas de Monfortinho	39	D2
Terme Luigiane	67	E2
Termini Imerese	68	B3
Terminillo	63	F2
Terminillo, Mte	63	F2
Termoli	64	B2
Terneuzen	16	B4
Terni	63	E2
Ternitz	57	E3
Ternopol'	113	D2
Térovo	82	C2
Térpilos	80	A2
Terpní	80	B2
Terpsithéa	83	D4
Ter, R	32	B3
Terracina	63	F3
Terra de Basto	34	B4
Terradets, Emb dels	37	F3
Terråk	97	D4
Terralba	66	B3
Terranova di Pollino	67	E2
Terranuova Bracciolini	61	D4
Terras de Bouro	34	A3
Terrassa	32	A4
Terrasson-la-Villedieu	29	D2
Terrenoire	30	B1
Terriente	41	D2
Terschelling	16	C1
Teruel	41	D2
Tervakoski	107	E2
Tervo	103	D2
Tervola	99	D2
Tervuren	50	C3
Terzaga	40	C2
Tešanj	71	E3
Teslić	71	E3
Tessin	48	C2
Tessy	18	C3
Teste, la	28	A2
Tetbury	9	E2
Teterev	113	E2
Teterow	49	D2
Tetijev	113	E2
Tetovo	77	D3
Tetrákomo	82	C2
Tettnang	55	D4
Teuchern	53	D2
Teufen	58	B2
Teulada	66	B4
Teupitz	53	E1
Teuva	102	B3
Tevere	63	E2
Teviot	5	D3
Tewkesbury	9	E2
Texel	16	C1
Thabor, Mt	31	D1
Thale	52	C2
Thalfang	54	B1
Thalgau	56	C3
Thalheim	53	E3
Thalmässing	55	F2
Thalwil	58	A2
Thame	9	F2
Thames, R	11	D2
Thanes, K e	76	C4
Thann	27	E1
Thannhausen	55	E3
Thaon	27	D1
Tharandt	53	E2
Tharsis	42	C2
Thássos	80	C3
Thássos, N	81	D3
Thaté, Mal i	77	D4
Thau, Bessin de	30	A4
Thaya	57	F1
Thégonnec	22	B2
Theil, le	23	F3
Themar	52	C3
Thenon	29	D2
Theológos (Stereá Eláda)	83	F3
Theológos (Thássos)	80	C3
Théoule	31	E4
Thérain	19	F3
Thérma (Ikaría)	89	D2
Thermá (Makedonía)	80	B2
Thérma (Samothráki)	81	E3
Thermaïkós Kólpos	80	A4
Thérma Lefkádas	89	D2
Thérmi	79	F3
Thermi	85	F2
Thermissia	87	E2
Thérmo	83	D4
Thermopiles	83	E3
Thérouanne	19	F1
Thespiés	83	F4
Thesprotía	82	B2
Thesprotikó	82	B2
Thessalía	83	D2
Thessaloníki	79	F3
Thessaloníki (Nomos)	80	A3
Thetford	11	D1
Theux	51	D4
The Wash	7	E3
Thèze	28	B4
Thézenay	24	C3
Thiamis	82	B1
Thiaucourt	21	D3
Thiberville	19	D4
Thiéblemont-Farémont	20	C4
Thiendorf	53	E2
Thiene	59	D4
Thiers	26	B4
Thiesi	66	B2

Torino

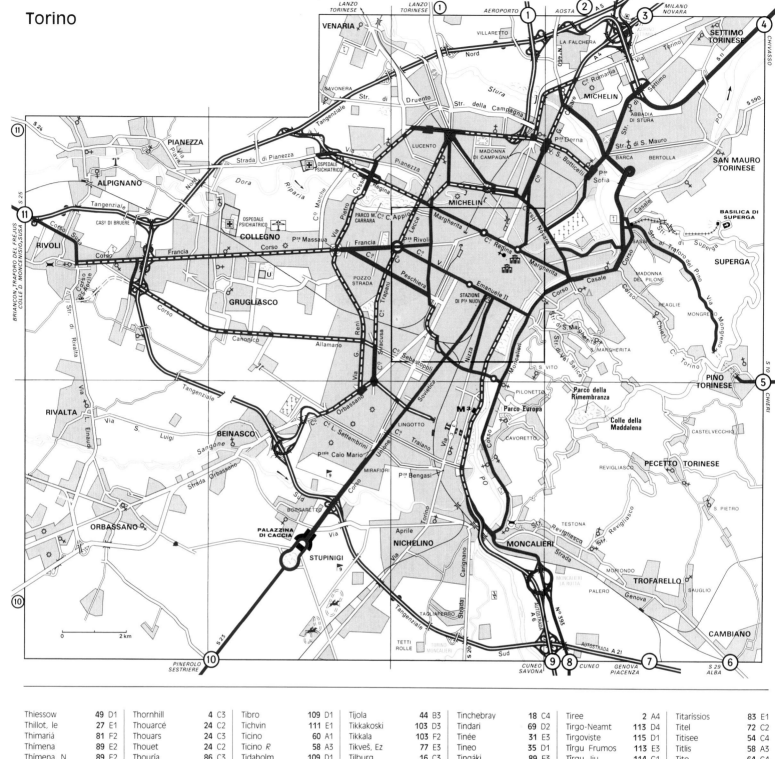

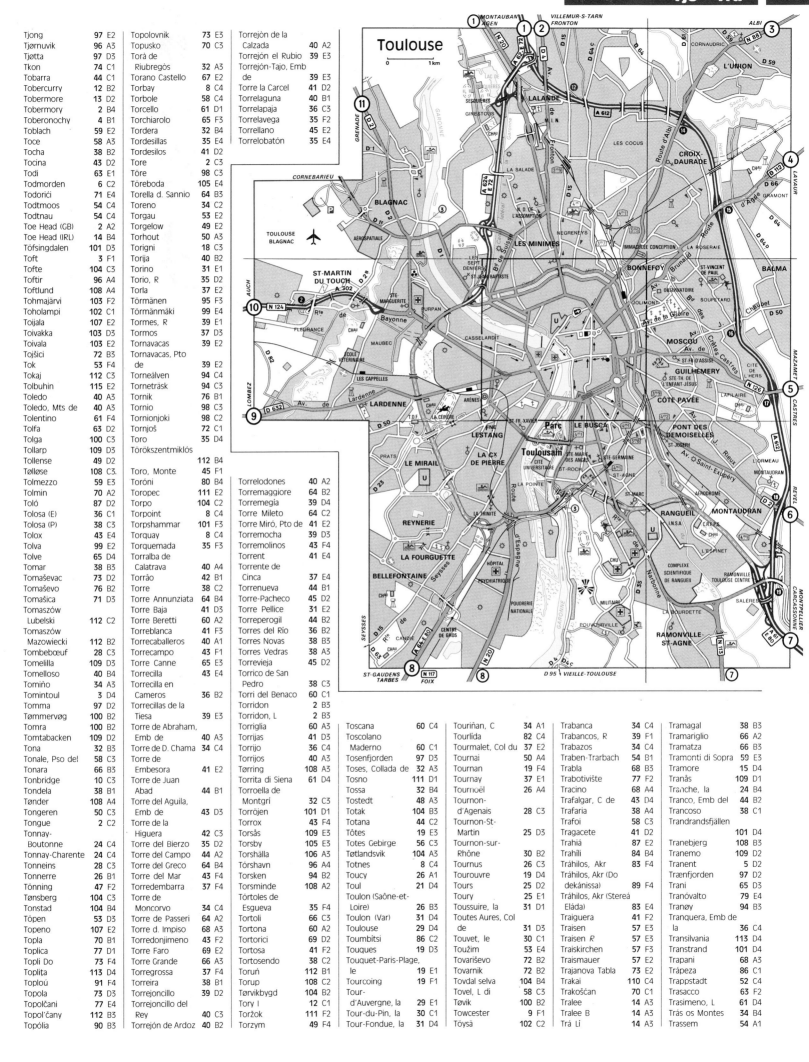

Toulouse

0   1km

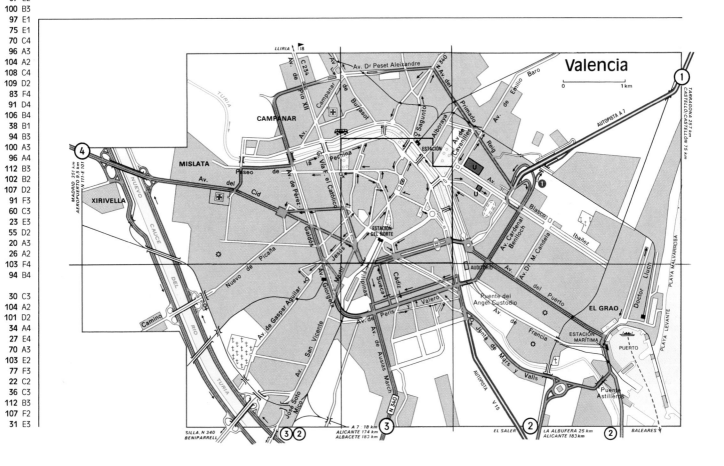

Valencia

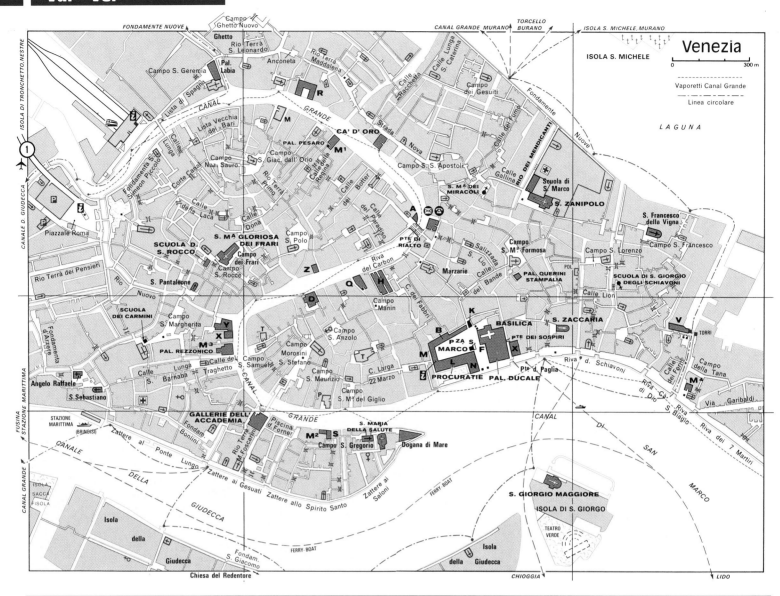

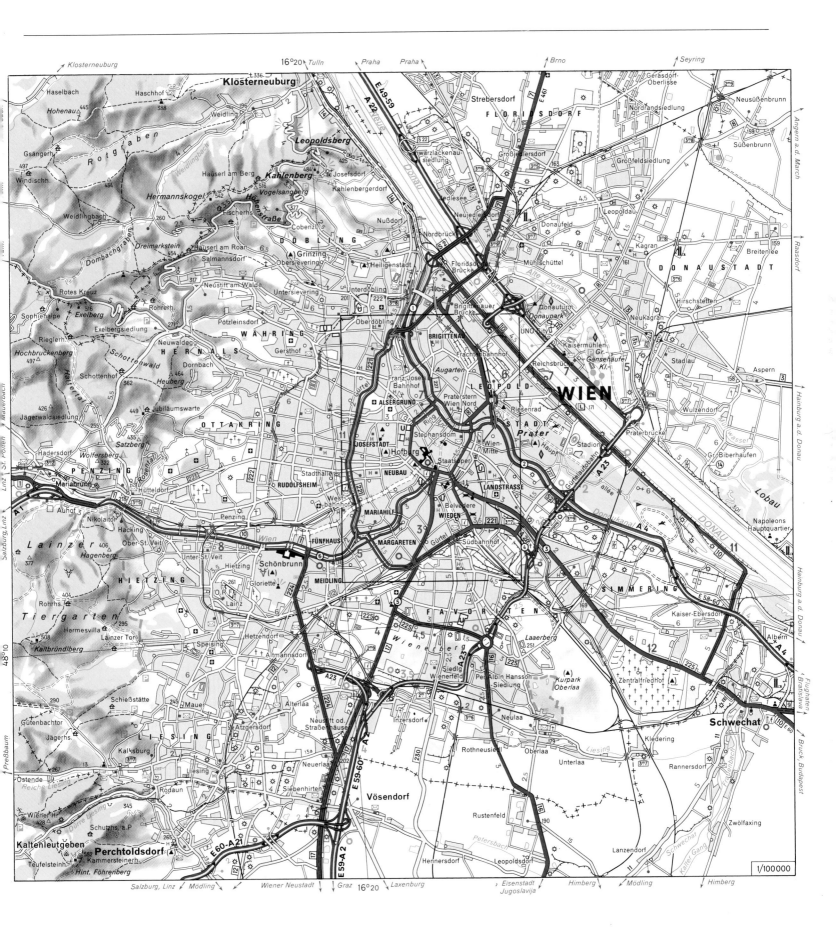

Wantzenau, la 21 F4
Wanzleben 52 C1
Warburg 52 A2
Wardenburg 47 F3
Ware 9 F2
Waregem 50 B3
Wareham 9 D3
Waremme 50 C3
Waren 49 D2
Warendorf 17 F3
Warin 48 C2
Warkworth 5 E3
Warmensteinach 53 D4
Warminster 9 E3
Warnemunde 48 C2
Warnow 48 C2
Warrenpoint 13 E3
Warrington 6 B2
Warstein 17 F3
Warszawa 112 B1
Warszów 49 E2
Warta 49 F3
Warth 58 B2
Wartha 52 B3
Warwick 9 E1
Warwickshire 9 E1
Washington 5 E4
Wasselonne 21 E4
Wassen 58 A3
Wassenaar 16 B3
Wassenberg 17 D4
Wasseralfingen 55 E2
Wasserbillig 21 D2
Wasserburg 56 B3
Wasser-Kuppe 52 B3
Wassertrüdingen 55 E2
Wassigny 20 A2
Wassy 20 C4
Wasungen 52 B3
Watchet 8 C3
Waterfoot 13 E1
Waterford 15 D4
Waterford (Co) 14 C4
Waterford Harbour 15 D4
Waterloo 50 B3
Waternish Pt 2 B3
Waterville 14 A4
Watford 9 F2
Wattens 59 D2
Watton 11 D1
Wattwil 58 A2
Watzmann 56 C4
Waulsort 50 C4
Waveney 11 D1
Wavre 50 C3
Waxweiler 51 D4
Wear 5 E4
Wechsel 57 E3
Wedel 48 A3
Wedemark-Mellendorf 48 A4
Weener 47 E3
Weert 17 D4
Weferlingen 48 C4
Wegberg 17 D4
Wegeleben 52 C1
Weggis 27 F2
Węgorzewo 110 B4
Węgorzyno 49 F2
Wegscheid 56 C2
Wehr 54 C4
Weibersbrunn 52 A4
Weichshofen 56 B2
Weida 53 D3
Weiden 56 A1
Weikersheim 55 D1
Weilburg 51 F4
Weil der Stadt 55 D2
Weilheim (Baden-Württemberg) 55 D3
Weilheim (Bayern) 56 A3
Weimar 52 C3
Weinfelden 58 A1
Weingarten 55 D4
Weinheim 54 C1
Weinsberg 55 D2
Weismain 52 C4
Weißbriach 59 F2
Weiße Elster 53 D3
Weißenbach 58 C1
Weißenberg 53 F2
Weißenburg 55 F2
Weißenfels 53 D2
Weißenhorn 55 E3
Weißenkirchen 57 E2
Weißensee 52 C2
Weißensee (L) 59 F2
Weissenstadt 53 D4
Weissenstein 27 E2
Weissfluhgipfel 58 B2
Weißkirchen 57 D4
Weißkugel 58 C2
Weißwasser 53 F1
Weitra 57 D2
Weiz 57 E4
Wejherowo 110 A4
Weldon 9 F1
Welgetschlag 57 D2
Welland 9 F1
Wellin 20 C2
Wellingborough 9 F1
Wellington 9 D3
Wellington Bridge 15 D4
Wells 9 D3
Wells-next-the-Sea 7 E3
Wels 56 C3
Welsberg 59 D2
Welschnofen 59 D3
Welshpool 9 D1
Weltenburg 55 F2
Welwyn Garden City 9 F2
Welzheim 55 D2
Wem 6 B3
Wemding 55 E2
Wemyss Bay 4 C2
Wendelstein 56 B4
Wenden 52 B1
Wengen 27 F3
Wenns 58 C2
Werbellinsee 49 E3
Werben 48 C3
Werdau 53 D3
Werder 49 D4
Werdohl 17 E4
Werfen 59 E1
Werl 17 F3
Werlte 17 E1
Wermelskirchen 17 E4
Wermsdorf 53 E2
Wernberg 56 B1
Werne 17 E3
Werneck 52 B4
Werneuchen 49 E4
Wernigerode 52 C1
Werra 52 B3
Wertach 55 E4
Wertach (R) 55 E3
Wertheim 55 D1
Werther 17 F2
Wertingen 55 E3
Wervik 50 A3
Wesel 17 D3
Wesenbeerg 49 D3
Wesendorf 48 B4
Weser 47 F3
Weser-Elbe-Kanal 48 C4
Wesselburen 47 F2
Wessobrunn 56 A3
West Auckland 5 E4
West Bridgford 7 D3
Westbury 9 D3
Westendorf 59 D1
Westenholz 48 A4
Westerburg 51 F4
Westerholt 47 E3
Westerland 47 F1
Westerlo 50 C3
Westernbödefeld 17 F4
Western Isles 2 B2
Wester Ross 2 C3
Westerstede 47 E3
Westerwald 51 E3
Westhofen 54 C1
West Kilbride 4 C2
West Linton 5 D2
West Loch Tarbert 2 A2
Westmeath 12 C3
West Mersea 11 D2
Weston-Super-Mare 9 D2
Westport 12 B3
Westray 3 E1
Westray Firth 3 E1
West Sussex 9 F3
West-Terschelling 16 C1
West-Vlaanderen 50 A3
Wetherby 7 D2
Wetter 17 E3
Wetteren 50 B3
Wettin 52 C2
Wettringen 17 E2
Wetwang 7 D1
Wetzikon 58 A2
Wetzlar 51 F3
Wexford 15 D3
Wexford (Co) 15 D3
Weyer-Markt 57 D3
Weyhausen 48 B4
Weyhill 9 E3
Weymouth 9 D3
Weyregg 56 C3
Whaley Bridge 6 C2
Whalsay 3 F1
Wharfe 6 C1
Whernside 6 C1
Whitburn 5 D2
Whitby 5 F4
Whitchurch 6 B3
White Bridge 2 C4
Whitehaven 5 D4
Whitehead 13 E2
Whiteness 3 F2
Whiten Head 2 C2
Whithorn 4 C4
Whitland 8 B2
Whitley Bay 5 E3
Whitstable 11 D3
Whittlesey 9 F1
Wick 3 D2
Wickford 11 D2
Wicklow 13 E4
Wicklow (Co) 13 D4
Wicklow Head 13 E4
Wicklow Mts 13 D4
Widnes 6 B2
Wiehe 52 C2
Wiek 49 D1
Wieliczka 112 B3
Wieluń 112 B2
Wien 57 F2
Wiener-Neudorf 57 F2
Wiener Neustadt 57 F3
Wienerwald 57 E3
Wies (A) 70 B1
Wies (D) 56 A4
Wiesau 53 D4
Wiesbaden 51 F4
Wieselburg 57 E3
Wiesenburg 53 D1
Wiesensteig 55 D3
Wiesentheid 55 E1
Wiesenttal 52 C4
Wiesing 59 D1
Wiesloch 54 C2
Wiesmath 57 F3
Wiesmoor 47 E3
Wigan 6 C2
Wight, I of 9 E4
Wigton 5 D4
Wigtown 4 C3
Wigtown B 4 C4
Wijhe 17 D2
Wil 58 A2
Wildalpen 57 D3
Wildbad 54 C2
Wildeck 52 B3
Wildeshausen 17 F1
Wildon 57 E4
Wildspitze 58 C2
Wildstrubel 27 E3
Wilfersdorf 57 F2
Wilhelmina kan 16 C3
Wilhelm Pieck-Stadt 53 F1
Wilhelmsburg (A) 57 E3
Wilhelmsburg (D) 48 A3
Wilhelmshaven 47 F3
Wilhering 57 D2
Wilkau-Haßlau 53 D3
Willebroek 50 B3
Willemstad 16 B3
Willingen 17 F4
Williton 8 C3
Wilmslow 6 C2
Wilnsdorf 17 F4
Wilsdruff 53 E2
Wilseder Berg 48 A3
Wilster 48 A2
Wilton 9 E3
Wiltshire 9 E3
Wiltz 21 D2
Wimborne Minster 9 E3
Wimereux 19 E1
Wincanton 9 D3
Winchcombe 9 E2
Winchelsea 11 D3
Winchester 9 E3
Windeck 51 E3
Windermere 5 D4
Windischeschenbach 53 D4
Windischgarsten 57 D3
Windsbach 55 E1
Windsor 9 F2
Winkleigh 8 C3
Winklern 59 E2
Winnenden 55 D2
Winnigstedt 52 B1
Winnweiler 54 B1
Winschoten 47 E3
Winsen (Celle) 48 A4
Winsen (Lüneburg) 48 B3
Winsford 6 C3
Winsum 47 D3
Winterberg 17 F4
Winterswijk 17 D3
Winterthur 58 A2
Wintzenheim 27 E1
Wipper 52 C2
Wipperfurth 17 E4
Wisbech 10 C1
Wischhafen 48 A2
Wiselka 49 E2
Wishaw 4 C2
Wisla 110 B4
Wismar 48 C2
Wissant 19 E1
Wissembourg 21 F3
Wissen 51 E3
Witham 7 D3
Witham 11 D2
Withernsea 7 E2
Witney 9 E2
Witnica 49 F3
Wittdün 47 F1
Witte 49 D1
Witten 17 E3
Wittenberg 53 D1
Wittenberge 48 C3
Wittenburg 48 B3
Wittichenau 53 F2
Wittingen 48 B4
Wittlich 51 E4
Wittmund 47 E3
Wittow 49 D1
Wittstock 49 D3
Witzenhausen 52 B2
Władysławowo 110 A4
Włocławek 112 B1
Włodawa 112 C2
Wöbbelin 48 C3
Woburn 9 F2
Woburn Abbey 9 F2
Woensdrecht 16 B4
Woerden 16 C3
Wohlen 27 F2
Woippy 21 D3
Woking 9 F3
Wokingham 9 F2
Wołczenica 49 F2
Woldegk 49 E2
Wolfach 54 C3
Wolfegg 55 E4
Wolfen 53 D2
Wolfenbüttel 52 B1
Wolfhagen 52 A2
Wolfratshausen 56 A3
Wolfsberg 70 B1
Wolfsburg 48 B4
Wolgast 49 E2
Wolin 49 E2
Wolin (Reg) 49 E2
Woliński Park Narodowy 49 E2
Wolkenstein 59 D3
Wolkersdorf 57 F2
Wöllersdorf 57 F3
Wollersheim 51 D3
Wollin 49 D4
Wolmirstedt 48 C4
Wolsingham 5 E4
Wolsztyn 112 A2
Wolvega 17 D1
Wolverhampton 9 E1
Wolverton 9 F1
Wolznach 55 F2
Woodbridge 11 D1
Woodhall Spa 7 E3
Woodstock 9 E2
Wooler 5 E3
Worb 27 E2
Worbis 52 B2
Worcester 9 D1
Wörgl 59 D1
Workington 5 D4
Worksop 7 D2
Workum 16 C1
Wörlitz 53 D1
Wormerveer 16 C2
Wormhout 19 F1
Worms 54 C1
Worms Head 8 C2
Wörnitz 55 E2
Wörrstadt 54 C1
Wœrth 21 E3
Wörth (Donau) 56 B2
Wörth (Main) 55 D1
Wörth (Rheinland-Pfalz) 54 C2
Worther See 70 A1
Worthing 10 C3
Woświn, Jez 49 F2
Wragby 7 D3
Wrath, Cape 2 C2
Wrecsam 6 B3
Wrexham 6 B3
Wriezen 49 E3
Wrocław 112 A2
Wroughton 9 E2
Września 112 A1
Wulfen 17 E3
Wullowitz 57 D2
Wümme 48 A3
Wümme *R* 48 A3
Wünnenberg 17 F3
Wünsdorf 49 E4
Wunsiedel 53 D4
Wunstorf 48 A4
Wuppertal 17 E4
Würzburg 55 D1
Wurzen 53 D2
Wurzen-Paß 59 F2
Wusterhausen 49 D3
Wustrow (Rostock) 48 C1
Wustrow (Wismar) 48 C2
Wuustwezel 50 C2
Wye, R 9 D2
Wyk 47 F1
Wymondham 11 D1

X

Xallas, R 34 A2
Xanten 17 D3
Xánthi 81 D2
Xánthi (Nomos) 81 D2
Xarrama, R 42 B1
Xàtiva 41 E4
Xeresa 41 E4
Xerovoúni 82 C2
Xerta 41 F2
Xertigny 27 D1
Xesta, Pto de la 34 C1
Xifianí 79 E2
Xilagani 81 E2
Xilikí 83 E3
Xilís, Akr 87 D4
Xilókastro 87 D1
Xilopáriko 83 D2
Xilópoli 80 A2
Xilóskalo 90 B3
Xiniáda 83 E3
Xinó Neró 79 D3
Xinzo de Limia 34 B3
Xiró 83 F3
Xirokámbi 87 D3
Xirókambos 89 E3
Xirolímni 79 D3
Xistral 34 B1
Xódoto, Akr 89 D3
Xubia 34 B1
Xunqueira de Ambía 34 B3

Y

Yaiza 42 C4
Yalova 115 F3
Yanguas 36 B3
Yare 7 F4
Yarmouth 9 E3
Yarmouth, Great 7 F4
Ybbs 57 D2
Ybbs *R* 57 D3
Yebra 40 B2
Yecla 45 D1
Yeguas, Emb de 43 F2
Yeguas, R de las 43 F1
Yell 3 F1
Yell Sd 3 F1
Yelmo 44 B2
Yeltes, R 39 D1
Yenne 27 D4
Yeovil 9 D3
Yepes 40 B3
Yerville 19 D3
Yesa 36 C2
Yesa, Emb de 37 D2
Yeşilova 115 F4
Yeste 44 C1
Yeu, I d' 24 A3
Yèvre 26 A2
Y-Fenni 9 D2
Yıldız Dağları 115 E3
Ylämaa 103 F4
Ylämylly 103 F2
Yläne 107 D2
Ylihärmä 102 C2
Yli-Kärppä 99 D3
Ylikiiminki 99 D3
Yli-Kitka 99 E2
Yli-li 99 D3
Yli-Muonio 95 D4
Yli-Nampa 99 D2
Yli-Olhava 99 D3
Ylistaro 102 B2
Ylitornio 98 C2
Ylivieska 102 C1
Yllás 95 D4
Ylläsjärvi 95 D4
Ylöjärvi 102 C3
Yngaren 106 A4
Yonne 20 A4
Yonne (Dépt) 26 A1
York 7 D2
Yorkshire Dales Nat Pk 6 C1
Youghal 14 C4
Youghal B 14 C4
Yoxford 11 E1
Ypäjä 107 E2
Yport 19 D2
Yppäri 99 D4
Ypres 50 A3
Yr Wyddgrug 6 B3
Yser 19 F1
Yssingeaux 30 B1
Ystad 109 D4
Y Trallwng 9 D1
Ytterhogdal 101 E3
Yttermalung 105 E2
Yuncos 40 A2
Yunquera 43 E4
Yunquera de Henares 40 B2
Yuste 39 E2
Yverdon 27 E3
Yvetot 19 D3
Yvoir 50 C4
Yvoire 27 D3

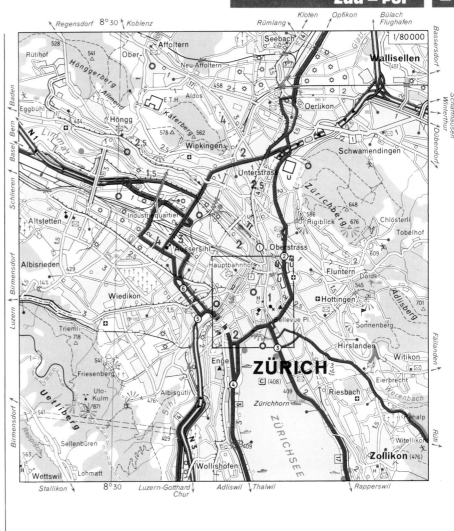

Notes

Notes